LUTHER'S WORKS

LUTHER'S WORKS

VOLUME 15

NOTES ON ECCLESIASTES

LECTURES ON
THE SONG OF SOLOMON

TREATISE ON
THE LAST WORDS OF DAVID

JAROSLAV PELIKAN
Editor

HILTON C. OSWALD
Associate Editor

CONCORDIA PUBLISHING • SAINT LOUIS

Copyright © 1972 by
CONCORDIA PUBLISHING HOUSE
Saint Louis, Missouri

Library of Congress Catalog Card No. 55-9893
ISBN 0-570-06415-5

MANUFACTURED IN THE UNITED STATES OF AMERICA

Contents

General Introduction	vii
Introduction to Volume 15	ix
NOTES ON ECCLESIASTES	
PREFACE	3
INTRODUCTION	7
CHAPTER ONE	12
CHAPTER TWO	29
CHAPTER THREE	49
CHAPTER FOUR	62
CHAPTER FIVE	74
CHAPTER SIX	94
CHAPTER SEVEN	105
CHAPTER EIGHT	134
CHAPTER NINE	144
CHAPTER TEN	155
CHAPTER ELEVEN	169
CHAPTER TWELVE	176
LECTURES ON THE SONG OF SOLOMON	
PREFACE	191
INTRODUCTION	194
CHAPTER ONE	196
CHAPTER TWO	211
CHAPTER THREE	223
CHAPTER FOUR	227
CHAPTER FIVE	236
CHAPTER SIX	243

CHAPTER SEVEN	249
CHAPTER EIGHT	254
TREATISE ON THE LAST WORDS OF DAVID (2 Sam. 23:1-7)	265
Indexes	353

General Introduction

THE first editions of Luther's collected works appeared in the sixteenth century, and so did the first efforts to make him "speak English." In America serious attempts in these directions were made for the first time in the nineteenth century. The Saint Louis edition of Luther was the first endeavor on American soil to publish a collected edition of his works, and the Henkel Press in Newmarket, Virginia, was the first to publish some of Luther's writings in an English translation. During the first decade of the twentieth century, J. N. Lenker produced translations of Luther's sermons and commentaries in thirteen volumes. A few years later the first of the six volumes in the Philadelphia (or Holman) edition of the *Works of Martin Luther* appeared. Miscellaneous other works were published at one time or another. But a growing recognition of the need for more of Luther's works in English has resulted in this American edition of Luther's works.

The edition is intended primarily for the reader whose knowledge of late medieval Latin and sixteenth-century German is too small to permit him to work with Luther in the original languages. Those who can, will continue to read Luther in his original words as these have been assembled in the monumental Weimar edition (*D. Martin Luthers Werke.* Kritische Gesamtausgabe; Weimar, 1883 ff.). Its texts and helps have formed a basis for this edition, though in certain places we have felt constrained to depart from its readings and findings. We have tried throughout to translate Luther as he thought translating should be done. That is, we have striven for faithfulness on the basis of the best lexicographical materials available. But where literal accuracy and clarity have conflicted, it is clarity that we have preferred, so that sometimes paraphrase seemed more faithful than literal fidelity. We have proceeded in a similar way in the matter of Bible versions, translating Luther's translations. Where this could be done by the use of an existing English version — King James, Douay, or Revised Standard — we have done so. Where it could not, we have supplied our own. To indicate this in each specific instance would have been pedantic; to adopt a uniform procedure would have been artificial — especially in view of Luther's own inconsistency in this regard. In each volume the translator will be responsible primarily for matters of text and language, while the responsibility of the editor will extend principally to the historical and theological matters reflected in the introductions and notes.

Although the edition as planned will include fifty-five volumes, Luther's writings are not being translated in their entirety. Nor should they be. As he was the first to insist, much of what he wrote and said was not that important. Thus the edition is a selection of works that have proved their importance for the faith, life, and history of the Christian Church. The first thirty volumes contain Luther's expositions of various Biblical books, while the remaining volumes include what are usually called his "Reformation writings" and other occasional pieces. The final volume of the set will be an index volume; in addition to an index of quotations, proper names, and topics, and a list of corrections and changes, it will contain a glossary of many of the technical terms that recur in Luther's works and that cannot be defined each time they appear. Obviously Luther cannot be forced into any neat set of rubrics. He can provide his reader with bits of autobiography or with political observations as he expounds a psalm, and he can speak tenderly about the meaning of the faith in the midst of polemics against his opponents. It is the hope of publishers, editors, and translators that through this edition the message of Luther's faith will speak more clearly to the modern church.

J. P.
H. L.

Introduction to Volume 15

THE three commentaries collected in this volume span a period of almost two decades in Luther's life and, as examples of Luther's exegesis of the Old Testament, are probably less familiar to most students of his thought than are most of the other lectures and expositions included in our edition.

What is presented here as Luther's *Notes on Ecclesiastes* (Weimar, XX, 7–203; Saint Louis, V, 1372–1579) was based on a series of lectures which he delivered in 1526. Together with much of the exegetical tradition, both Jewish and Christian, he had been puzzled by this book, whose seeming skepticism appeared to be out of place in the Book of faith; in addition, its linguistic peculiarities had been a problem to many earlier translators and interpreters. Although he, too, complained of its "Hebrew forms of expression" and struggled to solve the mystery of its vocabulary, sometimes without success (see p. 36 below), Luther came to believe that he had made sense of the Book of Ecclesiastes as few of his predecessors had. The dates of the lectures that can be determined are:

July 30	September 3
July 31	September 4
August 1	September 5
August 6	September 24
August 7	September 25
August 8	September 26
August 13	October 29
August 14	October 30
August 20	October 31
August 22	November 5
August 27	November 6
August 28	November 7

In addition, there must have been about three lectures between the one on September 26 and that on October 29. The scribe was George Rörer, to whom we are also indebted for several of the other exegetical lectures in our edition.

It seems that Luther intended to do with these lecture notes what he had done with a similar set on the Book of Deuteronomy (cf. *Luther's Works*, 9, pp. ix—x), namely, to make a proper book of them himself. He persuaded Philip Melanchthon to undertake a new translation of Ecclesiastes from Hebrew into Latin. Melanchthon reported to Johann Agricola in November 1526: "When I have completed the entire translation, it will be sent to you along with Luther's comments, which were taken down by some rapid writers." One year later, under the date of November 11, 1527, we find Luther expressing the hope that his colleagues would return to Wittenberg after the plague "to edit Ecclesiastes," presumably referring to his commentary on Ecclesiastes. In 1528 Luther's follower Johann Brenz published his own commentary, with a preface by Luther, in which Luther declared: "Although there is no book that I would rather have printed than my *Ecclesiastes*, which I delivered as lectures here in Wittenberg . . . I have not yet managed to have enough time and energy." Therefore he wished Brenz well in his efforts but did not give up the idea of publishing his own work eventually. He himself did not get to the assignment, but some of his friends did in 1532. As a basis for the printed edition they drew upon Rörer's lecture notes, but also upon those of some others who had attended the lectures. The result of this editorial work was the commentary which we present here in English translation. As in other printed versions of Luther's lectures, it is evident that the editors have smoothed out some of the rough spots, correcting and amplifying Luther's quotations, especially those from the Greek and Latin classics, and translating many (though not all) of Luther's German *obiter dicta* into Latin. We have followed our practice in this edition and have preferred the printed version to the raw notes of Luther's lectures.

The same volume of manuscripts in the library of the University of Jena that contains Rörer's notes from the lectures on Ecclesiastes has also preserved his notebook from Luther's *Lectures on the Song of Solomon* (Weimar, XXXI-2, 586—769; Saint Louis, V, 1580—1659), which were delivered during 1530 and 1531 on the

INTRODUCTION TO VOLUME 15

following dates:

March 7, 1530	December 6, 1530
March 8, 1530	May 15, 1531
March 10, 1530	May 16, 1531
March 15, 1530	May 22, 1531
March 21, 1530	May 23, 1531
March 31, 1530	June 5, 1531
November 8, 1530	June 6, 1531
November 14, 1530	June 12, 1531
November 21, 1530	June 13, 1531
November 28, 1530	June 22, 1531

There were two additional lectures between November 28 and December 6, 1530, as well as two more between June 13 and June 22, 1531; these are not dated. It was not until 1539 that the lectures appeared in print. The editor who prepared them for publication was Veit Dietrich, who had also been present in Luther's classroom when the lectures were being delivered. He had hesitated to issue them, hoping that other auditors would prepare them in a more ample version, but was finally persuaded to go ahead. Luther supplied a preface. Here again we have translated the printed version rather than the lecture notes.

The third part of this volume is a translation of Luther's treatise *On the Last Words of David* (Weimar, LIV, 28–100; Saint Louis, III, 1880–1973). In June 1543 he was reported by Johann Forster to be at work on a treatise entitled *On the Divinity of Christ on the Basis of the Last Words of David,* and by August 18 of that year he was able to send it to the printers. It was brought on by the need to defend the Christological exegesis of the Old Testament both against Jewish interpreters and against their Christian pupils. Luther acknowledged that he himself had followed the lead of the rabbis too closely in his translation of the Hebrew Bible and even in his interpretation of it, and now he set about to vindicate the Christian explanation of its Messianic prophecies and confessions. His own exegetical work on the Book of Genesis, with which he had begun in June of 1535 (cf. *Luther's Works,* 1, p. ix), and his continuing revision of the translation of the Old Testament gave him further concrete occasions to reconsider his understanding of many passages in the Old Testament. Among these passages, the words of David in 2 Sam. 23:1-7 were especially important, and Luther found in them proof that the doctrines of the Trinity and of the two natures in Christ were already taught in the Old Testament. In so doing, he set forth not only his exegesis of this passage, but also the hermeneutical principles that had guided him in the interpretation of the remainder of the Old Testament.

J. P.

NOTES ON ECCLESIASTES

Translated by
JAROSLAV PELIKAN

PREFACE OF DOCTOR MARTIN LUTHER TO HIS LECTURES ON THE ECCLESIASTES OF SOLOMON, DELIVERED IN THE SCHOOL AT WITTENBERG

BECAUSE this book has been translated obscurely from the Hebrew, all sorts of learned men have taken it upon themselves to expound it. All of them have striven to apply various of its statements to their own profession, or rather to their own opinion.[1] This may have been due to their curiosity, which delights in things that are obscure and novel or unusual, or it may have been because it is easy to make up whatever one pleases and to set it forth on the basis of writings that are obscure. The philosophers imagined that what the Preacher says at the very beginning (1:8), "All things are full of weariness; a man cannot utter it," applied to them, as though Solomon were speaking about their inane and speculative philosophy.[2] Others, offended at Solomon's saying (3:19), "As the beast dies, so dies man. They all have the same fate and the same breath," suspect him of having been an Epicurean, or at any rate of having spoken in the person of the Epicureans.[3]

But no one has abused this book more wickedly than those schools of theologians who have twisted the passage (9:1) "Man does not know whether he deserves love or hate" to apply to the conscience in relation to God.[4] They have twisted it in such a way that they utterly destroyed the consciences of all with their torture. They completely extinguished the certainty of faith in Christ and all knowledge of Christ, teaching and inculcating nothing more religious upon suffering hearts than to tell them that they must be in doubt and uncertainty about the grace and love of God toward

[1] Among the most recent of these had been Luther's associate Johann Brenz; see Introduction, p. x.

[2] See Luther's discussion of this passage, p. 18 below.

[3] See Luther's discussion of this passage, p. 59 below.

[4] See Luther's discussion of this passage, p. 144 below.

us, regardless of how blameless our lives may be. So dense was the darkness, worse than that of Egypt, that this statement of Solomon — or, rather, their own errors, smuggled into this statement — prevented them from seeing any longer the writings of the apostles and evangelists, which declare with such great signs, texts, and arguments that Christ is our Mediator and is the Author of an absolutely certain grace and salvation, freely offered to us and conferred upon us by God.

No less noxious for a proper understanding of this book has been the influence of many of the saintly and illustrious theologians in the church, who thought that in this book Solomon was teaching what they call "the contempt of the world," [5] that is, the contempt of things that have been created and established by God. Among these is St. Jerome, who by writing a commentary on this book urged Blesilla to accept the monastic life.[6] From this source there arose and spread over the entire church, like a flood, that theology of the religious orders or monasteries. It was taught that to be a Christian meant to forsake the household, the political order, even the episcopal (or, rather, the apostolic) office, to flee to the desert, to isolate oneself from human society, to live in stillness and silence; for it was impossible to serve God in the world. As though Solomon were calling "vanity" the very marriage, political office, and office of the ministry of the Word which he praises here in such a wonderful way and calls gifts of God! Although Solomon teaches that men themselves and their counsels are vain, they reverse everything; and, following their notions completely contrary to Solomon, they call the things themselves vain, while they regard themselves and their ideas as correct and solid. In short, all they have produced from this very beautiful and useful book are their own monstrosities. They have obviously used the gold of God to fashion abominable idols.

To illumine this darkness and to destroy such loathsome idols, I have found it easier to give my permission for these comments of mine, which were taken down by the hands of others and formu-

[5] The idea of the *contemptus mundi* had been prominent throughout medieval ascetic literature, but was most fully stated in the poem of Bernard of Cluny, *De contemptu mundi,* written around the middle of the 12th century.

[6] Jerome, *Commentarius in Ecclesiasten,* Preface, *Patrologia, Series Latina,* XXIII, 1009—12. (Future references to this work will be to Jerome, *Commentarius,* followed by the column numbers in the *Patrologia.*)

lated in these terms, to be published, although I myself have been prevented by other business from expounding this book in a proper commentary. My comments are slender and insignificant; but those who have nothing better or who, like me, were once led astray by false glosses can find here an opportunity in their wisdom to become better themselves and to find something better. It has given me great pleasure to have even a moderate taste of this book, after wearying myself over it all my life in vain, crucifying myself, and corrupting myself with wicked opinions contrary to the faith of Christ. I give joyful thanks to the Father of mercies for this, that He has deigned to renew this final period of history with so many revelations and so much light.

It would, therefore, be more correct to call this Book of Ecclesiastes the *Politics* or the *Economics* of Solomon. He does not, indeed, legislate or prescribe laws for the governance of the state or the family. This is taken care of in great detail by the natural law or human reason, to which, according to Gen. 1:28, earthly things have been subjected; this has been, is, and must remain the source, the criterion, and the end of all laws, whether political or domestic. But this book can give counsel to a man involved in the state or the household as he deals with difficult problems, and it can instruct and encourage his mind as he bears the troubles of such a position. Problems and troubles are endless here, as is evident both from all the histories in Holy Scripture and from the stories of all the poets. Consider the labors of Hercules, the monsters whom Ulysses and others had to overcome, the bear, the lion, and the Goliath with whom David had to contend. Anyone who is ignorant of this art will eventually grow weary, collapse, and come to utter ruin, as Timon, Demosthenes, Cicero, and many others fell. Because of such impatience the heretics in the church have also stirred up sects in the church, because they could not carry on their ministry on account of the malice of people. Thus, as it is said, "despair makes monks";[7] what the wise man said is true: "Government displays the man."[8] But unless there is some Solomon to exhort and console him, government crushes the man, extinguishes him, and utterly destroys him.

[7] See *Luther's Works*, 21, p. 27, n. 10.
[8] The same passage is quoted in *Luther's Works*, 9, p. 17.

Therefore I commend to devout brethren this Solomon of mine, which should more accurately be called an indication than an exposition. And I hope that someone endowed with a more abundant spirit and more eminent gifts will come forward to expound and adorn this book as it deserves, to the praise of God and of His creatures. To Him be glory forever through Jesus Christ, our Lord. Amen.

THE ECCLESIASTES OF SOLOMON, WITH ANNOTATIONS BY DR. MARTIN LUTHER

This book is one of the more difficult books in all of Scripture, one which no one has ever completely mastered. Indeed, it has been so distorted by the miserable commentaries of many writers that it is almost a bigger job to purify and defend the author from the notions which they have smuggled into him than it is to show his real meaning. There are two reasons why this book has been more obscure than others. In the first place, they did not see the purpose and aim of the author, which it is important to keep in mind and to follow in every kind of writing and even more important here. The other reason was the ignorance of the Hebrew language and the special style of this author, which often diverges from the ordinary usage of the language and is very strange to our way of speaking. As a result, this book, which on many counts deserves to be in everyone's hands and to be familiar to everyone, especially to government officials because of its graphic and unique description of the administration of human affairs both private and public, has until now been deprived of its reputation and dignity and has lain in miserable neglect, so that today we have neither the use nor the benefit from it that we should. This is the consequence of the temerity or of the ignorance of other people. Therefore our first task will be to hold to the certain aim of the book, what it seeks to accomplish and what it has in view. For if we do not know this, it will be impossible to understand its style and way of speaking.

The summary and aim of this book, then, is as follows: Solomon wants to put us at peace and to give us a quiet mind in the everyday affairs and business of this life, so that we live contentedly in the present without care and yearning about the future and are, as Paul says, without care and anxiety (Phil. 4:6). It is useless to plague oneself with anxiety about the future. By a sort of continuing induction from particulars, Solomon concludes that the efforts and endeavors of men are vain and useless, so that he draws a universal conclusion from particulars and shows that the efforts of all men are vain. He denies (9:11) that bread is to the wise or the race to the swift or the battle to the strong. In fact, the wiser or holier or busier someone claims to be, the less he accomplishes, and his wisdom, his righteousness, and his work are useless. And so if none of these things nor anything else amounts to anything, it follows that everything is vain and useless.

But here at the very beginning it is necessary to eradicate the error and dangerous opinion held by many, that the author is speaking about a contempt for creatures, which Scripture by no means wants to be despised or condemned. For all things that God has made are very good and have been made for the use of man, as Paul says in very clear words in 1 Tim. 4:4-5: "Everything created by God is good, and nothing is to be rejected if it is received with thanksgiving; for then it is consecrated by the Word of God and prayer." Therefore it is foolish and wicked when many preachers inveigh against glory, power, social position, wealth, gold, fame, beauty, or women, thus openly condemning a creation of God. Government, or power, is a divine ordinance. Gold is good, and riches are conferred by God. A woman is a good thing, made to be a helper for man (cf. Gen. 2:18). For God has made all things to be good and to be useful for some human purpose.

What is being condemned in this book, therefore, is not the creatures but the depraved affection and desire of us men, who are not content with the creatures of God that we have and with their use but are always anxious and concerned to accumulate riches, honors, glory, and fame, as though we were going to live here forever; and meanwhile we become bored with the things that are present and continually yearn for other things, and then still others. For this is the height of vanity and misery, to cheat oneself of the use of present goods and vainly to be troubled about future ones. Such depraved affection and human striving, I say, is what Solomon is condemning in this book, not the creatures themselves. For about the attitude toward creatures he himself says below (5:18) that there is nothing better for any man than to find enjoyment and make life pleasant for himself, to eat and drink and enjoy his toil, etc. He would be contradicting himself completely if he were to condemn these things themselves rather than the abuse of these things, which comes solely from the affections.

Some foolish men have not understood this and have therefore taught absurd ideas about contempt for the world and flight from it, and they themselves have also done many absurd things. Thus in the *Lives of the Fathers* we read that there were some who did not even want to look at the sun (such men would deserve to have their eyes gouged out) and who for the sake of religion ate the filthiest of foods.[1] The quality of such behavior is clear enough from what has already been said. The proper contempt of the world is not that of the man who lives in solitude away from human society, nor is the proper contempt of gold that of the man who throws it away or who abstains from money, as the Franciscans do, but that of the man who lives his life in the midst of these things and yet is not carried away by his affection for them. This is the first thing that should be considered by those who are about to read Solomon.

In the second place, this, too, should be diligently observed: in this book Solomon is speaking simply about the human race and is clearly confining himself within the limits of human nature. That is, he is speaking about the efforts, the endeavors, and the desires of man, about the counsels of man. Therefore we should not follow the imaginations of the interpreters who suppose that the knowledge of nature, the study of astronomy or of all of philosophy, is being condemned here and who teach that such things are to be despised as vain and useless speculations.[2] For the benefits of these arts are many and great, as is plain to see every day. In addition, there is not only utility, but also great pleasure in investigating the nature of things. Holy Scripture also points to things to show their properties and powers; for example, in the psalm (Ps. 103:5), "Your youth is renewed like the eagle's," or (Deut. 32:11), "As an eagle provokes its young to fly," or (Ps. 42:1), "As a hart longs for flowing streams," or (Prov. 6:6), "Go to the ant, O sluggard." The Scriptures are all so full of such metaphors and parables taken from the nature of things that if someone were to remove these things from the Holy Scriptures, he would also remove a great light.

[1] See p. 176, n. 2, below.
[2] See *Luther's Works*, 1, pp. 31—32, for a fuller statement.

Thus the subject or matter of this book is simply the human race, which is so foolish that it seeks and strives for many things by its efforts which it cannot attain or which, even if it does attain them, it does not enjoy but possesses to its sorrow and harm, as the fault not of the things themselves but of its own foolish affections. Julius Caesar was occupied with the effort to achieve the imperial power. How much danger and how much labor did this cost him? And when he had achieved it, he still was not satisfied. He still did not have what he wanted, but in the strenuous attempt to gain more he perished miserably. This is what happens in all human efforts. When things come flowing in, boredom soon takes over; if they do not flow in, there is an insatiable desire to have them, and there is no peace. This vice of the human spirit was seen by pagan writers. Thus Ovid says: "Whatever is permissible is unpleasant, but what is not permissible inflames us more violently. I run away from what follows me, and I follow what runs away from me."[3] Again: "No one lives content with his lot, and no one has learned to remain within his destiny."[4] This is the vanity of the human heart, that it is never content with the gifts of God that are present but rather thinks of them as negligible; it continually looks for others, and then still others, and is not satisfied until it achieves what it wishes, whereupon it despises what it has achieved and looks for something else.

To reiterate, the point and purpose of this book is to instruct us, so that with thanksgiving we may use the things that are present and the creatures of God that are generously given to us and conferred upon us by the blessing of God. This we are to do without anxiety about the things that are still in the future. The important thing is that we have a tranquil and quiet heart and a mind filled with joy, that is, that we be content with the Word and work of God. Thus in the verses that follow he exhorts us (9:7-9) to eat and drink and enjoy life with the wife of our youth; oil should not be lacking on our head, and our garments should always be white. This is in accord with the saying of Christ (Matt. 6:34): "The day's own trouble is sufficient for the day"; and Paul says (Rom. 13:14): "Make no provision for the flesh, to gratify its desires." If a man were to follow this, he would have a peaceful and

[3] Ovid, *Amores*, II, 19, 3, 36.
[4] Horace, *Sermones*, I, 1, 1—3.

tranquil heart, and God would abundantly supply everything. But now a man tortures himself with a twofold evil, depriving himself of the use of things that are present and uselessly troubling himself with anxiety about things that are in the future; or if some use is made of things, it is only in bitterness. Cicero was a man of such eloquence that he could have been completely happy if he had known how to use his tranquillity. But that good man always wanted something bigger and vainly pressed his plans, and see how many good things he robbed himself of and what calamity and ruin he brought down upon himself! Therefore St. Augustine says aptly: "Thou hast commanded, Lord, that a man who is not content with what he has receive a restless heart as a punishment." [5]

But if someone compares the good things he has with the bad things he does not have, he will finally recognize what a treasure of good things he has. Someone who has sound and healthy eyes does not estimate this blessing of God very highly nor take pleasure in it. But if he is deprived of them, what a treasure he would be willing to give in exchange for them! That is how it goes with health and with everything else. If God were to give me the eloquence of Cicero, the power of Caesar, or the wisdom of Solomon, I would still not be satisfied. We are always looking for something that is lacking, and we despise what is present. When a man does not have a wife, he looks for one; when he has one, he becomes bored with her. We are just like quicksilver, which never remains still. Such is the inconstancy of the human heart, which does not deserve to enjoy a single blessing of God. In this book Solomon inveighs against this miserable state of human affections. He denounces the inconstancy and vanity of the human heart, which enjoys neither present nor future goods; it does not acknowledge or give thanks for the blessings it has received, and it vainly pursues the things it does not have. This is really being suspended between heaven and earth!

[5] A paraphrase of the famous words in Augustine, *Confessions*, I, ch. 1.

CHAPTER ONE

1. *The sermon of the son of David, king in Jerusalem.*

IN my opinion, the title Ecclesiastes, or Preacher, should be applied to the name of the book itself rather than to that of the author, so that you understand that these are words that Solomon spoke publicly in some address to his princes and others. For since he was a king, it was not part of his duty or office to teach; this belonged to the priests and Levites. Therefore I think that these words were spoken by Solomon in some assembly of his retinue, perhaps after dinner or even during dinner to some great and prominent men who were present. He spoke this way after he had thought long and hard to himself about the condition and the vanity of human affairs, or rather of human affections. Then he poured this out to those who were present, as usually happens, and afterwards what he said was put down and assembled by the leaders of the community or of the church. Therefore they also acknowledge at the end (12:11) that they have received and gathered these things from one Shepherd. In the same way it could happen that one of us would discourse about human affairs while seated at table and others would take it down.[1] This is, then, a public sermon which they heard from Solomon, on the basis of which it seemed appropriate to call this book Koheleth—not in the sense that Solomon himself was a preacher but that this book was preached as though it had been a public sermon.

2. *Vanity of vanities, says the Preacher.*

The content of this book and its aim have now been determined. Henceforth the difficulty will be chiefly in the Hebrew words and figures of speech, which abound in the books of Solomon more than in those of others. For Solomon has a singular way of speaking. He wants to seem more elegant than his father David, and his language is much more picturesque and adorned with

---

[1] Luther is, of course, describing just what was happening to him in his discourses at table, as preserved in the *Table Talk*.

many more figures of speech. He speaks in a courtly style, not in the manner of the common people. David's language is simpler, even though it is not lacking in common figures of speech. But Solomon introduced courtly language; and as courtiers make it a practice to avoid the simple language of their fathers, especially in writing, so Solomon does also, to avoid giving the impression that he speaks as the common people do. He departs from the simplicity not only of his father but also of Moses, who is the simplest of all but nevertheless has as many striking figures of speech as David does, only commonplace ones.

Vanity of vanities.

This is a Hebraism. Because the Hebrews have neither a comparative nor a superlative, they are obliged to form the superlative and even the comparative by means of compounds. Thus they say "Song of Songs," that is, the supreme and most excellent song that Solomon composed. Vanity of vanities, that is, the greatest and highest vanity of all, total and utter vanity. All of this he says not about things themselves but about the human heart, which abuses things to its own disadvantage. The reduplication, *Vanity of vanities! All is vanity*, is a typically Solomonic pleonasm.

With these opening words he announces the theme and argument of the entire book, what he wants to talk about. He says that he is speaking about the highest and greatest of vanities, that men are extremely vain in all their endeavors, because they are not content with the things that are in the present; because they neither use these nor are able to enjoy the things that are in the future, they turn even the best of things to misery and vanity by their own fault and not by that of the things themselves. That this is the summary, you will easily see from the following, where you find him speaking about vanity, which men have in their own labors and endeavors, not in the things themselves.

3. *What does man gain by all his toil at which he toils under the sun?*

That is, what vanity! Men are led and dragged along by their plans and endeavors, and yet what do they have of such efforts? Nothing but vanity, because their labors are vain and "there isn't any use." They enjoy neither the things that are present nor those that are absent, because their heart is not at rest. Suspended this way between heaven and earth, they are borne along and accomplish nothing whatever. The word "vanity" means precisely what we mean when we say "nothing." They gather treasures, riches, power, etc., and yet all these things are nothing. Gold is, of course, something, but to you it is nothing because you do not use it. His phrase *by all his toil* is therefore to be interpreted in an emphatic sense. By this phrase he indicates that he will be dealing not with the works of God, in which there is holiness and salvation—and this includes all creatures—but with the works of men, who are driven and carried along by their own counsels; in this way he wants to limit their calamities and toilsome chores. Nor is he speaking about the labor of man's hands, which was commanded by God in Gen. 3:19, "In toil shall you eat bread," but he is speaking about our striving and planning, by which we try to accomplish what we please. For the word עָמָל means tribulation and calamity rather than work, that is, that toil by which men afflict themselves and torture themselves in vain. For it is the most miserable toil to try so hard to work out our plans and to carry out our endeavors and yet to accomplish nothing at all. Therefore he says: *What does man gain?* That is, when a man tries to carry out his plans, what does he gain by all the effort and the toil but the vainest of vanities?

Under the sun.

He is about to describe the realm of vanity and the location of this realm. He calls this entire realm of vanity *existence under the sun,* a unique phrase that we do not read elsewhere in Scripture. In this way he seeks to exclude the works of God, which God Himself either works in us or has commanded us to work; these are above the sun and beyond the efforts of men. For the sun rises, as Ps. 104:22-23 says, so that man may go forth to his work, so that it may serve as the light of the world, so that it may be of service in physical matters. Under that sun, I say, are carried on those vain strivings with which men are afflicted. This must be noted again, in refutation of the vain notion of the interpreters, that this applies to the vanity of the creatures. The creatures are indeed subjected to vanity, as Paul declares in Rom. 8:20, but they themselves are good things. Otherwise he would have said that the sun is vain; but he makes the sun an exception, for he says: "under the sun." Therefore he is dealing not with the works of God, which are good, true, and above the sun, but with works that are under the sun, works that we carry on in this physical and earthly life.

4. *A generation goes, and a generation comes, but the earth remains forever.*

You see that he is discussing not works under the sun but the very works and creatures of God, such as human generation, the sun, water, and earth. He includes the four elements, for the philosophers distinguished in this way the four elements within which everything in the world carries on its activity. They placed fire above the other three elements.[2] Solomon, too, seems to take the sun as this elementary fire. In these words, then, he explains what he wanted to be understood by his words *under the sun.* Thus his meaning can be summarized as follows: The things of the world, such as sun, air, and water, in which men have their existence, continue in accordance with their sure laws. They come and go and are moved just as they have been constituted. They have an assigned station; they neither fluctuate nor wander about but do what they ought to do, as the sun is moved in its path and prescribed movement. But human beings, who have their existence in these four elements (things that are, as I have said, stable) cannot behave this way. They fluctuate and waver, utterly unstable in the variety of their endeavors and desires, dissatisfied with their limitations, their business, their vocations, etc. Therefore it is not correct when some explain the first "generation" to refer to the Jews and the second to the Christians,[3] because here he is speaking about the continual succession of generations, or ages.

5. *The sun rises and the sun goes down, drawing its breath to its place where it rises.*

6. *It goes to the south, and goes round to the north. Round and round goes the wind, and on its circuits the wind returns.*

Solomon continues with his description of the realm and

[2] See also *Luther's Works,* 1, p. 26.
[3] Jerome, *Commentarius,* 1015.

location of vanity, and he proves the stability of the sun from its perpetual and constant rising, setting, and course. Then Solomon wants to indicate that the wind, or air, follows the impulse of the sun in its course, which he makes practically the lord and the director of the elements.[4] This sun, I mean, controls the wind; it moderates everything by its governance, and it tempers the air, the water, and the wind by its course. When it rises, it makes one kind of air; and, as we can see, it makes another when it sets. So also it affects the water differently at different times. For when the sun sets, the earth becomes humid, the water becomes cold, the air becomes humid, etc. In fact, the whole of creation is affected differently by the rising and the setting of the sun.

Drawing its breath to its place.

The word שׁאָף, which our translator incorrectly rendered as "is returned," means "to draw a breath." Therefore it means that by the powerful impulse with which it is moved the sun is a kind of cause of all the winds and breaths, just as when someone runs, he agitates the air and excites his breath. Therefore "to draw breath" means to be carried by a very rapid impulse from the east to the west and then back to the east, which is what happens every day and every night.

Round and round goes the wind, and on its circuits the wind returns.

That is, when the sun returns to the east in order to rise there again, it takes the wind with it and has the wind in its hand. All this is a typically Solomonic pleonasm; the only thing he wants to say by it is that the sun rises and sets daily and that the wind is moved by its impulse.

7. *All streams run to the sea, but the sea is not full; to the place where the streams flow, there they flow again.*

Aristotle disputes about where springs and winds come from and really sweats over this investigation, as do many others.[5] But nowhere do we find what Solomon says here, that all streams come

[4] The original reads *elementorem,* but we have read *elementorum.*
[5] See *Luther's Works,* 2, pp. 93—95.

from the sea and in turn fill the sea. He makes the sea the origin and beginning of all waters and streams, which gush out and break forth from it through hidden passageways. Most philosophers suppose that each stream has its own origin beneath the earth and gushes forth from this. But Solomon's opinion is the correct one, namely, that all the waters, whether of springs or of streams, flow from the sea and flow back to the sea. These are very great miracles: first, the course and movement of that huge light, about which I have just been speaking; second, the fact that streams run to the sea and yet the sea is never full. Otherwise, if even the Elbe had been flowing since the beginning of the world, it could have filled the entire sphere of the air all the way to the sphere of the moon. But now, even though it has been flowing more than five thousand years, it is still being held within its banks and does not overflow.

Therefore he says that everything is borne along in its proper order and that one thing follows another in perpetual motion, just as the sun continually moves and never stops. Thus also the air is always in motion. The streams, too, continually run into the sea, and the sea in turn, as it were, is distilled and sweats itself out through hidden passageways of the earth and channels of the mountains into rivers and springs. The earth is a veritable bag of lye, by which water is purified. Thus you see that in a few words Solomon embraces the marvelous arrangement and interaction of the four elements, as he mentions the earth, the sun, the wind, and the streams.

I believe, however, that Solomon intends this as an allegory of these changes in nature in order to direct us to the matter he is discussing and that he applies this allegory as a comparison with us. It is as though he were saying: "Just as all those things remain in their assigned places, so our things should as well." The sun never grows weary in its continual rounds, and the waters run to the sea but are not exhausted. So it is with human beings. They do not cease imitating their ancestors, who strove after vanity. Just as they never accomplished anything, so we never accomplish anything. No one is improved by the example of others or becomes more careful because of the danger of others. Julius Caesar was occupied with the vainest of strivings. Cicero strove for eloquence, but what was the outcome of his striving?

An utterly vain outcome, for he never attained what he wanted. If he had used his eloquence not for the sake of his own schemes but for the circumstances and benefit of other people, he would have been truly happy. We, too, follow their example. Therefore all the strivings of men rise and set, go and return and remain just as they always have been. Thus, as I have said, these words contain not only a description of the realm of vanity but also an analogy and a picture of human striving.

8. *All things are full of weariness; a man cannot utter it.*

The sophists corrupted this text because they thought that here the study of the philosophers was being reproached, the investigation of the nature of things and of their causes, as though this were something evil and beyond explanation.[6] But it is not an evil thing to investigate the nature and the qualities of things. Besides, the causes and the objects of this world are the most evident of all, far from difficult to know. The meaning, therefore, is this: he wants to speak about human vanity, but these vanities are so many and so great that he thinks he cannot say enough about them. The greatness of the vanity of men, he says, is unspeakable. Thus also Persius exclaims: "Oh, what vanity there is in things!"[7] And someone else says: "No one lives content with his lot, and no one has learned to remain within his destiny."[8] Vanity is too widespread to be counted throughout all the affairs of men. Therefore I shall be saying very little about vanity if you consider the magnitude of the subject. For vanity is so vast that I cannot comprehend it in any words. It is too big a thing either for them to grasp or for me to explain. It is simply too great, and there is too much of it. It is difficult to recount the variety of human desires and efforts — what Julius Caesar or Alexander or Solomon or Cato or Scipio or Pompey wanted. Feelings are always greater than words can express. He shows what he is saying by means of an example.

[6] Cf. Bonaventure, *Commentarius in Ecclesiasten, Opera* (Quaracchi, 1882 ff.), VI, pp. 17—18.

[7] Persius, *Satires*, I, 1.

[8] See p. 10, n. 4, above.

The eye is not satisfied with seeing, nor the ear filled with hearing.

That is, man has restless eyes and senses. If I were to begin recounting only the efforts we undertake with our eyes or our ears, I would be beginning an endless labor. If the eye is not satisfied with seeing, how could I express all the vanity of man with words? In short, "the heart of man is depraved and inscrutable" (Jer. 17:9). So great is the variety of human affections and desires that the eyes are never satisfied. They want first one thing, then another, and when they obtain it, the heart still is not satisfied. The heart is a constantly yawning chasm; it wants everything, and even if it obtained everything, it would go on looking for still more. Look at Alexander the Great. He was lord of almost the whole world. Yet when he heard that there were more worlds, he sighed: "And I have not yet conquered even one!"[9] Thus his heart wanted innumerable worlds. How could anyone, even the most eloquent, adequately describe the enormous vanity of this man's heart? The vanity and insatiability of the human heart are unspeakable. What a man has does not please him; what he does not have, that he yearns for. The words *The eye is not satisfied with seeing* you should explain in a general way, not as they have explained it: "The eye is not satisfied with seeing heaven."[10]

9. *What has been is what will be, and what has been done is what will be done; and there is nothing new under the sun.*

10. *Is there a thing of which it is said, "See, this is new"? It has been already, in the ages before us.*

11. *There is no remembrance of former things, nor will there be any remembrance of later things yet to happen among those who come after.*

Here again the sophists are trifling when they interpret these words as referring to things themselves, even though he clearly shows that he is speaking about affections and desires when he says: "The eye is not satisfied, etc." For hearing and sight are the senses that feel things most and are affected by things most.

[9] Plutarch, *Lives*, "Alexander," ch. 5.
[10] Cf. Bonaventure, *Commentarius in Ecclesiasten, Opera*, VI, pp. 16—17.

This, then, is the meaning:

What has been, etc.

That is, after you have achieved what you wanted, your mind is still not at peace. You feel the same after you have achieved the thing as you did before you achieved the thing. The heart never finds fulfillment. When Alexander has gained the world, he has no more than he did before, because his heart is no more satisfied than it was. As he accomplished nothing before his attempt, so he accomplishes nothing after it either. Julius Caesar thinks about establishing the republic, and Brutus thinks about establishing it also; but neither of them accomplishes it. This is what it means when it says: *What has been is what will be.* That is, the feeling that is never satisfied is always the same. What it wants and strives to have or to achieve is the very same thing it now has. In short, whatever one has today he will have even more of tomorrow. This refers to that restless and insatiable appetite and the vanity of the human heart, which cannot be satisfied with the things that are present, no matter what they may be. What I have achieved today means nothing to me. If I have something, if I achieve something, I still am not content. I always want to do something else. This is the way all men behave—Julius Caesar, Pompey, Alexander. As those men behaved, so everyone behaves, wishing for the things that are future and being bored with the things that are present. Remember, therefore, that in these words he is speaking about human actions, not about the things that are to be created or have been created, for he is always referring to the things that take place under the sun, in this realm of the world. Therefore it continues:

There is nothing new under the sun. There is no thing of which it can be said: See, this is new.

This passage creates very great difficulties for the sophists, because they read in Sacred Scripture that many new things have been done.[11] For example, the nativity of Christ is something new, and it is a new thing that His mother was a virgin. Again (Is. 65:17): "I create new heavens and a new earth"; also (Rev.

[11] Cf. Augustine, *De Genesi ad litteram*, IV, chs. 11—12, *Patrologia, Series Latina*, XXXIV, 303—306; also *Luther's Works*, 2, pp. 148—49.

21:5): "I make all things new"; and again (Num. 16:30): "The Lord creates something new on the earth." These passages caused them to perpetrate enormous kinds of nonsense as they sought to harmonize what Solomon says here with what these passages say. But this happened because of an ignorance of Solomon's way of speaking, because they did not pay attention to what he means when he says *under the sun.* For if you take this to refer to the things and works of God themselves, it is not true; for God is constantly doing new things. But it is we who do nothing new, because the same old Adam is present in all of us. Our ancestors abused things in exactly the same way as we do. Julius Caesar had the same attitude as Alexander had; so did all the emperors and kings, and so do we. Just as they could not find fulfillment, so it is with us. They were wicked, so are we. We want to fill all our senses, but we cannot because our heart is insatiable. Therefore we do nothing new under the sun. There are no new affections in man, but we always remain the same and do not refrain from curiosity even when we have been warned by the example of such men. The human heart ought to be content with the things that are present and to stifle its affection for the things that are future. The fact that it does not is truly the vainest of vanities. Therefore this is what he is saying when he says *there is nothing new under the sun:* there is nothing new in human beings, but God does many new things.

But he says later on in this same chapter (1:16): "I have surpassed in wisdom all the kings who were before me." Was this not something new? Of course. But this was a gift of God, and therefore genuinely new. But all men go on with the same affections, and you will not find even one man whose affections have been new in any way. Other men have built buildings as we do, have waged war as we do. And as they did not achieve what they wanted by their affections and efforts, so we do not either. But God by His works and gifts does many great and ever new things.

There is no remembrance of those who have gone before.

That is, men follow their own desires and push their own schemes, and they do not permit themselves to be moved by the examples of their ancestors, who accomplished nothing. No one considers that the schemes of Alexander and Julius Caesar were in vain. Brutus was not moved by the example of Dion, who unsuccessfully pressed his plans to recall Dionysius and to reestablish his government.[12] These things are a kind of theme of the entire book, announcing the subject about which he will be speaking, namely, human vanity, by which we attempt much and accomplish nothing, or in other words, the inconstancy and insatiability of the human heart.

12. *I the Preacher have been king over Israel in Jerusalem.*

13. *And I applied my mind to seek and to search out by wisdom all that is done under the sun.*

Thus far we have heard the general theme or argument of the book: he has proposed to speak about the unsuccessful strivings and efforts of men, on which they rely for the achievement and fulfillment of their plans; these God makes useless, as something which He always resists. Now, by a dialectical induction, he begins to enumerate particulars, in order to support the universal proposition with which he opened the book, namely, "Vanity of vanities, etc." This vanity or misery is increased when a man sees that the strivings of men who have gone before have been frustrated and their efforts useless and that they have tormented themselves in vain, and yet he does not learn from this. The flesh is so foolish, the reason so blind, that it will not be corrected by any examples.

But he begins with himself and sets himself up as an example of vanity. He says: "I tried to establish my reign wisely and brilliantly, but I failed, even though I was a king by divine right." It is well known that this king had been commended and ennobled in Holy Scripture for his divine wisdom, as we read in 1 Kings 3: 11-12: "Because you have asked this, and have not asked for yourself long life or riches, etc., behold, I give you a wise and discerning mind, so that none like you has been before you and none like you shall arise after you." This was a great testimony to the wisdom of this king. And yet so wise and prudent a king did not achieve what he wanted. His schemes did not meet with success, and properly so, for God did not give him this wisdom to make him capable of everything. God did not say: "I shall give a wisdom

[12] A reference to Dion of Syracuse, who died in 354 B. C., a pupil of Plato.

that others will hear about." Therefore Solomon had more labor and sorrow from this wisdom than he did success. He saw that God was pleased when he established his reign properly and laid down the laws for the people; but no one, neither princes nor people, followed him.

Therefore he says: "If even I have not succeeded in my schemes and no one went along with them, what will happen to those who are not as wise as I? First, I shall cite my experience. I the Preacher have been king of the Israelites." All his words are emphatic and magnificent: "I am king, and yet I achieve nothing. Who will resist a king, one who is lord of all? Besides, I am not simply a king of some people or other but of the people of God, in which there have been many holy men, prophets, doctors of the Law, etc. Finally, I am king in Jerusalem, this supremely holy place which God chose as His habitation. If a king so powerful, free, and wise, ruling over the holiest of peoples in the holiest of cities, with God and the Word of God present, still cannot carry out his good and holy plans, what shall we say about others?"

And I applied my mind to seek and to search out by wisdom all that is done under the sun.

Once more we must remain with the theme. He is not speaking about the deeds of God, which are not confined to the area under the sun but are everywhere, but about those things that are done by men and that happen under heaven. This is the place and the realm committed to us, for the works of God are above heaven, below heaven, and everywhere. It is, therefore, of works that we do by our plans and our powers that he says, *I applied my mind.* That is to say: "In order to arrange everything in the best possible way, in order to have a government set up with the best possible order. But God performed only as much as He Himself ordained. Otherwise, where God did not add His hand, I went ahead with pressing my own plans, wisdom, and efforts to make everything come out right, but in vain. I accomplished nothing except to plague and torture myself miserably." Thus it now follows:

It is an unhappy business that God has given to the sons of men to be troubled with.

That is: "God gave me this thought as a punishment, so that

I would finally learn that I should not trust in my wisdom and that if God does not will things, they are all in vain, even if they have been undertaken very wisely. I could not bear it if there was any defect or any error. Therefore it was just of Him to afflict me with this thought, to teach me to resign everything to His will and to see that my wisdom is nothing." But it is an evil affliction, because we refuse to yield to the wisdom of God and claim to know better. We do not bear what the wisdom of God brings and do not commit ourselves to His will.

Otherwise, the thought and investigation by which we want to be of counsel to the state is not only not evil but pious. It is a good man indeed who wants to be of counsel to the world. Someone who feels this way and argues as follows, "Would that this state and this prince had the right ideas!" is not thinking or feeling wrongly. For a solicitude about the establishment and preservation of the state is certainly a fine virtue, in fact the highest virtue among men. "This very fine investigation," I say, "by which I wanted to be of counsel to the state, was a vain one. It did not succeed, but only brought me misery." Cicero and Demosthenes, the most prudent of men, wanted to be of the best possible counsel to the state, but instead they only entangled it with all sorts of evils. Thus God made their wisdom vain. So it is, then, that this book condemns the solicitude and anxiety to be of assistance to things, whether public or private, with our own counsels and wisdom. Look at Adam, Abraham, Isaac, and all the saintly fathers. As soon as they began to rely on their own counsels apart from the Word of God, everything immediately slipped away from them, and they accomplished nothing. For unless God has preceded men with His Word, they accomplish nothing good. Without the action and the Word of God we do nothing, even though we may begin something. Thus when Adam and Eve at the birth of Cain said (Gen. 4:1), "I have gotten a man with the help of the Lord," [13] they were frustrated, because this was a human thought without the Word. They had magnificent hopes that this would be the promised Seed. He was brought up and established as the heir of the world. Soon Cain killed his brother, and with that all their thinking fell and became vain. Thus also Isaac was deceived in Esau, his firstborn.

[13] See Luther's more extended discussion of Gen. 4:1, pp. 319—21.

Saul's plan to pass his reign on to his sons was vain. Thus also David was in error when he gave a preferential position to Absalom. So it is that God puts to naught the thoughts and plans that do not depend on the Word, and rightly so. For why do we want to prescribe to Him and add to His wisdom?

Let us learn, therefore, to submit ourselves to the counsels of God and to refrain from the cares and thoughts that God has not commanded. There is nothing safer or more acceptable to God than if we refrain from our own counsels and rely on His Word. There we shall find sufficient guidance about what we ought to do. His commands to us are faith, love, and bearing the cross. With these things, I say, we can happily occupy ourselves. Let us deal with everything else as it comes into our hands, leaving to Him the concern about its outcome. But now, because we despise His Word, God punishes us in turn by having us plague ourselves in vain. For God resists in such a way as to prevent the realization either of the good or of the evil that wise men and princes plan to the neglect of the Word. As Ps. 33:10 says, "The Lord brings the counsel of the nations to naught." Where there is the most impressive wisdom and the most diligent activity, therefore, there God most thoroughly frustrates the plans. This is obviously happening in our times, when the princes and bishops of Germany have been unable to accomplish anything with all their assemblies and all their counsels. Nevertheless, not even in this way can God bring us to the point that we submit our plans to His will. Therefore it is said to be "an unhappy business," that is, one that afflicts and tortures — not as though the things themselves, such as wisdom, plans, etc. were evil, but in keeping with the usage of Scripture, as in Matt. 6:34: "The day's own trouble is sufficient for the day." But God has given men this trouble or affliction not in order to destroy them but in order to call them back from their foolish wisdom and schemes and to teach us that our wisdom amounts to nothing. Cicero did indeed say many wise things in his writings; but if, when we read them, we try to carry them out, everything goes crabwise and nothing comes of it, because we have gone at it with our own plans. For it is not wisdom that accomplishes anything, not even genuine wisdom, but the will of God, so that we learn to pray (Matt. 6:10): "Thy will be done."

14. *I have seen everything that is done under the sun; and behold, all is vanity and vexation of spirit.*

15. *What is crooked cannot be made straight, and what is lacking cannot be numbered.*

This is a confirmation of the preceding statement. "Not only have I learned about this vanity by my own experience, but I have watched all the others and have seen that their plans are frustrated as well as mine. Just as my own plans did not succeed, so I saw that no one else's in the world succeeded either. The plans of the wise are frustrated just as much as those of the foolish." With this word, therefore, that attitude which is called "good intentions" is rejected, as is commonly said: "I meant it for the best." But a good intention is nothing unless it is regulated by the Word of God and takes its beginning from faith. Other intentions, even those that appear to be very good, are deceptive and extremely harmful. Cicero himself testified to this from his own experience: "The best plans come out worst." [14] And God does rightly when He frustrates our plans this way, because when there is even a bit of success, men are soon inflated and arrogate the glory to themselves, which is contrary to the glory of God, who wants the glory to be given to Him alone.

Iniquity or crookedness cannot be corrected, and what is lacking cannot be numbered.

He adds the cause for the affliction of everything with useless care and anxiety. It is, he says, because the defects are infinite. They cannot be corrected, and they are so many and so great that they overcome all human counsel. Thus he wants to say: "To be sure, I understand with considerable wisdom what is useful and appropriate. But what am I to do to counteract these things?" There is such great crookedness and depravity in human affairs that they can never be corrected. Look at the Roman empire. Although it was administered prudently, it was never able by its own counsels to find a lasting peace or to achieve it. In place of one enemy who fell there arose many others. And when there were no foreign wars, there arose internal conflicts, until the state perished. This is what happens to all men. Let everyone look at the

---

[14] Cf. Cicero, *De natura deorum*, II, 12; *De divinatione*, I, 131; I, 24.

course of his own life. If anyone's life has gone at all times just as he had proposed, he may accuse this book of lying. Therefore it would be best to commit everything to God and to follow those who say: "Let it happen as it happens, because it wants to happen as it happens." [15] The German proverb also admonishes: "You are much too rakish around the beak to be able to make old rascals pious." Therefore you see that princes who want to reform and correct everything in the best possible way often do a great deal of harm. It is impossible in human affairs to act so well that everything comes out right and no more evils remain. It is most right, therefore, to walk by faith, which permits God to reign and prays that the kingdom of God may come, but meanwhile tolerates and bears with all evils, turning the matter over "to Him who judges justly" (1 Peter 2:23). So Christ "did not trust Himself to" men (John 2:24), but He did tolerate the defects and iniquities of all men. When the murder of John the Baptist was announced, that horrible crime, He was silent, went away into the desert, fed the people, and did not make an issue of it, but only preached the Word and did His duty. Christian wisdom, therefore, means to commit oneself to the power of God and to turn one's cause over to Him who judges justly. A Christian can indeed, by the office of the Word, judge sin, but he should not raise [16] his hand against it unless he is compelled to do so by God or commanded by the Word. And so when you are alone and unable to set everything right and straight, commit your cause to Him who has more powers and who alone can do everything.

16. *I communed with my own heart, saying: Behold, I have come to greatness, surpassing in wisdom all who were over me in Jerusalem before me; and my mind has considered many things wisely.*

17. *And I applied my mind to know wisdom and knowledge and to know madness and folly. I perceived that this also is vexation of spirit.*

---

[15] Luther frequently quoted this "trite proverbial saying," e. g., *Luther's Works*, 7, p. 192.

[16] We have accepted the conjecture suggested by the Weimar editors and have read *admovere* rather than *admoliri*.

18. *For in much wisdom is much vexation, and he who increases knowledge increases sorrow.*

This is almost identical with what he said earlier. "I have," he says, "often thought how it happens that my efforts and plans do not succeed, even though I have come to greatness and surpass all others in wisdom." For in addition to the divine wisdom, which had been granted by God, he was also outstanding in his admirable human or political wisdom, so much so that even the seating of his officials was like a miracle to the queen of Sheba (2 Chron. 9:4).

Wisdom and knowledge. Knowledge does not refer to speculative knowledge, but to a practical and experiential insight, a discretion in the performance of actions, what we call experience and practice in human affairs, as in the psalm (Ps. 119:66): "Teach me good judgment and knowledge." Wisdom, on the other hand, is the insight by which I know how the state ought to be established and administered; this is then modified by knowledge or experience, in accordance with things as they are at present and with circumstances, in the manner and pattern that the facts and the times warrant.

Madness and folly. That is, to keep these away from myself and from my kingdom, but to promote the other qualities. But how did it come out? I learned that even this was a vexation of spirit and a useless anxiety, which does not attain its purpose. Therefore the wisest thing is to compose oneself in such a way that one can stand anything. Why?

For in much wisdom is much vexation. Anyone who sees much and who knows how it is to go cannot help becoming angry. He thinks: Oh, how miserably and dreadfully things happen in this world! What is the source of this anger and indignation except much wisdom? For anyone who is very wise has many reasons to become angry, as one who daily sees many things that are wrong. Someone whose eyes are closed knows nothing and does not become indignant. Therefore learn to keep quiet, to commit the kingdom to God, and to pray: "Lord, Thy will be done." Otherwise you will wear out your heart and your body, and you will waste time and eventually your life.

CHAPTER TWO

1. *I said to myself: Come now, I will make a test of pleasure; enjoy yourself. But behold, this also was vanity.*

IN the preceding chapter he showed that the anxiety and solicitude and planning of men, particularly when we want to be of aid and counsel to others, are vain and empty. He teaches that we should be content with the Word and work of God, so that we are not presumptuous about anything except what the Word of God prescribes or His work requires. Often this seems to be contrary to the Word, as when He oppresses us in some way even though we have acted correctly according to the Word. Then we need faith and patience, so that we do not seek our own counsels and try to evade what He has sent, but commit ourselves to Him and bear the hand of God in His work. Now he turns to the other side.

I said to myself: Come now, I will make a test of pleasure.

It is as though he were saying: "Since anxieties and my own plans cannot achieve anything, I shall refrain from them. I shall turn to the right hand and make a more tranquil life for myself. I shall create ease and tranquillity, take delight in good things, let everything happen as it happens and chooses, and live a life of pleasure." But this, too, was useless and was no more successful than his earlier reliance on human wisdom and anxiety, for God resists this also. Tranquillity is not attainable except from the Word and work of God. Experience itself teaches this. Often dinner parties are arranged to create a happy atmosphere, with foods and entertainment intended to make the guests happy. But usually it comes out just the opposite way, and only seldom does a good party result. Either there are gloomy and solemn faces present, or something else upsets all the arrangements, especially when there is such deliberation and planning about how much fun it will be. By contrast, it often happens that someone happens upon a most joyful dinner party by accident, that is, by the gift of God. The same thing happens in other areas of life. One seeks pleasure in love but soon experiences bitterness. Augustine also complains in his *Confessions* that he was tormented horribly in the very midst of his amorous affairs.[1] Thus when we seize upon pleasure, it is soon covered with bitterness. Therefore, the best thing is to abide in the Word and work of God, to instruct the heart this way in how to be peaceful and content with the things that are present. If the Lord has given one a wife, one should now hold on to her and enjoy her. If you want to exceed these limits and add to this gift which you have in the present, you will get grief and sorrow instead of pleasure. One should therefore simply stick to what the Lord wills and gives. If you want joy and delight, wait to receive it from Him. As He offers it to you, accept it. "Rejoice with those who rejoice" (Rom. 12:15). Do not try to be wise and solemn in the midst of those who are rejoicing, as sanctimonious people do, who dampen the happiness of other people, which God has given. Just be sure to acknowledge that all of this comes to you from God; accept it from His hand and use it as His gift.

In sum, we should not find enjoyment in happiness, goods, our own counsels, or any other thing; only as God has given them should we use them. One should let God have His way. It is not up to us to prescribe the place, the person, or the manner; if we do, we shall go wrong. This does not mean that happiness is condemned as something evil or vain. What is condemned is human striving and planning, when we ourselves want or try to create happiness without respect to the will of God. But as both come from God, so let us use them. As it is a sin to invite anxiety and sorrow by our own counsels and also a sin to refuse to suffer them when they are imposed on us by God, so it is also to be condemned if we run away from happiness and do not accept it when it is given by God. This is what those sanctimonious killjoys do when they "disfigure their faces" (Matt. 6:16). They seek out places, times, and persons that are gloomy, and they prescribe strict regulations, which is hypocritical and vain. They want us to weep with those who weep, but they themselves refuse to rejoice with those who rejoice (cf. Rom. 12:15). Sorrow, happiness, and all such things, whether external or internal, must not be measured on the basis of places, times, etc.; but as they come from God in His complete freedom, so one should use them in complete freedom.

---

[1] Augustine, *Confessions,* II, ch. 3.

Therefore he says: *I said to myself: Come now, I will make a test of pleasure*, that is, "I wanted to measure it by manners and rules, but this was nothing but vanity." Here again it is appropriate to warn that we should not stray from the theme, as Jerome did when he foolishly boasted that from this book he had learned contempt for the world and for all things.[2] He was then followed by monks and sophists, who did not know what it was to flee the world—in fact, did not know what the world was. For this is in fact to teach a contempt for the good creatures of God and to forbid their use, contrary to the clear words of Holy Scripture. Fleeing the world, therefore, does not mean abstaining from things, but it means abstaining from one's own counsels. This would have been the right way for Jerome to teach his disciple Blesilla: "Do not despise things, but rather despise the strivings, plans, affections, and concerns by which you seek to obtain everything for yourself by your own exertions. It is not honor and desire for things that is evil, but an anxiety about things and your schemes to obtain them are to be despised. Nor is a contempt for the world the same as wearing dirty clothes, wearying your flesh with vigils, growing weak through fasting, and the like, but using these very things as they come. If God has given you food, eat it; if fasting, bear it; if honor, accept it; if condemnation, suffer it; if He casts you into prison, put up with it; if He wants you to be king, obey Him when He calls; if He casts you down, do not worry." So David was a real despiser of the world when with equanimity he administered his kingdom and bore his exile. The real despisers of the world are those who accept everything as God sends it to them, using everything with thanksgiving while it is present and freely doing without it if the Lord takes it away.

2. *I said of laughter: It is mad, and of pleasure: What use is it?*

You should take all these things as referring to human counsels. He wants to say: "I wanted to use skill to seek the good, to seek pleasures and happiness. But this thought was sheer madness, which brought me double affliction. In the first place, the very labor of thinking and seeking brings affliction to the heart. In the second place, when I was hoping that I had achieved it, suddenly there came another conflict or trouble, and I lost both the labor and

[2] See p. 4 above.

the joy." By "laughter" he means what I myself seek, and by "pleasure" what I try to accomplish. *What use is it?* "Because it never turns out right for me, and some kind of trouble always arises." Therefore the best happiness and gaiety is that which is not sought but is offered unexpectedly by God without your caring or planning. Thus outward happiness is indeed a good thing, but only for those who know how to use it well. The wicked, by contrast, even when they are lost in revelry, still are not happy, because they do not recognize that this is a gift of God and are always bored, dissatisfied with the things that are present and looking for something else.

3. *And I thought in my heart that I would abstain from wine and govern my heart wisely and comprehend prudence, till I might see what was good for the sons of men to do under the sun during all the days of their life.*

Now for the third time he undertakes to experience something else, to see whether perhaps this would succeed: "In the world and in human society, where I have lived, I find success neither in the anxieties with which I trouble myself as I seek to give counsel to others nor in my own pleasures. They are all useless. Therefore I shall undertake a rigid and austere way of life, one of total abstinence and strictness." I am amazed that those false despisers of the world and of creation have not referred to this passage of Solomon, where he calls an austere way of life and severe rigor "vanity." Therefore he is condemning here those extremely strict observances of the monks, and especially those of the Carthusians, which the world nevertheless admires and regards as marks of piety and sanctity. This passage is like a thunderbolt against all the regulations and the religiosity of the monks, by which they subject to themselves and to their own planning such things as do not belong to them. This is not to say that abstinence is evil; what is evil is to seek it out by one's own planning and to bind oneself to it as something necessary. For time, things, and places are gifts of God, which they nevertheless want to take captive through their rules and prescriptions. Besides, all they get out of it is sorrow and misery, while they torture the flesh and torment themselves in vain. For this is what the Carthusians prescribe: One is not to eat meat even if one were dying of hunger. The worst part of it is that they look for sanctity in such things, as though the devil himself could not be a saint this way, since, after all, he neither drinks wine nor dresses in purple, etc.

Therefore he is saying: "All things would be good for me, whether abstaining or eating and drinking, but they become very evil when I add my own ideas." God has not prescribed place or time, food or abstinence, but in our foolishness we prescribe: "Now I shall eat meat, now I shall not eat it." God Himself says: "When you have it, eat; if you do not have it, abstain." Therefore if you want to be abstinent, wait for the counsel of the Lord. He is able to cast you into prison, into hunger, into infirmity, and the like. There you should be abstinent, for there you have a rule that has been prescribed for you not by yourself but by God Himself. But now by your own ideas you make up a form of abstinence that is contrary to the will of God. These outstanding despisers of the world, moreover, everywhere abstain from things in such a way that they never lack for anything. They act in such a way as never to have to abstain. In short, just as they are puffed up above God through their own righteousness, so they are puffed up above the creation through their own ordinances.

And govern my heart wisely.

That is: "By my own counsel I wanted to control myself wisely and to be wise in abstinence, so that I might understand prudence"—or perhaps foolishness. For the Hebrew term is ambiguous, meaning sometimes wisdom, sometimes foolishness. But usually it means foolishness, so that it would mean here "to understand foolishness," that is, to know how to warn others about what is foolish and what is wise, to understand, I say, how one may do this avoiding, since it belongs to wisdom not only to know the good but also to avoid the evil.

He is almost reciting a catalog of the works he undertook, to teach others. "I began to attempt many things. Occupied as I was with them, I abstained from wine and pleasure. By working and building I looked for experience and wisdom, to teach others, so that on the basis of my example others would live rightly, wisely abstain, and rule their households. (He is speaking about human and political wisdom, not about divine or spiritual wisdom, by which we understand the things that pertain to our relation with

God.) Therefore I began to build, to plant vineyards, and omitted no labor or effort. But all I got from all these labors was vanity, because I wanted to direct myself by my own counsel." The wish to direct oneself by one's own counsel is a vain one. In fact, anyone who seeks to direct himself by his own counsel afflicts himself with a double disadvantage: first, he tortures himself with his own counsels; second, he accomplishes nothing, or if he does accomplish something, sorrow intervenes and undoes it. So Nero built a magnificent royal palace but did not enjoy it. That is the way it usually happens, that one man builds but another possesses and enjoys what has been built; as the parable in the Gospel says (John 4:37), "One sows and another reaps." Thus Frederick, our prince of blessed memory, built many things, but now others possess them.[3] He gave his attention to things that were in the future and was not content with things that were in the present. As soon as he had built one thing, he was looking for another. The prince who is ruling now does not enjoy the things that were built but is building still others, fortifying his cities, and following an altogether different course. And his successor, in turn, will find his pleasure in yet a different course.

Therefore this is truly a great vanity and misery, to be troubled in one's own work with care and anxiety until it is finished, but when it is done, to die or become ill or be deprived of its use and its good by some other hindrance. Similarly, the one who succeeds to a thing that has been done does not use it or even destroys it. Such is the course of all of human life. God always battles against the counsels of men, and we in turn battle against the counsels of God. It is easy for Him to destroy whatever we have begun. Indeed, so great is the vanity of the heart that it never agrees with itself; nor can it be so stable that it can stick to present reality and find its peace there. When a thing has been attempted and accomplished by a man, the curiosity about doing something remains. There is boredom with what has been done, and something else is sought, as he has also said earlier (1:9): "What has been is what will be." The human mind remains the same after achieving a thing as it was before achieving the thing—always inconstant and restless. If someone has a gulden, he concerns himself with his wish for ten; if he has ten, he wishes for a hundred;

---

[3] Frederick the Wise, Elector of Saxony, had died in 1525.

if he has a hundred, he wishes for a thousand. If a prince has one castle, well constructed, he wants two. If he has one kingdom, he tries to gain a second. In sum, Alexander wants many worlds.

This is also how it happens in domestic matters, in marriage and in the rearing of children. You think about marrying a wife, one who is well-mannered, chaste, pleasant, a good mother. But it can happen that you get a wife whose manner is completely different, one who is very bad, or who, even though she may be truly good, still leaves much to be desired for you. You think about how to rear your sons to be decent and useful to the state. But behold, contrary to your expectation they become criminals or scoundrels of some other kind, useless burdens on the earth. Is that a reason to desert my home and my domestic responsibilities, because I see that nothing succeeds for all my diligence and that nothing responds to my labors? No. What, then? One must rule his household, found a family, educate his children, and rule his wife, but in such a way that it happens without your measure and rule, that you do not trust in your own wisdom. If your son is suited for learning the liberal arts, let him learn them; if he is suited for a craft, let him learn that. The important thing is that you do not exceed your own limits, but commit the entire outcome and success to God. Otherwise you will have the double disadvantage mentioned above. On this basis it is easy to understand what follows:

4. *I made great works; I built houses and planted vineyards for myself;*

5. *I made myself gardens and paradises, planted with all kinds of fruit trees.*

6. *I made myself pools from which to water the forest of growing trees.*

7. *I obtained male and female slaves, also domestic ones; I also had great possessions of herds and flocks, more than any who had been before me in Jerusalem.*

8. *I also gathered for myself silver and gold and the treasure of kings and provinces; I got singers, both men and women, man's delight, and every kind of musical instrument.*

9. *So I became great and surpassed all who were before me in Jerusalem; also my wisdom remained with me.*

10. *And whatever my eyes desired I did not keep from them; I kept my heart from no pleasure, for my heart found pleasure in all my toil, and this was my reward for all my toil.*

11. *Then I considered all that my hands had done and the toil I had spent in doing it, and behold, all was vanity and vexation of spirit, and there was nothing to be gained under the sun.*

As I have said, Solomon is reciting here a catalog of the works that he did to achieve happiness and pleasure and to administer his household properly. From what has been said before, these are easy to understand. *I made great works.* Our translator has rendered this as "I magnified," that is, "I made outstanding and great works," about which you can read in 1 Kings 3 and 7. But what were the fruits that I had from this? Nothing but labor, while others had the fruit and the benefit.

Paradises or gardens of pleasure. The Hebrew word means a garden of pleasure, where one makes beautiful plantings of flowers and the loveliest plants. *Domestic servants,* that is, servants who were born in the house. The children of slaves born in the house were called "domestic" and served in perpetuity the master whose slave their father had been, regardless of whether he had been purchased or had come into slavery by some other means. *I obtained male and female slaves,* that is, "I was an outstanding householder and head of the family, and I sought to rule my household by my own counsel." "I made a treasure" or Gaza. "Whatever there was of beautiful and precious things in other regions," he says, "that I gathered for the pomp of my kingdom, as great and wealthy kings are accustomed to do."

I got singers, both men and women, man's delight, etc.

Here there is a grammatical quarrel about what שִׁדָּה and שִׁדּוֹת mean.[4] I have translated them as "male and female dancers," but this does not satisfy me. Meanwhile I am following those who think that these were musical instruments; this is on the basis of the preceding, where he writes: "I got singers, both men and women, man's delight, namely, musical instruments." He repeats the term,

---

[4] The Septuagint had translated these words with οἰνοχόους καὶ οἰνοχόας, but even the translators of the Revised Standard Version note that "the meaning of the Hebrew word is uncertain."

saying שָׂדֶה וְשִׂדּוֹת, perhaps because he wants to indicate the harmony between them or their antiphonal music. *I became great, etc.*, that is, all these things were obtained and arranged in the most appropriate manner. He continues *My wisdom remained with me.* By "wisdom" he understands not speculative wisdom, but the wisdom to govern life and all things; in this, of course, divine wisdom is included. He acknowledges that he had not only an abundance of all things but with it also the wisdom to administer, carry on, and govern all these things properly, which is the greatest gift of God. But he did not have success, because he wanted to make everything succeed by his own counsel, the things that he himself had prudently arranged, etc., although the unanimous statement of all men on [5] earth is: "It doesn't work!" They see that many things are defined and set prudently up but still do not meet with success. Therefore the greatest part of wisdom is to know this, that success does not follow except in its own time and that things are not governed either by the counsel of the wise or by the temerity of the foolish.

Whatever my eyes desired I did not keep from them. That is, "I extended myself even further and wanted to enjoy all these good things that I had prepared, but it was not allowed. I wanted this to be my portion in life, but God does not permit me to decide these pleasures by my own counsel; He continually put various obstacles in my way. When I wanted to enjoy my pleasures and my gardens, the business of the realm called me away; there were judicial decisions to be handed down, conflicts to be adjudicated and settled, etc. Thus I could not decide my happiness by my own counsel." The same thing happens to our princes. When they propose to enjoy themselves, some sad business interferes to disturb their fun and make them sorrowful. Thus God always acts to hinder our plans and the rule that we prescribe for ourselves. He gives us enough for our use and happiness, but at the same time He wants us to have and to keep His things pure and unalloyed in their freedom. *Behold, all was vanity and vexation of spirit.* Is this not the height of vanity, that a king who has such wealth and such an abundance of everything is not able by his own counsel to enjoy even one of this infinite number of things? And if he does enjoy one, he must enjoy it in snatches. So utterly are we unable to con-

[5] The Weimar text reads *iu*, which should certainly be *in*.

trol or govern or comprehend things by our own counsel. Therefore let everyone freely enjoy the things that are present, as God has given them. Let him permit them to be granted or withdrawn, to come or to go, according to the Lord's will. When things are going well, let him think that they can go badly, and vice versa, so that he does not, like the wicked, wallow and drown in pleasures. *And there was nothing to be gained under the sun.* On the basis of his own plans he has nothing but trouble and misery. The things themselves are good, to be sure, but our efforts are vain. We prescribe rules or methods of use for them, even though they do not permit themselves to be regulated by us.

12. *So I turned to consider wisdom and madness and folly; for what man can imitate the King who has previously made him?*
13. *Then I saw that wisdom excels folly as light excels darkness.*
14. *The wise man has his eyes in his head, but the fool walks in darkness; and yet I perceived that one fate comes to all of them.*

Another experience proves that everything is vanity, namely, the efforts and plans of men. "Whatever happened to me," he says, "I saw that it also happened to others. My counsels and even my wisdom were vain and useless; they did not have the success that I wanted. I observed the same thing in others as well. I observed the wisdom and the madness of others and compared them with each other. I saw that some men behave very wisely and attempt many things prudently. I also saw mad fools acting without any plan. Yet their folly and madness was somehow lucky and successful, while the plans of the wise men were utterly useless and the wise men themselves were so unfortunate that the madness merited the proverb 'Fortune helps the bold.'"[6] Cicero and Demosthenes were very wise men, who brilliantly established the state and prescribed its laws. They thought that the outcome and the success would correspond to this, but it turned out otherwise, so that one of them exclaims about himself: "Oh, I have never been a wise man, and yet somehow I was mistakenly regarded as something I was not. How deceived your opinion of me has been,

---

[6] Vergil, *Aeneid*, X, 284.

Roman people!" [7] But the other one, bent with age and broken by trouble, said that he would rather die than return to government office, after having experienced for himself that things are not decided by the counsels of the wise, not even by their good counsels.[8] By contrast, Julius and Octavius Caesar, who pursued their plans not always with wisdom but often with boldness, were much more fortunate. Philip of Macedon acted against the counsels of Demosthenes and was himself more fortunate than prudent.[9] The counsels were indeed good ones, but urging them in order to bring about certain success is vain, for human affairs refuse to be taken captive by human counsels. In short, a thing is not decided by the wisdom of the wise nor by the temerity of the foolish, so that the counsels of the wise are made foolish and we do not glory in ourselves. Thus in war victory does not come immediately, even though the army may be highly trained and everything may be very wisely thought out, as some years ago certain victory was expected by the French over the emperor, but the opposite came out.[10]

Therefore he says: You see that the foolish succeed as well as the wise, so that there is no difference apparent between the wise man and the madman as far as success is concerned, in fact, so that it seems that there is no God who would allow things to be carried on so madly. But Solomon answers: "No, wisdom is far more excellent than folly," even though it is true that human wisdom does not accomplish things but God Himself accomplishes them. God is able by His wisdom to accomplish whatever He wishes, but man does not accomplish it. For God has not only wisdom but also the power to accomplish it, so that what He has decreed succeeds; man is not able to do this. In short, the counsel of God is not deceived, but the counsels of men, even of wise men, are deceived. Therefore he correctly says:

Then I saw that wisdom excels folly as light excels darkness. Wisdom is indeed a good thing; nevertheless, it lacks power and cannot accomplish things or decide events.

[7] Cicero died in 43 B. C., having failed at the end of his political career to bring Rome back from dictatorship to the principles of the Republic.

[8] Demosthenes died in 322 B. C. after having attempted unsuccessfully to achieve the independence of Greece from Macedon.

[9] Cf. Plutarch, *Lives*, "Demosthenes," 20.

[10] Luther is apparently referring to the Peace of Cambrai, signed on August 3, 1529, between Charles V and Francis I of France.

The wise man has his eyes in his head, but the fool, etc. I see that the same thing happens to both of them. Wisdom errs, and so does temerity; nevertheless, wisdom excels folly. To have one's eyes in one's head is a Hebraism, which we express commonly in German this way: "Whoever wants to play chess, had better not hide his eyes in his pocket." By this we mean that he must not only be an expert at the game but must also be a watchful and diligent player. Thus he says here also *The wise man has his eyes in his head.* That is, they are not only prudent administrators of affairs, but circumspect, diligent, and watchful. They do indeed see how affairs are to be administered, but they cannot bring about the outcome. The fool, on the other hand, does not have his eyes in his forehead, because he is carried along by temerity and boldness. Eventually the affairs of both are decided by luck and fortune, that is, by God's determination of the outcome, and not by either our counsel or our temerity. Both of them sometimes fall and sometimes prosper. But God does not want this to become the basis of rules. For the creatures are not in our hand, but in God's, who gives them to us to use and who through us does what He wishes. What we add on our own, however, when we wish to determine this use by our own counsels and efforts, is in vain. Therefore he instructs us not to trust in our own wisdom and counsel but to do what He has given us to do; if it does not succeed, we should commit it to God.

What man can imitate the King who has previously made him? In a beautiful and fitting periphrasis he describes God, as though he were to say: "God is our King. Not only has He made us, but He also continues to rule us, so that everything comes out for us according to His will. He alone persists from beginning to end, and His counsel and will cannot be hindered by anyone." This is why Solomon preferred to call Him King rather than God. Some have wisdom, others temerity; but none can imitate his King, none can do what He does. For what He prescribes happens; His will and counsel have success. "He has previously made us, that is, before we existed." There is a similar phrase in Paul (Rom. 11:35): "Who has given a gift to Him that he might be repaid?" Therefore as this King commands and rules, so everything comes out. In this way, therefore, he indicates that our counsels are nothing, because we have been made and are not the King. God does not want us and His creatures to be ruled by us, but the opposite; otherwise we would be Kings and Gods. Nothing is decided by our wisdom or our temerity, except that many have brought about evil by their temerity, and some by their wisdom, such as the very wise men Dio,[11] Cicero, Brutus, Demosthenes, etc. God makes human counsels and efforts useless and makes sport of them, and everywhere He is provoking us to fear Him, so that we learn to concede to Him the laws of government and not to prescribe anything to Him.

And yet I perceived that one fate comes to all of them. That is, "I saw that both had the same fortune, that the wise man accomplishes nothing just as the madman accomplishes nothing. Things cannot be decided either by temerity or by wisdom, even though God may permit them to be decided both ways, but this does not become a rule. For if our counsel did prevail, it would always prosper; if temerity were an obstacle, it should never prosper. Marius, Antony, and others like them accomplished more by their temerity than Cicero accomplished by his wisdom.[12] Nowhere is it better to note the examples of human temerity and wisdom than among the Romans and the Gentiles. For among the Jews the wars were mostly waged at the command of the prophets and on the basis of the Word of God.

15. *Then I said to myself: What befalls the fool will befall me also; why then have I been so very wise? And I said to myself that this also is vanity.*

This, too, is intended to make us refrain from trust in our own counsels. "I administered my kingdom very wisely," he says, "and yet it did not succeed as I wished. On the other hand, I had a prefect who did not rule as wisely, and yet he did succeed. Therefore when I see that fools have almost the same success or even greater success, why have I made such an effort to act wisely? That is, why do I trust in my own counsels and my own wisdom, adding sorrow to labor? And I said to myself that this also is vanity. By my experience I learned that one should trust neither in counsel nor in temerity." Earlier it was shown that wisdom excels folly,

[11] See p. 22, n. 12, above.

[12] A reference to the military exploits of Gaius Marius (d. 86 B. C.) and of Mark Antony (d. 30 B. C.).

even though affairs are decided neither by folly nor by wisdom. One should, therefore, travel by the middle way: affairs should be commended to the King, who has made us. If He has granted us some opportunity, let us use it; if He has given us something, let us accept it; if He takes it away, let us bear it. Whatever you can do, do; whatever you cannot do, leave alone. What you cannot budge, let lie. Wisdom is beneficial, then, if I do what I know is pleasing to God and commit to Him what He wishes to be accomplished through me. If we did this, then at last we would be truly wise.

16. *For of the wise man as of the fool there is no enduring remembrance, seeing that in the days to come all will have been long forgotten.*

What the wise man has decided and established by his own counsels as well as what the fool has done by his temerity, whether it turned out well or badly, will be consigned to oblivion. For neither they themselves nor others become better, so that they commit everything to God; but their descendants follow their own counsels and are not content with the ordinances of their ancestors but look for new ones. They are tired of what they have, and they look for what they do not have. This is what they imagine: "If it succeeded before, it will succeed again. If it did not succeed, it will succeed now. We will act more wisely than they did." Look at the Roman republic, how the consuls and emperors who followed always revoked what had been done by those who had preceded them; they were bored with the present and the past, and they looked to the future. Why then do you afflict yourself with many cares, as though your descendants were going to approve of what you are doing or even were going to feel the same way? They will not, for whatever one has one despises as useless. Therefore it is impossible for things or constitutions to remain in the same esteem among the descendants that they had among the ancestors. Lycurgus thought that he had given laws to the Lacedemonians that they would keep until he returned, that is, forever. With this in mind he departed never to return, hoping for the future and supposing that in this way his laws would be perpetuated.[13] But he accomplished nothing. Augustus used to say that he had laid such foundations

---

[13] Cf. Herodotus, *History*, I, chs. 65—66.

for the state that he hoped it would stand forever,[14] but those who followed soon overthrew it all. The Roman people longed for the death of Nero, supposing that then the state would be better, but afterwards the state was no better off. Solomon governed his realm in such a way that he hoped it would last forever, but it was divided right after his death. For Rehoboam, who succeeded Solomon, was not content with his father's wise administration of the state; he ruined everything, and his kingdom was cut into two parts.

But this does not happen only in external and political affairs, where such foolishness is more tolerable, since it does damage only to physical matters, but also in religion and in the Word of God. The descendants always neglect the purity of the doctrine handed down to them by the fathers and look for something new. This is what is now being done by those who, after the Gospel has once more become known, are not content with the purity of faith and the doctrine of the Gospel but are stirring up new controversies about the sacraments; and when these controversies have run their course, an infinite number of new sects will arise. For the flesh cannot remain content with the one simple and true doctrine.

But you should understand that Solomon is not speaking about persons but about the things that men do, be they wise or foolish, because these things are overlooked. The memory of men abides in books but not in the government of the state. Their historic accomplishments are recorded in the annals, but no one pays attention or cares. The descendants are not stirred by the example of their ancestors and are always interested in something new. Whatever is present is boring, whatever is absent is intriguing. And yet there is nothing new. For once it is present, it is already old; it brings no pleasure, and something else seems desirable. In sum, the ability to be content with what one has is simply a gift of the Holy Spirit and is impossible for the flesh, which is always being drawn away from what it has to the things that are to be and, in following the latter, loses the former and thus is deprived of the use of both. The greedy man is deprived both of what he has and of what he does not have. What happens to the greedy man in the case of money happens to the entire human race in the case of desires and plans; that is, they have nothing, even if they have everything. Alexander the Great may serve as an example. Even

---

[14] Cf. Vergil, *Aeneid*, I, lines 278—79, lines often quoted by Luther.

after he had conquered all of Asia, his heart was not satisfied. If this is true of outward affairs, why would it be surprising that it is true of the Gospel? When we have it, we still do not have it, because we are not moved by it but want something else. Christians, on the other hand, even while having nothing, possess everything (cf. 2 Cor. 6:10).

How the wise man dies just like the fool!

There is a similar statement in Ps. 49:10: "He shall see that even the wise die, the fool and the stupid alike must perish and leave their wealth to others." This, too, is to be understood as speaking about historic accomplishments. The wise man dies with his accomplishments just as the stupid man does. There is no notice taken of the things that they achieved so well. And if you have done everything as well as possible, you get the reward that everything you did becomes boring and you yourself are condemned to exile or death. In fact, many men despise you and destroy you.

17. *So I hated life, because what is done under the sun was grievous to me; for all is vanity and vexation of spirit.*

That is, whatever was being done under the sun was completely displeasing to me, because it was nothing but vain labor and a source of useless trouble. This does not imply that Solomon wishes for death, but that he regards it as a misery and a calamity to deal with these matters. He intends to say: "I became sick and tired of it." For who can bear having nothing but labor in establishing something and nothing but contempt once it has been established or done? In Scriptural phraseology, "to live" or "life" means to live well, to live in plenty. Ps. 22:29 says: "And they did not keep their soul alive," that is, their soul did not live well, they lived a difficult and grinding life like paupers, like those who have been oppressed and who are otherwise miserable and destined for death. Such people are called in Scripture "not living." Therefore he is not saying that he yearns for death, but he is displeased with the way of life that wearies and afflicts a man with human counsels. Therefore Solomon means that we should stand ready for death or for life, and he recalls us to the use of things in the present. We should be content with these things, without anxiety about the future, and should commit everything to God, who does indeed want to work through us but in such a way as though we were ignorant of the process. As an ox that threshes and eats does not know what he is doing and has no anxiety about food or about the success of his labor, so we also ought to do what the Lord has assigned and carry out what He has willed. Yet all these things ought to be like a crust of bread that we have on earth, so that we do not strive for the cultivation of this life by our own efforts; for that way lies perpetual disquiet, as now follows:

18. *I hated all my toil in which I had toiled under the sun, seeing that I must leave it to the man who will come after me;*

19. *and who knows whether he will be a wise man or a fool? Yet he will be master of all for which I toiled.*

This is exactly the same sentiment as the preceding. For Solomon is abundant in his use of words and treats this subject at great length. "Thus," he says, "I am tired of life. For even though I have carried on and administered all my affairs very well, I still do not know whether I am going to have a wise heir or a foolish one. If a wise one, he will grow weary and look for something else, since after all I myself grow tired of my own things and wish for something new. If he is a madman, he will destroy things and will have the same labor in wrecking that I had in establishing them." As the proverb says, "One man builds and the other destroys." Thus Octavius Caesar decorated the city, and Nero laid it waste. Pompey had collected an enormous amount of money in the public treasury, with the intention of helping the state. Caesar later confiscated it, and that money contributed more to the downfall of the state than to its welfare. "Therefore regardless of whether my heir is wise or foolish, I have labored in vain and have destroyed my life with silly cares by wanting to provide for the future instead of using the present." Therefore he adds:

20. *So I turned about and gave my heart up to despair over all the toil of my labors under the sun,*

21. *because sometimes a man who has toiled with wisdom and knowledge and industry must leave all to be enjoyed by a man who did not toil for it. This also is vanity and a great evil.*

22. *What has a man from all the toil and strain with which he toils beneath the sun?*

23. *For all his days are full of pain, and his work is a vexation; even in the night his mind does not rest. This also is vanity.*

"I called a halt," he says, "and refrained from all the anxiety about the business that goes on under the sun." This is the voice of a wise man, who calls his heart back from anxiety to peace. "I shall be content with present things and shall do what lies at hand. I shall bear what God wills and shall not be anxious about tomorrow" (cf. Matt. 6:34). This is the conclusion which he then confirms at great length when he says *Sometimes a man who has toiled with wisdom and knowledge and industry, etc.* You see here what he means by wisdom, namely, not speculative wisdom but the practical wisdom of administering things. By "industry" or congruity he is referring to skill, the arrangement of all things according to order and time, as when he himself set up 12 officers in the land (cf. 1 Kings 4:7), apportioned provisions (cf. 1 Kings 4:22) and horses (cf. 1 Kings 4:26). This, I say, is what he calls toiling with wisdom. But he must relinquish this labor or portion to a man who has not labored at this work, or what is even more unfortunate, to a man who neglects it and consigns it to oblivion. "When I do a lot of work," he says, "I leave the results either to a despiser or to a destroyer." This is certainly utter vanity. *What has a man from all the toil, etc.?* This is a further elaboration. *Even in the night.* His heart does not rest even at night when he labors this way, so that he not only achieves and establishes his business during the day, but even at night he works out plans about how to conserve and increase it.

24. *There is nothing better for a man than that he should eat and drink, and find enjoyment in his toil. This also, I saw, is from the hand of God.*

This is the principal conclusion, in fact the point, of the whole book, which he will often repeat. This is a remarkable passage, one that explains everything preceding and following it. This is how it agrees with the preceding: Those pleasures are to be condemned which we by our own counsels seek to achieve for the future, and those labors are to be condemned which we strive to carry out by our own counsels. But those pleasures and labors which God gives are good, and they are to be used for the present without anxiety about either future afflictions or future pleasures. But who is capable of such things? It is rightly said, but what is wisely set forth does not happen. Indeed, hearing we do not hear and seeing we do not see, and no one follows it. We are immersed in striving and anxiety about planning and carrying out our affairs. The heart is averse to plans, and every day it becomes more irritated and restless. Those who are pious refrain from anxiety; the rest of the human race have a restless life until they die. Therefore he says *This also, I saw, is from the hand of God.* This is a noteworthy statement and an outstanding doctrine, but he stresses it less than he did the earlier one. This is because an affirmative statement affects us less than a negative one, as, for example, even the affirmative statement "I am the Lord your God, who brought you out of the land of Egypt" (Ex. 20:2) is quickly said but does not affect us, while there is greater force in the negative statement "You shall have no other gods before Me" (Ex. 20:3). Thus here also he treats the affirmative statement "It is good for a man to eat, etc." in few words; but he uses many words in the negative statement, to prove and show us our foolishness, namely, that we accomplish nothing by all our counsels and our toil, distracted as we are by anxiety so that we do not use the things that are present. To crude people it is necessary that he speak in crude and lengthy terms and with examples. To wise people he could have said it all in one word: "The Lord Himself is your God."

25. *For who has eaten or enjoyed himself more than I?*

He is citing his own experience. "For if I who achieved many things and had an abundance of good things still have not attained what I wanted, how much less will others do so if God does not grant happiness?"

26. *For to the man who pleases Him God gives wisdom and knowledge and joy; but to the sinner He gives the work of gathering and heaping, only to give to one who pleases God. This also is vanity and vexation of spirit.*

He proves that it is a gift of God to be content with the things that are present, for this is given to the man who pleases God without any preceding merits. He divides the world into the pious and the impious. In addition to other common gifts, especially wisdom and prudence, joy is conferred on the pious, because they are content with things that are present and are not vexed with thoughts and desires as the impious are. They acknowledge in joy and peace that they are intelligent and wise in administering their affairs. But the impious suffer affliction, so that they continually add more and more, heap things up, and yet are never satisfied. In addition, even if they have wisdom and skill, it is still so mixed with troubles that it becomes more of a punishment for them. They do not enjoy their labors when they till the fields or build, but others enjoy them and get happiness from them. What the impious work at and build is not used rightly by anyone except the pious. Thus what sinners [15] heap up belongs to the pious, because only they use it with thanksgiving and joy, even when they have very little. The impious, on the other hand, for all their anxiety and trouble, do not even use it. In short, the pious truly possess the whole world, because they enjoy it with happiness and tranquillity. But the impious do not possess it even when they have it. This is the vanity which the impious possess.

[15] The Weimar text has *principes*, but we have read *peccatores*, which fits the context.

CHAPTER THREE

1. *For everything there is a season, and a time for every matter under heaven.*

HERE too, as has been said before, Solomon is speaking about human works, that is, about works undertaken by human counsel. Because they do not observe this, the interpreters suppose that he is speaking here about the corruption of created things.[1] Therefore you should understand this as follows: All human works and efforts have a certain and definite time of acting, of beginning, and of ending, beyond human control. Thus this is spoken in opposition to free will. It is not up to us to prescribe the time, the manner, or the effect of the things that are to be done; and so it is obvious that here our strivings and efforts are unreliable. Everything comes and goes at the time that God has appointed. He proves this on the basis of examples of human works whose times lie outside the choice of man. From this he draws the conclusion that it is useless for men to be tormented by their strivings and that they do not accomplish anything, even though they were to burst, unless the proper time and the hour appointed by God has come. Here the statement in the Gospel is pertinent (John 7:30): "His hour had not yet come"; and again (John 16:21): "When a woman is in travail, she has sorrow, because her hour has come." So the power of God comprehends all things in definite hours, so that they cannot be hindered by anyone.

But you will say: How then has man been installed as the lord over things, according to Gen. 1:26,[2] if he cannot have dominion over them according to his own will and use them in keeping with his own desire? The answer is: We are installed as lords over things in such a way that we are able to use them for the present, but we are not able to have dominion over them by our anxiety and effort.

[1] Cf. Hugh of St. Victor, *In Ecclesiasten Homiliae*, XIII, *Patrologia, Series Latina*, CLXXV, 206—209.

[2] The original has "Gen. 2."

No one is able by his effort to accomplish anything for the future. For how can someone who is uncertain about the future determine something about the future? Therefore God wants us to make use of creatures, but freely, as He has provided them, without our prescribing the time, the manner, and the hour. These are in the hand of the Lord, so that we should not think that it is in our hands to use things as we wish if He does not give them. Therefore Ecclesiasticus says (Ecclus. 15:14): "God left man in the power of his own inclination," but He added the commandments by which man was to regulate his inclinations and actions.

"All things have their time," that is, a definite hour.[3] If a man transgresses this and wants to accomplish everything by his own counsel and effort, he will have nothing from it but vanity. Many people work to get rich but gain nothing. Others, however, get rich without work, because God has granted them the hour but has not granted it to the others. *Every matter, etc.* The Hebrew word is חֵפֶץ, which is usually translated as "effort" or "will." It seems to me that "delight" would not be an inappropriate translation, as in Ps. 1:2: "His delight is in the law of the Lord." For חֵפֶץ means something with which one deals and toward which he is inclined, in this case the desire to keep the Law. So also in the present passage: everything that men wish and desire. They strive for it and desire it, but they are merely undone; because they do not hit the precise hour that they have in mind, they accomplish nothing. Therefore one should commit things to God and make use of present things, refraining from a lust for future things. If you do otherwise, you will have nothing but affliction.

2. *A time to be born, and a time to die.*

He now cites examples to prove what he has said about human affairs and human efforts. Birth, he says, has its own time, and death has its own time. And as we do not have our birth in our own hand, so we do not have our death either. Yet there is nothing that is more our own than our life and the various parts of our body — but only in the sense of use, for we have not been granted dominion over them even for a moment, and therefore it is useless for us to try to define them with laws. An infant is in the hand of God and

---

[3] Luther's Latin *definita hora* is equivalent to his German *stündlin (Stündlein)*, "the appointed hour."

is not born until its hour of birth comes. Women labor and are concerned about the birth of an infant, and they predict its time, but there is nothing certain about it. Nor do we die, in spite of great danger and extreme desperation, except at our appointed hour. Why then do we fear death? You cannot live any longer than the Lord has prescribed, nor die any sooner. For this is also what Job says in chapter 14:5: "The days of man are determined, and the number of his months is with Thee, and Thou hast appointed his bounds that he cannot pass."

But you say: Many people die of their own initiative and rashness, and they would otherwise have lived longer; and others have hurled themselves into death alive. Could they not have saved their lives? I reply: No, God has set this hour and even this means and kind of death. Experience teaches this also. Some men receive mortal wounds and yet are easily cured and survive, while others who are lightly wounded die nevertheless. The astrologers ascribe this to the stars, others ascribe it to fortune. But Holy Scripture attributes this to God, with whom the moments of our life and of our death are fixed, to whom it does not matter whether you perish of a large wound or of a small one, so that He may confound all the wisdom and counsel of man. To Christians this is a great comfort, so that they know that death has not been placed into the power of tyrants nor into the hands of any creature and so that they are not extremely fearful about death but die like children when it pleases God. Therefore what has been said about the time of being born and of dying should be said about all the other works of man, as now follows:

A time to plant, and a time to pluck up what is planted.

These are works of human life, but they are not in our hands any more than life itself is. In the spring there is planting, in the autumn there is plucking up. All of this is as God gives and ordains it, and it cannot be done otherwise by us.

3. *A time to kill,   and a time to heal;*
   a time to break down,   and a time to build up;

4. *a time to weep,   and a time to laugh;*
   a time to mourn,   and a time to dance;

5. *a time to cast away*	*and a time to gather stones together;*
a time to embrace,	*and a time to refrain from embracing;*
6. *a time to seek,*	*and a time to lose;*
a time to keep,	*and a time to cast away;*
7. *a time to rend,*	*and a time to sew;*
a time to keep silence,	*and a time to speak;*
8. *a time to love,*	*and a time to hate;*
a time for war,	*and a time for peace.*

This catalog requires experience, so that it may be applied to the entire course of life. For this is what happens: one man plants, and another plucks; or one man acquires, and another tears down. In short, for each of the works of human life there is a defined time, outside of which, regardless of what you do, you will accomplish nothing and work in vain. There is a time to weep, there is a time to laugh. It often happens that when we want to be very joyous, a sudden disturbance arises. Therefore joy has its appointed time. Experience proves all of this, namely, that by our own counsels we can achieve nothing, but whatever is to be done is presented to us at its appointed time. Therefore let us not torment ourselves about future things, but enjoy present things.

9. *What gain has the worker from his toil?*

That is, unless the appointed time, or καιρός, is here, he achieves nothing. The worker has nothing else except his own appointed time. If this does not come, he can achieve nothing. But if the appointed time is right, then he is right, too.

10. *I have seen the travail, which God has given to the sons of men to be exercised in it.*

This is a clarification of everything that has preceded it. "In all those labors," he says, "I have seen that men cannot achieve anything by themselves unless their appointed time is here." But those who want to anticipate their appointed time prematurely have travail, care, and anxieties; this is intended to make them learn from their experience and to refrain from care about future things, but to use the things that are present.

11. *He has made everything beautiful in its time.*

Now this is the second part. Those who do not expect their appointed time are afflicted, while those who do expect it are delighted. For everything that God makes or that happens through the gift of God in its appointed time is pleasant. That is to say, when the heart is empty of cares and yet something happens to it that is pleasant or some interesting sight comes along, this is very delightful. Therefore such people have pleasure where others have affliction, because they do things at the time which has been appointed by God.

Also he has given the world into man's heart, yet so that he cannot find out what God has done from the beginning to the end.

This is a confirmation of the preceding. "Although God has given the world into the hearts of men," he says, "they still cannot govern it by their own counsels." "To give into the heart" or "to speak into the heart" is a Hebraism for giving or speaking in a sweet and flattering way. He wants to say: God not only gives the world into the hand of men, so that they can use the things that are present, but also into their heart, so that they can use them joyfully and with pleasure and so that they have fun and delight from it. Nevertheless, man cannot know what the beginning or the end of the work is, when or for how long he is to have these things. Therefore man should be content that he has the world for his use. Paul speaks in similar terms in Acts 14:17: "Yet He did not leave Himself without witness, for He did good and gave from heaven rains and fruitful seasons, satisfying their hearts with food and gladness." And elsewhere (1 Tim. 6:17): "Who richly furnishes everything." This happiness the Christian has, and everyone else would have it also if he could be content with the things that are present. St. Jerome says correctly in his preface to the Bible: "The believer has a world of riches, but the unbeliever does not have a penny; as the proverb says, 'the miser lacks not only what he does not have but also what he does have.'" [4]

---

[4] Jerome, Epistle LIII, 10, *Patrologia, Series Latina*, XXII, 549; this epistle to Paulinus was sometimes printed as one of the prefaces to Jerome's translation of the Bible.

Yet man does not find out or discover what God has done, etc. That is: Man cannot know, even if he torments himself, when God wants to do him good, when He wants to start or to stop, just as no one, regardless of how he works at it, can investigate or identify the hour when someone is to be born, to live, or to die. Therefore one should say: "Lord, it is up to Thee to give future things; meanwhile I shall enjoy the life that is present and that has already been given by Thee." Thus also the other activities of life which he has just cataloged lie outside the power of man. For if this were placed in the hands of men, many would always be waging war, while others would always be playing or building; for there are many who labor at this. The whole world is ours. Only let us not prescribe to God the time or the method of using it. "I refuse to be measured by your counsels," says God; "otherwise everything will belong to you, including Me." Therefore he draws the same conclusion that he drew in the preceding chapter.

12. *I know that there is nothing better for them than to be happy and enjoy themselves as long as they live;*

13. *also that it is God's gift to man that everyone should eat and drink and take pleasure in all his toil.*

This can be understood satisfactorily on the basis of what has been said above. He wants to say: There is nothing better for a man in such a disastrous business than to enjoy the things that are present and to have a happy and joyful heart, without anxiety and care about the future. But the ability to do this is a gift of God. "I can teach this," Solomon says, "but it is not in my ability to do it or to grant that it be done." He shows what is to be done, and at the same time he teaches where it is to be obtained. He teaches that our cares only bring affliction, but he urges that we call upon God to take away these cares and to give success and peace of heart.

14. *I know that whatever God does endures forever; nothing can be added to it, nor anything taken from it; God has made it so in order that MEN SHOULD FEAR BEFORE HIM.*

That is: "I have seen that everything God does lasts forever, but our works are unsure and vain." And one must note the antithesis. He says that only God can carry out His counsels and set a definite time for them. To whom He has given this gift of finding enjoyment in the present, he has it. He is faithful and sure; whatever He gives, no one takes away. If He grants life, no one snatches it away, even though the world and Satan should rage; for He is sure and eternal. If He gives me good eyes, I shall keep them, even though Satan should sprinkle all the dust of the earth into them. If He gives me healthy and robust arms or legs, no one will deprive me of them. All our works have their appointed time, which we do not set. Who sets it, then? God Himself determines this time—not fortune or fate, as the philosophers suppose. When He who made the time permits it to come, then it comes.

Why, therefore, does He afflict men with this vain supposition when He has reserved the appointed time for things to Himself? For this reason, he says, in order that men should fear, that we should not be rash in our works or attempt things proudly and presumptuously as though they came from us. Thus also Paul teaches (Rom. 9:16; Phil. 2:12-13): "Walking in fear, so that you know that it does not depend upon man's will or exertion, because He Himself is at work both to will and to work." Anyone who believes this, that matters have not been placed into our hands, will not do anything rashly, but will attribute everything to God in His working and will expect everything from Him. If He grants it, he enjoys it; if He does not, he does without it; and if He takes it away, he bears it. Thus there abide the glory of God and our humiliation and the true worship of God among us. This is what it means to fear God: to have God in view, to know that He looks at all our works, and to acknowledge Him as the Author of all things, both good and evil.

15. *That which is, already has been; that which is to be, already has been; and God seeks it even though it hinders Him.*

Earlier in chapter one (1:9) he said: "What has been is what will be." This is quite different from what he says here: "That which has been, already is." There he was speaking about the works and things of men, here about the deeds of God. The human heart cannot be content with the things that are present; nor can it wish for what merely is, but only for what is to be. But once it has what is to be, it is still not content but looks for something else again. The heart is not satisfied. This is the condition of the human heart, always to be looking for future things but never to be satisfied. But

God works and acts in the opposite way. With Him "whatever has been, is present"; that is, He does not turn away to future things. For it is said of Him (Gen. 1:31): "He saw everything that He had made, and it was very good." God abides in the work that He does, and He does not overthrow it or run off to other and still other desires for the future, as the mind of man does. Those who walk according to God do this also; they are not diverted toward future things, to the neglect of the things that are present. The pious man does his work steadily and enjoys things steadily. *Because God seeks it even though it hinders Him.* As I have said, he is using antithesis to compare our efforts with the efforts of God. Our efforts are directed toward neglecting what we have, growing bored with it, and looking to what we shall have. God, on the other hand, follows through on what is and perseveres in His work, so that what He does may be stable. The efforts of the pious are of this kind also. Therefore he wants to say: Even when man wants and tries to hinder the work of God, God still seeks and defends His work, which men try to hinder and molest. Thus God has established David as king, but Absalom persecuted and molested him; but God in turn restored what Absalom hindered. The things that are done by God are not inconstant, as human counsels are, nor does God become bored with His counsels.

16. *I saw under the sun that in the place of justice, even there was wickedness, and in the place of righteousness, even there was wickedness.*

17. *I said in my heart, God will judge the righteous and the wicked, for He has appointed a time for every matter, and for every work.*

What am I to say about the faults and the vanity of human efforts when even in the place of justice, that is, in the administration of law and of judgments, wicked men and wickedness are found? Solomon is not complaining because there is wickedness in the place of justice but because the wickedness in the place of justice cannot be corrected. It is as though he were saying: "Thus all things are vain, so that even a concern about correcting the injustice of the magistrates is of no avail. When I saw wickedness, I thought I would correct it, but I realized that I could not do so until God corrected it." Thus our Prince Frederick used to say: "The longer I rule, the less I know about ruling." Again: "Where shall I finally find someone whom I can trust?"[5] You see that in all the courts of princes, regardless of how many people there are who are good, interested in the welfare of the state, and ready to give advice, you will always find others who cause plenty of trouble for all the plans of everyone and who make trouble for everything. The malice of men is so great that you cannot set them all straight. Therefore Solomon wants to say: "If someone torments himself here in order to set them all straight, he will have nothing but affliction and sorrow." Therefore one must commit it to God. A stone that can be lifted and carried should be lifted and carried, but one that cannot be lifted should be allowed to lie there. "Therefore," he says, "I who have been a wise king of the holy people and a diligent custodian of justice was obliged to retain wicked men in public office. Even though I deposed some, others always sneaked in." What is to happen to anyone else? Therefore it would be best to do what God gives and to commit the rest to God, who in His own time will judge the righteous and the wicked. Men do not want to do so, and they cannot even if they want to very much.

He has appointed a time for every matter, and for every work. All things, he says, have their own time. Faults cannot be corrected earlier than their appointed time arrives. Therefore it is useless for us to occupy this time prematurely by trying to correct everything for the future. "My trying did not succeed even in public office. Therefore I acted according to my ability, I corrected what I could, and I committed the rest to God."

18. *I said in my heart concerning the estate of the sons of men that God is testing them to show them that they are but beasts.*

19. *For the fate of the sons of men and the fate of beasts is the same; as one dies, so dies the other.*

This passage is a little more obscure, not by its own fault but by that of the interpreters, who torment themselves very much, since they usually suppose that Solomon is speaking in the person of the

---

[5] Apparently this information came to Luther through Staupitz; cf. *Luther's Works,* 13, pp. 213—14.

wicked. But this interpretation is quite frigid, even though it is widely accepted.[6] It seems to me that the meaning should be taken in a simple way. He made a comparison or a discourse about the efforts and strivings of men and concluded that all human plans and efforts are vain. Finally he came to the troubles of the public official, namely, that those who ought to be a norm for the rest are also vanity. And so from the special instances that preceded he comes down to generalities. What shall I say about individuals, when all of us are like the beasts? Is it not a miserable business among men? How are they different from the brutes, which do not remember anything of God either? But the question is: Why did he compare men with beasts, as though they did not have anything more than the beasts, when on the contrary he had earlier taught piety, or the fear of God, and had said that after this life there is an eternal life? This is what troubled the interpreters most. A brief answer: Here the interpreters do not notice the purpose of the book, nor do they remember what he inculcates so many times, that he is speaking about things "under the sun," what in the New Testament and in common usage is called "in the world." For this book distinguishes the life of godliness from the life of the world, or life "under the sun." To have a happy heart and to rejoice in present things with the fear of God is not a thing of the world but a gift of God. It comes from heaven, from beyond the sun. But being afflicted with these things means being no different from the beasts.

Concerning the estate of the sons of men.

In Hebrew this is a word that is very broad in its meaning, but in this form it means "manner, habitude, order, or way of life." Thus in Ps. 110:4: "You are a priest forever after the order of Melchizedek." I think that it properly means "a state."[7] The Epistle to the Hebrews has interpreted this term from the psalm in an outstanding way (Heb. 7:1-17). "For as Melchizedek did not have father or mother," it says, "so Thou also art in the same manner or mode." The word comes from דָּבָר, which means "thing" or "cause." Therefore it means "habitude" or "how things go," so that the meaning is: "I said in my heart concerning the estate, that is,

---

[6] Cf. Gregory I, *Dialogi*, IV, chs. 3—4, *Patrologia, Series Latina*, LXXVII, 321—25.

[7] Luther uses the German *ein wesen*.

For the fate of the sons of men and the fate of beasts is the same.

That is, the same things happen to, the same things befall, both men and beasts. He wants to say: "The human race wanders around just as the beasts do, and it does not gain any more from life than the beasts do." "As the beasts die, so men die also." He is speaking about the hour of death, not about death itself. That is, as the hour of death for the beasts is unsure, so it is with men. A beast does not know when it will have sickness or health or when it will die, and neither does a man. Why then are we proud, when we have no more information about the hour of death than the beasts do?

They all have the same breath, and man has no advantage over the beasts; for all is vanity.

20. *All go to one place; all are from the dust, and all turn to dust again.*

This passage cannot be twisted to refer to the mortality of the soul,[8] for he is speaking about things under the sun. The world, of course, cannot understand or believe that the soul is immortal. In fact, if you look at how things go and at the appearance, about which Solomon is speaking when he says, "Man dies as the beast does," they do have the same breath as the beast. In appearance, therefore, we coincide. The philosophers have indeed disputed about the immortality of the soul, but so coldly that they seem to be setting forth mere fables. Aristotle above all argues about the soul in such a way that he diligently and shrewdly avoids discussing its immortality anywhere; nor did he want to express what he thought about it.[9] Plato related what he had heard rather than his own opinion.[10] Nor can its immortality be proved by any human reason, for it is not a thing "under the sun" to believe that the soul is immortal. In the world it is neither seen nor understood as certain that souls are immortal.

[8] The Weimar text has *animi*, but *animae* would seem to be more appropriate.

[9] Cf. Aristotle, *De anima*, I, ch. 1, on the relation of soul and body.

[10] Apparently Luther is referring to Plato's use of Socrates in his discussion of the soul in such dialogs as the *Phaedo*.

All go to one place, etc.

That is, if the Lord did not give His Spirit to man, no one could say that man is different from the beast, because men and cattle, being made of the same dust, also return to the same dust. This return to the same place is an argument for the similarity between men and beasts—not because it is so, but because the world, which judges on the basis of appearance and their common outcome, thinks this way and cannot think otherwise, since believing otherwise requires something more sublime than the world.

God is testing them.

The Hebrew word means "to purify" or "to elect." God, he says, permits both men and cattle to go about and live in the same manner and form. But God permits this in order to test men, whether they look only at these external things, and whether they are persuaded by these arguments, to which the wicked pay attention without believing otherwise. But the godly are exercised in this way so that they may acquire more faith. They go in the same way as the wicked and the beasts do, but inwardly, in the spirit, they receive comfort and peace.

21. *Who knows whether the spirit of man goes upward and the spirit of the beast goes down to the earth?*

"Simply show me," he says, "one man who is not among the godly but among those who are under the sun, or in the world, one man who can assert that the soul lives after this life, when he sees that the spirit of men and that of cattle are not different from each other; for death comes immediately to both of them when their breath fails." No one among men knows this. That we do know it is not on the basis of what we know as men but of what we know as sons of God and above the sun, inasmuch as we are in the heavenly places (cf. Eph. 2:6) and belong to heaven. But in the world there is neither this knowledge nor peace, but everything is carried on as it is among the beasts. There were outstanding geniuses in Greece, who nevertheless did not say anything solid about this matter. Lucian, a man of great understanding and delight, argues about it vigorously but only ridicules the opinions of the philosophers about the soul.[11]

---

[11] Apparently a reference to the satire *De morte Peregrini*, by Lucian of Samosata (d. ca. 180), in which the Christian attitude toward death is ridiculed.

22. *So I saw that there is nothing better than that a man should enjoy his work, for that is his lot; who can bring him to see what will be after him?*

This is how godly men feel, for they have comprehended this teaching. The ungodly are vexed by their similarity to the beasts, and they get nothing out of their labors but vanity; for they neither know nor believe this teaching, because their reason does not persuade them of it. This passage also convicts the whole mob of the philosophers, who compile many arguments about the immortality of the soul, although they themselves do not believe it. This, therefore, is the portion of the righteous: to enjoy the things that are present and not to be afflicted by the things that are in the future. But this does not happen under the sun. Those who act otherwise, take a double burden upon themselves: they do not make use of the things that are present, and they do not gain the things that are in the future. The same thing happens to them that happened to the dog in Aesop, which snapped at its shadow and lost the meat.[12] Thus they also become bored with the things that are present and look for other things. Until now Solomon has been setting forth general arguments about the vanity of the world. Now the particular arguments follow.

[12] Luther had frequently busied himself with Aesop and in 1530 was to undertake a translation of some of the *Fables*.

CHAPTER FOUR

1. *So I returned and considered all those that are oppressed under the sun. And behold, the tears of the oppressed, and they had no one to comfort them or rescue them from the hands of their oppressors; and there was no one to comfort them.*

HE has reviewed the empty counsels of the human heart when God hinders it, namely, that only those things that God establishes and does attain their goal and cannot be hindered. Now he goes on to enumerate the hindrances to human counsels, that is, the means and causes by which God usually calls us away from our own efforts and counsels and compels us to make use of the things that are present. "I have seen," he says, "that neither rulers nor kings are able to remove oppression and injury from human affairs. In fact, God casts depraved and violent spirits in their way, from which they cannot be set free. David, that very fine prince, wants to make good plans for the state, but Joab and Absalom get in his way. He tried to get rid of Joab, but he could not do so. That is the way of the men who trouble their princes; yet the princes are obliged to bear them, for it is through them that God hinders the counsels of the wise. I have also seen that judges are corrupt and that tyrants oppress widows and orphans." And surely the violence and the ferocity of men is too great to be ruled and corrected by any human being; only God can do it.

2. *And I thought the dead who are already dead more fortunate than the living who are still alive;*

3. *but better than both is he who has not yet been, and has not seen the evil deeds that are done under the sun.*

Here again the babblers argue as though Solomon were speaking as an ungodly man, who prefers the dead to the living,[1] when Augustine, in his interpretation of the passage from John (Matt.

[1] On this interpretation of Ecclesiastes, see p. 4, n. 6, above.

26:24; Mark 14:21), "It would have been better for that man if he had not been born," says: "It is better to be in an evil way than not to be at all." [2] But these men are guilty of sophistry. Those who have been condemned and who have suffered calamity feel and judge the way Solomon is speaking in this passage, for they would certainly prefer not to be rather than to be continually tormented this way; and this would simply be better for them. Therefore he says correctly here: "If you consider the misery of human afflictions and if you look only at this life, you will think that the dead are more fortunate than the living." One would rather be dead than see such misery and such calamities. Therefore he is speaking not about the future judgment but about things that happen under the sun, where it is better not to exist than to see human affliction. The Gentiles felt this way, for they say that it is best not to be born or, if one is born, to die early.[3] Therefore this passage must simply be understood in a comparative sense.

4. *Then I saw that all toil and all skill among craftsmen come from a man's envy of his neighbor. This also is vanity and affliction of spirit.*

This is another kind of calamity and hindrance to the efforts and counsels of men. Just as slander and oppression are dominant among those who are great and powerful, so among the common people there is nothing but envy, rivalry, hatred, etc. "Come down to the common people," he says, "and look at the craftsmen. You will find craftsmen with an evil will; you will sense their wickedness, fraud, cheating, and disparagement of one another, how they constantly hate and envy one another." If someone has ability, he arouses hostility. Anyone who is a good craftsman has a thousand people who hate him, and it happens as the poet says: "The potter envies the potter, the smith envies the smith, and the poet envies the poet." [4] This is the downfall and the normal course of all craftsmen. Imagine someone who wants to learn a craft from which he hopes in the future to have a happy life or a livelihood. If he learns

---

[2] There does not seem to be any such comment in Augustine's exposition of the Gospel of John, but Jerome, *Commentarius*, 1044—45, may be what Luther has in mind.

[3] Sophocles, *Oedipus Coloneus*, line 1224.

[4] Hesiod, *Works and Days*, line 25.

it well and is preeminent over others, he will have the envy and the hatred of many. What is he to do then? Should he stop? Should he not learn anything? No, he should do his work in accordance with his abilities and commit his work to God. What are we to do in our studies? Should we stop because our students do not accept this or that, or because the learned despise us? No, you do what you are doing, and meanwhile wait for the appointed time. You know that it is a good thing to teach others, and so do not pay attention to the world or to your own counsels. Wherever you look, there will be troubles. We today want to be of service to Germany through the Gospel, and we used to hope that everyone would embrace it. But the very people whom we were aiding to be free from the tyranny of the pope are covering us with their excrement, and those whose helpers we thought we would be are treading us underfoot. What are we to do here? Should we not become indignant? Should we not let everything go? No. Let other people envy, despise, and persecute. We, in accordance with our abilities, will stick to our teaching, working, writing, and learning, because this is what God wills. For no one who only wants to do the right thing will ever be without envy in the world. We should not prematurely define the hour in which our labor is to succeed; God will see to that. But you just do your job and do what God places into your hands. Nor should you suppose that everything can be set right by you, that all rulers will be good and all craftsmen harmonious and honest.

Therefore he says *I saw that all skill among craftsmen, etc.*, that is, "I saw men who were very well fitted for their positions but who could not accomplish anything the way they wanted it, because it was not in their hands; the hatred of their neighbors got in their way and hindered them." Therefore these are completely evangelical admonitions and consolations, which call us away from care and anxiety about human affairs. There is indeed a great number of human vanities and afflictions everywhere; there is no place where they do not occur. When I was new as a preacher, I seriously undertook to make everyone good. But people said to me, and truly: "He has too rakish [5] a bill to be able to make old rascals pious." The same thing happens in all positions. This evil is present in every

---

[5] The Weimar text has *gelben* ("yellow"), but from the manuscript of the lectures it appears that *geelen* may be the proper reading, one that would agree with the form in which this proverb is quoted on p. 27 above.

way of life. Therefore the best thing is to enjoy the things that you have in the present, to do everything in the present, and to let what is evil flow past you. This is the way to make fun of the world. In short, anyone who wants to live quietly should put the proposition to himself that in the world he will see nothing but vanity. He should not be sad if something evil happens, but he should rather be happy with the good things that are present. If you are thrust into the obligation of having to help make things better, do what is permissible, and God will do what He wills. But if you want to go beyond this and mingle with the world, straighten every curve, cure every evil, and throw Satan out of the world, you will cause yourself nothing but labor and sorrow. You will accomplish no more than if you wanted to forbid the Elbe to flow. Human affairs refuse to be, and cannot be, governed by the will of man, but He who created all things also rules them by His will.

This also is vanity and affliction of spirit.

If, that is, you want to cure this envy and these very evil things. Let those people envy and hinder, let them act wickedly. If the Lord wants to use your works and counsel, He will do so at His own time and place; you just wait for that. Thus if He now wants to preserve study and the schools, He knows the time and the persons through whom He will achieve this. Those whom we regard as useful for this purpose are often the most unfitted.

5. *The fool folds his hands and eats his own flesh.*

"Fool" in this passage does not mean, as we usually understand it, a man who is stupid or silly, but one who is wicked and good-for-nothing, one whom in German we call "a useless reprobate." Such are, for example, those envious people who, while they themselves are incapable of anything, nevertheless trouble and hinder others. Such good-for-nothings, without industry or ability, have no other purpose in life than to be a nuisance to others, as, for example, the foolish and ignorant preachers who teach or learn badly. Among the craftsmen there are those drones whom we call "bunglers," who only get into other people's way since they themselves do not do anything right. In public office such people are a hindrance to the state, just as those who most want to help do the most to disturb the state, education, and other good things. In the same way, foolish preachers do more to hinder the Gospel than do the overt enemies of the Gospel.

The fool folds his hands; he is not an energetic worker. He is not watchful, but drowsy and lazy, a man who is not seriously concerned about his own work, but instead hinders, despises, and slanders others. That is what it means to fold one's hands, to do nothing oneself but also to get into other people's way. The same phrase occurs in Prov. 6:10-11: "A little folding of the hands to rest, and poverty will come upon you like a vagabond." This appears to be the source of Pliny's statement that the folding of the hands is an ominous thing.[6] That was correctly said, but not correctly understood by them. On the other hand, it is said of an industrious and energetic housewife (Prov. 31:19): "Her hands hold the spindle," that is, she grasps it. Therefore God arouses these stupid and good-for-nothing men for us to frustrate our counsels and efforts.

He eats his own flesh. This again is a Hebrew phrase, meaning, "He torments himself." There is a similar statement in Job (13:14): "I will take my flesh in my teeth." He wants to say: "An inept and foolish man of this kind does not do himself any good, but he harms and opposes others, he envies others and tortures himself." In the state such a man is a rust or a worm, harmful to himself and to others. That is why there are always bunglers.

6. *Better a handful of quietness than two hands full of toil and vexation of spirit.*

This can be understood as spoken by the fool in imitation or as spoken simply and declaratively by Solomon. If it is in imitation, it must be taken as the wise counsel of a foolish man, who abuses a very good statement for the support of his own sloth, as such people usually do. It is as though he were saying: "Why should I toil the way that hard worker is wearing himself out with his labors and his diligence? Why should I torment myself? I get as much as the next man." In this way he excuses his sloth, just as a certain monk used to say that it was pointless to torment himself with studying when he received just as fat a portion at table as a doctor

---

[6] This may be a reference to Pliny, *Natural History*, XI, 274; but it is not at all clear what Luther has in mind.

did.⁷ It is among such people that we have to live, even though they are unbearable; we are forced to walk as though through woods and thickets, where one must get out, regardless of how much the thorns may hinder and delay him. For this world is nothing but sheer thorns. If the statement is to be understood as a declaration, you should take it as the words and counsel of Solomon; this appeals to me much more. Then the meaning will be: "When you see that there are hindrances in every endeavor, what are you going to do? Do not torment yourself if those fools get in your way. Rather, if a fool torments you, you just go on working and enjoy your share with joy. If you cannot have both hands full, then accept even a handful by the gift of God and be satisfied. No matter how tiny your possessions may be, just be content and live happily."

7. *Again, I saw vanity under the sun:*

8. *a person who has no one, either son or brother, yet there is no end to all his toil, and his eyes are never satisfied with riches, so that he never asks, "For whom am I toiling and depriving myself of pleasure?" This also is vanity and an unhappy business.*

Solomon continues with his enumeration of the strivings and cares of human vanity, in the course of which he refers to that miser Euclio, who amasses a lot of things and yet does not enjoy them.⁸ Almost the entire world is caught up in this vice. Everyone "seeks his own" (1 Cor. 13:5) and serves his own belly (cf. Rom. 16:18). Chiefly, however, he is attacking those who are tormented by the desire to get rich and nevertheless only amass things for others. They do not look forward either to the time when they acquire things or to the time when they are to enjoy them. *A person who has no one.* The poets also condemn this vice and ridicule it with appropriate fables. The miser does not derive any enjoyment from his gold; he only looks at it, and his eyes are never satisfied. That is how the poets make fun of Tantalus; so, for example, Horace: "Tantalus, in thirst, snatches at the streams that run from his lips.

---

⁷ This is apparently a personal reminiscence of Luther's days in the monastery.

⁸ Euclio is the miser in the *Aulularia* of Plautus.

Why are you laughing? With no more than a change of names, the story could be told about you. With your moneybags filled from all over, you restlessly open your mouth for more; yet you are forced to refrain from touching it as though it were something sacred, or you must merely enjoy it as though it were a picture." [9]

9. *Two are better than one, because they have a good reward for their toil.*

10. *For if they fall, one will lift up his fellow; but woe to him who is alone when he falls and has not another to lift him up.*

11. *Again, if two lie together, they are warm; but how can one be warm alone?*

12. *And though a man might prevail against one who is alone, two will withstand him. A threefold cord is not quickly broken.*

This is counsel from Solomon, in which he recommends a social existence and a community of goods. He commands us to use the things that are present and to work, not for ourselves alone but also for the benefit of others. Community is good for the preservation of things. A miser, however, cannot stand an associate and condemns the community of goods. He amasses things only for himself and is a regular dog in the manger. Such solitary accumulators, who are not human beings but beasts and dogs, are condemned by Solomon. It is more beautiful, he says, to live a social existence with a community of goods, because *if they fall, etc.*

The interpreters distort this passage by applying it to sin and confession. This is how they understand and interpret the text: If someone has fallen into sin and does not have a holy man to whom he can confess, he cannot rise to a life of godliness and grace.[10] But it has already been shown that Solomon is speaking about the course of human life under the sun, in opposition to vain affliction. He is recommending human community and association in the enjoyment of things, against the solitary life of the miser. He wants to say: "The miser is of no use either to himself or to other people. No one can share his pleasure, because he does not live with anyone else and keeps his property all to himself; indeed, in having it

---

[9] Horace, *Satires*, I, 1, lines 68—72.

[10] The exegetical tradition, represented for example by the comments of Bonaventure on this passage, connected these words with those of Gal. 6:4.

he does not have it. Someone whose style of life is not so solitary, on the other hand, has certain definite advantages. Being himself of benefit to others, he also receives benefits from others." As I have said, this community serves to preserve and to increase goods. That is what it means when he adds *He does not have anyone to lift him up* and *How can one be warm alone?* He does not have help, does not have counsel, does not have comfort in affliction. What does he have when he amasses things only for himself? He merely looks at his money as though it were a picture.

A threefold cord is not quickly broken.

He introduces an excellent proverb, as he often does below, and does so after the fashion of a good preacher. The meaning is: It is better to be in association with others and to enjoy things in common than to be a solitary miser who only cares about himself and grabs things for himself. In society there is mutual help, common work, common solace; meanwhile, the life of the miser is a sorry one, useless and afflicted, and finally he must come to a miserable end. This, then, he establishes with a proverb, which seems to be taken from this source: A certain wise father, when he was about to die, commands his sons to be present. He gives them a bundle of of sticks to break. Although they could not break them all at the same time, they did break them individually. In this way he taught his sons that their riches would be secure if they were in concord with one another and mutually assisted one another.[11] For through concord small things grow, but through discord they are scattered and brought to naught.

13. *Better is a poor and wise youth than an old and foolish king who has not provided for his successor.*

After the misers, who are useless both to themselves and to other people, he discusses another way of life. As he has said that there is vanity in avarice, so now he says that there is in ambition as well. For many are born in royal office and still do not keep it, while others come to royal office out of prison and get rich and still others come out of royal office and become slaves. All of this is intended to make us know that our efforts are nothing and that our counsel and our striving achieve nothing. Therefore these prisoners

[11] This story had been told about various men, notably about Charlemagne.

become kings and rule well, simply because God gives them this good fortune. Those who have been born to royal office rule badly. I have seen many youths, excellently brought up and very well educated, who nevertheless became completely corrupt once they lost their teachers and came into their inheritance; others, lacking in upbringing and education, were good men. What are we to do, then? Are we to neglect our children, stop educating them, neglect everything? No. This book does indeed give the appearance of teaching that we should neglect things and quit, but nothing is farther from the truth. Rather, it teaches us to neglect our own counsels and anxieties, by which our heart is troubled. So it is that when the Gospel rejects the righteousness of works, it sets our consciences free, not our hands. For God has commanded the work, but forbidden the anxiety. Therefore children should be educated, but the care for the result should be committed to God, just as a farmer ought to do his planting but commit to God the care for what it will yield. Thus also through the Law that was given to this people God overlooked nothing that pertained to their government, even though what was necessary was not carried out and in many ways things turned out badly. In the same way a magistrate ought to take diligent care that the state be well established and fortified, but he ought not trust in his own industry and counsel. One must pay attention and do the work, but one must avoid anxiety and affliction. Nor should we prescribe either the manner or the place or the time to God. Thus a farmer casts the seed into the field and then goes away and sleeps, with no anxiety about what it will yield; otherwise he would never have any rest. And so let no one suppose that Solomon is condemning human toil. He is forbidding care and anxiety, but demanding toil.

14. *For out of prison he comes to reign, whereas also he that is born in his kingdom becomes poor.*

This is related and combined with the preceding in the following way: A wise youth is better than a foolish old man because it often happens that someone comes out of prison to reign. On the other hand, one is changed from a king to a shameful and foolish man, as Manasseh and Zedekiah were, while by contrast Joseph was in prison and was made prince of Egypt. In our own age, too, Matthias, the king of Hungary, was taken from prison to be made a very powerful king.[12] Such things happen often in human affairs, as Roman history attests perhaps most clearly. Valerian, who was not an evil emperor, was taken captive and made the footstool of the king of Persia, remaining so all the way to his death.[13] But why did this happen to him? Because his appointed time, as set by God, had arrived. What, then, is the point of anxiety? "The day's own trouble is sufficient for the day" (Matt. 6:34). Therefore a king's son should be brought up in a royal manner; but wanting to prescribe what he ought to do in the future and how good a king he is to be—this is really a vexation. One should commend this to the plan and the will of God and say: "Lord, God, I am indeed bringing up this boy, but do Thou make him a king if it be Thy will."

15. *I saw all the living who move about under the sun, as well as the second youth, who was to stand in his place;*

16. *there was no end of all the people before him and after him. Yet they will not rejoice in him. Surely this also is vanity and vexation of spirit.*

By *the living* Solomon means those who lead a luxurious life and who live as though this life belonged to them and as though the world had been established for their benefit, as the nobles at court live. But he continues with his example of the education of a king either for political or for military affairs. Education, he says, is a good thing, but human willing and striving does not accomplish what it desires. The plans for an education are deceptive. The effort is necessary, but the outcome and the anxiety often deceive one. Therefore he teaches that our plans are vain. For if the anxiety and the planning are deceptive in the education of a king, how much more deceptive will they be in the case of other people, where there is less care and where the education is less closely supervised!

When he speaks of *all the living or the nobles who move about under the sun, as well as the second youth,* he is referring not to all the living or all the nobles who are under the sun but to the

[12] See *Luther's Works,* 8, p. 103, n. 2.

[13] The emperor Valerian was engaged in war against Persia beginning A. D. 256 and was captured by the Persian king, Sapor. He died in captivity in 260.

people of that kingdom and king or to a majority among them. Thus the meaning is: All the people who are around the king pay attention to the king's son. They all clung to him, hoping the best for him. For he was the young prince, *the second youth,* who stood in the place of the other king; that is, he was to be the king after the present king and was supposed to succeed his father in the kingdom. *There was no end of all the people before him and after him.* That is, he was surrounded by a large multitude, or company, of his people, with satellites and ministers in front of him and in back of him, as is customary for a king. There was great hope for this youth, that he was to be greater than his father. They all prophesied good things, and yet they were not happy with him. Why? Because he did not come up to their expectation but became stupid and foolish; as the proverb says, "either a king or a fool is born." Thus Nero became king amid great hope and congratulations, so much so that his first five years were celebrated and praised; but his later years were as different as they could be.[14] Thus also Heliogabalus and Commodus became princes and emperors amid great expectations, but they disappointed the hopes and expectations of everyone. The former degenerated into the filthiest sort of human being, in fact, a beast rather than a human being, while the latter became quite incommodious and another Nero.[15] Therefore a good prince is a phoenix, and a very rare one at that. For human plans are deceptive, so that we often come to regret most the very thing for which we had such hope. Thus Rehoboam was the son of a very wise father and one about whom people undoubtedly had the highest hopes, since he had received the best possible education from his father; nevertheless, he turned out to be as different from his father as he could be. If, therefore, human plans are deceptive at the highest level of life, they will certainly be far more deceptive in private life, in your home, in your work, etc. For there, too, one must be born either an artisan or a fool.

He is speaking about kings because in the case of illustrious persons their deeds are also illustrious, that is, conspicuous to everyone. The deeds of private persons are usually overlooked

[14] Cf. Suetonius, *Lives of the Twelve Caesars,* "Nero," 37 and *passim.*

[15] Heliogabalus, a Syrian priest, was emperor from 218 to 222 (cf. Dio Cassius, *History,* LXXIX); Commodus, on whose name Luther is punning here, was emperor from 180 to 192 (ibid., LXXII).

or, at any rate, are less noticed. But as the German proverb says, "a wise man does not make little mistakes." If some ordinary person commits a sin or does something foolish, he does not attract very much attention. Otherwise the condition of private individuals is the same as that of kings. Therefore Solomon is not condemning the effort to educate a king, make a son rich, or rule a household, but our plans, by which we want to control this. He commands the work but forbids the anxiety. Work hard, but leave the outcome and the effect to God. Remember the example of the king who had been carefully trained and who nevertheless changed, so that you know that affairs are not governed by our plans and efforts but by the will of God, who has determined for everything its time and hour, apart from which nothing whatever succeeds. Therefore if someone responds to an education, we should give thanks not to our effort or care, but to God, who gives His blessing. If the crops grow, this too is owing to God, not to us. For what human being could defend his crops, either from the birds or from wild animals or from caterpillars or from wolves,[16] indeed, from the envy of Satan? Therefore it does not depend on our efforts but on the benevolence and benediction of God, so that we give thanks only to Him, who does all in all, for His good will. The situation in the education of children is the same. If you have a good child, say: "The Lord has given him and made him this way." If you do not, say: "That is the condition of human life. I did my work, but the Lord has not willed it. Blessed be His name!"

[16] The Weimar text has *lupis,* and we have translated accordingly; but the St. Louis Edition suggests the reading *bruchis* ("locusts"), which would seem to fit the context better.

CHAPTER FIVE

1. *Guard your steps when you go to the house of God; to draw near to listen is better than to offer the sacrifice of fools; for they do not know that they are doing evil.*

I BEGIN the fifth chapter at this point, for this is a new topic.[1] The reading of this book has the same effect on senseless people that the preaching of the Gospel has on wicked people. For when the latter hear the righteousness of faith and Christian liberty being preached and the righteousness of works being denied, they soon draw the inference: "Then let us not do any works. In fact, let us sin! For faith is sufficient." On the other hand, if works and the fruits of faith are preached, they soon attribute justification to these and look for salvation from that source. Thus it is that the Word of God is always followed by these two effects, presumption and despair, so that it is extremely difficult to stick to the royal road.[2] This little book has the same effects. For when senseless people hear this doctrine, that we should have such a quiet and peaceful heart that we commit everything to God, they draw this inference: "If everything is in the hand of God, we shall not do any works." In the same way others sin in the opposite direction by being excessively solicitous and wanting to measure and control everything in every way. But one should travel on the royal road. Let us work hard and do whatever we can in accordance with the Word of God; let us not, however, measure the work on the basis of our efforts, but commit every effort and plan and outcome to the wisdom of God.

Therefore Solomon seems to me to be anticipating an objection[3] here and addressing a salutary exhortation to those who are not traveling on the middle road but are either too negligent of their work or too concerned about it. He advises them to let themselves

[1] In the Hebrew this was chapter 4:17.

[2] Luther ordinarily uses the phrase *via regia* to refer to the middle way between two extremes, rather than to something easy (as in the words ascribed to Euclid, "There is no royal road to geometry").

[3] The technical term in Latin rhetoric is *praeoccupationem facere*.

be governed by the Word of God and meanwhile to work diligently.

Guard your steps when you go to the house of God.

The house of God, or the temple, was instituted not so much for the purpose of sacrificing as for the purpose of preaching, so that there would be a gathering of the people of God there to listen to the Word from their God. In the same way a prince calls his people together, not only for them to eat and drink but also for them to hear his word. Therefore where there is not the hearing of the Word of God, there is not the gathering of the people of God or the house of God. Therefore he commands that one guard one's steps rather than one's heart, that is, that one be not offended when one hears such a doctrine. "See to it," he says, "that you do not err when you hear this doctrine," as that man says in the psalm (Ps. 73:2): "My feet had almost stumbled." For every Word of God, whether it deals with the peace of conscience or with external peace, is followed by offense. It is a sign that is spoken against for the fall and rising of many (Luke 2:34), as Christ also says (Matt. 11:6): "Blessed is he who takes no offense at Me." In sum, the Word is an offense and foolishness to the flesh.

Therefore he is saying: "You hear me teaching, but see to it that you are not offended or do not take offense at it. Thus when you hear that you should have a peaceful heart and that your efforts are vain, you should not say: 'Then I will not do any work!' or feel that one should not care about anything at all. On the other hand, you should not be too concerned and want to control everything by your reason. Human cares, arguments, and counsels are as ineffective as the republic of Plato. But if you want to avoid all offenses, turn yourself over to the Word and work of God, putting aside and casting away all your own thoughts and counsels. Let yourself be spoken to, prick up your ears, and come close to listen." For in all the affairs of man and God our way is never safe unless we turn ourselves over completely to the Word and work of God and take our stand on it without any debate about it in our mind.

To draw near to listen is better than to offer the sacrifice of fools.

This is added after the fashion of a proverb to confirm this statement. Listening to the Word is superior to, or better than, all those sacrifices, acts of worship, and offerings of fools. The reason he says this is to extol listening to and obeying the Word above all other works. For it is eminently proper that above all we should listen to the counsel of our God whenever we gather in the house of God. But the ungodly torment themselves with works, while the counsel of God is neglected. And here you see what "fool" means to the Hebrews, namely, not the one whom we call a moron, but one who does not listen to the Word of God or does not believe it wholeheartedly, even though in other ways he may be very wise. Because such people do not know God or the things of God, they care even less about them, but are racked with their own cares and are anxious about things that should not be treated with anxiety. Their zeal is intent on sacrificing. But you, take hold of the good portion (Luke 10:42)! Listen to the Word of God, and be careful that you are not offended.

For they do not know that they are doing evil. With these words he himself interprets the word "fools." For certainly no one is so evil that he would do evil if he knew that it is so evil in the sight of God. That is why he calls them fools, ignorant and blind men, who do many things as though they were good, and do them with great seriousness, but do not know that these sacrifices, which they carry out with such zeal, are utterly wicked. Thus Christ called the Pharisees "blind" (Matt. 23:26) because they sacrificed much, tormented themselves with works, but neglected faith and love, in fact, did not even know about them, calling evil good and vice versa. Therefore it was right for him to call them fools. But you see that the highest and best zeal in religion is called foolish and evil. For he is speaking about sacrifice, which they carry out with the best of intentions and with seriousness, because it is performed to the neglect of the Word of God. Remain therefore in the Word, lest by your neglect of it you follow your own zeal and end up with the sacrifice of fools. That is what happened to those who, by their neglect of the Word of God, ended up with the vows of chastity, poverty, and obedience, and other such things. These men were brought to offense by the outward appearance, and their feet stumbled.

2. *Do not be rash with your mouth, nor let your heart be hasty to utter a word before God, for God is in heaven, and you upon earth; therefore let your words be few.*

3. *For a dream comes with much business, and a fool's voice with many words.*

This pertains to those who are offended and who deviate toward the right, who are excessively troubled and who dispute about the counsels of God. Just as others say, "If we do not need to do anything but only believe, we shall do no good works," so these people say: "If our own counsels are nothing, what are we to do? Why did God create us this way? Why does He give success to one, but not to another?" Therefore Solomon warns us here not to give in to such thoughts or imitate those who argue this way. Instead, let us remain in the Word and do what he prescribes for us here. Let us not incline either toward the anxiety of these people or toward the negligence of those, but remain on the highway and the royal road.

Before God. That is, in the house of God, in that place where the Word is taught, where God is worshiped and preached—there you should not speak rashly. In other words, you should not be the teacher and you should not do the teaching, but you should permit yourself to be taught. The wicked, however, after they have heard the Word, immediately rail and murmur, some on the left side and others on the right. On the left side the papists battle, the sectarians on our right. Both of them are quick at speaking before God, since they want to prove that their doctrines are divine. Therefore you should not follow your own word or anyone else's, but you should listen to the Lord, as James also says (James 3:1): "Let not many of you become teachers." The meaning, therefore, is this: "Do not be your own teacher or anyone else's, and do not listen to yourself or to anyone else but only to the Word of God." "You have one Master, Christ" (Matt. 23:10), who is in heaven. "Listen to Him" (Matt. 17:5).

For a dream comes with much business. These are two proverbs, which he applies to his statement. For it happens that when there is much business and thought during the day, various dreams follow at night, also according to the judgment of the physicians.[4] This general proverb he applies as follows: If you think anxious thoughts and dispute about how affairs are to be governed and want to take solicitous care for everything, nothing but dreams will follow; when you wake up, they will frustrate you, that is, they will

---

[4] See Luther's fuller discussion, *Luther's Works*, 7, pp. 118—22.

finally seem vain to you. 1 Tim. 1:7 calls this "without understanding either what they are saying or the things about which they make assertions." Thus when we and others prescribe many things for people, still none of them happen. Much more is this true when we prefer our thoughts and plans to the Word of God. *And a fool's voice with many words.* That is, arguing about various things, being too much of a wiseacre, wanting to prescribe to and to instruct everyone—these are indications of a fool. The way to recognize a fool is by his trying to appear wise. A wisdom and a justice that are in too much of a hurry never reach perfection; as the man said, "I hate a boy with precocious wisdom!" [5] That is why he warns us this way not to dispute but to listen and to do. This text could be summarized in two words: Listen and be silent! For if someone is able to listen well, we say in the German proverb that he will be wise. But if someone, by many words and arguments, wants to give the impression that he is helping things, he is a fool and is getting in the way of things instead. Therefore these are very appropriate proverbs for morality, and they can be spoken against those who want to prepare food by their own efforts or who want by their works to prescribe a rule for God. Thus also Jude calls such men dreamers who want to help the church without the Word of God (Jude 8).

For God is in heaven, and you upon earth.

That is, remember your situation: God is such a great majesty in heaven, and you are a worm upon earth. You cannot speak about the works of God on the basis of your own judgment. Let God rather do the speaking; do not dispute about the counsels of God and do not try to control things by your own counsels. It is God who can arrange things and perfect them, for He Himself is in heaven. We express all of this in German by saying: "Don't use many words, but keep your mouth shut!" You will not impose a rule on God. Therefore these people sin on the left side when they refuse to listen to the Word of God but themselves want to help things along; in fact, they teach the Lord what He ought to do. He restrains such people in the following way: "Listen, keep quiet, and do what He commands and offers. If you do not do this, you will fall into offense and will become a dreamer and a fool."

[5] Otto Ribbeck, ed., *Scenicae Romanorum Poesis Fragmenta*, 63.

4. *When you vow a vow to God, do not delay paying it; for He has no pleasure in fools. Pay what you vow.*

5. *It is better that you should not vow than that you should vow and not pay.*

This passage has really been thrown around in the church and in the kingdom of the pope, and it is almost the only one with which they urge and support monastic vows.[6] We have spoken about this matter at greater length elsewhere.[7] We do not dispute whether vows should be paid or not paid but whether what they discuss are truly vows. Jerome and Lyra are agreed that a vow should be one that is possible and that redounds to the honor of God. A foolish vow they call something like picking up a piece of straw from the ground or scratching your head with your finger.[8] Moses also lists the kinds of vows and which things may be vowed, namely, a field, a house, food, clothing, our own body, all of which are in our power (Lev. 27:14-25). Thus the Jews would vow their soul or body to the priests, promising to serve them at some definite time. Beyond this, Moses has no perpetual vow, except for one which he calls anathema, namely, the vow of death, in the last chapter of Leviticus (Lev. 27:28-29); whatever had been vowed was to be killed, whether it was from among human beings or cattle, as in the case of Jephthah in Judges 11. Therefore if the monks want to make such a thing of perpetual vows, they would soon be strangled, if, that is, they want to defend their vows on the basis of Moses. Otherwise all vows must be possible and temporary, as you could, for example, vow your body to the Lord, or a field, a meadow, a garment for a certain time, so that a priest or a Levite would use it. This method of vowing was very valuable for the Levites, to provide for them more easily and more comfortably. God established rules about these things in order to provide for them this way. But our vows are completely foolish, not to say wicked, because we vow poverty and obedience, which are commanded in the Gospel and apply to all Christians. But the vow of virginity is impossible; therefore, on the basis of the judgment

[6] Cf. *Luther's Works,* 46, pp. 148, 152—53.

[7] Apparently a reference to his major work *On Monastic Vows* of 1521, *Luther's Works,* 44, pp. 251—400.

[8] See *Luther's Works,* 44, p. 282, n. 36.

of Jerome and Lyra, these vows are null and void. Besides, this passage of Solomon seems to me to pertain obviously to those who deviate to the right, who upon hearing that their efforts do not avail do not want to do any works at all. For that is how a fool argues: "If I do not accomplish anything by my cares and efforts, I will not do anything. I will not pay even what I have vowed." In opposition to these despisers he says: "Do what God commands. I am not setting you free from toil, but commanding you to do what God has commanded. He has commanded, however, that if you vow you must pay what you have vowed. Therefore if you have vowed something and if you have something to pay it from, it must be paid." Summarize all of this as follows: "Listen, keep silent, and do what is to be done, what the Lord commands."

For He has no pleasure in fools.

Now he confirms this statement with a divine threat. He is speaking, however, about fools in the Scriptural sense, those who despise the Word of God or do not care: "Do not be reckless, do not cast it into the wind. For you will not remain unpunished, but there is a sure punishment awaiting you, as it usually awaits those to whom God is averse and with whom He is wrathful. For He is wrathful with you too."

6. *Let not your mouth cause your flesh to sin and do not say before the angel that it was a mistake, lest God be angry at your voice and destroy the work of your hands.*

7. *For a multitude of words is only a dream and futility; but do you fear God.*

This is a reinforcement of the same statement, by which he warns that they should not be arrogant and refuse to do anything, just as he warned earlier that they should not be overanxious and try to control everything by their reason. "Do not," he says, "speak in so carnal, so rash, and so imprudent a way that you listen to your flesh, but speak in accordance with the Word of God. Nor should you say: 'This is ignorance or a trivial sin, namely, if I do not work or do not pay what I have vowed.' This is how easy consciences usually commit a sin and suppose that God does not care about sins and does not demand our good works. But do not excuse or overlook it if you sin!" For this is where heresies come from, because they throw the Word of God to the wind and stand firm where they are, as though it were not a sin; they are so spiritual that they suppose they do not need the ministry of the Word. This smugness or negligence is indicated by the Hebrew word שִׁגָּיוֹן, which also appears in the title of Psalm 7 and in the title of the canticle of Habakkuk (Hab. 3:1). It means ignorance, but not what we call unknowing, rather what we would more properly call "unconsciousness," if this were a Latin word;[9] that is, when someone is not aware of a thing or has no consciousness of it, so that you do not refer it to the angel but to the words of the one who is speaking, who says: "I am not conscious of any evil as far as I am concerned; therefore God will not rebuke me."

Before the angel. This is because God ruled this people through the mediation of angels, and it is said in Galatians (3:19) that the Law "was ordained by angels through an intermediary." Moses says to the people (Ex. 32:34), "My angel shall go before you," recommending to them the angel as the director of the people. In this manner Solomon says: "Do not say before the angel," namely, the one whom God has given as our director. "Before the angel," however, is the same as "before God." *Lest God be angry at your voice,* that is, see to it that you are not a despiser of your vow and that you do not become unfortunate in everything you do.

Next he concludes this entire passage in almost the same way and with almost the same statement as above: *only a dream and futility.* For where there are many cares, many dreams follow; and where there are many counsels and disputes, there is much futility. Do you therefore fear God, be content with the Word, and let Him rule by His counsel. For He is in heaven, and you upon earth, as was said above. Do you indeed labor, but let Him rule your labors and let Him grant success. For what do you accomplish with all your words, plans, and arguments but affliction? For where there are many words, there there are many dreams, and vice versa. This is a universal principle, which is simply converted: Where there are many thoughts or disputes, there there are many dreams; and where there are many dreams, there there are also many words and disputes. Therefore it adds up to this: Fear God,

---

[9] The word Luther is coining is *inconscientia;* there was, however, a late Latin adjective, *inconscius.*

that is, revere and regard Him in your heart. In this way Paul commands the wife to fear her husband (Eph. 5:33), that is, to revere him in such a way that she does not easily commit something that will offend him. This is also how we shall fear God; that is, we shall revere Him and neither do nor commit anything that would offend Him. Solomon means to say: "You should neither agree with those who are overanxious nor with those who are overnegligent. That way you will not be either a wicked despiser or a presumptuous adviser and investigator."

This is now the end of this topic and of the admonition not to be offended at the course of this life. "Do not argue," he says, "and do not despise, but revere God and keep in mind that the work belongs to God." For God does all of this to confound our plans and our flesh and to show that He is God. For the flesh is either too troubled or too contemptuous. Thus Solomon, in the middle of his sermon, is concerned to beware of offense; he wants no one to take offense at his doctrine, and he wants to avoid either anxiety about things or presumption. Therefore he warns us to pay our vow, so that we fear God and observe His commandment. By a vow, however, Scripture understands not only something pertaining to ceremonial matters but the entire worship of God. In this sense the psalm says (Ps. 50:14): "Pay your vows to the Most High." This is also the meaning of what the Jews cried (cf. Ex. 19:8): "All that the Lord has commanded we will do." This was the greatest vow. You, therefore, having promised that you will do His will, stick to this vow and put aside other things, which God does not want you to investigate or worry about. Now Solomon returns to his catalog of human affairs.

8. *If you see in a province the poor oppressed and justice and right violently taken away, do not be amazed at the matter; for the high official is watched by a higher, and there are yet higher ones over them.*

9. *Beyond this, a king is over the whole land for the cultivation of the region.*

After his treatise on piety he returns nicely to his catalog of vanities. He often repeats the same thing, as happens in sermons. Therefore he says: "I have said that you should fear God. Otherwise you will not do anything good. In fact, you will say that there is no God, unless you are fortified with the fear of God and the acknowledgment of the truth. For you will see the oppression of the poor and the subversion of justice. Then you will murmur, 'How unjustly these things happen!' and you will say: 'Where is God? Why does He put up with these things?'" It is against these thoughts and these offenses that Solomon is strengthening us. "As for you," he says, "fear God and think to yourself: 'This will have its Judge.' If you cannot improve the judge, think to yourself that such is the course of the world and that no one can bring it about that all judges should be just. This belongs only to God and the Highest King." No one understands this except people who have been in public administration. I myself have seen and experienced in the monastery that many incompetent people there were promoted to the position of directing affairs or of holding office, a situation that cannot be corrected. Thus when our Staupitz wished and desired to promote the best men to all positions, he could not do so. "One must," he used to say, "plow with the horses one has." [10] Or, as the proverb says, "he who does not have horses must plow with oxen." That is how it is in human affairs. Sometimes there is a good prince, but he still cannot set all the judges straight or bring it about that all the officials and judges are good and just; nevertheless, he is obliged to have magistrates. Thus wise men are concerned and take care that the common people be provided with good laws and are obedient, but the latter only murmur and complain about the violence and incompetence of the judges. When you see such things, keep in mind that these are the vanities of the world, and do not flee from the world, as the monks flee into the desert. They act just like the farmer who, when he has wild horses, wants to let them go when he ought to use his care and diligence to make them not so wild. Thus certain heads of the household are extremely rigorous taskmasters, and yet they accomplish nothing except to disturb everything by their incompetence. Emperor Frederick III's famous saying is often quoted: "He who does not know how to dissemble does not know how to rule." [11] You should add: "He who does not know how to dissemble does not know how to live." If you want to live in the world, learn to see this.

[10] See also *Luther's Works,* 7, p. 192.

[11] Elsewhere Luther quotes this saying, but suggests that Emperor Frederick III did not follow it (*Luther's Works,* 29, p. 75).

Is it a matter of doing nothing, then? By no means. One must act and work; but what you cannot bring about, you must dissemble. Thus a wise head of the household must dissemble many things and overlook the things that offend him. For it is impossible that everything be done rightly and without injustice. Therefore this book teaches you to have a quiet and peaceful heart in the affairs of this life, so that when you hear or see evil, you do not become indignant but say: "Such is the trouble in the course of the world. There is no other way here." On the other hand, when you see good things, you should say: "Blessed be God, who governs things in such a way that He does not permit only evil to happen or to be committed, but mixes good with evil." Do what you can; commit the rest to God and bear it, in accordance with the proverb: "Whoever cannot lift a heavy stone should let it lie and lift a stone that he can pick up." Therefore when you see evil in princes, the abuse of vested authority by magistrates, wicked judgments by judges, the murmuring of the common people, quarrels among the wise, etc., just keep in mind: "God will set these things straight."

Do not be amazed at the matter.

He wants to set our hearts at rest. "Do not be amazed," he says, "if you see such things, but be content. You will not set these things straight, for you are not even able to give aid or counsel. Therefore fear God and commit them to Him. That way you will have peace. Anyone who does not do this will have nothing but affliction."

For the high official is watched by a higher. That is, do not torment yourself if you cannot change things, but leave it to a higher judge. What a lesser person cannot do, he should think of as pertaining to a higher person. If the prince is evil, defer to the higher Prince, God. Thus if I become very vexed on account of the Sacramentarians and the sects who are disturbing the church of God and contaminating the Gospel, what will I accomplish? Therefore I commit the matter to God the Judge, in whose hand everything lies. Although I myself lament it that souls are being deceived and led astray so miserably, I cannot do any more except to oppose them in accordance with my office and to say: "Stop it! There has been enough error. Come to your senses!" When you have given this advice to the other person, you should commit the matter to God, in accordance with Paul's statement (Titus 3:10): "A man that is a heretic after the first and second admonition reject"; and again (2 Tim. 3:13): "Evil men will go on from bad to worse" and will not escape their judge. Everyone has his judge. If the assessor does not do it, the bailiff or the captain will. And if the latter does not judge him, the prince will do the judging. And if the prince neglects it also, the emperor will do it. If the emperor despises his duty, God will neither despise it nor neglect it. This is what he means when he says: "Above these there is a king over the whole land." Solomon did not have any magistrate higher than the king. "Let the king carry out what you cannot."

For the cultivation of the region.

This seems to be an epithet for the royal authority, signifying the office he occupies and the task of the secular authority. For this, he says, the king was made a magistrate, to cultivate the earth and to avenge the injuries and evils of those beneath him. The king has a sword to protect the innocent and to punish the guilty. Nor does God permit any evildoing in the land which He does not punish through the magistrates. If the lower magistrate does not do it, the superior will; that is, it eventually comes under the power of the sword. It is, moreover, lovely to have the king called the cultivator of the earth, which does not refer only to the practice of agriculture but to the conservation of the entire state, as this goes on through laws, judgments, etc. It is the king's duty both to protect and to nourish and enhance the goods and the property of people. Agriculture prepares things; the army, or the sword, protects them and restrains wicked men so that others are able to cultivate and to do the things they should. Thus it depends on the king that things be grown and that they be preserved; for unless he defends them, others cannot cultivate the earth. In this way, therefore, he strengthens us against offenses and at the same time teaches us that our counsels are in vain. "I," he says, "am a king by the grace of God. If I cannot set things straight, I still do what I can. The rest I am compelled to tolerate, for otherwise the whole land would be laid waste. Meanwhile I commend it to a higher Judge, to God, to whom all the power of the sword belongs." This is what others do too, each doing in his own office whatever he can; the rest they commit to a higher power.

10. *He who loves money will not be satisfied with money; nor he who loves wealth, with gain; this also is vanity.*

11. *When goods increase, they increase who eat them; and what gain has their owner but to see them with his eyes?*

This pertains to what he had said in the first chapter (1:8): "The ear is not filled with hearing, nor the eye satisfied with seeing." For here the vanity of the heart and of human desires is being treated. One world was not enough for Alexander. So it is in all other matters, in honors, riches, and the like. For the miserable life of man is so arranged that the miser is an example to everyone. He has money and still is not satisfied. In fact, he does not enjoy the things that are present, but only thirsts for other money that is not present yet. Therefore what is a miser but a heart that is distracted by what it does not have and is turned away from what it does have? This, then, is vanity of heart. Would it not be preferable to be content with the things that are present and to cast away the anxiety about the things that are in the future? Soldiers are happier than misers, even though they are filled with every vice, are extremely dissolute, and live a very hard life. For otherwise all men are misers, except for such in whom other similar vices have extinguished this one. But only the godly have this blessing, that they are content with the things that are present and that they also use them with thanksgiving and joy. A miser does not have a larger mouth or stomach than a godly poor man, nor does he eat more; yet the latter is content with the little he has and is in fact rich, while the former in the midst of his riches is needy and in want. These things are said and pointed out in a healthful and godly way, but the flesh in its smugness despises whatever you say or do.

When goods increase, etc. This is a remarkable statement. The miser is not satisfied but goes on gathering. For whom? The stingy man needs a spendthrift.[12] For even if he has an enormous amount of money, it will still be used up whether he lives or dies; and he gets nothing out of it but toil and trouble. King Solomon has houses filled with gold and silver, but who uses these goods? His courtiers. He himself gets only clothing and food from it. Who at the courts of princes uses the property of the princes? The

---

[12] The saying, which sounds proverbial, is: *Tenax requirit prodigum.*

knights, the scribes, the Thrasos,[13] and the great scoundrels. To gather riches, therefore, is to gather many who eat them. Why, then, do you torment yourself this way to scrape things together? Be content with what you have. Even if you accumulate riches, they will not come without bringing along as guests those who will eat them, if not during your life, then certainly after your death. Beyond this you will have nothing from all your goods except something to fill your mouth and stomach and to clothe your body. But if the riches flow in, use your portion, but leave the rest to others and put away the anxiety of collecting and accumulating; if you do not, it will happen nevertheless, for you hear it said here: *When goods increase, they increase who eat them.*

And what gain has their owner?

This is a striking taunt of avarice. There is a word of Horace: "With your moneybags filled from all over, you restlessly open your mouth for more; yet you are forced to refrain from touching it as though it were something sacred, or you must merely enjoy it as though it were a picture." [14] And again: "Poor in the midst of great riches." [15] Solomon expresses exactly the same sentiment. A miser has only one benefit, that he can look at his florins as I look at a picture that has been drawn; beyond that he gets nothing out of them. A miser cannot use his money for the purpose for which it was established, namely, to eat, drink, and clothe himself, and to serve others with what is left. For this is why wine and grain grow and why gold and silver circulate, that we should put them to such use. But the flesh does not care about this; in fact, it despises it and follows its own desires. Therefore it also attains to an utterly miserable life, without rest or peace.

12. *Sweet is the sleep of a laborer, whether he eats little or much; but the surfeit of the rich will not let him sleep.*

Solomon continues to condemn riches, that is, the anxiety and effort to accumulate riches and to keep them. For the more a miser accumulates riches, the more his mind or his greed is stimulated.

[13] Thraso is a braggart in Terence's *Eunuchus,* a character to whom Luther frequently refers, e. g., *Luther's Works,* 13, p. 182.

[14] See p. 68, n. 9, above.

[15] Horace, *Odes,* III, 16, 28.

A miser is always in need and is poor in the midst of his riches. In fact, miserliness is such a monster, says Sallust, that it is not diminished either by bounty or by poverty.[16] And someone has said: "The love of money grows more as the money grows more." [17] Among the troubles of the miser he now lists another: even if a miser is surfeited, he still cannot sleep. Therefore the life of the miser is miserable in every way, for he has no rest either by day or by night. Nature is so constituted that a body which has been fed in a moderate way sleeps and rests sweetly. For drunkards are neither asleep nor awake, neither dead nor alive. The man who exerts himself with a moderate amount of labor sleeps easily and sweetly, even though he may have little to eat, as it is said (Ps. 104:23): "Man goes forth to his work and to his labor until the evening." But misers continue their labor until midnight, and they tire and wear out their bodies. The miser's body is overloaded with food and broken with toil, but his mind is overloaded and broken with cares and will not let him sleep. Therefore when Solomon says *laborer*, he is commanding us to work and is not forbidding us to acquire riches. And when he says *Sweet is the sleep*, he is calling for moderate labor which exercises the body but does not wear it out. Therefore he demands labor but condemns greed and anxiety, because "the blessing of the Lord makes rich" (Prov. 10:22). Enormous labor does not make rich; as Ps. 127:2 says, "It is vain that you rise up early, etc.," and "He gives to His beloved sleep." So it was that Abraham, Isaac, Jacob, David, and Solomon were made rich by the gift and the blessing of God. Moreover, they used their riches in such a way that they helped others by means of them. Therefore what Epicurus taught is wrong: [18] riches should not be rejected; magistrates should not be deposed; one's wife should not be put away; one's family should not be driven away. Instead, one must labor and be patient. We must carry out our existence in the midst of things; things should not be rejected, but we should endure to the end whatever God has given. Where God has appointed you, there you remain; only do not try to control things by your own counsels. Whatever evil does not befall you,

---

[16] Cf. Publilius Syrus, *Sententiae*, 440—41.

[17] Juvenal, *Satires*, XIV, 139.

[18] The first of these ideas is more usually identified with the teaching of Epicurus than is the second.

regard as a gain. For that is how it is in this life, that we should expect evil things daily, but good things are beyond expectation, and that is how they come. But when they do come, we should give thanks to God for a special act of kindness. If you happen to have a chaste wife or obedient children, give thanks to God. If the magistrate at any time manages to administer the state in a good and worthy way, or if your field produces a crop, etc., regard all of this as a gain. But when the opposite happens to you, do not fret. Therefore Solomon does not want to move us out of human affairs but to thrust us into them. We should not make Solomon into a Crates or a Diogenes, those foolish despisers of riches and of the world.[19] For it is a wicked philosophical saying λάθε βιώσας ["Do not draw attention to yourself by the way you live"].[20] For when they saw that this world and its affairs are administered unjustly, they concluded that it is best to live a solitary life and not to become entangled in such affairs or in public business, so as not to be compelled to see and to bear such injustice. This statement of Solomon about using and bearing things was hidden and unknown to all the philosophers. But let us, who have Solomon as our teacher, do what we can; what we cannot do, let us permit to slip away.

13. *There is a grievous evil which I have seen under the sun: riches were kept by their owner to his hurt,*

14. *and those riches were lost in a great calamity; and he is father of a son, but the son has nothing in his hand.*

This, too, is the vainest of miseries in human life. It is not an evil that is common to all, and yet it does come to our attention often, that riches serve to bring harm to the one who owns them and has accumulated them. For Solomon is complaining not merely that there is affliction in such things but also that one must see such things in the world, even if one is free of them himself. How many men in our own century have been murdered in their own homes on account of riches? Did not the duke of Bavaria in our age have a large amount of gold, a tower filled with gold? But this gold

---

[19] Crates the Cynic, who died in 285 B.C., taught the ideal of poverty; Diogenes, who died about 325 B.C., founded the Cynic philosophy and taught the ascetic renunciation of luxury.

[20] Epicurus, *Fragments*, 551.

brought war to the duke and calamity to the entire land.[21] There are hardly any princes who have left great riches behind them without bringing trouble to their entire country. Just as Julius Caesar made use of the Roman treasury to bring harm to the city,[22] so our bishops have accumulated treasure, but only for an evil end; for they did not do anyone any service with it, and this fact aroused the peasants.[23] Now they persist in their accumulating and in their skinning the people, but they will not stop doing this until the people arrive who will take these things too and bring destruction upon them. Should one on this account reject wealth? No. In fact, it should be acquired, especially by princes, but in such a way that we benefit and help others. Because this does not happen, God permits the very riches in which people trust to bring about the ruin of those who own them. Thus Ezekiel prophesies against the wicked Jews and misers (Ezek. 16:49): they did not aid the poor; therefore they will be led away into captivity and will perish along with their riches. The same thing is happening to our wealthy misers, the bishops and despisers of the Gospel. Because they refuse their gold and riches to the needs of the poor, the soldiers and the tax collector will come and will take away whatever Christ does not get. *They were lost in a great calamity.* The rich man himself suffers great misery. He is in danger every day at home from thieves, and away from home from robbers, who may capture and murder him. Merchants know this little ditty very well.

And he is father of a son, but the son has nothing in his hand. This is the reason why the Lord overthrows Sodom and Gomorrah, that they have riches but do not aid the poor (Ezek. 16:49). The miser accumulates, but someone else will dissipate what has been accumulated. The miser thinks: "My son will have these riches." But look, God lets in some thieves or robbers to deprive him of all the riches, so that neither he nor his son has anything left. Therefore one should persist in his toil, but should look for the blessing of God and should aid the poor. Indeed, all our toil should be like that of those who, in the winepress or in the harvest, sing as they work. In the midst of our labor and sweat we should be

---

[21] The duke of Bavaria at the time was William IV, grandson of Emperor Frederick III.

[22] This account is taken from Plutarch, *Lives*, "Caesar."

[23] Luther is referring to the abuses that had led to the Peasants' War of 1525.

happy and have the feeling that we can lose everything with equanimity. This is how we should think to ourselves: "To be sure, I shall work for myself and for my children. If God gives something, we shall use it. If there is something left after me, my son will have it. If there is nothing, God will provide for him as He has provided for me."

15. *As he came from his mother's womb he shall go again, naked as he came, and shall take nothing for his toil, which he may carry away in his hand.*

16. *This also is a grievous evil: just as he came, so shall he go; and what gain has he that he toiled for the wind?*

The same thing appears in Job 1:21: "Naked I came from my mother's womb, etc."; and in Paul, 1 Tim. 6:7: "We brought nothing into the world, and we cannot take anything out of the world." Even the richest of men cannot boast of anything more than of that from which he has been eating and drinking while he has been alive. Since, therefore, we shall not take anything with us, let us share it with others, using our riches as though they were flowing water or air. This is how we should think: "As I shall forsake my riches when I die, so I forsake them while I am living, Why, then, should I accumulate them with such great anxiety, when we cannot have anything more than a small mouthful? That is how I use water: I wash myself, and others wash themselves also. What we do not need, we let flow away. That is how we use fire or air." Riches also should be used this way, that you are merely their administrator. *What gain has he that he toiled for the wind?* "To toil for the wind" is a Hebrew phrase which Paul imitated in 1 Cor. 9:26: "I do not box as one beating the air"; and in 1 Cor. 14:9: "You will be speaking into the air." It means the same as speaking in vain. This is what Solomon is saying: "A miser toils for the wind, that is, he toils in vain." It is labor lost.

17. *All his days also he eats in darkness and grief, in much vexation and sickness and resentment.*

Once more a Hebrew phrase: *he eats in darkness* for "he eats in sadness." It is derived from the gestures and facial expressions of men. For when the heart is sorrowful, the eyes are covered over as though by some kind of cloud. But when it is happy, they are lit up as though by some kind of rays and a new light. This phrase occurs frequently in the Psalms. Light is used for happiness and darkness for sadness, as in Ps. 27:1: "The Lord is my Light and my Salvation" and again (Ps. 13:3): "Lighten my eyes." To eat in darkness, therefore, means to toil in sadness. A greedy workman, in fact, any greedy person, constantly finds something that he does not like and that he criticizes, because he is filled with cares and anxieties. He cannot eat his bread in happiness; he is always making accusations; he is always finding fault with his household. So it is that the only cases that are referred to the prince and the magistrate are the bad ones. Hence a magistrate who is not wise will torture himself and wear himself out with cares because he does not see his efforts and strivings succeeding. But a wise one will say this: "I help and do as much as I can. But what I cannot set straight, that I bear and am obliged to bear. Meanwhile I commit it to God, who alone knows how to set everything straight according to His will and how to grant success to our endeavors." So it is that we are disturbed when we hear that among such a large number of preachers there are so few who are faithful and good and to whom it is a matter of the heart. But what shall we do? Shall we grow indignant over this and wear ourselves out with grief? We would not accomplish any more that way. But we turn the matter over to God. Therefore our ears and eyes should become accustomed to hearing and seeing evil things that we do not want. Nor should we suppose that we are to see the good things that bring us pleasure. This world does not bring such things. Whoever does not want ever to be offended will find more things that offend him than anyone else does. Therefore let us be armed against all evils in this way, by knowing that this is the course of the present life.

18. *Behold, what I have seen to be good and to be fitting is to eat and drink and find enjoyment in all the toil with which one toils under the sun the few days of his life which God has given him, for this is his lot.*

19. *Every man also to whom God has given wealth and possessions and power to enjoy them, and to accept his lot and find enjoyment in his toil — this is the gift of God.*

20. *For he will not much remember the days of his life because God keeps him occupied with joy in his heart.*

This is the conclusion of this entire book or argument, which was also stated earlier in chapters two and three. And here you see that Solomon does not condemn riches, nor does he forbid that we acquire riches or food or drink. But he calls these things gifts of God in order to teach us to put down our anxieties; then we shall wait for all of these things from God by faith and when God wills shall surrender them with patience, just as Abraham gave his son back to God. Therefore riches are not to be rejected. Nor are they granted to us by God for the purpose of our rejecting them or abstaining from them, but rather so that we use them and distribute them to the poor. This statement is the interpreter of the entire book: Solomon intends to forbid vain anxieties, so that we may happily enjoy the things that are present and not care at all about the things that are in the future, lest we permit the present moment, our moment, to slip away. *For this is his lot,* that is, this is what he gets out of it. *For he will not remember the days of his life,* that is, his heart is not swollen with anxiety and care either about the things that are present or about the things that are in the future. *Because God keeps him occupied with joy in his heart.* In this way he has joy in his toil here, and here in the midst of evils he enters into Paradise. On the other hand, wicked men and misers and as many as do not follow this example in using the things of this life, begin already here to suffer torment and to be thrust down into hell.

CHAPTER SIX

1. *There is an evil which I have seen under the sun, and it lies heavy upon men:*

2. *a man to whom God gives wealth, possessions, and honor, so that he lacks nothing of all that he desires, yet God does not give him power to enjoy them, but a stranger enjoys them; this is vanity; it is a sore affliction.*

AFTER interposing his teaching, or exhortation, he returns to his catalog of the various endeavors in human life in which vanity and misery reign. What he recounts here about the rich man seems similar to what he said above. But here he is speaking about the rich man who keeps his great riches and his family in peace, who lives without loss or damage to his property. Yet in the very midst of his wealth and his superb honors he is still tormented and cannot enjoy them, either because illness interferes or because he is hindered by hatred and anxiety about preserving and increasing his property. Thus he is tortured and he perishes through the very things he has. If a son is born to him, this is now another source of anxiety. How is he to make and to bequeath as much as possible to him, especially if he is already a full-grown man? For as the common saying goes, "Small children are a small anxiety, big children a big anxiety." People accumulate things for their children and want to leave them wealthy and to gain the highest possible honors for them. Everyone has these wishes and desires, which are nevertheless vain in the extreme. For what good is it when a living man has everything and yet does not make use of anything but is constantly being distracted by things that are in the future and that do not exist, while neglecting the things that are present? This is therefore a description of a rich man who lacks nothing for a good and happy life and yet does not have one. Look at many of our noblemen. They could live comfortably in their homes, for they own plenty in their fields. But not content with this, they proceed to the courts of the princes, where they expect to receive more but live very miserably.[1] One can see the same thing in rich men and merchants; although they too could live at home in tranquillity, they venture forth by land or sail by sea at great peril to their lives and with jeopardy to their goods. Is this not vanity and sore affliction? Therefore he also goes on to say:

3. *If a man begets a hundred children, and lives many years, so that the days of his years are many, but he does not enjoy life's good things, and also has no burial, I say that an untimely birth is better off than he.*

4. *For he comes into vanity and goes into darkness, and in darkness his name is covered.*

He is enlarging upon the woes of the rich miser. No one, he says, should suppose that he will make his heirs rich by his own stinginess. For there are many people who toil anxiously to gain wealth and still do not make it. On the other hand, there are many people who grow wealthy without having anxiously sought to do so. Therefore you should acknowledge that riches are completely the gift of God. Nor does it lie in your powers to make this or that heir rich. The command is: "Poor people are not to be rich." You can do whatever you wish, but you will not make rich a man whom God wants to be a pauper. Besides, it can also happen that this rich miser will not die rich but will be deprived of everything.

And also has no burial. He continues to enlarge upon the misery. These words mean that he would be thrown out of his property and would die somewhere else rather than in his own home. *I say that an untimely birth is better off than he.* That is, it would be preferable not to exist rather than to be so miserable and to be a pauper in the midst of enormous wealth. This is true quite apart from any question of piety. For if you compare the life of a rich and unhappy miser with that of someone who has not yet been born, you will feel the same way. Nor is Solomon speaking in the manner of foolish men or dressing up in the mask of a foolish man, as some interpreters say,[2] but he is here describing the life of foolish men in their external behavior. In this respect, he says,

---

[1] The economic and political changes of the period had driven some of the knights and lesser nobility to the courts of the German princes; others had rebelled.

[2] See p. 58, n. 6, above.

it is truly better not to be born than to live this way. Therefore this is to be understood as pertaining to the miserable rich man, who has the things that are necessary for happiness but whose unhappy mind does not permit him to make use of them. Surely a poor man who bears his lot with equanimity is better off than this rich man. For "the traveler with an empty purse can sing in the presence of a robber." [3] But the rich man is frightened by every bramblebush, and at the height of his happiness he is as miserable as possible. Truly the world is ruled by opinions. God rules by realities, but we are troubled by opinions and lose the reality, just as that dog did in Aesop.[4] *For he comes into vanity and goes into darkness.* That is, he comes into the world naked, empty, and poor. That is how he lives, that is how he dies; for he does not enjoy things but is only distracted and troubled by what is in the future. But this is nothing else than having nothing and being empty and poor. *And in darkness his name is covered.* That is, he does nothing either worthy or memorable, not even in his own household, except that it is said of him: "He lived neither for himself nor for others." A miserable man, whom no one would want to imitate!

5. *Moreover he does not see the sun or know rest either here or elsewhere.*

"To see the sun" is Hebrew for "to enjoy things and take pleasure in them." For this physical life has the sun as a sort of very sacred divine power, one that is supremely necessary for moral men. Without it everything seems and is sad, as Christ also says (John 12:35; 11:9): "He who walks in the darkness does not know where he goes. But if anyone walks in the day, he does not stumble, because he sees the light of this world." Therefore it is a most pleasant thing that the sun shines. But the miser does not look at the light, he does not view the sun; that is, he does not think what a good thing light is, nor does he look at any creature as something to enjoy and to use well. For he has lost every consideration of the blessings, the creatures, and the things of God on account of his greed. He never sees what an outstanding gift of God it is that the sun rises every day. He thinks of nothing, wonders at nothing, yearns for nothing—except money. In the same way the ambitious

---

[3] Juvenal, *Satires*, X, 22.

[4] See also p. 61 above.

man looks at nothing except honors. The lover does not look at his own wife but is always looking at another woman. That is, such people do not enjoy the good creatures that are present now. Thus the wicked begin their hell in this life, because [5] they are deprived of the use of all the creatures and gifts of God, so that they never see the sun, which we nevertheless have every day. In other words, they do not rejoice in the gifts of God but are always looking for something else.

6. *Even though he should live a thousand years twice told, yet enjoy no good — do not all go to the one place?*

Look how he enlarges upon the woes of the miser. He means to say that nothing will happen to this man except that the more his life is prolonged, the more he will accumulate and prolong his miseries and calamities. This is human life, sheer vanity and misery, whether you experience it yourself or see it in others. For even the saints, although they do not live in accordance with the flesh, are nevertheless troubled by the flesh and compelled to feel the vanity of the flesh. *Do not all go, etc.?* He is repeating what he had said earlier, in chapter one (1:5, 7, 4): "The sun rises and the sun goes down, and hastens to the place where it rises. To the place where the streams flow, there they flow again. A generation goes, etc." Everything goes back to where it came from. Everything finally passes away. Human life, kingdoms, and whatever belongs to men — all of these return to where they came from, from the earth to the earth, just as the wind blows back and forth and just as the sun returns to where it rose. This, then, is what Solomon means: One should get rid of care and anxiety about the things that are in the future and are still to be acquired, and should rather enjoy the things that are in the present. Therefore he continues:

7. *Toil is meted out to all men after the fashion of each, yet his soul is not satisfied.*

In Hebrew it reads: "All the toil of man is according to his mouth," a phraseology that is peculiar to them. Moses uses this word "mouth" to mean fashion, or measure, this way in Gen. 47:12, speaking of Joseph: "And he provided them and all his father's household with food, furnishing rations to each." The Hebrew

---

[5] The Weimar text has *qua*, but we have read *quia*.

reads: "And he provided for them by providing according to the mouth"; that is, he provided for the entire household of his father after the fashion of infants, to whom rations are furnished even though they do no work. And Ex. 12:4 says: "According to the mouth of each you shall eat the Passover," that is, according to the measure of those who can eat the lamb. Thus also Solomon says here: "All their toil is according to their mouth," that is, according to the fashion or the measure of each; in other words, each man has a certain amount of toil. God assigns to each man his toil in accordance with his powers and in keeping with his calling. In German we say it this way: "Each one has his allotted share." To each one God has assigned his portion. A boy ought to toil in one way, a man in another; a magistrate ought to toil in one way, a private citizen in another. He wants you to be trained by means of infantile duties or labors, as though you were an infant, while the prince is trained with arduous and great ones. This is the source of the common saying: "Whatever one's official position is, that is the apron he receives." In this way, therefore, he calls us away from alien anxieties to our own business. Nor does he forbid toil. In fact, he declares that one must toil, but he wants you to do your duty happily in accordance with your assigned task and to leave other things to other people. He wants us to enjoy our pleasure, but in God, so that we do not abandon ourselves to pleasure when it is present, as the wicked do, nor grieve when it is absent but bear it with equanimity. You should, he says, have a happy spirit and an active body, but in such a way that you abide in your assigned place. Do not be like the envious person, who pursues what belongs to others: the merchant envies the soldier; the soldier counts his troubles and envies the merchant; the old man envies the youth. We turn our gaze away from our own real happiness, and with intense distress we look at the happiness of other people. No one is able to consider the good things he has or to be content with his lot; if he were to consider himself, he would not long so much for what belongs to others. If, for example, old men could see the dangers that afflict youth, they would not want to be young. On the other hand, if young men could see the many discomforts of old age, they would be willing to bear their own discomforts and would not begrudge the elderly their comforts. But we do not do this; instead, we are always looking at what belongs to others and despising what belongs to us. Thus the rich miser looks at and desires what he does not have, but neglects what he does have. For "his soul is not satisfied," that is, he does not stick to his assigned task. No one is content with his lot. The spectator of a play always imagines that he would perform it better. If I hear someone else preach, I think that I would be able to surpass him in many ways. A servant thinks likewise: "If I were king, I would administer everything with the utmost prudence." Similarly, that character in Terence says: "I should have been king!" [6] If the kingdom were turned over to him, no one would be a greater fool than he. But as the saying goes, "May God visit palsy on the man who claims to do something better than he knows how!" But the soul neglects its own job and is completely preoccupied with someone else's job, and so it does not do either one right. For whoever does not take care of his own things will do very poorly at taking care of other people's things. God has given me an assignment to keep me from becoming idle. But look how I desert my own work and become busy with someone else's. This is truly what he said above (1:8): "The eye is not satisfied with seeing." In the same way the heart or soul is not satisfied with longing, but is always inconstant and fickle.

8. *For what advantage has the wise man over the fool? And what does the poor man have who knows how to conduct himself before the living?*

That is, both wise men and fools are troubled by lusts that go beyond the bounds of their assigned tasks, and there is no difference between wise men and fools. For they both yearn for things beyond measure, and both are overwhelmed by a yearning for what belongs to someone else. By wise men he means not those who are truly wise but those who are wise ψυχικῶς ("in an unspiritual way," cf. James 3:15); by fools, moreover, he means the wicked, the unrestrained, reckless, and impudent people. Both of them, he says, have their assigned tasks, apart from which they will accomplish nothing; one will get as far as the other. Therefore someone can suppose, or even say, that if he were in public office, he would accomplish a great deal. But if he actually were in public office, he would accomplish no more than is now being accomplished by

---

[6] Terence, *Phormio,* 70.

the man whom he judges and condemns. What follows is to the same effect:

What does the poor man have? By "the living" here he means not only those who have life, but, as above,[7] those who enjoy life, that is, those who have a good and sweet life. Therefore he says: "It is foolish for private citizens to prescribe to others how they ought to arrange everything and carry it out, on the supposition that they would take care of things better; for, after all, nothing ever happens except what ought to happen."

9. *Better is the sight of the eyes than the wandering of the desire; this also is vanity and vexation of spirit.*

All of this is a Hebrew way of speaking that is altogether unfamiliar to us. The Hebrew word literally means "mirror," that is, a thing that presents itself to the eyes or into the sight of the eyes. Thus Ex. 38:8 says: "And he made the laver of bronze and its base of bronze, from the mirrors of the ministering women who ministered at the door of the tent of meeting." This should have been translated from the Hebrew as follows: "And he made the laver, etc., in the sight of the armies that performed military service at the door of the tent of testimony." For the Jewish people had women votaries who continued in prayers and petitions and who served God and performed military service day and night, as it is written in 1 Sam. 2:22 and as in Luke 2:37 Anna is said to have performed military service.[8] On the basis of this military service the women were called the army of the Lord performing military service at the door of the tent of testimony. Later, as time went on, however, religion declined and, as Jude says (Jude 4), it was "perverted into licentiousness." It is said of Rachel, the wife of Jacob (Gen. 29:17): "She was beautiful in the mirror,"[9] that is, beautiful in face and appearance: she was lovely to look at.

The meaning, then, is this: It is better to enjoy the things that are in sight, right before your eyes, than to have a wandering desire. That is, use the things that are present and do not wander

[7] See p. 71 above.

[8] We have translated the text as it stands, but Luther seems to be referring "day and night" rather than "to have performed military service" to Anna.

[9] The translation "mirror" is apparently Luther's own, based on the use of the same Hebrew noun for "appearance" in Gen. 29:17 and for "mirror" in Ex. 38:8.

in your desires, as that dog in Aesop did when he desired the reflection and lost the meat that was present. What the Lord has given you here within your sight, that you should use and be content. Do not follow your desire, which will not be fulfilled, as he has also said earlier. You should, therefore, understand "the sight of the eyes" to mean not the sight which the eyes themselves make but the sight which they have from their objects. It is a passive sight; that is, you should make use of what is presented to you here and now. So it is said of God in Gen. 1:31: "And God saw everything that He had made"; that is, He rejoiced in His works, He clung to them. He sees them, they please Him, they are very good. Thus a man who is godly also clings to what he has and is pleased by it as something that God has granted to him and offers to him now. The ungodly man is not so. Everything he sees is a vexation of spirit, because he does not use it as a mirror but permits his desire to wander. If he has money, he finds no pleasure in it; he does not enjoy it but constantly desires something else. He has taken a wife, but he desires another; he has acquired a kingdom, but he is not content with only one. Alexander seeks and desires another world. All things ought to be a "mirror" to us, for us to delight in them and to fix our eyes and gaze upon them, enjoying them and giving thanks to God. Therefore he forbids our soul to wander (as the Hebrew has it), that is, to roam in its thoughts and opinions about things. Therefore the conclusion of this passage is: Use the things that are present and do not wander in your desires. "For this is vanity," namely, for the soul to wander.

10. *Whatever has come to be has already been named, and it is known what man is, and that he is not able to dispute with one stronger than he.*

11. *The more words, the more vanity, and what is man the better?*

This can be adequately understood on the basis of the preceding. Earlier we spoke about the phrase *What has been is what will be.*[10] In all these words there is a Hebraism at work, which we would express in German this way: "As things have been, so they still are; and as things are, so they will be." That is, men will always be vain in the extreme, desiring and seeking things that are

---

[10] See p. 20 above.

vain because they are outside the Word of God and their assigned task. Nor do they listen to the counsels of God. God has determined and preordained certain boundaries for all men, when they are to be born, when they are to die, what name they are to have, and what office they are to fill. After we are born, He presents us with these things for us to use. But men, not content with the ordinance and counsel of God, immediately choose and desire something else, yet in vain. For only God accomplishes what He thinks. Therefore the meaning is: What is it that is? That is: What is a man who is now alive or others who will be born later? It has already been decided for a man what is going to happen to him and what name he is going to receive. By "name" you should understand what is ascribed to a man on the basis of his deeds and what is worthy of being celebrated about a man; thus Caesar was called "the Victor" and Catiline "the Parricide." [11] These names, I am saying, have been determined ahead of time and assigned in the presence of God before we are born. Thus also it has been determined that this man is to be a shoemaker, that man a parish pastor, yet another a preacher, etc. If, therefore, all these things, both our professions and our names, have already been defined and foreknown, why does a man wander about in his opinions, attempt many things, and desire things that are beyond limits? Why does he act outside his assigned station? For he does not accomplish anything except to bring greater and greater affliction upon himself. *He is not able to dispute with one stronger than he,* that is, with something that has been placed above him; for "all things stand according to a definite law." [12] The heathen also saw that human affairs are not carried out by the schemes of wise men, but they attributed this to fate or even to fortune, but not to God. Thus also Solomon looks here at the very course of history, how things happen in the world. This is what he sees there: men are not able to accomplish or to attain what they desire and strive for. The reason is that events themselves resist it; they refuse to be dominated or controlled by our plans. If someone disputes with them and wants to break through and to push his plans, so that what he has in mind will happen, he accomplishes nothing; the reality resists him, and God hinders him. Therefore it is useless for us to kick against the goad (cf. Acts 26:14),

[11] Cf. Julius Caesar, *Gallic War*, VII, 70; Sallust, *Catiline*, LI, 25.
[12] Vergil, *Aeneid*, X, 467.

as though someone were to try to break through the wall with his head. For that which is stronger than he and higher than he resists his plan. Thus Antony wanted to break through the wall when he invaded Italy and made his two sons kings, one in the East and the other in the West; but he was frustrated in this plan.[13] Look at the thoughts Caesar had and how he was frustrated. The pope's efforts have not succeeded either. This was because their name had been called and defined, but they went beyond the assigned limit. Therefore they were struggling against Someone stronger than they, and all they attained was sorrow, anguish, and calamity.

When you see, therefore, that all things have been established by a definite law, including your name and your profession, and when you nevertheless refuse to be contented with this but strive and strain in opposition to it, you are navigating against the stream. Nor will you accomplish anything, regardless of how wisely you plan and proceed, except to multiply words. Nothing will come of it except a lot of talk. Thus Plato wrote a great deal, and so did Aristotle, about the administration of the state and about civic morality. But these were mere words and remain words, with no consequences. Later, when they saw that these ideas did not succeed, they tried to improve the situation with yet other plans and laws. They said, "If only we had acted this way!"—wising up after the fact. Therefore the history both of the Gentiles and of the Jews teaches us that work undertaken outside one's assigned station cannot accomplish anything, whether it be done by a wise man or by a fool, except that the history of the Jews was carried on in the Word of God and teaches us that everything happens by the ordinance of God and that therefore it is safer for us to stick to this. Otherwise, the history of the Gentiles is equally wonderful and great, but it was carried on apart from the Word of God.

12. *For who knows what is good for man while he lives the few days of his vain life, which he passes like a shadow? For who can tell man what will be after him under the sun?*

That is, no man knows what is good for him in life. Men do not know how to enjoy things, nor do they know how to have a peaceful heart. The plans of men vary. One man seeks for imperial power, another for riches. But they do not know whether they will attain

---

[13] Luther seems to be referring to the account in Plutarch, *Lives*, "Antony."

these goals, and so they do not enjoy either the things that are present or the things that are in the future. The only good thing they want is the one that they neither have nor see. This is a general conclusion about all men: no one knows what he is bringing upon himself. Thus although Cicero and Demosthenes had written a great deal about the state and wanted to help it with their counsels, they administered it in a very unfortunate manner.[14] Similarly, the monks and the papists want to govern the world, but see how they lead it astray and plunge it into the gravest of danger and the deepest of darkness. *For who can tell a man what will be, etc.?* He is not speaking about what is to be after this life but about what is to be after this hour in which we make use of the things that are present. Here no one knows what is to take place: whether Antony will live, whether Brutus and Cassius will be victorious. When Julius had once succeeded, he began to think about establishing an empire, but he perished in the very midst of his thinking. Why, then, are we so upset about our ideas, when the things that are to come are never in our power for a single moment? Let us, therefore, be content with the things that are present and commit ourselves into the hand of God, who alone knows and controls both the past and the future.

[14] See p. 38 above.

CHAPTER SEVEN

1. *A good name is better than precious ointment; and the day of death, than the day of birth.*

2. *It is better to go to the house of mourning than to go to the house of feasting; for this is the end of all men, and the living will lay it to heart.*

THIS passage seems difficult because of our ignorance of the Hebrew language, which has its own figures of speech that cannot be understood except through the usage of the language; this passage does not seem to be related by any logical connection to the preceding. To me this seems to be the point of this passage: Solomon wants to comfort the impatient in their fruitless efforts, just as heretofore he was concerned, after reciting a catalog of human vanities, to interject comfort and exhortation to fear God, urging our hearts to rise toward God, encouraging us to listen to the Word of God, not to be hasty in speaking, etc. So here again he inserts an exhortation after he has completed a catalog; later on he will return to the catalog.

Therefore let this be a passage of exhortation or comfort inserted into the midst of the catalog of vain efforts and desires addressed to those who are impatient. For in this life the human heart experiences nothing but offenses and impatience. This is especially true of those who are the best of men, because, as he said above (1:18): "He who increases knowledge increases sorrow." He who sees and hears much has a great opportunity for sorrow and indignation, because [1] he sees and experiences the things that bring injury to the heart. Look at Timon, who was transformed into a wild animal and became a misanthrope, an enemy of the human race, when, after performing many great deeds of help for his fellow citizens, he received nothing in return but envy and persecution.[2] Even now this could be the reaction of anyone if all he ever got out of his

---

[1] The Weimar text has *qui*, but we have read *quia*.
[2] Timon of Athens appears in Plutarch, *Lives*, "Alcibiades" and "Antony."

labors was extreme ingratitude. A man's spirit is broken, so that he does not want to do anything more. Solomon is not speaking about foolish men, who do not care at all about wisdom and human affairs, but about the best of men, those who want to help human affairs, men such as those in public office and in the management of households. For those who administer public or private business come to experience the fraud and perfidy of men. This fact has frightened many men away from public office. Thus that old man in Terence thinks that he is fortunate never to have married.[3] By contrast, another says: "I married—and then what misery I had to behold! Children were born—still more trouble!" The human spirit is offended by all these things unless it has been forearmed by the Word of God. Therefore those who have seen these things exhort others as follows: "The man who has lived obscurely has lived well."[4] But Christians should be exhorted to live in the very midst of the crowd, to marry, to govern their household, etc. Moreover, when their efforts are hindered by the malice of men, they should bear it patiently and not cease their good works. Do not desert the battlefield but stick it out. Do not let yourself be broken by trouble or impatience, and do not let yourself be overcome by anger. Therefore this is a very good and joyful exhortation, yet one which no one but a Christian will listen to.

He begins this statement of comfort with a proverb, saying: *A good name is better, etc.* This is his style, for Solomon is full of proverbs. This is what he wants to say: "I have enumerated so many evils of human vanity that someone could despair and choose death rather than to see and bear so many calamities and vanities, or he could even give up all effort and work and do nothing. Not so! Do not give up, but endure! Do not be like the man who is not going to have any name or any fame. Remember that you will have this good fame if you remain in your assigned labor, whether in public life or in the household. Look at what a lazy life is led by those who live for themselves. Therefore do not let yourself be broken by misfortunes, but hold out against these evils. For it is better to prove that you are a man and to develop into a great man, an example to others and an advantage to yourself, than to be a snoring and lazy man, of no use to anyone. For a good name is not

---

[3] Terence, *Adelphoe*, 42—44.
[4] See p. 89, n. 20, above.

conferred on those who snore and are lazy, who disdain courage, but on those who are vigorous and energetic, who are undismayed and push right on through. To have it said of him that he had fled the world, St. Jerome fled from Rome and from the crowds and came to Bethlehem.[5] There he intended to remain in hiding as a recluse, and yet he also wanted to make a name for himself; but he did not have a sufficiently firm resolve, for he was very impatient and anything but a manly spirit. Therefore Solomon says: *A good name is better than precious ointment.* In this passage "name" again means reputation. This proverb must be understood on the basis of Jewish customs. Only in this realm does balsam, the best of ointments, grow.[6] Among these people ointment was regarded as among the most precious things in the realm, as can be seen in the Books of Kings (cf. 2 Kings 20:13). Therefore this proverb was appropriate among the Jews; it would not be so among other nations, where jewels are regarded as more precious. Therefore the figure of speech is: Just as a precious aroma affects the nose, so a good name affects the spiritual sense of smell. Paul frequently employs this figure of speech, as in 2 Cor. 2:15: "We are," he says, "the aroma of Christ." Paul was a good teacher and a sincere preacher, blameless in his way of life. Therefore the meaning of this passage is: "Do not let yourself go to pieces in anger. As I have taught you fear before God, so I am teaching you perseverance and good works before men. For what does it matter if some people take offense and are jealous at your labors? Just continue, and the divine aroma, the good reputation, which you will gain from this will attract more people, who will themselves be preserved in their works."

The day of death is better than the day of birth.

It seems to me that this, too, is said proverbially. Now, it seems to sound pagan and carnal if someone prefers death to life. But he is not speaking simply about death and life, but about what must be done and has been done even by the most prudent of men. Show me a man in public life or in household management, one who deals with business affairs, and let him tell us whether it is not better to choose death than to live amid so many dangers and labors.

[5] Jerome came to Bethlehem in 386 and remained there until his death in 420.

[6] It seems that the "balsam," or "balm," referred to in the Bible is the so-called *Commiphora opobalsamum*, which is probably what Luther means here.

Therefore Solomon is comparing this life with itself, not with the life to come. He wants to say: If human life is to be considered, then it is certainly true that the day of death is better than the day of birth. For what can be worse than that those who administer public affairs and sincerely wish to serve the state, and who do and suffer everything for the sake of this, eventually receive no reward but extreme ingratitude, contempt, condemnation, and exile? Thus the text is to be understood just as it stands. It is not speaking about the works of God or about the life that comes after this life but about the affairs of man, the things that lie within our own use and administration, the things from which we get nothing but an occasion for anger and impatience. The day of birth involves you in evil, but death rescues you from it. To be sure, birth is a good thing and a creature of God. Solomon is not speaking about this but about the use to which birth is put; for there is a difference between birth as it has been created by God and birth as I use it. We get nothing out of our birth except cares, not by the fault of our birth but by the wickedness both of ourselves and of the world in our abuse of the creatures of God. Therefore life as it has been created by God has nothing to do with this book. It would be most wicked to say of that life that death is better than it, since God has made us men and wants us to live. Therefore this is an exhortation to us not to despair, but to keep our courage unbroken in order to bear these evils to the end. It is as though he were saying: "Suffer and bear. Do not yield to evils, but rather go forth ever more boldly!" [7]

It is better to go to the house of mourning than to go to the house of feasting; for this is the end of all men.

This is stated in the form of a maxim, for on the basis of those two proverbs he has formulated maxims and exhortations. A fool says the opposite: "Do not become involved in mournful occasions and do not lead a life of mourning," which is what Jerome taught when he said that one should lead a celibate life, that is, a pleasant life. But Solomon says something else: "It is better to bear the cross and to go into the house of mourning, for in such a house one can see what is the end of all men and of the whole world." In public life and in the household everything is filled with trouble and with mourning, but it is better to bear this cross than to flee;

---

[7] Vergil, *Aeneid*, VI, 95.

for he who lives his life amid mourning and mortification is himself becoming accustomed to dying, satiated with living, and prepared to die without sorrow. But someone who does not become accustomed to this way to dying, who wants to live forever amid pleasure and without the cross, is not training his spirit; he is living his life in danger, threatened by great trouble, and he will die in a very sad state. But the one who lives his life in the midst of things, who trains himself and who endures in bearing them, he will become a real man. Therefore Solomon says: "Although a fool desires and does things that are contrary to this, do not you let the reins drop. Accept the fact that you have more trouble than fun. It is better to bear it to the end than to give in to the evils. For on the basis of bearing the evils you will get a good name, and people will say of you: 'This is a brave man, one who has endured in the midst of evils. He has managed to overcome all the insults and wickedness of the world and of Satan.'" It is in the very midst of evils that a man learns to despise evil, as Ovid says: "Accustom yourself to the evil you are bearing, and you will bear it well."[8] Thus that well-known woman who drank poison did not die of it because she had accustomed herself to it, and the proverb says: "Familiar evils are the best."[9] Therefore we should not run away or shrink so much from evils, since we know that the end of all men is envy, slander, evil, and death. And so if you want to endure despite these things, you will have to learn how through contiuous experience. To a fool these troubles always come when he is least prepared; but to a godly man they have been done away with by long experience. The godly find this life vile and death sweet; they go on living only for the sake of God, who wants them to live.

And the living will lay it to heart. "The living" means one who is well provided for and who lives high. The Hebrews usually call the natural life "soul," while they call a pleasant or usual [10] life "living." This passage explains in a beautiful way what effect the experience of evil has, namely, that someone who is living high lays it to heart; that is, he is compelled to let his heart be instructed by

---

[8] Ovid, *Ars amandi*, II, 647.

[9] Plautus, *Trinummus*, Act I, scene 2, line 25.

[10] The printed text has *usualem*, but the lecture notes add *in bono usu*.

these evils. But the man who [11] refuses to bear evil learns nothing and always remains a fool.

3. *Anger is better than laughter, for by sadness of countenance the heart is made better.*

This has the same meaning as the preceding. But how does it harmonize with what he had said earlier (5:18), that one should not become angry but should find enjoyment in all his toil, whereas here he says that anger is better than laughter? My answer is: He is speaking about sorrow rather than about anger, not about the foolish sorrow which people make up for themselves; but as he speaks about the house of mourning, so he speaks about anger, so that anger is equivalent to sorrow or to trouble which brings sorrow. Thus when it was announced to David that all the king's sons had been slain (2 Sam. 13:30), "the king was very sorrowful" (2 Sam. 13:21). The same term is used there as is used in this passage, and there it certainly cannot mean anger, but sorrow. Thus it means the same as when we say in German: "He was shocked and became very troubled." Adversities make the face cloudy and the brow sorrowful. If someone is in public office or manages a household, he soon forgets how to laugh. If he is a good man and one who carries out his duty in a worthy manner, he will be so overwhelmed by such troubles that he will feel like saying: "Let the devil be a mayor or a ruler!" There is nothing but annoyance and displeasure in public or in domestic life. Such troubles wrinkle the brow of those who want to help things along, until they think to themselves: "Give in, quit! You are not accomplishing anything except burdening yourself with trouble and envy." Solomon is opposing such thoughts here, advising and warning: "Do not yield, but stick it out. It is better that you should be angry, or sad, that you should swallow your laughter, that you should have a grave countenance and bearing and should be obliged to show it (on account of trouble, that is) than that you should laugh." The reason is that *by sadness of countenance the heart is made better.* This can be understood in two ways. First, it can mean that by sadness of countenance the heart of other people is made better. Thus Paul requires σεμνότης "gravity" in morals and conduct, in a bishop (1 Tim. 3:4), so that he does not offend others with his

[11] The Weimar text has *quia,* but we have read *qui.*

levity. Thus also Solomon wants the man who administers things to rejoice in his heart but to conduct himself with gravity on the outside, so that others may be made better. For if a man is of the sort that has a joyful heart and a grave countenance, one who is not frivolous either in dress or in bearing, he will be one whom other people respect and whose family will not be unrestrained. Second, the passage can be explained this way: When the countenance looks bad, the heart is well off; that is, there is nothing in the way of the heart's being happy even though externally the countenance may be grave. Then the meaning would be: It is better to lead a strict and grave life than an unrestrained one. The Hebrews use the word "laughter" for the sort of life led by our papists, who live utterly without restraint, despising and ridiculing everything that is good. I like this interpretation better than the other one, according to which it is supposed that the heart of a foolish or wicked man can be made better by the sadness or gravity of someone else. It can, of course, seem that a wicked man respects the gravity of another, but his heart does not become any different.

Therefore I accept this meaning, that you understand this as applying to your own heart: When things are troubled, the heart is made better. "A good heart" is a Hebrew phrase meaning a joyful and happy heart. Solomon speaks this way to direct his hearers toward his goal, for his intention is to make them happy regardless of how things fall. Although he had said above that it is good to be happy, here he seems to be asserting the opposite: *Sorrow is better than laughter.* These two things surely do not seem to be in agreement. But matters that have to do with godliness are difficult and are always being carried to the opposite extreme. If we teach that nothing but faith alone justifies, then wicked people neglect all works. On the other hand, if we teach that faith must be attested by works, they immediately attribute justification to these. A fool always veers to one or the other extreme. It is so difficult to remain on the royal road, as, for example, here: neither sadness alone nor happiness alone, but the middle between them is what one is to keep. One must keep one's spirit happy, free, and peaceful; it must keep its equanimity in human affairs, regardless of whether happy things or sad things occur. Therefore he says: "In evil or distress the heart, etc." It is as though he were saying: "I distinguish between the sadness of the countenance and the sadness of the spirit. I always want to be happy in spirit, on the inside; but on the outside this cannot be, because [12] sad things happen." Thus the apostle says in 2 Cor. 6:10: "as sorrowful, yet always rejoicing." You should refer the first to the outside, the second to the inside.

4. *The heart of the wise is in the house of mourning; but the heart of fools is in the house of mirth.*

All of this seems to conflict with the preceding, unless we distinguish between the two kinds of happiness, that of the spirit and outward happiness, as well as between inward and outward sorrow. But he continues with his statement of consolation and exhortation: "Do not follow those fools who change their minds when outward circumstances change and whose hearts are attached to circumstances. When happy things come, they are happy; when sad things come, on the other hand, they are sad." *In the house of mourning.* The Hebrews call "house" not only the building made of stone and wood but any place in which something is carried on and done. Therefore their grammarians call each letter the "house" of the words that begin with that letter.[13] Why is the heart of the wise in the house of mourning? Because the wise do not go to pieces when things are bad, nor do they change when things change. Fools pursue outward happiness and run away from adversity. They are the most troublesome sort of people. They start a thing with great fervor and energy; but as soon as any little trouble gets in their way, they quit. When something is succeeding, they go ahead bravely; but when it is not, they are dejected in spirit and run away from the field of battle. Therefore they are useless in the management of either public or private life, since it is impossible to live in any way of life without discomfort and trouble. The courageous spirit or heart of the wise, however, bears the adversity and pushes on through. He deliberately speaks of the heart of the wise and the heart of the fool, for he is judging on the basis of attitude rather than of the things themselves. The heart of the fool is always looking for happiness, that of the wise man for sadness, even if the latter often has happy things happen to him and the

---

[12] The Weimar text has *quin,* but we have read *quia.*

[13] Recent research suggests that Luther may have been acquainted not only with the work of Reuchlin (see *Luther's Works,* 4, p. 393, n. 79) but with Conrad Pellicanus, *De modo legendi et intelligendi Hebraeum* (1504).

former has sad things. Therefore these are confirmations and exhortations for good men.

5. *It is better for a man to hear the rebuke of the wise than to hear the song of fools.*

6. *For as the crackling of thorns under a pot, so is the laughter of the fools; this also is vanity.*

He calls the opinions of fools a song. That is a striking figure of speech. It is not to be translated or understood as applying to music any more than the preceding applies to feasting but to the whole conduct of this life, according to the Hebrew manner or figure of speech. Rebuke, on the other hand, is instruction and exhortation about how to manage things. Therefore he is saying: "Even if you do not seem to be gaining any advantage for yourself, you must nevertheless do what lies at hand. And you must not desist from rebuke, even though fools do not listen to it." This is what Paul said in 2 Tim. 4:2: [14] "Convince, rebuke, be urgent in season and out of season." I have taught and I teach that things are vanity and that results are not achieved by our own plans, etc. When a fool hears these rebukes, he is carried to opposite extremes. Are we then to do nothing? But this is no reason to refrain either from acting or from rebuking vanity, either from teaching or from preaching, regardless of how much we see it being despised. We should rather push right ahead and denounce the wicked. If I for my part were bound to discontinue my ministry of the Word because I do not see any results except among the very few but only the extreme perversity of almost the whole world and the height of ingratitude, I would long ago have had to be silent. But God does well not to permit us to see such things ahead of time, before we are right in the middle of them, when we can no longer turn back. It is much better to go on doing one's job amid these evils than to retreat. Therefore listening to rebuke from the wise, who want to give us good advice, is preferable to "hearing the song of fools," that is, the things that the flesh enjoys hearing and that fools find pleasant. For they demand that we say only pleasant things to them. In short, Solomon is doing this to keep us from using

---

[14] The original has "1 Tim."

his preceding teaching as an occasion for snoring and for discontinuing our work.

For as the crackling of thorns under a pot, so is the laughter of the fools.

"Laughter" refers to the entire life of the fools, which gives them pleasure but is only an outward mask of happiness, not the true joy of the heart. The comparison of the laughter of fools to the crackling of thorns is wonderful. The Jews have many comparisons derived from the things of their life. They made very extensive use of cooking and of building fires because of their constant washings, sacrifices, and the like. Their priests were veritable butchers and cooks. This was the source of the proverbial saying about the crackling of thorns here and in the Psalms (Ps. 58:9; 118:12). This seems hard to us because it is out of keeping with our customs. In the same way, our proverbs would seem hard to them, as when we say, "A copper's worth of money gets you a copper's worth of Requiem Mass"; although this is familiar among us and was taken from our forms of worship, they would be completely unable to understand it. Therefore almost this entire passage is a kind of allegory based on a fire of bramblebushes (which are thorns that have intertwined with one another). This is a sudden fire and one which makes a lot of noise, but it is over very quickly, with more flame than fire in it. It threatens a horrible conflagration, but soon, when the flame and the noise have passed, the fire is out. Thus the psalm says (Ps. 118:12): "They were extinguished like a fire of thorns." And Vergil says in the third book of the *Georgics:* "As fire in stubble blusters without strength, he rages idly." [15] Therefore a fire of thorns or of stubble does not give any heat and does not penetrate, and yet it gives a greater appearance of burning than a fire of live coals, which do not have much flame but a great deal of heat. In the same way the happiness of the fools gives the impression that it will last forever, and one thinks that it has as much strength as it has flame; but it is nothing of the kind, for they are happy for a moment, but soon adversities come, and they go to pieces and are in utter despair. Thus I think that this statement is clear and that it harmonizes beautifully with the preceding and with the following. *This also is vanity,* because

[15] Vergil, *Georgics,* III, 99—100.

when the happiness is over, there remains trouble in the spirit. For this is how it is with all carnal happiness; it ends in confusion, and it leaves evil stings when it departs.

7. *Because a slanderer disturbs a wise man and destroys a generous heart.*

This, too, pertains to the topic of consolation. But he is saying this by way of concession; that is, it could happen that a slanderer would disturb a wise man and make a fool of him and destroy a heart disposed to give (for that is how it reads in Hebrew), namely, a generous and liberal heart. For when a wise man wants to help the world and be of aid and counsel to things and when he does everything with the utmost correctness, he is still covered with filth by fools, and he experiences the extreme of ingratitude. This is attested by the histories of the Gentiles and of the Jews, indeed by daily experience. So Antiochus horribly murdered a man of outstanding merit, after having murdered two of his children before his very eyes.[16] This was the thanks paid for merit! Belisarius, a very good and wise man, was most wickedly murdered by Emperor Justinian.[17] Everything is full of such instances. Therefore let anyone who wants to serve in either public or domestic affairs expect to waste his kindness. Thus God wastes the blessing of the sun and of all His gifts on the ungrateful and wicked, as Matt. 5:45 says. This sort of slander leaves the generous heart undone, so that in his impatience a man decides to stop doing anything and permits himself to lose heart through ingratitude, unless his heart has been instructed by the Word of God. So it happens even to wise men, as Jerome says: "When his patience has been tried too often, a man goes crazy." [18] Nor can a human being do otherwise; but God can do otherwise. God grants the sun, kingdoms, principalities, etc., to the wicked. What do they do? What do they give in return? They crucify His Son! This is their way of giving thanks. He is able to bear it, but human beings are not. But what Solomon says here is what happens to them: "*Slander disturbs a wise man and destroys*

---

[16] Apparently a reference to Antiochus IV Epiphanes, of the Seleucid dynasty, who died in 163 B. C.

[17] Belisarius, who died A. D. 565, was general of the Byzantine empire under Justinian; the story of his murder seems to be a medieval legend.

[18] The saying of Jerome, which had apparently become proverbial, was: *Furit saepius laesa patientia.*

a generous heart. But you, do not let yourself be overcome by evil, but continue": for

8. *Better is the end of a thing than its beginning.*

That is, perseverance crowns the work;[19] wait for the end. It is not how you begin that matters, but how you follow through. It is much better to have reached the end than to have attempted the beginning. Do not praise anyone before the Last Day.[20] Not he who has begun, but "he who endures to the end will be saved" (Matt. 10:22). What I am saying about matters of religion may also be said about all other matters, in accordance with the common saying: "The beginning is hot, the middle is warm, the end is obnoxious," so that it lies completely in ashes. We Germans are especially subject to criticism on account of this vice, that we are lustful for new things. We begin many things, but we do not continue or persist in anything. This affects us above all in the area of doctrine, where every day we embrace new ones. But this is the fickleness of the human heart. Therefore one must think not about the beginning but about the end. See to it, then, that you persevere. You will suffer slander on account of your wisdom; you will experience ingratitude; people will forget your acts of kindness; they will disparage your best advice and will return evil for good. If one's spirit has been unsure, this will cause it to quit. But you, continue bravely and persevere, because God will eventually grant you the fruit of your work.

And the patient in spirit is better than the proud in spirit.

He is still continuing with his exhortation. In human affairs it is required that one consider the end. What is needed for this is not a proud spirit, which changes immediately because it wants everything to be done at once and does everything with a certain force, but a patient spirit, which overcomes with patience and forbearance the evils that occur and hinder it. This is what the sayings of the wise also teach: "Make haste slowly" and "Bear it and endure." [21]

[19] An adaptation of the more familiar proverb *Finis coronat opus.*

[20] Apparently an echo of Eccl. 11:28.

[21] Suetonius, *Lives of the Twelve Caesars,* "Augustus," II, 2, 25; Ovid, *Amores,* III, 11, 7.

9. *Be not quick to anger, for anger lodges in the bosom of fools.*

There is an abundance of exhortations from Solomon that we should persevere in what we have begun, even though our plans are not carried out. He is speaking about the anger of the spirit, as he spoke earlier about outward anger. "Do not," he says, "be quick to anger, even though occasions for anger may arise. Let the fools become angry." Fools have anger in their heart and outwardly at the same time. But you, preserve a happy spirit even when you are severe on the outside. *Anger lodges in the bosom of the fool* is a Hebraism for what we in German would say this way: "Anger clings to fools," that is, they enjoy getting angry.

10. *Say not, "Why were the former days better than these?" For it is not from wisdom that you ask this.*

This is how the human heart customarily complains whenever it experiences the ingratitude of the world: "Things are worse than they used to be." But you, do not talk this way, for you are not asking or arguing the right way. Old men usually speak this way: "When I was a boy, everything was better." They are what the poet calls "glorifiers of times past." [22] But Solomon says: "This is false; things were never right." The reason you see and understand this only now is that as we grow, our experiences of things and our occasions to be angry grow also. A boy does not care and is not moved when someone cheats or murders someone else, but goes on playing, hunting, and riding; to his mind the highest of crimes is when someone steals another's marbles, and this makes him angry. But when he becomes the head of a household, then he is sensitive to the annoyance and unfaithfulness of his household, and he becomes angry if a horse breaks a leg or an ox is not properly fattened. Therefore the world has always been evil, but we have not always been in the world and are not now. When we were children, nothing disturbed us; we ourselves did indeed lead a more peaceful life, but the world has always been the same. To be sure, it is true that in one era wickedness erupts more than in another, but this happens because different situations and greater opportunities exist for it to erupt; the wickedness of the world, however, always remains the same. Julius

[22] Horace, *De arte poetica*, 173.

Caesar shook up the whole world because he had a great opportunity to do so; if Esau or Absalom had had such an opportunity, they would have done the same thing. Therefore the evil in the world is always the same. See to it, then, that you have a peaceful and tranquil heart and that you do not get angry when you see this evil. You will never change the world, but see to it that you change into another kind of man.

11. *Wisdom is good with an inheritance, excelling those who see the sun.*

12. *For the protection of wisdom is like the protection of money; and the advantage of knowledge is that wisdom preserves the life of him who has it.*

Solomon's only purpose here is to avoid giving the impression that he approves of laziness, which is what those who hear the teaching of godliness usually claim. "If all our efforts are condemned," they say, "let us not do anything; let us be absolutely lazy." But Solomon rejects this and says: "I am not condemning work nor approving of laziness. In fact, I approve both of riches and of wisdom, but I prefer wisdom to riches because it gives life to man. In addition, I am condemning human counsels in acquiring riches and all other things. I am saying to you that you should be neither laborious nor idle, neither foolish nor wise; for neither of them matters. That is, do not scheme or strive to obtain either riches or wisdom; but be concerned about the things about which God wants you to be concerned, and get rid of your own concerns, which are only vanity. For the wisdom of God is not set forth to you so that you should do something. But look up and see how God brings about justice and wisdom." In this way, therefore, he condemns human counsel in the acquisition of anything; and yet at the same time he also urges that people be active in things, manage and direct them, but in the present, and that they wait for the hand of God to intervene when they see that things are not succeeding. For if you begin to insist upon your own plans, you will get nothing out of it but vanity and affliction.

Wisdom with an inheritance is better than those who see the sun.

To see the sun means to rejoice and be happy in this life, to live high. He wants to say: Wisdom with an inheritance is superior to the very happiest life in this world. And he adds a comparison: Wisdom protects, and money protects also. As the saying goes, "Wealth makes a person bold"; that is, those who have wealth have confidence, and those who have wisdom have confidence (this is his concession), but I make a distinction between them. Wisdom is superior to riches or money in this way, that wisdom brings life to the one who possesses it. Money cannot do this; it neither preserves life nor liberates from death. He is saying this to avoid the impression that he is simply condemning wealth, for what he is condemning is only the use to which wicked people put it. In addition, he prefers wisdom, because a knowledge of wisdom preserves life for its possessor.

13. *Consider the work of God; who can make straight what He has made crooked?*

He concludes this entire passage, which he began in order to comfort impatient and angry people, with a beautiful closing flourish.[23] "Why," he says, "are you angry? Why are you impatient in your opposition to ungrateful people? Look at the works of God. No one can make straight someone whom He has made crooked. Let this give you comfort. For by this argument you can come to acknowledge that God rules all things and that it is not required of you that all men be good or grateful, and that it does not lie with you to make them so. Therefore be calm and let things happen as they happen, for they will happen as they happen." [24] It does not lie in my hands to make the crooked straight. I am kind to many people, and look what I get in return — calumny and ingratitude. But when this happens, it is nothing strange or new, because unless God has granted an understanding and grateful heart, you will waste all your acts of kindness. Therefore this passage contains an outstanding teaching, namely, that it is not in the power of the human will to make the human heart straight and that it is impossible for anything troublesome to be corrected by the human will. You can teach, warn, etc., but no one except God can correct. The knowledge of this is our only remedy against such great ingratitude and so much calumny. And so when your rebuke

[23] The technical rhetorical term used here is ἐπιφώνημα.
[24] See p. 27, n. 15, above.

and instruction have not helped, observe Paul's rule (Titus 3:10): "A man that is a heretic after the first and second admonition reject." When you have done your part, let God do His part. To refuse to quit unless you have corrected things first is to put yourself in the place of God, that is, to be obviously insane. Therefore:

14. *In the day of prosperity be joyful, but remember also the day of adversity. God has made the one as well as the other, so that man may not find out anything beyond.*

This is the other part of his closing flourish. If you get a day of prosperity, this is what you should do: be happy, that is, enjoy the things that are present, lay aside your cares, lay aside your own counsels, put a limit on all your emotions. Let God be your wisdom; commit your past and your future to Him. And be happy over the present in such a way that you *remember also the day of adversity*. That is, prepare yourself in such a way that you are also able to be sorrowful; enjoy the things that are present in such a way that you do not base your confidence on them, as though they were going to last forever. Do not be smug, looking only at the good things, but be prepared for the day of adversity as well. Always be free and equable. Thus he takes away the attitude and the confidence of the fools who cling to the joys that are present and immerse themselves in these as though the day of prosperity would have to endure. But we should be happy in such a way that we do not immerse ourselves, but reserve part of our heart for God, so that with it we can bear the day of adversity. Thus it will happen that the adversities foreseen for us will bother us less.

For God has made the one as well as the other in His fashion.

He leads all our thoughts back to God and takes them away from things. God, he says, has made all these things, the day of adversity as well as the day of prosperity; He sends unhappiness as well as happiness. And He does so "according to His way, according to His order" (here again there is a Hebraism in the use of the word דָּבָר, as there was above in the third chapter [25] and as there is in the psalm [Ps. 110:4], "after the order of Melchizedek"); that is, in accordance with the way it is written and spoken of Him, in His fashion, as He is wont to do. If you observe this,

---

[25] See p. 58 above.

you will overcome temptations easily. But we become completely immersed either in prosperity or in adversity. But when godly people suffer the vicissitudes of good and evil, they say, "This is the order, or the fashion, of God," and they do not go to pieces.

So that man may not find out anything that will be after him.

That is, so that man may learn that he cannot have more good than God has given him, even if he seeks it. Man does indeed seek beyond what God has done, but he does not find. God has given happiness, and you seek for more happiness but you will not find it. For no one can add even a particle to the works of God. If the Lord God has decided something, you will not add anything to it. When the heart is filled with happiness, it is not able to be sad, and vice versa. Thus God determines everything, so that you may learn to be content with what He has offered and will use even that moderately; then your joy will be in the Lord.

15. *In my vain life I have seen everything; there is a righteous man who perishes in his righteousness, and there is a wicked man who prolongs his life in his evildoing.*

Now that his exhortations and consolations are finished, he looks around at everything and returns to his catalog. "As I was reviewing everything," he says, "there occurred to me, among all the other vanities, also the ones that I am now going to enumerate."

There is a righteous man who perishes. Here again it is necessary to watch Solomon closely, so that we do not suppose that he is speaking about the righteousness of God or the righteousness of faith. But he is speaking about political righteousness, so that you understand the "righteous man" to be the one who exacts righteousness from others, the one who wants to make people upright; such a man is a public official or the administrator of a household. "I have seen a righteous man," he says, "one who had outstanding laws and statutes. But when he began to enforce them and demanded that everything be done according to the rules, he accomplished nothing except that everything went backwards." This is like what a certain idiot did: he was standing crooked in the sunlight and accusing his shadow of being crooked, although he did not straighten himself out meanwhile.[26] This is how we are, too. We see the speck that is in the eye of another, but do not notice the log that is in our own eye (cf. Matt. 7:3). In summary, "The highest law brings the deepest injustice." [27] Anyone who wants to govern everything according to the rules and to set everything straight in the state or in the household will have a lot of work but no results. On the other hand, someone else does not want to do anything and is a despiser of the enforcement of justice. Neither of these prevails. One must be neither wise nor unwise, neither righteous nor wicked. Then what is to be done? This will be the middle way:

16. *Be not righteous overmuch, and do not make yourself overwise; why should you destroy yourself?*

17. *Be not wicked overmuch, neither be a fool; why should you die before your time?*

That is, forget about the highest law; measure yourself by your own foot and sing, "Know thyself." [28] Then you will find in your own breast a lengthy catalog of vices, and you will say: "Look, I myself am still unrighteous, and yet I am tolerated by God and am not banished by people. Then why am I so carried away with fury that I harshly require of others what I do not achieve myself?" This is what it means to be "righteous overmuch." The things of this world cannot bear it. Therefore observe the laws by teaching and preaching, and give thanks to God when your household or your audience acknowledge that the laws and teachings are holy and just, even though they do not observe everything as it is prescribed. In this way you will be truly holy and wise. You will be "overwise" and "righteous overmuch" if in your administration either of public or of private affairs you have good laws but insist on them and want them to be observed in such a way that there is not one iota of transgression. For this is what it means that "the highest law brings the deepest injustice." A prudent public official or head of a household ought to make a distinction

---

[26] This seems not to be a literary allusion, but a reference either to folklore or to Luther's own experience.

[27] Cicero, *De officiis*, I, ch. 10, sec. 33, who quotes it as a proverb.

[28] This injunction, quoted here in Greek, was attributed to Thales of Miletus.

between the goodness of the law and the obedience of his subordinates. It is better to bear with and to endure a moderate amount of rebellion than to let the entire state perish. This is what usually happens to the rigid enforcers of laws. Therefore laws should be enforced and insisted upon as far as the situation allows, but no further. This is also what physicians do. They do not diagnose and cure diseases only on the basis of books or of what is prescribed but are often obliged to make adjustments in keeping with the state of the body. Thus also the minds of men are influenced in the most diverse possible ways, so that it is often necessary to modify the laws themselves. This calls for extremely wise men, of whom there are few in the world. Therefore all those chosen as heads of households or as public officials should be men like David, Abraham, Solomon, and Joshua, if they were available, men who could administer the laws properly. For this is how important it is to administer the state well.

Be not wicked overmuch.

This is the second part of the conclusion. See to it that just as you are not righteous overmuch, you are not wicked overmuch either. That is, do not despise and neglect all the duties of government committed to your charge, and do not permit everything to fall apart. It is good to overlook some things, but not to neglect all things. If wisdom does not succeed, that is no reason to go crazy with anger and revenge. Finally, do not give in to idleness, so that you do not want to care about anything. Do not behave like that wicked servant who buried his talent and did not want to trade with it at all (Matt. 25:24-30). Well then, be just and let others be just with you; demand uprightness; persevere, regardless of the outcome. Why? "Why should you destroy yourself, or die before your time?" There is reason to fear that He may come suddenly and call you to judgment, as He took away the soul of the rich man at night when the rich man was not thinking about it (Luke 12:20). If this life were heavenly and angelic, nothing would happen unjustly; but our sinful nature cannot do anything but sin and be foolish. Anyone who does not know this has not yet learned about the world. We should think that here we are as though we were in a shipwreck or a fire, where one must labor to snatch at least some brand from the fire when one cannot control or extinguish the whole fire. Therefore if you are in a household, be content to snatch even one person from the public fire of wicked people. If you are a teacher of children, labor to educate at least one of them and to bring him up properly. If you are a preacher of the Gospel, do not preach as though you could gain all men for Christ, for not all heed the Gospel (cf. Rom. 10:16); but if you convert three or four souls and lead them to Christ, like the tips of burning brands (cf. Amos 4:11), give thanks. For one should not quit simply because so few are changed for the better to hear the preaching of the Gospel. But do what Christ did: He rescued the elect and left the rest behind. This is what the apostles did also. It will not be better for you. You are foolish if you either presume that you alone can accomplish everything or despair of everything when it does not go your way.

18. *It is good that you should take hold of this, and from that withhold not your hand; for he who fears God shall come forth from them all.*

Christ makes a similar statement in Matt. 23:23 when He says: "These you ought to have done without neglecting the others." Thus here, too, he demands both: justice and yet not the highest justice, so that you are neither too remiss nor too exacting. Sometimes you must overlook the laws and judge as though you were wicked, and sometimes you must take hold of the laws and become just once more. But remember, as has also been said earlier, that he is here speaking not of personal righteousness but of communal or political justice, not of righteousness before God but of justice in governing others and before the world. For in personal righteousness there cannot be too much righteousness. *He who fears God shall come forth from them all.* That is, the fear of the Lord will easily judge both. If I fear the Lord, my heart says: "I have often lived this way, and I still live shamefully. Therefore I will have compassion on those delinquents. If I can restrain them by moderating my discipline, I will do so. If not, I will let them continue until they collide with the law of the sword. If they escape all of this, they still will not escape the judgment of God." Thus he who fears God proceeds correctly in these matters; when he sees that he cannot prevail, he calls upon the Lord. Therefore do your duty, warn, exhort, and never stop. He who does not hear you will bring on his own punishment, even though not through your punishing him; for there is One who will punish. This is what happened recently to our peasants. When they did not accept our rebuke, they were thoroughly punished by others.[29]

19. *Wisdom gives strength to the wise man more than ten rulers that are in a city.*

This is a commendation of the sort of wisdom just mentioned, namely, of equity. Things are not preserved by force, but it is by prudence that everything is accomplished and progresses in a kingdom, in laws, in administration, and in the arts. Thus we, too, have been created as human beings so that we might act by reason and accomplish more through it than all the animals with their strength. In this way a man by reason tames a wild horse and an enormous lion. Therefore regardless of how many laws are enacted or of how well states are ordered and established, unless prudence is present, things often go very badly. For when a wise man sets down the laws, it is impossible for him to be able to see all the conditions and circumstances. Therefore much is left to the administrators of the laws. Thus legal experts call the emperor "the living law," [30] because he has been placed into a position to moderate the laws as a driver does with a wagon and to adjust everything in accordance with places, times, persons, etc. A foolish man does more harm through laws that are rigidly observed than a wise man through laws that are overlooked. All of this is still intended to be spoken as an exhortation. Do not, he says, become angry when things do not succeed as you had wished. Be satisfied with having the laws observed in such a way that everything is not trampled upon. For the highest wisdom is not the knowledge of the laws and statutes themselves but the knowledge that wisdom is not heeded in this world. This life does not allow everything to be done right. Therefore the summary of this passage is: One should not trust to force but rule by wisdom, which often saves everything in the kingdom when force ruins everything. Why is this so?

---

[29] Once again, as on p. 90 above, a reference to the Peasants' War of 1525.
[30] See also *Luther's Works,* 13, pp. 161—62.

20. *Surely there is not a righteous man on earth who does good and never sins.*

Always keep in mind that Solomon is speaking about things that are under the sun and about things that can be carried out. Nor is he, strictly speaking, instructing consciences here; rather, he is teaching how to have a peaceful heart amid the difficult and troublesome affairs of this world. Therefore he expressly adds *on earth,* namely, to show that he is thinking about earthly righteousness and about the sins that we commit against one another. It is as though he were saying: "Why do you try to enforce everything exactly according to the laws? It will never happen that everything will be done exactly right. If you want to live in the political order, you must overlook a great deal, bear a great deal, and ignore a great deal, in order to preserve at least some bit of righteousness. Look into yourself, and you will see how often you yourself act unrighteously and do things that are with good reason displeasing to many people. Therefore do not be righteous overmuch, because you yourself sin and offend in many ways." Thus also Christ says in Matt. 7:3: "You see the speck that is in your brother's eye but do not notice the log that is in your own eye." There, however, He is speaking about heavenly righteousness. If we were to look at ourselves at home, we would undoubtedly find the defects which with good reason offend others. This fact ought to prompt us not to be such severe judges of others, so righteous overmuch or so insistent upon the righteousness of others. For from this it comes that the most rigid enforcers of the law are themselves the greatest criminals. They do not know the feeling of mercy and compassion; they are cruel and intolerable to themselves and also to others. Therefore Solomon means: "Do not become angry if you see carryings-on and activities that are offensive to you. You do not always do what you ought to do either." One must overlook and tolerate in many situations. For just as it belongs to the righteousness of faith and spiritual righteousness to bear the weak in faith and to instruct them gently, so it belongs to political righteousness (of which he is speaking here) to bear the defects of others, so that there is a mutual toleration, by which we tolerate one another and wink at faults. In his book *On Friendship* Cicero wants us not to overlook anything in our friends.[31] In

[31] Cf. Cicero, *De amicitia,* ch. 21.

The Praise of Folly Erasmus wants us to correct all the faults of our friends.[32] These are the speculations of men who have often been moved by very great passion. Foolish men govern the world according to books and fail to see that no one is able to achieve what is prescribed there. Thus the Stoics very foolishly depicted the wise man as someone without feelings, while they themselves were extremely cruel to everyone. What remains, then, is that we bear with one another and wink at one another's faults; for there is no man who does not sin, who does not do what is troublesome to others.

21. *Do not give heed to all the things that men say, lest you hear your servant cursing you;*

22. *your heart knows that many times you have yourself cursed others.*

What I have said about the experience of looking at yourself, I also say about listening to others. The household must be governed, and the wicked must be punished. But if, beyond this, there is something that you cannot correct, let it go. The wicked will not remain unpunished, for the proverb is true: "You will not escape the executioner, for God Himself is the executioner." *Lest you hear your servant cursing you.* Some people are so curious about their reputation that they pay close attention to every word and every nod of every person. They listen at windows and at cracks in the walls to find out what someone is saying about them. It serves such people right if they hear something about their family that causes them grief. Therefore if you want to give ear to what everyone is saying, you will have to expect to hear even your own people cursing you. In fact, this may well happen by accident even when you are not thinking about it. For just as you will experience many things that you do not like, so you will hear many things that you do not like. There is no need to reach out curiously for what everyone is saying. Nor should you immediately lose your temper and seize your weapons on this account. You should rather overlook it, for you, too, have committed many sins

---

[32] In his *Praise of Folly* Erasmus wrote: "Conniving at your friends' vices, passing over them, being blind to them . . . does this not seem to be folly? . . . But it is this same folly that makes friendships and keeps them after they are made."

against others. If Jupiter were to hurl his lightnings as often as men deserve, Horace says, he would soon run out of weapons.[33]

Therefore both of these are necessary in the administration of human affairs, a lawgiver and a moderator of the law: a lawgiver, to formulate good laws and to give a foundation to the state; but also a moderator, to apply the laws rightly and to employ them correctly and prudently in accordance with the conditions of various places, people, and persons.[34] A moderator of the law is more necessary in the state than the lawgiver himself, as can be seen also in household affairs. A prudent head of the household assigns to each his duty, at specific times and places, and he apportions specific food and clothing to his servants and maids. But if some accident intervenes—a servant gets sick, for example—the law must be broken and the conditions of the time must be observed. One does not exact assigned labor from a sick man. Instead, one gives him better food and drink and more comfortable sleeping quarters than the others, and one excuses him from his assignment. Unless one does this, he is foolish and wicked. And so the prescription of the law steps aside here because the person has been changed. Therefore if we ourselves often fall short of the Law and if we sin in word and deed, let us bear with the same thing in others.

23. *All this I have tested by wisdom; I said, "I will be wise"; but it was far from me.*

24. *That which is, is far off, and deep, very deep; who can find it out?*

He refers to his own experience, telling the story of what happened to him earlier, when he was searching for these things. "I am instructing you by my example," he says. "I teach that one should abstain from this wisdom. There is indeed such a thing as wisdom, but there is no such thing as a wise man of this kind. I was compelled by this experience [35] to learn my lesson when

---

[33] The words do not come from Horace but from Ovid, *Tristia*, II, 33; see also *Luther's Works*, 13, p. 153.

[34] We have translated the Latin *persona* with the English "person," but it refers to one's public role, or "office."

[35] The Weimar text has *haec*, but we have read *hac*.

I wanted to be overly wise and to bring it about that the world would be governed by the strictest laws possible. But nothing was less successful than my attempt." As I have said, therefore, human life must have these two, a lawgiver and a moderator, and it does not need the latter any less than the former. Thus it is not enough for a coachman to have good horses and to know the way he is traveling, unless he also controls his wagon in accordance with road conditions. Therefore ἐπιείκεια [36] must be combined with the law, saying: "You have established this or that law well, and it ought to be observed. But exceptions have to be made."

Deep, very deep.

Thus also he said above (1:8): "All things are full of weariness; a man cannot utter it." Those who write the laws intend them only as universal statements of what ought to be done. But those who are in administration are forced to get down to particular and individual cases and to see whether what ought to be done can be done. Here there are an infinite number of cases, with an infinite number of different circumstances. The depths of this are beyond measure. Therefore the summary of the seventh chapter and of this exhortation is: As far as you can, sustain the law; and as far as you can, moderate the law. Do not try to have everything observed as strictly as possible, and do not break all laws through negligence. Only fear the Lord, and He will teach you all things correctly. For those who are without fear are either righteous overmuch or overly impatient.

25. *I turned my mind to know and to search out and to seek wisdom and knowledge and to know the foolishness of the wicked and the errors of the stupid.*

This is a sort of addition to the exhortation and teaching that has preceded, as though he were saying: "I have noted with sufficient care what happens to those who want to do everything righteously and to have everything done righteously by others and who are righteous overmuch in enforcing righteousness. They do not succeed, and by being wise overmuch they become foolish. I have also found that being unwise instead may be the height of wisdom. On the other hand, I have also investigated every way

---

[36] On this notion, see also *Luther's Works*, 26, p. 84.

of life to discover how things are done by the wicked and how the foolish succeed, to see whether it is better to cast away all care (as foolish people do) or to be righteous overmuch." He is speaking again about the things that are done or ought to be done by the foolish and the wicked, just as earlier he spoke about the things that are done by the righteous — both in political terms.

26. *And I found more bitter than death the woman whose heart is snares and nets and whose hands are fetters; he who pleases God escapes her, but the sinner is taken by her.*

"Among the things I have noticed about fools is this one, which has to do with women." For when he was writing a catalog of vanities, it would not do to pass over this. What happens to fools who try to keep hands off and to do nothing and to be free of everything is that they fall into the hands of women and are obliged to serve women. He is speaking about a woman who administers things and arrogates wisdom and ruling power to herself. He is not speaking about the wrath of women, although it is true that a woman has a more tempestuous nature than a man. This is not a condemnation of the female sex, which is a creation of God. For the sex must be kept distinct from its weaknesses, just as earlier he made a distinction between the works of God and the counsels of men. A human being is a work of God, but beyond this work he wants to follow also his own counsels and not to be controlled solely by God, by whom he has nevertheless been created and made. In the same way the sex must be kept distinct from its weaknesses. As a creature of God, a woman is to be looked upon with reverence. For she was created to be around the man, to care for children and to bring them up in an honest and godly way, and to be subject to the man. Men, on the other hand, are commanded to govern and have the rule over women and the rest of the household. But if a woman forsakes her office and assumes authority over her husband, she is no longer doing her own work, for which she was created, but a work that comes from her own fault and from evil. For God did not create this sex for ruling, and therefore they never rule successfully.

In opposition to this one could cite the histories about the Amazons, celebrated by Greek writers.[37] They are said to have

---

[37] See, for example, Homer, *Iliad*, VI, 186 ff.

exercised authority and to have waged war. For my part, however, I believe that what is said of them is a fable. The Ethiopians select women as both kings and princes, as is their custom; thus Candace, the queen of Ethiopia, is mentioned in the Book of Acts (Acts 8:27). But this is a foolish thing to do, as foolish princes are often put in charge of a kingdom. Never has there been divine permission for a woman to rule. Of course, it can happen that she is put into the place of the king and of the kingdom; but then she always has a senate of leading men, by whose counsel everything should be administered. Therefore even though a woman may occupy the king's place, this does not confirm the right of women to rule. For the text is clear (Gen. 3:16): "You shall be under the power of your husband, and he shall rule over you." The woman was created for her special purpose, namely, to use prudence and reason in the rearing of children. For everyone functions most efficiently in that for which he was created. A woman can handle a child better with her little finger than a man can with both fists. Therefore let everyone remain in that work to which he has been called and ordained by God.

Therefore the sum and substance of this passage is: Among the other hindrances to that peace which the human heart ought to have is a woman, namely, one who does not permit a man to accomplish what he is able to. Thus Samson, that outstandingly noble man, was seduced by Delilah, the wicked woman. For they are not content with their distaff and their wool but want to prescribe for men even in those matters that pertain to the governance of public affairs. "I say I truly hate such women," says Solomon, "for they are more bitter than death and are a major cause of our vanity." If men begin to give in to such women, everything goes wrong. This is what happened to Samson. Solomon, too, was made a fool of by women. Therefore this is what he says: "Just as I have seen overly righteous and overly wicked men, so I have also seen domineering women. This is great vanity, not because of their sex but because of their snares and nets. Therefore those who are wise in the Word of God run away from these snares but not from the female sex."

27. *Behold, this is what I found, says the Preacher, adding one thing to another to find the sum,*

28. *which my mind has sought repeatedly but I have not found. One man among a thousand I found, but a woman among all these I have not found.*

That is, by my own experience and by my observation of others I have learned many things, namely, that all things are vanity. Others may learn this also. For this is the height of human wisdom, to know that no wisdom is worth anything or achieves anything unless God grants success. Thus Socrates said: "This I know, that I do not know," if he understood this correctly.[38] *Adding one thing to another.* "One thing after another"; that is, I have investigated each individual effort, and everywhere I found that no one can live correctly by his own counsel. *Which my mind has sought repeatedly;* that is, I see vanity in myself and in others, and yet I do not cease my madness nor restrain myself to keep from seeking what I know I shall never find. *One man among a thousand;* that is, one who sees that his wisdom is nothing. Regardless of how much men may see that things always come out differently from the way they themselves have planned, those who have attained to this negative wisdom are rare indeed. Thus Demosthenes, after using up all his wisdom, said that wisdom was worthless.[39] For this reason philosophers said that everything happens by chance and by the turn of fortune. They were unable to think that the wisdom of God is greater and higher than our plans and efforts. *But a woman among all these I have not found.* If men do not achieve this, or at best only a few, how much less will women do so! Once more he is speaking about the female sex as it is outside the state of grace, in the state of nature, and "under the sun." Nature does not make prescriptions for the works and miracles of God. Among a thousand men, he says, one could be found somewhere who through his experience of things has come to the point that he can say, "My plans and efforts do not succeed, and they accomplish nothing," and who thereby has been made fit to rule. But among women not even one has come to this point, and this because of a divine ordinance. Therefore one should not listen to them in these matters.

[38] See, for example, Plato, *Meno,* 71.
[39] See p. 39, n. 8, above.

29. Behold, this alone I found, that God made man upright, but they have sought out many devices.

The scholastics have twisted this passage until the present day to prove the freedom of the will in opposition to grace.[40] This is contrary to Solomon's meaning, since Solomon throughout this book is speaking about bodily matters. As has already been said earlier, he is not instructing consciences before God, except that he occasionally refers to the fear of the Lord, but he is instructing man about political life, telling him to control his heart. The meaning, therefore, is this: God has placed man into things, has given him certain works and a certain task. But man does not remain in these tasks, but by his lusts he seeks for those that belong to someone else. God made man upright, straightforward, to look at what is in front of him and before his eyes, that is, at the things that are present, and to be content with these. But man, forsaking this uprightness, argues about the things that are in the future. Therefore Solomon wants to say: "On the basis of my investigation I have found that no one lives content with his lot, but that everyone has crossed and oblique eyes." As Ovid said, "The crops in someone else's field are always more productive, and the neighbor's cattle have larger udders." [41] And again: "The lazy ox wants to wear a saddle, and the riding horse wants to plow." [42] Peter had such eyes when he said (John 21:21): "What about this man?" Uprightness in external matters, therefore, consists in this, that everyone look straight ahead in his acting and in his ruling and that he not look elsewhere. *But they have sought out many devices.* That is, they occupy themselves with many plans and with anxious thoughts about how they will govern everything in the future, meanwhile neglecting the things that are present and that God has put before their very eyes. Thus a woman pursues a man's job, and a man pursues a woman's job. This statement, then, is a kind of final flourish [43] in his discussion of human vanity.

---

[40] See Luther's discussion of this passage in *Against Latomus, Luther's Works,* 32, pp. 212—13.

[41] Ovid, *Tristia,* V, 12, 23.

[42] Horace, *Epistles,* I, 14, 43.

[43] See p. 119, n. 23, above.

CHAPTER EIGHT

1. *Who is so wise as that? And who will interpret these things?*

ALL things are difficult, as cannot be stated often enough. For we are so immersed in our plans and counsels that we do not even understand how immersed we are. It is as though he were saying: "I want to keep silent about the fact itself; indeed, men do not understand the dogma and the law and are even further from being able to achieve it." The meaning is: how vain is the human heart!

The wisdom of the righteous man makes his face shine, but the shameless man is deserving of hatred.

I think that this pertains to what has gone before. The figure of speech that Solomon uses here is partly familiar to us from other passages of Scripture which have a similar figure. In Prov. 7:13 we read of a prostitute whom a young man meets: "With impudent face she says." And again (Prov. 7:10): "A woman meets him, wily of heart." Thus also in Dan. 8:23: "A king of bold countenance." This figure of speech refers to an impudence and daring of countenance. Where there is no fear, there is no reverence. As it is said of the fool in the proverb, "A fool puts on a bold face" (cf. Prov. 21:29); that is, he has an erect neck and is devoid of fear or shame.

This passage can be understood in two ways. One way is actively, so that it means: "Wisdom illumines the face of the righteous man," which is the same as: "Wisdom makes him a man of happy countenance." On the other hand, hypocrites go about in sadness, as Christ says of the Pharisees in Matt. 6:16: "They disfigure their faces," that is, they have a sour expression. A wise man, however, always goes about with a serene countenance, because he does what he can. The wicked man always has a hateful and cloudy countenance. This is therefore a kind of proverbial saying, as though he were saying: "One can readily tell by the eyes where there is a happy heart." Wicked men almost always have a rumpled forehead; for as their heart is, so their face is. Secondly, the passage can be understood the same way in a passive sense, namely, that a man who has a happy face is also pleasant to others and makes others happy. His conduct is joyful and happy. In this way also this is a flourish in praise of wisdom.

2. *I keep the king's command and the oath of God.*

It is evident that in this book Solomon is active in deterring men from being active. Since this is what he is doing, it will take no less an effort to summon them back to work. Thus also when we preach faith, we exhort men away from works altogether in order to proclaim a day of rest. On the other hand, when faith has been planted, one must act to make Christians very busy on behalf of their neighbor. Here they must not keep any day of rest at all but must be zealous for good deeds (Titus 2:14), ardent in their love for the neighbor, and keeping a day of rest only in relation to God. So he teaches here that we should not do anything according to our own counsels and efforts but should do everything according to the Word of God. He deals with this for about half of this chapter. Therefore when he says *I keep the king's command,* he is urging political obedience. For this is to be understood regarding a political king and kingdom, although it could also be applied to God, but not in this context. He assumes the role of his subjects, saying: "I would keep the king's command. I advise you to be subject to the king and not to follow your own efforts. There is enough for you to do in the state. Just do what the king commands. He has been established by God for you to listen to him." It is noteworthy that he says *the king's command,* because he wants us to be bound by the word and to obey it. Whatever the magistrate commands in accordance with the laws, that you must do. *And keep the oath of God.* Understand this oath to be not that by which God swears but that which one swears to God. "Obey the magistrate," he says, "in accordance with the oath of God, that is, as you have sworn to God." For he who swears to the magistrate, swears not to man but to God. Here you see in a remarkable way that political obedience is included in obedience to God. Thus also Paul wants servants to be obedient to their masters not as to men but as to God (Eph. 6:7).

3. *Be not hasty to go out of his sight, stand not in an evil thing, for he does whatever he pleases.*

4. *For the word of the king is supreme, and who may say to him: What are you doing?*

To go out of sight is a Hebraism that occurs frequently in Holy Scripture, in Jonah (1:3), in Job (1:12), as well as in Matt. 18:28: "The servant went out of the sight of his master and came upon one of his fellow servants." "To go out of sight" means nothing else than to turn away from obedience or to deny or neglect it. *Stand not in an evil thing.* "Do not persevere in disobedience, but persevere in obedience." It is as though he were saying: "Even though the thing that the king has commanded does not succeed immediately, even though the king has a lapse, nevertheless, you persevere and act in such a way that the command of the king retains its majesty. Do not act counter to his command, for you will not escape his punishment." *For he does whatever he pleases,* namely, within his own realm, for he is speaking about political administration. "The king," he says, "will protect and defend justice. It was for this that he was appointed by God. Therefore you should fear him." This is exactly the same as what Paul says in Rom. 13:2: "Those who resist will incur judgment." It is impossible for someone who resists the magistrate to escape this judgment. Therefore the safest thing would be simply to obey the magistrate. He also asserts the power of the king: *He does whatever he pleases,* because this is an ordinance of God. For this reason you will not accomplish anything or be able to resist him, even though you stir up revolt and violence. You must therefore either obey for your own good or run away to your own hurt, *for the word of the king is supreme.* The word of the king is a real sultan; for this comes from the word שָׁלִיט, which means "to rule." [1] All of this is said to exhort us to yield our obedience and to persevere in the work we have been commanded to do, even though it does not immediately succeed according to our wish.

5. *He who obeys a command will meet no harm.*

This is the conclusion of what has gone before. Now, this can

---

[1] Unlike some of Luther's etymologies, this derivation of the title "Sultan" seems to be accurate.

be explained in two ways. The first is this: He who obeys a command will not want to meet any harm, that is, he will be careful and watch himself to avoid doing evil. The second is this: He who obeys a command will suffer no harm. Both interpretations are good, but I like the first one better.

A wise man's heart discerns both time and judgment.

When the word *judgment* is employed alone, it generally means revenge or punishment. Thus in Rom. 13:2: "will incur judgment," that is, will not go unpunished. That is also how it is used here: A wise man knows that an appointed time against the disobedient has been set by judgment and that no one can escape this appointed time. Therefore he fears God and does nothing evil.

6. *Because to every purpose there is time and judgment, therefore the misery of man is great upon him.*

7. *For he knows not what the present means, and who can tell him what will be?*

This is a warning to the disobedient about the punishments that follow their disobedience; as though he were saying: "I advise you to be obedient and subject to your magistrates." But if someone is not obedient to his magistrate and refuses to be subject to him, he may of course go ahead. But the reward he will get for this will be that he will become involved in many evils and will bring many afflictions and calamities upon himself. He is afraid of every hour, but he cannot escape. Therefore the best thing for him to do is simply to be obedient. For what good does it do to refuse to obey when you cannot escape the judgment? That is what happened to the peasants.[2] This is how preachers ought to exhort rioters and seditionists. For there is a judgment ordained and defined by God and a vengeance or punishment for all those who are disobedient; and none can escape it. This is a great consolation for magistrates, heads of households, and teachers. When they do what they can but the disobedient and stubborn ones are incorrigible and escape their hands, then they may retain their equanimity in the certainty that such people still will not escape punishment.

[2] See also pp. 90 and 125 above.

Because the misery of man is great upon him. Not that of the man who is obedient, that is, obedient to the mouth of the king, *for he knows not what the present means.* He proves a particular statement with a general principle, as though he were saying: "The disobedient man has his eyes turned away and does not see what is before his very eyes. He does not see what he should do, nor how great an evil his disobedience is. *And who can tell him what will be?* That is, the disobedient man does not know what lies in the future. By his disobedience he yearns for all sorts of things and hopes that he will achieve great things, but he is deceived. He promises himself that he will go unpunished; but when he least expects it, his appointed time of judgment arrives, and he perishes in his disobedience. In short, the wicked man despises obedience in the present and overlooks punishment in the future; on the other hand, the wise man does not act this way but knows what evils await those who are disobedient, and therefore he is obedient.

8. *No man has power to retain the spirit or authority over the day of death; there is no discharge from war.*

He explains himself and tells what it meant that he said above about obedience to the king: "The word of the king is full of power." For it has been ordained this way by God that someone who despises obedience cannot escape with impunity. A man does not have enough power to be able to fight back against a king. Then why does he not obey? *He does not have power to restrain his spirit,* that is, he is not able to forbid life, the breath of life, but must give in. He will not escape. *He does not have authority over the day of death; there is no discharge from war.* In short, God has so many judgments and so many ways of punishing that no one can escape His hands. Even if someone has escaped everything else, He will cast him into war, where he will perish. Therefore he concludes:

Nor will wickedness deliver those who are given to it. That is, therefore be obedient and do what you ought to do, because there will be no redemption for you, nor any impunity for your disobedience. This is to keep anyone from thinking that I am teaching rebellion or idleness.

9. *All this I observed while applying my mind to all that is done under the sun, while man lords it over man to his hurt.*

Now he returns to his catalog, as he once more enumerates the miseries caused by human vanity. "Among all these things that I have been reciting I have also seen that man lords it over man to his hurt." This should be referred to the person who is a subject; that is, it often happens that tyrants reign, but reign in such a way that they bring affliction on their subjects. And in spite of this the mouth of the king must be obeyed, and sedition must not be set in motion. For even if there is a good ruler, he still gets no thanks for it. Not only is there no thanks, but people themselves become worse, as is the case now with the rabble who have been set free from the laws and restrictions of the pope. Everyone wants tyranny to be abolished; but when they are set free, they cannot bear this either. Therefore he concedes that wicked magistrates exist in order to punish their subjects, but he also teaches that one should nevertheless put up with them.

10. *Then I saw the wicked buried; they used to go in and out of the holy place and were praised in the city where they had done such things. This also is vanity.*

There is a similar passage in Amos 6:1: "Woe to you who are rich in Zion, who enter the house of Israel with pomp!" Entering the church, or the house of God, is a Hebrew figure of speech for holding office in the people of God. So it is that in Deut. 23:3 [3] the Ammonites are forbidden to enter the assembly of God, that is, to have dominance in the Jewish state.[4] The Ammonites could be among the people of God but could not hold office. Thus here, too, they were "in the holy place," that is, they administered the state. This is why he says *I saw the wicked buried*, that is, the tyrants extinguished and succeeded by a good prince, as David succeeded when Saul had been extinguished. But when the wicked have been set free from tyranny, they forget their liberation. Thus people simply do not recognize their blessings, as we have immediately forgotten Prince Frederick, the author of our peace.[5]

[3] The original has "Deut. 22."

[4] See the discussion in *Luther's Works*, 9, p. 230.

[5] It seems that Frederick is called "the author of our peace" on account of his efforts in support of the Reformation.

No one thinks what good things we have received through him and from what evil things we have been set free by him. We always want something else; we neglect and forget the things that are in the present. All of this is being said by Solomon so that we might learn to know the world and to use the foolishness of this world wisely. Therefore this book should especially be read by new rulers, who have their heads swollen with opinions and want to rule the world according to their own plans and require everything to toe the mark. But such people should first learn to know the world, that is, to know that it is unjust, stubborn, disobedient, malicious, and, in short, ungrateful. Let them be grateful if they can motivate even one percent to keep the laws. Thus our sectarians are not content with the good things in the present, the preaching of faith and the grace of the Gospel; they disturb everything with their novel and vain teachings. Therefore it is Solomon's counsel that we should know this to be their vanity and should teach in opposition to it as much as we can. Finally, those whom we cannot convert to faith or keep by our admonitions, those we should let go; for the wicked become obdurate through continuous punishment. And therefore he says:

11. *Because sentence against an evil deed is not executed speedily, the heart of the sons of men is fully set to do evil.*

This can be expounded in two ways. In an active sense it would mean: The wicked persist in doing evil because of the delay in their punishment; because God does not take revenge immediately, as men do, they become insolent. In a passive sense it would mean: Because we see that they go unpunished, we ourselves are filled with many evils, become indignant, are tired of waiting, and stop doing good. For the postponement of punishment has both effects: first it makes men worse and makes them obdurate; then it also causes others who see this to become lukewarm and to quit. Both meanings are good.

12. *Though a sinner does evil a hundred times and prolongs his life, yet I know that it will be well with those who fear God, because they fear before Him;*

13. *but it will not be well with the wicked, neither will he prolong his days like a shadow, because he does not fear God.*

Now he is consoling not the human being but the pious heart. For the human being cannot stand this, nor can he see such ingratitude. David could not stand the ungrateful Nabal; as 1 Sam. 25:13 shows, he wanted to kill him, as far as human plans went. Therefore he says: "Learn to know the world. You will not be able to make it over in another way. It will not adjust itself to you, but you must adjust yourself to it. You must know that it is ungrateful and forgetful of every good deed. When you know this, you will be well off." Therefore he wants to say *Though a sinner does evil a hundred times,* that is: "Even though you postpone the punishment and do not take revenge against the injury, still eventually there will be a punishment. It cannot be otherwise than that those ingrates be punished. Therefore do not be in a hurry to make the world righteous or to avenge everything. Be content with even one one-thousandth, if you are able to convert that many to gratitude. Let the world sin, not you, for it will not escape the revenge that is due." So it was that the Jews found their punisher in Vespasian, even though the slayers of the prophets and of Christ had had their punishment postponed for ever so long.[6] *Neither will he prolong his days.* The punishment of the wicked seems to be postponed for a long time, especially to those who have been afflicted by them. But when the day and the punishment of the wicked arrive, it will seem to us to be too sudden. Thus Job says that the day of the wicked will come upon them before their time (Job 15:32), and the psalm says (Ps. 55:23): "Wicked men shall not live out half their days"; that is, since they always strive and hope for things that are endless, they will die before they achieve or reach even half of these.

14. *There is a vanity which takes place on earth, that there are righteous men to whom it happens according to the deeds of the wicked, and there are wicked men to whom it happens according to the deeds of the righteous. I said that this also is vanity.*

These two things are extremely offensive to the human heart: that the punishment of the ungrateful is postponed and that evil

---

[6] A reference to the fall of Jerusalem to the Romans A. D. 70, which was interpreted by Luther and many other Christian theologians as a punishment for the death of Christ.

things befall good men, that the good men are resented and the evil are cherished; yet this is what happens. Formerly everything used to be given to the wicked priests, but now faithful ones do not receive support, and those who teach in the schools are not fed. There is no gratitude for the liberators of the world, except that they are trodden underfoot. But everything is given, and in abundance, to those who are destroying the world and drowning it in evils. So it is that nowadays soldiers have a higher standing than do those who teach aright. This is said so often so that we might instruct our hearts and teach good people what the world is, a raging and ungrateful beast, one that is elated by the good deeds that are done to it, one that cannot do anything but to exalt the wicked and oppress the godly. We should not expect anything else.

15. *And I commend enjoyment, for man has no good thing under the sun but to eat and drink and enjoy himself, for this will go with him in his toil through the days of life which God gives him under the sun.*

This is a repetition, but a necessary one; for he has said so many sad things that he seems to have forgotten his purpose. The world is ungrateful; it is always looking elsewhere and becoming bored with the things that are present, no matter how good they are. It lets you labor and grow tired, and it despises and persecutes you. Therefore you must also make fun of the world, just as it has made fun of you. Do what you ought to do and put away your cares and troubles. Have a happy and tranquil mind, for you know that this is how the world is: good people do not get their reward.

16. *When I applied my mind to know wisdom and to see the business that is done on earth, how neither day nor night one's eyes see sleep.*

This means: "When I concerned myself with this, troubling my heart and meditating on the wisdom with which everything in the world might be set right, I accomplished nothing except to spend sleepless nights." The same thing will also happen to you if you refuse to be happy and if you wear yourself out with your striving and planning. For this is nothing other than the story told about the fool who tried to carry the whole world on his shoulders;⁷ this means that he wanted to govern it with his own effort and by the laws which he prescribed. Therefore you should rather commit everything to God and not be curious about things that are none of your business.

17. *Then I saw all the work of God, that man cannot find out the work that is done under the sun. However much man may toil in seeking, he will not find it out; even though a wise man claims to know, he cannot find it out.*

This is Solomonic extravagance. The meaning is similar to that which was stated earlier (cf. 1:15): "Consider the works of God, that what is crooked cannot be made straight." So it stands here also. Let no one presume that he can set everything right, for this is a work of God alone, not of man. It is impossible that men should be brought to the point of doing what God alone does. A human being does not pay attention to what is in the present and is not satisfied with it, but he looks only to what is in the future. The human heart is filled with its various plans; God, on the other hand, has everything defined by a fixed boundary, so that present things are present to Him and future things future. We for our part are never content with the things that are in the present, nor are we satisfied with the things that are in the future; this is as though the present were not present, nor the future future. It was the experience of this that caused the poets to say that everything is governed by fate and to imagine that the goddesses of fate tear up our web even when we suppose that we are living in the prime of life.⁸ Thus Julius Caesar did not "find," that is, did not complete his work; his thinking left him in the midst of the action. For while he was thinking about establishing or, more accurately, reestablishing the Roman republic, he died in the very effort.⁹ And while Absalom was contemplating the royal office, he perished miserably (2 Sam. 18:9-15).

⁷ Perhaps a reference to the story of how Hercules took over the carrying of the burden of the world from Atlas, who then refused to take it back.

⁸ Here as elsewhere, Luther used *Parcae*, goddesses of fate, as proof against the doctrine of free will.

⁹ That is, according to some historians Julius Caesar was not attempting to become king but was attempting to restore the Roman republic, when he was assassinated.

CHAPTER NINE

1. *But all this I laid to heart, examining it all, how the righteous and the wise and their deeds are in the hand of God; whether it is love or hate man does not know.*

HERE one must be careful to remember the argument of the book, so that we do not listen to those who have applied this text to the question of man's worthiness of the hate or love of God and who wickedly teach that no one can be certain about grace.[1] Solomon is speaking only about works that are done "under the sun," that is, among men in the administration of political affairs. Look, he says, how crooked the world is, where I find that there are men who govern justly and wisely, whose servants and subjects are in the hand of God and are blessed and protected by Him, as was the case with Solomon and with David. *And yet whether it is love or hate man does not know* (I take both of these in an active sense); that is, "men are so depraved that they do not acknowledge as their benefactors even those just and wise men whose servants they see being governed and blessed by God; nor do they acknowledge either the love or the hate of these men." There is nothing they forget more rapidly than kindnesses. Solomon reigned wisely, in peace and with great wealth; but as soon as Solomon had died, they immediately began to complain about "the yoke of Solomon" (2 Chron. 10:4), and there was no remembrance of his deeds of kindness. Regardless of what the state of the world has been, it has always seemed intolerable to the world. Italy is an example of this to us; whether it has war or peace, it cannot bear it. In the time of peace they look for war, in time of war they yearn for peace. The world cannot stand on the things that are present, and it is always tormented by the things that are in the future. So it is that Germany is always looking for something new. When the Gospel began, everyone ran to it eagerly; but once the Gospel has prevailed, we are bored and forget the great blessings. Now there is a rush for the Sacramentarians; but when they have

[1] See also *Luther's Works*, 26, p. 386.

grown old, people will become bored with them and will want something else. In short, the world cannot stand it, whether it is governed well or poorly. He whom the Lord does not help in governing could not live even a single day without peril. Therefore if anyone wants to serve the world with wisdom, justice, or any other good things, let him expect nothing from it except the worst. Thus David and Solomon, the best of kings, loved good men and hated evil men. But the people did not acknowledge their love and forgot all their kindnesses and good deeds. Therefore John wrote correctly (1 John 5:19), "the world lies in wickedness," because there is nothing there but ingratitude and utter wickedness. Who could be pleased with this life, where no matter how long he lives, he lives in the highest danger and in extreme disturbance?

2. *One fate comes to all, to the righteous and the wicked, to the good and the clean and the unclean, to him who sacrifices and him who does not sacrifice. As is the good man, so is the sinner; and he who swears is as he who shuns an oath.*

3. *This is an evil in all that is done under the sun, that one fate comes to all; also the hearts of men are full of evil, and madness is in their hearts while they live; and after that they go to the dead.*

This is another Solomonic extravagance, as though he were saying: "The world is altogether disturbed and ungrateful; there is no memory in it either of the good or of the evil." Therefore this must be understood as applying to the world, not to God. Those who live righteously are despised in the presence of the world and within the world. But in the presence of God they are well off, as he said earlier (cf. 7:18): "He who fears God will be well off." The world, however, gives the same reward to the good and to the evil. "Everything is displeasing to it, and doing a favor means nothing."[2] *This is an evil in all that is done under the sun.* That is, the human heart is too weak to be able to bear this perversity of the world. Those who do not have the fear of the Lord cannot bear this ingratitude with patience. Again, there is no difference between the good and the evil, but one fate comes to all. *Also the*

---

[2] These words are attributed by some of Luther's editors to Catullus, perhaps as a paraphrase of his *Carmina,* LXXXIII.

hearts of men are full of evil, that is, of indignation and annoyance, because they do not understand and cannot make themselves imitate God, who sends rain on the evil and on the good (cf. Matt. 5:45). I believe that this is an attack on the philosophers and the monks, who deserted the world because they could not bear all of this. They did not want to serve a world that was ungrateful. But Solomon wants us to deal with human affairs and to acknowledge the world; we are not to be deterred from action by its ingratitude but are to imitate our Father, who daily causes His sun to shine on the evil and on the good, as Matt. 5:45 says.

And madness is in their hearts while they live, and after that they go to the dead. That is, they die without any works, as though they had never lived. They are shadows in this life, of no use to anyone. No one has a share in their work or in their property, and what they hope for in the future is prevented by death. Therefore their end is nothing but death; they leave nothing good to others. But you must use your life in such a way that you are happy from it and that you are of benefit to others.

4. *Because that which is chosen among all the living is hope, for a living dog is better than a dead lion.*

With this passage Solomon opens an exhortation that we do good as long as we can. We should not be affected by the ingratitude of the world but persist in our duty and hold on to our hope; for hope still survives among all men. It is as though he were saying: "Do not despise life in such a way that you either despair or shun the company of people." For hope is *that which is chosen,* that is, the best thing there is among mortals is hope or confidence. For those who are living among men still have hope remaining. Therefore one must do what one can; for the sake of the remnant one must serve the whole mass. Thus a good minister of the Word of God preaches the Word of God on account of the good citizens, regardless of how many people find fault with him. If a teacher has two good pupils, he should work for the sake of these, even though he may have 20 others who are lazy and hopeless. A magistrate should also do his duty even if he cannot keep the entire state in its appointed task; he will still find one or another citizen with whom he can accomplish something. Therefore Solomon is saying this to keep us from either being crushed by despair or becoming presumptuous. One should not despair about the living as one does about the dead, about whom one cannot have any hope. One must continue to bear with the annoyance of people, and one must not despair of all even though there are many who perish.

For a living dog is better than a dead lion. He inserts a proverb and means to say: "It is enough if one sets some part of the world straight, just as a living dog, no matter how contemptible an animal it is, is superior to the magnificent carcass of a powerful lion." We say the same thing this way: "A sparrow in the hand is better than a crane in doubt." And in German we say: "One must not throw out the baby with the bathwater."

5. *For the living know that they will die, but the dead know nothing, and they have no more reward; but the memory of them is lost.*

6. *Their love and their hate and their envy have already perished, and they have no more in the world any share in all that is done under the sun.*

The living, he says, know that they will die, and therefore in life they use this hope. Therefore they should not postpone acting or doing well from one day to the next, as do the fools and softies, who always pay attention to the examples of others and will not do right until they see others do right. *But the dead know nothing, and they have no more reward.* Jerome has clumsily distorted this passage to apply to the reward of the dead in purgatory.[3] Solomon seems to feel that the dead are asleep in such a way that they know nothing whatever. And I do not believe that there is a more powerful passage in Scripture to show that the dead are asleep and do not know anything about our affairs—this in opposition to the invocation of the saints and the fiction of purgatory. *They have no reward* is a Hebraism for what we would say in German this way: "It is all over for those who are dead." All that was theirs is nothing; they no longer do what would have been beneficial. As we read elsewhere, "There is a reward for your work";[4] and Paul says (1 Cor. 15:58): "Your labor is not in vain." *Their love and their*

---

[3] Jerome, *Commentarius*, 1081—82.

[4] Apparently a quotation from 2 Chron. 15:7.

hate. You must understand all of this in an active sense, as it was understood earlier, that all the good deeds they did by loving, obeying, etc., are handed over to oblivion. But when Jerome raises the quibble that although the dead do not know anything of what goes on in the world, they do know other things, namely, those that go on in heaven, this is an error, and a foolish one at that. *And they have no more in the world any share,* that is, they have no traffic with us. He describes the dead as unfeeling corpses. Therefore he wants us to use life as much as is permitted and to work as much as we can. For we are forced to relinquish the larger part of the world to Satan and can scarcely gain a thousandth part of it for God. And so if your lion dies, you had better not kill your dog.

7. *Go, eat your bread with enjoyment, and drink your wine with a merry heart; for God has already approved what you do.*

Just as Solomon made it a point, after recalling the vanity in the world, to add comfort and exhortation, so that we might have a happy and peaceful spirit, so he does here also. It is as though he were saying: "As long as we are obliged to live in the midst of such perversity, it is best for us to be happy and relaxed." We cannot change things and we will not accomplish anything, no matter how much we may torture ourselves with worrying. Now, he says *your bread* and *your wine,* namely, that which you have earned by your labor, with the blessing of God. Thus Is. 4:1 says: "We will eat our own bread," and Paul says to the Thessalonians (2 Thess. 3:12): "Let them eat their own bread."

For God has already approved what you do. This exhortation applies to the godly, to those who fear God, as though he were saying: "You who are godly, do what you can, because you know that God approves what you do." This is the height of spiritual wisdom, to know that one has a gracious God, who approves our works and actions. Thus Rom. 8:16 says: "It is the Spirit Himself bearing witness with our spirit that we are children of God." For unless our heart immerses itself in the will and good pleasure of God, it can never sweeten its bitterness of heart; it will always remain bitter unless the heart is filled with the good pleasure of God. This passage ought to refute those who conclude from the mistranslation of the earlier words (v. 1), *whether it is love or hate man does not know,* that men should be uncertain about the will of God toward us.[5]

8. *Let your garments be always white; let not oil be lacking on your head,* .

    Solomon is speaking in accordance with the customs of that area. The Romans and Greeks favor a purple garment; but the Orientals, and especially the Jews, favor a white one, on account of the washings and cleanliness which they practiced so scrupulously. Thus the Turk wears linen garments as the most splendid, and we under the papacy wore the alb for the highest festivals. Therefore he says: "Always be happy. Use the garments that you are accustomed to wear for banquets and festivals." *Let not oil be lacking on your head,* that is, "Use the ointments which God has given you." Once more he is speaking in accordance with the custom of his people, who took the greatest pleasure in ointments. Therefore he says: "You are living in the midst of vanity. Therefore enjoy life, and do not let yourself come to ruin through your indignation, but drive the grief from your mind. You cannot mock the world more effectively than by laughing when it grows angry. Let it be enough for you that you have a gracious God. For what is the malice of the world in comparison with the sweetness of God?" He is not urging a life of pleasure and luxury characteristic of those who do not sense this vanity, for that would be putting oil on fire; but he is speaking of godly men, who sense the vexation and troubles of the world. It is their downcast hearts that he wants to encourage. It is to them that he recommends merriment, not to men who are incorrigible and wicked, who are already overflowing with pleasures and delights. He does the same when he says:

9. *Enjoy life with the wife whom you love, all the days of your vain life which He has given you under the sun, because that is your portion in life and in your toil at which you toil under the sun.*

    It is as though he were saying: "You will not get any more out of it anyway." Thus Paul says in 1 Tim. 6:8: "If we have food and clothing, with these we shall be content." But those who are not content with these, but yearn for other things in addition and torture themselves with indignation over troublesome and painful

---

[5] See p. 144, n. 1, above.

things will simply add sorrow to sorrow, vanity to vanity, and in the process deprive themselves of everything good.

10. *Whatever your hand finds to do, do it with your might; for there is no work or thought or knowledge or wisdom in the pit, to which you are going.*

This is the second part of the exhortation. In it he opposes those idle men who, because they see that the world is ungrateful and because they are aware of its pain, refuse to achieve anything at all or to do any good. Therefore he commands both, that we should be merry, but in such a way that we do not become idle but labor in accordance with the command in Gen. 3:17-19. The labor must be present, but the burdensome and troublesome anxieties must not. One must tire his body with labor, but one's heart must be free of anxiety and be content with what is in the present. Add a third element: Do not afflict your heart with grief because you see that the world is ungrateful. Now, he says *finds* deliberately; that is, "do not pursue your own plans but what lies at hand, what God has commanded and provided, without any concern about the future." When he says *with your might*, he is demanding industry and diligence. *For there is no work, etc., in the pit.* This is another passage which proves that the dead do not feel anything. There is, he says, no thought or art or knowledge or wisdom there. Therefore Solomon thought that the dead are completely asleep and do not feel anything at all. The dead lie there without counting days or years; but when they are raised, it will seem to them that they have only slept for a moment. *Pit* means the grave or the sepulcher. In my opinion it refers to the hidden resting-place in which the dead sleep outside of the present life, where the soul departs to its place. Whatever it may be, it cannot be physical. Thus you should understand the pit to mean the place where the souls are kept, a sort of sepulcher of the soul outside this physical world, just as the earth is the sepulcher of the body. What this is, however, is unknown to us. So in Gen. 42:38 and 44:29: "I shall descend with sorrow to the pit" and "You will bring down my gray hairs in sorrow to the pit." For true saints do not descend to the pit in order to suffer something there. Therefore the dead are outside of space, because whatever is outside of this life is outside of space. In the same way we shall be removed from space and time after the resurrection. Thus also Christ is outside of space. This we say in opposition to those who want to take Christ captive in space, although He is everywhere.[6] The Word of God is not separated from the flesh. Where God is, there the flesh of Christ is. But God is everywhere; therefore Christ is everywhere also.

11. *Again I saw that under the sun the race is not to the swift nor the battle to the strong nor bread to the wise nor riches to the intelligent nor favor to the men of skill; but time and chance happen to them all.*

This is a sort of summary and epilog to his catalog, as though to say: "It does not matter what someone is able to do." Therefore do not work at your own plans and endeavors, but at what your hand finds to do. That is, stick to the definite work which has been assigned and commanded by God, leaving behind the things that try to hinder you, as Samuel said to Saul (1 Sam. 10:6-7): "You will be turned into another man; and whatever your hand finds to do, that you do." He has not prescribed any law for him; but whatever matter presents itself, that he should take on, on that he should work. That is what Solomon teaches here also: Always stick to that which lies at hand and belongs to your calling. If you are a preacher or minister of the Word of God, stay with the reading of Scripture and the office of preaching; do not get caught up into something else until the Lord Himself catches you up. For whatever the Lord has not said or commanded will be worthless. Solomon proves this on the basis of his own experience when he says: "Look at the swift runners who do not win the race and at the many strong fighters who do not win the battle. Again, I have seen many very wise men who still did not succeed, as well as many who administered human affairs very well and were quite industrious, who nevertheless accomplished nothing." It does not depend on the person, regardless of how skillful he may be. In war the strong are often defeated by the weak, and great armies have often been vanquished by smaller ones; this is because the outcome does not depend on strength. Thus Troy was mightily fortified, lacking neither armed forces nor military might; and yet it was captured and overthrown, because the hour appointed for them by God had come. For the same reason a few years ago, the king of France was defeated and

[6] See *Luther's Works*, 37, pp. 215—29.

captured by the Emperor Charles, even though he was far superior to him in armed forces and weapons.[7] When he says that *the race is not to the swift,* this is a Hebraism. For among them "to run" means to carry out some office, as Paul says to the Corinthians (1 Cor. 9:26): "I do not run aimlessly"; and again (2 Tim. 4:7): "I have finished the race."

Nor favor to the men of skill. That is, many are skilled in outstanding arts and acquainted with good literature, and yet they remain objects of contempt. No one cares about them or follows them. Similarly, there is enough of the Word among us, and there are enough brilliant men; and yet we cannot convert everyone to faith. Nevertheless, this should not cause us to forsake the Gospel. For the Lord reigns in our very weakness; He will rule, He will perform it. The Lord is able to stir up a great fire and flame, so long as we preserve even a spark. We are stirred up and troubled by various thoughts as we seek to make a living. A man becomes a printer in order to get rich; and behold, he loses all his property.[8] Therefore it is not enough to be clever or wise, for many very clever ideas and many outstanding craftsmen become objects of contempt. This is what he means when he says:

Chance happens to them all.

That is, I cannot determine the outcome or the success, regardless of how much I may labor. You simply do what is your duty, and the Lord will find His appointed time to make use of your labor. We cannot make any judgments about these matters; we ought to labor, but not to prescribe the end and the outcome of our work.

12. *For man does not know his time. Like fish which are taken in an evil net, and like birds which are caught in a snare, so the sons of men are snared at an evil time, when it suddenly falls upon them.*

You should understand "time" here not to refer only to the end of life but to every appointed time and outcome; as though he were saying: "You should labor even though you do not know what will come of it." Therefore get an education; if God wills, He will grant

[7] See p. 39, n. 10, above.
[8] Cf. *Luther's Works,* 48, pp. 292—93.

success and fruit through your study. We should do the same in all the other affairs and business of life. We should labor but commit the outcome to God. For the time of success is hidden from us.

Like fish. He uses two lovely analogies to prove that things happen usually contrary to our plans and hope. A fish snaps at the bait and swallows the hook. Birds confidently enter and eat, with nothing further from their minds than a trap; and then suddenly they are captured. So it is that when we have chosen something good and hoped for it, we are deceived. And when it seems that something evil is impending, it is something good that is impending. In such a way do we stumble into things from which we then cannot extricate ourselves that we obviously do not know how we are deceived. All of this is so because the appointed time is unknown to us. There experience itself teaches us that human affairs are carried out not by our plans but usually contrary to our plans. This is the source of the statement of luckless people: "That is not what I had in mind!"

13. *I have also seen this example of wisdom under the sun, and it seemed great to me.*
14. *There was a little city with few men in it; and a great king came against it and besieged it, building great siegeworks against it.*
15. *But there was found in it a poor wise man, and he by his wisdom delivered the city. Yet no one remembered that poor man.*
16. *But I say that wisdom is better than might, though the poor man's wisdom is despised and his words are not heeded.*

I think that this is put after the epilogue as an example by which he states everything that he has said before. It is a general example, the likes of which can be found in many histories. So in Judg. 9:53 a woman set a city free by killing King Abimelech with a piece of millstone. He calls the wisdom great because it is the greatest kind of political wisdom to rescue a small and poorly armed city from powerful enemies. Besides, it is the height of ingratitude to forget such wisdom and such deeds of generosity, and yet that is what most commonly happens. Thus Themistocles did many good things for his fellow citizens, but he experienced extreme ingratitude.[9] Thus David did great things for all of Israel, and so did Solomon; yet afterwards the ten tribes forgot these great deeds and fell away from the house of David. To do something good for the world, therefore, is nothing else than to lose one's good deeds, to cast gold into the manure or pearls before swine (cf. Matt. 7:6). Therefore it is best to be happy and to work for the present, casting away all anxiety about the future; for it is better to lose my good deeds than to be lost myself along with my good deeds, as Phaedria says in the *Eunuchus*.[10]

Yet no one remembered that poor man.

The words of the wise man were listened to as long as he was giving good advice, but afterwards they were immediately forgotten.

[9] Themistocles was ostracized by the Athenians about 470 B. C. and died in exile in 462 B. C.

[10] This is an allusion, but a garbled one, to Terence, *Eunuchus*, 210—12.

CHAPTER TEN

9:17. *The words of the wise heard in quiet are better than the shouting of a ruler among fools.*

THE summary of this passage is consolation and exhortation for those who administer affairs, as well as rebuke for those who stand in the way and see to it that the plans of godly and wise people do not succeed. Thus he began with the example of the poor man who accomplished great things in his wisdom, but as soon as his great deed had been achieved, it was consigned to oblivion. As has been said above, everything that is in the present becomes boring. "Seeing this," he wants to say, "it seems to me: Do not grow weary, for you cannot make the world or people over to be something different. If things do not develop according to your good plans, commit them to God."

The words of the wise heard in quiet, etc. The words of the wise are not heard, and therefore fools are forced to hear the words of a foolish ruler. The shouting of the ruler prevails among fools, and the words of a foolish counselor are heard by the foolish ruler because he tells the ruler what the ruler wants to hear. This, I say, you have to see, as it is said also in Proverbs (18:2): "A fool does not hear unless you tell him what is already in his heart." The reason is this: because his own feelings are predominant in the heart of a fool, he does not hear whatever you say, unless you say what he wants. They do not hear because they are preoccupied with their own feelings or with their own wisdom. You will accomplish nothing else, and you will not be heard where there are not quiet hearts, that is, hearts that have not been made blind by their own feelings. So today it does not matter that you write against heretics or Sacramentarians, for you accomplish nothing. This is also what Paul says (Titus 3:10): "As for a heretic, after admonishing him once or twice, have nothing more to do with him." This is the way things are not only in matters of religion but also in government. In the affairs of the world this is how things happen: if you give wise advice, you will accomplish nothing and will not be heard except among those who are neutral, who have a calm mind and are not partisans. Those who have a calm mind and are quiet can truly judge that the shouting of the ruler is foolish. Therefore one must wait until the feelings have become calm, for then someone will hear. Just as roiled water is not clear, but someone who wants to see the bottom must wait for the water to settle, so everyone who has conceived something in his mind is beyond persuasion unless that conception settles, because it holds him captive as though by a charm. He has said the same thing elsewhere (cf. Prov. 17:12): "Let a man meet a she-bear or a lioness robbed of her cubs, rather than a fool confident in his folly."

9:18. *Wisdom is better than weapons of war, but one sinner destroys much good.*

He has proved this statement by the example given above. And nowadays all those who are experienced in warfare have proved the same, namely, that weapons of war are nothing without prudence and good counsel, and that wisdom accomplishes and prevails in war more than military might. There are all sorts of sudden emergencies, plots, etc.; unless they are immediately dealt with by a direct plan, the army and its weapons are done for. Thus the Romans boast that they conquered the world not by military might but by wisdom.[1] Therefore wisdom is indeed dominant in the world, and yet it is not heard; for *one sinner destroys much good.* In war and in peace there are always such pests around who ruin everything. Some senator gives good advice in favor of peace, but soon some other rascal or Thraso distorts everything.[2] It is useless to fight back at such a man, for people are the captives of their own feelings. They follow these and do not hear those who give contrary advice; as Homer also said, "the worse part usually prevails."[3]

10:1. *Dead flies make the best ointment give off an evil odor.*

This is a proverbial statement against fools. Solomon really makes some harsh transitions! The transition would have been less

[1] Cf., for example, Vergil, *Aeneid,* VI, 851 ff.
[2] See p. 87, n. 13, above.
[3] Cf. Homer, *Iliad,* IX, 318.

harsh if he had added: "As it is said in the proverb," or "As it is said." The proverb is taken from the customs of that nation, which regarded ointments as among the most precious of things. The comparison seems to us harsh and cold, because the customs and manners of that people do not prevail among us. Therefore just as dead flies ruin the best of ointments, so it happens to the best of counsel in the state, in the senate, or in war; along comes some wicked rascal and ruins everything. Therefore just as we are forced to bear those nasty flies, so we are also forced to bear these destructive counselors.

So a little folly is sometimes better than wisdom and glory.

This is a comfort against these troubles in the world and against evil counselors. By *a little folly* he means one that lasts a short time; as the poets say, "Foolishness in its place is the height of wisdom." [4] And so when you see a wicked scoundrel having his own way in a council or in a senate, forget about your advice and put aside your wisdom; for you see that they are not welcome, and you will only make yourself miserable. It is better for you to be a little foolish and to let them continue in their folly, for they will not listen to you, and you cannot break through by force. A fool cannot be changed by any advice unless you tell him what is already in his heart. After you have given your advice and have done what you can, you should let them go. For if you wanted to break through, you would only stir up the hornets, run into an angry she-bear, and bring upon yourself all kinds of unnecessary danger. This advice is very good for us who have our existence in a world that is as evil as it is ungrateful, a world that does not listen regardless of what we advise or say or warn.

Glory refers not only to fame but to wealth, pomp, decoration, and riches, from all of which fame comes. Thus Matt. 6:29 says: "God clothes the lilies of the field in a way that not even Solomon in all his glory was arrayed"; that is, he was arrayed in all his wealth and in all his pomp.

2. *A wise man's heart inclines him toward the right, but a fool's heart toward the left.*

This, too, is a proverbial saying. It means: A wise man has con-

[4] Cf. Horace, *Odes,* IV, 12, 28.

trol over his heart. If he sees people acting foolishly and refusing to listen, he can temporarily refrain from giving advice. He is able to make use of his wisdom according to the place and the person, on the basis of his seeing that his advice will be neglected on the right or on the left. But a fool does not have control over his heart, and so he makes up his mind to break things up just because he feels like it. It is a great thing to be able to control and moderate one's heart, something that no one has ever done or can ever do unless he knows the world and respects the judgment of God.

3. *Even when the fool walks on the road, he lacks sense, and he regards everyone else as a fool.*

That is, it is not enough for him that he himself has his way with his twisted counsels and that you are obliged to give in to him, but you are obliged to stand for it that he receives glory for his foolishness and twisted counsel and that he slanders the wisdom of everyone else. For if you give some good advice, he will immediately insult it and will slander the best things you say and counsel. But this is how you should reply: "I have given my counsel. I am not forcing anyone to accept it, and I have simply said what seemed good to me." First of all, the fool does not listen. Then he begins to break things up. Finally, he will ridicule and slander as foolish and wicked whatever you said in opposition to him—something you, of course, ought to do anyway but not insist on. We are seeing and experiencing this very thing among ourselves today.

4. *If the spirit of the ruler rises against you, do not leave your place, for deference will make amends for great offenses.*

We say the same thing in our proverb: "He who knows how not to hear will become wise." Therefore he says: "If their spirit, that is, their insistence or their counsel, should prevail, do not let yourself become impatient; do not forsake your post, stick tight, hold still. But if you resist and if you do not want your counsel to be rejected, you will only stir up the hornets and kick against the goads (cf. Acts 26:14), for a large part of wisdom is the ability to overlook things or to yield. For this restrains great evils, which are put to rest by being quiet, that is, by yielding, even though ultimately they come to rest on their own; on the other hand, they will stir up huge upheavals if you insist upon taking a stand against them.

Thus the Romans boast of their man Fabius that he smashed Hannibal by his tactics of delay.[5] In the same way our elector, Frederick of Saxony, held back the rebels of Erfurt by keeping silence and took his revenge upon them.[6] Vergil also says the same thing: "Every turn of fortune should be overcome by being borne."[7] These statements are derived from a central experience of human affairs.

5. *There is an evil which I have seen under the sun, as it were an error proceeding from the ruler:*

6. *folly is set in many high places, and the rich sit in a low place.*

7. *I have seen slaves on horses, and princes walking on foot like slaves.*

It is not surprising, he says, if the insistence or the counsel of fools prevails against wise men or against those who give good advice. I have seen that among princes it is a rare one who is not foolish and who does not come up with wrong ideas about things on his own. So it is that the fool is in charge everywhere, prevailing in the senate, in the courts of rulers, etc. The world is foolish, and it is ruled by fools and by foolish opinions. Therefore if you give some other kind of advice, it will not listen. On the other hand, if you break things up, the fool is irritated even more and in his anger will do something that may bring harm on the whole country.

When he speaks of the rich sitting in a low place, he is referring to those who ought to have a preeminent position and who could reign well. When he speaks of slaves, he is referring to those who ought to be under someone else's rule. It is as though he were saying: "Those who ought to be under someone else's rule are the ones I see reigning and in high position, namely, slaves and fools. On the other hand, I have seen the wisest of men in poverty, with hardly enough to eat. Therefore when you see such centaurs and Thrasos reigning, men who really ought to be serving you, do not be surprised. Just remember that this is how the world is governed."

---

[5] Quintus Fabius, who died in 203 B. C., was originally surnamed *Cunctator* ("Delayer") as a criticism for his inaction against Carthage; but when this had worn down Hannibal's armies, the epithet became a title of honor.

[6] On riots in Erfurt, see *Luther's Works,* 45, p. 64, n. 21.

[7] Vergil, *Aeneid,* V, 710.

8. *He who digs a pit will fall into it; and a serpent will bite him who breaks through a wall.*

9. *He who quarries stones is hurt by them; and he who splits logs is endangered by them.*

Here Solomon inserts a kind of collection of proverbs, all of which he applies to the experience of governing human affairs. It is as though he were saying: "In human affairs, what these proverbs say is what happens. Whatever you undertake in human affairs, you will have the same experience as is described here: 'He who digs a pit, etc.'; that is, one does not get out of it without trouble. Similarly, governing people is the same as breaking through a wall, where it often happens that you are bitten by a serpent. Therefore even if evil things happen to you, do not be a quitter, but remember that it cannot be otherwise in human affairs." Governing men belongs only to God. Therefore anyone who has charge of administration should know that he is administering matters which cannot be controlled by any human counsel. The hearts of men do not lie in our own power. Only those who have the fear of God are easy to govern.

The proverb is taken from the experience of gravediggers, to whom it tends to happen that they will unknowingly fall into their pits. Thus governing human affairs is the same as digging a pit, where you should be forewarned that you will never be out of danger: for unless you are forewarned, you will fall into much greater and more unforeseen dangers. Dangers that one has foreseen do not strike as hard. Demipho in Terence's *Phormio* has wisely warned about this when he says: "Therefore when things are going well, all men should above all think about how they will bear the opposite kind of fate—danger, condemnation, exile."[8] A man returning from a journey should always consider the possibility that his son has committed some sin or that his wife has died or that his daughter has been taken ill. These are common things and can happen, and therefore this should not be something novel for his spirit. Whatever happens beyond your expectation you should regard as a gain, so that if something like this happens, you can say, "This is what I expected," and can recall that nothing is happening to you which is contrary to general human experience.

[8] Terence, *Phormio*, 241—43.

In fact, if something good happens to you, you should regard it as your daily gain. Therefore one must not immediately quit digging, even though a careless person may fall in. Human life is filled with dangers. And just as in breaking through a wall there is often a danger that a hidden serpent will bite, so we must be careful in the administration of human affairs that we don't get hurt. But if you are bitten or get hurt, you must bear it; for what is happening to you is nothing new.

He who quarries stones. Someone who rolls stones can easily hurt a hand or a foot. He is thinking of larger stones, which cannot be rolled along without great trouble. And so governing human affairs is like rolling a stone along. When you get hurt, therefore, you should say: "If I were not rolling stones around, I would not get hurt. But because I am transporting them and rolling them around, it is no wonder that I get hurt." If you are the head of a household, you should keep in mind that for you, too, there is a stone to be rolled. What follows is similar.

He who splits logs is endangered by them. That is, one cannot carry things out without harm and danger. Therefore it is best to fortify one's heart and to expect some difficulties, so that if anything succeeds well in the state, it will be a kind of miracle. The more unhoped-for your good luck is, the happier it makes you, just as the more foreseen your troubles are, the less they hurt you. Therefore we should always keep in mind that we are carrying on our lives in danger, not in good times.

10. *If the iron be corroded by rust and the rust has gone so far that one cannot whet the edge, then what is left is that there must be a wise artisan.*

Once again he is comforting those who are in the administration of human affairs. Just as a piece of iron that has been corroded by rust is hard to polish or to make sharp again, so the world is a piece of iron corroded by rust, an ax that is pitted and loose in the handle, one that no one can wield properly. This is a very appropriate comparison. As it is a lot of work and trouble to chop with a pitted and rusty axe, so it is a miserable and troublesome thing to administer the government of the world, the state, or even the home. The instrument is simply wretched and useless for its purpose, and yet we are obliged to carry on in it and with it. In the same way, because men are evil and filled with wicked feelings, great wisdom is necessary to rule them and to control them.

Therefore he says: "If the iron has become rusty or dull and it, that is, the rust, has gained the upper hand, then what is left is that there must be a wise artisan." That is, it takes a good craftsman to sharpen an old rusty ax. Thus it is necessary that there be a wise man who will make good use of things that are so bad, that is, of the world and of men who are so evil and perverse. By nature men are contemptuous, but God has interposed His own authority so that they will at least obey. For He says: "It is My will that you obey this man. If you do not obey him, you will be despising Me also." But they do not obey even then. Therefore the state or the home is nothing but this kind of rusty iron. Use the ax you have, therefore, if you cannot use any other. As the proverb says, "He who does not have plaster, will have to build his wall with manure or putty." If you are the head of a household or in the government, keep in mind that you have a rusty piece of iron (that is, people who neither want to be nor can be governed). Use it and cut as best you can, so that you may at least retain and restore some part and form of a state. For in human affairs things will never be done so well that there will not be a greater share of evils left behind. Therefore there is need of an artisan who will sharpen the iron, corroded though it is with old rust, so that he can at least use it. This is what ought to comfort us in the midst of human affairs.

11. *If the serpent bites before it is charmed, it is no better than a babbler.*

This also applies to the state. Just as a serpent that has not been charmed, that is, one that is unknown or unforeseen, will bite (for a charmed serpent does not bite, because it obeys the voice of the charmer), so also a babbler will bite. A babbler is no better than a biting serpent, that is, a man who does not have control of his tongue, one who curses his ruler or the person who is placed over him. This is what happens in political and even in domestic affairs. If you are the head of a household, you will do many things that will be displeasing to your wife, family, etc. Among these you will find some who, if you do something good, will distort it and slander you; but if you do something wrong, they will betray you and carry the story to your neighbors and fellow citizens. This, too, you must bear. You may, of course, resist it according to your ability, but what you cannot prohibit must be borne. Of course, it is tiring and difficult to be betrayed so bitterly by the mouth of evil-minded people even when you do not know about it, but what can you do about it? You will not be able to restrain these slanders and these detractors. Simply shut your eyes and ears and do what you can. We, too, are obliged to bear it that in words and actions we meet with resistance, for the world never stops persecuting its magistrates and those who urge the right path.

12. *The words of a wise man's mouth are grace, but the lips of a fool consume him.*

That is, the wise man arranges his words correctly and graciously; but because he is situated in the midst of evil tongues, he does not succeed. The slanderer comes along and consumes him, he overwhelms the good man with his words. Therefore I apply the word *him* to the wise man, not to the fool. The gracious word of the wise man becomes useless because of the lips of fools. If some good and wise man gives very good advice, a slanderer and scoundrel will nevertheless come along and overthrow it. This is what happened to Paul in Acts (27:21) when they were suffering shipwreck. "Men and brethren," he says, "you should have listened to me, and should not have set sail from Crete." In short, the fool consumes the wise man, and "the worse part always wins." [9]

13. *The beginning of the words of his mouth is foolishness, and the end of his talk is wicked madness.*

That is, this is what happens to fools, who want to give the appearance of being wise and who regard everyone else except themselves as foolish: whether they are beginning or concluding, their entire speech is sheer foolishness. The more a fool wants to appear wise, the more foolish he is; and yet he prevails over the wise man and consumes the best of counsels. So the Pharisees prevailed over Christ, the best of teachers, and the Jews and false apostles over the apostles. The Arians consumed the good teachers. Today, too, we are preaching Christ, but the heretical persecutors come along and consume us. But let us await greater things to come, and mean-

[9] See p. 156, n. 3, above.

while let us count it a gain that we still retain some good things and that there are still some who retain the correct doctrine.

14. *A fool multiplies words.*

A wise man teaches with few words and says what he feels with brevity. The statement of truth is simple. Fools, on the other hand, spill over with words, and cannot be restrained or put down with words so that they will keep quiet, but will answer one word with a thousand. Thus Christ always answered the scribes and Pharisees with few words when they accused His doctrine of being not from God, but from Satan.

No man knows what is before him, and who can tell him what will be after him?

That is, a man does not see the things that are present, the things that are in view. He is never content with the things that are present but always looks for things that belong to others and are in the future; he forsakes what has been given to him and prescribed for him by God. Nowadays the Gospel has been given to us, but look, we are carried away to other things. But this has been said earlier at greater length.[10]

15. *The toil of fools wearies them, because they do not know the way to the city.*

That is, even though the words of the fool have prevailed and have multiplied, they do not accomplish anything; all they achieve is to multiply toil and to increase its woe. Night and day they are agitated and think about protecting their property. But this toil does not bring them any benefit, except that they torment themselves even more. One must observe these two antitheses: the fool finds misery in his toil; the wise man finds happiness. When the fool sees that his efforts are not succeeding, his spirit becomes restless. He has neither the ability nor the knowledge to commit his success to God. On the other hand, the wise man keeps his equanimity at both times, for he knows that things do not happen because of our counsels or efforts but because of the will of God. It is to Him that he commits the success or outcome of his plans. *Because they do not know the way to the city.* This is a Hebrew

[10] See pp. 19—22 above.

phrase, like the phrase in the psalms (Ps. 107:4): "finding no way to a city." That is, they wander around all over the place and do not know where to go to find rest. All the ways lead to some place where people live, but these people are wanderers all their way and do not stay still anywhere. Wise men, by contrast, stick to their path and preserve their place, even though various dangers and obstacles may arise; for they have seen ahead of time that this is how it would be. Therefore let everyone act and do his job with a happy heart. One will act with a happy heart if he knows that he is in the world and in the midst of danger. This is how evil can be conquered before it arises.

16. *Woe to the land whose king is a child, whose princes feast in the morning!*

Thus far we have heard that human affairs are conducted in such a way that fools usually have their way and prevail, although usually to their own harm, so that when they have suppressed the words of the wise, they bring upon themselves the consequences of their own foolishness. Since this is how things are, it is extremely dangerous to have a child as a king, when among so many fools, who fill everything, even the king has no sense. This is the condition of the government in Germany and Spain today, where the princes, who are regarded as the wisest of men, govern and direct everything for their own advantage and seek their own gain. Meanwhile all the others do not know anything except to ride their horses, to go whoring around, and to get drunk; they leave everything to their counselors, who are out for their own advantage and do not care about the welfare of the state. And all of Germany is a kind of desert, in which there is nothing like civic morals, no concern for the education of the youth, where the laws, discipline, and the liberal arts have all gone to pieces, and there is no reason in the courts. A good prince is a great gift, one who ponders and understands what will be of benefit to his land, one who can foresee what will be of benefit to individuals so that everything is carried out and administered according to the law and every person gets his rights. Even such a prince does not have success in everything; in fact, many things come out contrary to his expectations. But he does not therefore quit what he has begun but continues to do what he can, although in the manner that has been described above. In this way Solomon was a very good and prudent prince, or king, for he wrote proverbs for the instruction of the young; and yet all he got out of it was trouble and much toil. Therefore if even the best of princes did not find success, what is going to happen when the king is a child and does not do anything worthy of a prince? *Whose princes feast in the morning.* That is, they do not delegate their work and their tasks, do not take care that the affairs of their government are properly administered; all they care about is that they themselves have a good time. In fact, when there are some who want to be of use to the situation and to their princes, they are oppressed by the likes of these. *In the morning* therefore means the same as "in the first place" or "above all." The morning is the first hour for work or activity. These men *feast in the morning,* that is, they look out for themselves first, providing for their own profit and appetite, putting off the affairs of the realm to the evening and dealing with them after everything else is finished.

17. *Happy are you, O land, when your king is the son of wise men and your princes feast at the proper time, for strength and not for drunkenness!*

Phrases like "the son of death" or "the son of life" or "the son of a year" are Hebraisms. And so here "the son of חוֹרִים," that is, of noblemen, one who has חוֹרִים, that is, leading men of the state. (We translate the Hebrew "son of" with "one who has"; thus it is said of Pharaoh in Isaiah [11] [19:11], "I am a son of the wise," that is, I have many wise men.) Now, חוֹרִים means "white." The Oriental people had the custom of using white garments the way the Romans used purple ones or robes of state. Therefore these men are called "white" on the basis of the garment worn by princes, just as some of the Romans were called Torquati.[12]

And your princes feast at the proper time; that is, they do not give their own appetites preference over the business and the cares of the realm, they do not seek their own advantage. But where are such men to be found? Avarice reigns at court; the

[11] The original has "in Ezekiel."

[12] Titus Manlius Torquatus, who lived in the fourth century B. C., was said to have acquired this cognomen by depriving an enemy of his collar *(torques)* and putting it on himself.

nobles are nothing but sheer avarice. You can see this in our princes. The principalities are being bled white while the leading men of the state and the nobles are getting rich. On account of the good-for-nothing nobles we are unable to get anything done about providing for the poor, establishing schools, providing poor girls with a dowry, and similar godly works; but meanwhile there is nothing that these men do not extort from the princes. Truly happy, then, is the land whose princes feast *for strength and not for drunkenness*, that is, who enjoy the generosity of the prince in order to have something to eat for themselves and for their families, not in order to accumulate enormous treasures.

18. *Through sloth the roof sinks in, and through indolence the house leaks.*

He inserts a proverbial saying, as though he were to say: "In a realm where the princes, or nobles, seek their own advantage and the king is a fool, the situation is just like that of a negligent head of a household who fails to act when for a few cents he could see to it that the timbers of the building do not go to pieces, and so the whole house goes to ruin." Where the head of the household does not pay constant attention, repairing every day whatever has fallen down, there one misfortune usually follows after another. A man who pays attention will fix right away whatever has gone wrong; he will not only preserve what he has, but also restore and repair what is broken and add something to his property and its ornamentation. What he says here about the house he wants understood of the entire household. Just as a building goes to ruin when it is neglected, so the entire household goes to ruin when it is neglected. A diligent head of the household is always busy with improving things, a lazy one with ruining them. Thus many dioceses and principalities have gone to ruin because no one kept them in repair, no one lifted a hand. He who despises trifles, gradually ruins everything. The head of a household must be both frugal and generous. He must not neglect even the smallest detail; then he will be able to give generously when giving is called for. Our prince, Frederick, was a very admirable administrator of his household, so that he seemed to be niggardly when he counted things out individually into the hands of his cooks, stewards, etc. But when it came to giving things to his guests, he poured out everything with the greatest generosity—something he could not have done unless he had saved it up by his parsimony. In this way he saw to it that he had a very orderly home and household.[13] So it is also with a prince. If he neglects one or two usurers or other public criminals, he will finally get to the point that he will not punish anyone at all and the whole state will go to ruin. Thus the Roman generals did not want any enemy to be overlooked, not even the least.[14] In short, where there is a foolish king, there is also a foolish administration and the kind of realm that must go to ruin. The state is like the household, and letting a house leak is the same as wrecking it.

19. *They make bread with laughter, and wine makes the living happy.*

That is, these good-for-nothing gluttons and gullets do not carry on any honest work but earn their wages with nothing but silly works and deeds; they get rich by flattery, tickling, and guzzling. This is how the majority of those in the courts of princes are. Indeed, among four hundred there are hardly four or five who earn their wages by serious and honest work and who are of benefit to the commonwealth. *And wine makes the living happy,* as though he were saying: "They care about nothing except high living; they are of no use to the princes, except to drink their cellars empty and burden them with unnecessary expenses."

And they answer everything with money.

We say this just this way in German: "Money is all that matters." Everywhere they are after money, whether it is of advantage to the commonwealth and the realm or not.

[13] Cf. *Luther's Works,* 54, pp. 194—95.
[14] A reference to Publilius Syrus, *Sententiae.*

CHAPTER ELEVEN

10:20. *Even in your thought, do not curse the king, nor in your bedchamber curse the rich; for a bird of the air will carry your voice, or some winged creature tell the matter.*

THE preceding chapter was a kind of invective against fools and a description of how the kingdom of the world is, so that anyone who deals with human affairs would recognize that he holds a very unhappy position. It is, I say, the height of wisdom to know this, that the kingdom of the world is very wicked and cannot be set straight. This chapter, on the other hand, is an exhortation to good works. For when it has been taught that the kingdom of the world is so wicked, the hearts of men begin to grow weary, and they think of quitting the direction of human affairs, of forsaking the world because they have been overcome by the malice of men, as has been said above. But Solomon teaches that the more wicked and evil the world is, the more one must persist and work, so that at least something is done. He begins with respect for the government. Government is an ordinance of God and a very important element in the world, or *under the sun.* Through this ordinance God directs everything that happens under the sun. Wicked men most often begin by despising government when they hear God rebuking it in the Scriptures. But it is God's business to rebuke and denounce governments. If you hear this, this does not mean that you are to imitate it. You are not God, neither the founder nor the restorer of the divine ordinance. But God rebukes you no less than them in the Scriptures, so that you, too, will do your duty. But you forget about the log in your own eye and begin to see the speck in someone else's eye (cf. Matt. 7:3-5) and to rebuke those who are placed above you, by whom you ought rather to be corrected. If you were to hold their office, you would sin much more than they and would not even accomplish what they accomplish. Therefore let us hear how God rebukes the government, but let us not imitate God in this.

The meaning, therefore, is this: "I have said much about

princes and about how they bring the world to ruin. But you, do not curse the king even to yourself, that is, in your thought, nor in your bedchamber curse the rich." That is, those who have been established in authority are to be revered, for this is not a human ordinance but a divine one. Even though Peter calls government a "human institution" (1 Peter 2:13) because it is taken over from human beings, nevertheless, its authority is divine; and even though rulers are evil, they are still to be respected on account of the ordinance of God. Why, then, do you want to curse those who, if they are good men, are troubled with so many cares and such great labors for the sake of your peace? But if they are evil and stupid men, their wickedness is and brings enough evil upon them. Therefore you should rather feel sorry for them. But this is not what happens; in fact, the world does the opposite: it deals out ingratitude to good men, it curses other men, it praises foolish men. Indeed, good men are torn away from their lands. In short, we cannot bear either ourselves or others, either good fortune or misfortune. If God puts us to the test with moderate afflictions, with illness or poverty, we grow impatient and make accusations against God. But if He accedes to our wishes, we cannot bear this either. Great indeed is the patience of God, which is able to bear with us despite such ingratitude! Therefore let us desist from cursing our rulers, and let us begin to show them respect, whether they be good or evil. Give thanks to God if they are good, suffer and bear with them if they are evil. Those who occupy the ministry of the Word have the right to issue rebukes, but not the common people.

For a bird of the air will carry your voice, and a man of wings will tell the matter.

The Hebrews call a bird *a man of wings* or "a husband of pinions" or one who has pinions. He means to say: "If you curse the king, this will not be hidden but will become known, and thus you will be punished," for "a king's wrath is a messenger of death, and his favor is like the clouds that bring the spring rain" (Prov. 16:14-15).

11:1. *Cast your bread upon the waters, for you will find it after many days.*

This again is a Hebraism, as Solomon abounds in figures of speech. He wants to say: "Be generous to everyone while you can, use your riches wherever you can possibly do any good." And he adds a promise: "For if you live long enough, you will receive back a hundredfold." So we read in Proverbs (19:17): "He who is kind to the poor lends to the Lord"; so also Christ says (Luke 6:38): "Give, and it will be given to you"; and Paul says (2 Cor. 9:7): "God loves a cheerful giver." Whoever wants to be poor, let him not give anything to others. Therefore he says *Cast your bread*, that is, "share your food, which the Lord has given to you." *Upon the waters*, that is, "give it simply and generously, even though your kindness seems to you to perish and your bread seems to sink into the water." Solomon is using a metaphor, with which he merely wants to say: "Being mortal yourself, feed those who are mortal." *For you will find it after many days*, that is, "if you live long, you will find that bread which you have cast upon the waters." It is as though he were saying: "The fact that you have been generous to others will not perish, even though it may seem to perish. Indeed, after a long time the Lord will grant bread." Ps. 37:26 says: "He is ever giving liberally and lending"; and again (Ps. 37:19): "In the days of famine they have abundance." For God does not let Himself be surpassed in generosity, but surpasses our generosity in endless ways.

2. *Give a portion to seven, or even to eight, for you know not what evil may happen on earth.*

Here again he is exhorting, and to his exhortation he adds a threat. Distribute your bread, he says, to seven or to eight; that is, give it generously. For as Paul says, "he who sows bountifully will also reap bountifully, and he who sows sparingly will also reap sparingly" (2 Cor. 9:6). Do not think too highly of yourself for giving. Even if you were to give everything away, you would still not be poor. Just see to it that you give of your own and that what you give is there, as Christ says in the Gospel.[1]

For you know not what evil, etc.

That is, it can happen that you will die tomorrow and leave everything to completely unworthy men, or that some other calam-

[1] Perhaps a reference to such passages as Luke 6:35-38.

ity will suddenly strike that will make you regret not having distributed or given away your goods; and then when you want to do so, you will not be able to. Therefore give while you have something and while you can. You are not sure what the evening will bring with it. For when princes accumulate treasures, they do nothing but provide a cause for war; and rich men accumulate many things, which are a source of quarrels and dissensions.

3. *If the clouds are full of rain, they empty themselves on the earth.*

These are nothing but exhortations and threats. If the *clouds*, that is, the poor, are full, they will empty their rain on the earth. This can be understood in two ways. The first is this: "Imitate the clouds, which pour out rain when they are full; do the same and pour out upon the poor." The second is as though it were a promise, which I prefer: "If you have property, give to those who are like a wandering cloud and who have nothing. Fill those clouds, I say, and you will see that you, too, will be filled again." Now there follows a threat.

If a tree falls to the south or to the north, in the place where the tree falls, there it will lie.

That is, you do not know how long you will be alive and will possess things. Just as a tree, when it is chopped down, whether it falls to the south or to the north, will remain there; so just as death strikes you, regardless of the place or the situation, so you will remain. If the Lord finds you in the south, that is, fertile and rich in good works, good. But if He finds you in the north, that is, not abounding in good works, too bad for you. As you are found, so you will be judged and so you will receive.

4. *He who observes the wind will not sow; and he who regards the clouds will not reap.*

This also pertains to exhortation. We express this sentiment in German this way: "He who is afraid of the bushes will never get into the woods." To the person who is giving, it seems that he will have nothing left at home but will lose everything. This is the reason why we are so reluctant to give things away. Therefore he says: "If you want to be afraid of poverty or of ingratitude, you will never do good to anyone." He who looks not at the Word of

Him who has promised but at the property given does not believe that he will eventually be fed or will have plenty. Therefore you must look at the Word of God and at the promises (Matt. 4:4): "Man shall not live by bread alone." If you listen to His Word, I say, He will bless you in the field and at home. Therefore he who observes the wind will not sow, and he who regards the clouds will not reap. For at harvesttime rain is not good. Sunny weather is what is expected for this, and there is no harvest until it comes. "I would be happy to give," people say, "if I could see that I shall not be in need." You are willing to give only from that which you do not need. But you should know that the poor man ought to eat with you, so that you would rather do without something than that he should be in want. But he who does not believe the Lord does not do anything good. He who overlooks the Word, overlooks the work as well.

5. *As you do not know the way of the wind or how the bones grow in the womb, so you do not know the work of God who makes everything.*

Solomon heaps up his exhortation in order to stir up our sleepiness and laziness. "Just as you do not know," he says, "what is the way of the wind and how the bones grow, etc., so you do not know the work of God which He does everywhere or in everything." You do not know what God intends to do to you or to someone else, whether tomorrow you will die or live or get sick or what other evil may befall you. If we had knowledge of God's prolonging or shortening our lives, we would be very badly off in every way. Now we do not know about our lives even one hour ahead, and yet even so we do not stop doing evil. Christ uses this comparison in John 3:8: "You hear the sound of the wind, and yet you do not see whence it comes or whither it goes." So also you do not know where you will go or where you are traveling. Therefore just as you do feel the wind that is present, so also you should make use of the things that are present. *Or how the bones grow, etc.* So it is, he says, that animals and human beings come into being in their mothers' wombs without your knowing about it. As Psalm 139:15 [2] says: "My frame was not hidden from Thee, when I was being made in secret." This is what the entire Psalm 139, "O Lord, Thou

[2] The original has "Ps. 38."

hast searched me," says. Even if the womb were open, we still would not see how these things happen. For the trees grow in plain sight of all of us, and yet we do not see how leaves, branches, and fruit grow, nor can we assign any reason to it. Thus also we ourselves grow in the sight of other people. Since, therefore, we do not understand these things which are present and which are going on before our very eyes, how are we to do so with future things? Therefore the summary of this is: The works of God are not known to us, and things that are in the future are not sure.

6. *In the morning (therefore) sow your seed, and at evening withhold not your hand; for you do not know which will prosper, this or that, or whether both alike will be good.*

He is saying this not only about farming but in general about all human works, above all, however, about doing good; as Paul says (Gal. 6:10): "As we have opportunity, let us do good." *In the morning,* that is, be busy at the proper time or constantly. The reason: "For you do not know what will come up better." You do the sowing and do what you should, but commit your works and their outcome to God. Do good to all men, do not observe the winds, and do not be concerned about what will be the outcome. Thus one should do his job and should not look for gratitude. If the world does not thank you, God will thank you; and if they both do, so much the better! But if dangers come, be prepared to accept them.

We see, therefore, that in this whole book Solomon is teaching how to use the things that are in the present and is arming us beforehand against future dangers and calamities, so that when they do come we accept them as a matter of course. What follows is a kind of applause or rather supplication, as in German we customarily add to our sermons or exhortations something like: "God grant that it happen this way!"

7. *Light is sweet, and it is pleasant for the eyes to behold the sun.*

This is allegorical. He wants to say: "It would be a happy thing if someone were to produce an example of this teaching, if the princes of the people or the people themselves were to follow the teaching which I have taught and am teaching in this book.

8. *If a man lives many years and rejoices in them all, he will remember that the days of darkness were many; for all that comes is vanity.*

As I have said, this is nothing but supplication; as though he were saying: "I would love to see an age in which this book would be observed. That would be a fine man!" As the sun is sweet and the light joyful, so joyful it is to see a man whose heart has been aroused, who for many years has experienced these things with a happy heart and has despised the world in the midst of dangers. Such a man would also see much darkness, that is, the evil of the world. But this would bring him delight, that he would be able to despise these things, as a man who knew and foresaw long beforehand that this is the way the world is.

CHAPTER TWELVE

11:9. Rejoice, O young man, in your youth, and let your heart cheer you in the days of your youth.

AFTER defining that rare bird, the man who has lived throughout his life with a happy spirit and has made fun of the onrushing evils and the malice of the world, he now adds an exhortation. "Therefore," he says, "O young man, you who are inexperienced in human affairs, if you want to live happily, listen to what I am writing to you and teaching you, so that you do not go too far astray. Live in such a way that you are a despiser of the world and that you conquer its malice." Here you see what he calls "the contempt of the world" [1] — not that we human beings should run away but that we should carry on within the world, in the midst of dangers, yet in such a way that we preserve a quiet and peaceful heart in any and every adversity. Therefore he says: "If you want to attain this goal, to have a quiet heart in the midst of evil, get used to evil from your very boyhood. Then you will be able to anticipate any danger securely."

And let your heart cheer you. That is, "joyfully enjoy the joyful things when they are present, but do not be crushed by the difficult things when they come." This is how the youth ought to be instructed and educated. Unless the youth follow such admonition, they will never accomplish anything worthy of a man. For youth burns with passions and is inexperienced. This inexperience is then an obstacle so that it cannot bear the malice, or go along with the ingratitude, of the world. Solomon is, therefore, the best of teachers of youth. He does not forbid joys and pleasures, as those foolish teachers, the monks, did. For this is nothing else than making young people into stumps and, as even Anselm, the most monkish of monks, said, trying to plant a tree in a narrow pot.[2] So the monks confined their pupils as though in a cage and forbade

---

[1] See p. 4, n. 5, above.

[2] Anselm, who died in 1109, had been abbot of Bec in Normandy, 1078—93, before becoming archbishop of Canterbury.

them to see or talk with people, with the result that they learned and experienced nothing, even though there is nothing more dangerous to youth than solitude. The mind needs to be trained with good sense and ideas, so that people are not corrupted by association and contact with evil men, since according to the body they have to live in the very midst of such things. Therefore one must see and hear the world, so long as there is a good teacher present. Above all, young people should avoid sadness and loneliness. Joy is as necessary for youth as food and drink, for the body is invigorated by a happy spirit. Education should not begin with the body but with the spirit, so that this is not overlooked; for when the spirit has been properly instructed, it is easy to govern the body. Therefore one must be indulgent with youth, and must let them be happy and do everything with a happy spirit. Yet one must see to it that they are not corrupted by the desires of the flesh. For carousals, drinking-bouts, and love affairs are not the happiness of the heart of which he is speaking here but rather make the spirit sad.

Walk in the ways of your heart and the sight of your eyes. But know that for all these things God will bring you into judgment.

This passage made me think that this entire text, from the beginning of the chapter, is meant to be ironic; for it almost sounds like something bad to say that someone walks in the ways of his heart. But one must remain with the argument of the text and with its context. Therefore this is what he wants to say: When the heart has been correctly instructed, no joy or happiness will harm it, so long as it is a genuine joy and not a happiness that brings corruption or affliction — a subject about which we have already spoken. *And walk in the sight of your eyes,* that is, "whatever is offered to your eyes, that you should enjoy." Do not be diverted to the things that are in the future, lest you become like the monks, some of whom, as for example the monk Silvanus, taught that one should not even look at the sun.[3] They wanted to deprive the youth of sight, hearing, speech, and all the senses and to enclose them in a cage as though they were birds. That is what these obviously wicked and truly misanthropic men wanted to do! But you, on the contrary, if something is pleasant to the sight or the hearing, etc., enjoy it, just so long as you do not sin against God. Do not set up

[3] *Vitae Patrum,* V, ch. 3, sec. 15, *Patrologia, Series Latina,* LXXIII, 862.

laws for yourself in such matters but enjoy everything, only with the fear of God. See to it that you do not follow the perverse desires of the world, which can corrupt your heart. So far the first section.

11:10. *Remove vexation from your mind, and put away pain from your body; for youth and the dawn of life are vanity.*

It is as though he were saying: "As I want you to be restrained by the fear of God, so that you do not follow your wicked and harmful desires, so I want to preserve you from being troubled by sadness and broken up by adversity. Therefore remove anger from your spirit, that is, accustom yourself not to become angry or to be overcome by indignation when you see that everything is going very badly. If something sad happens, you should know that this belongs to the world. Let other people envy and hate, but you refuse to do so, because such things destroy a happy life; as the proverb says (Prov. 14:30), "envy is the rottenness of the bones." Envy is a disease that corrodes [4] and melts things. Preserve your heart for me in its integrity, and do not corrupt it with too many desires of this world or sorrows. *And put away pain from your body,* that is, "whatever can afflict your flesh, that you must put away." This does not mean that he wants to forbid the castigation of the flesh, but your affliction is in vain if you torture and vex yourself with such things. Therefore do not wrinkle your brow this way but have a serene countenance. Just see to it that you fear God. A serene countenance is an indication of a happy heart. And as I want you to be happy in spirit, so I also want your body to be serene. *For youth and the dawn of life, etc.,* that is, "remember that you are a youth and are situated completely in a life of vanity." For youth in itself is vain and is caught up in various passions. Therefore you be wise and do not, as the saying goes, pour oil on the fire. As far as things are concerned, do not love them nor be sad about them, but be happy with them and enjoy them. And get used to this in your youth, so that you may know it in your old age. For those who have lived quietly and joyfully in their youth will also come to a joyful old age.

12:1. *Remember also your Creator in the days of your youth, before the evil days come, and the years draw nigh, when you will say: I have no pleasure in them.*

---

[4] The original has *corradens,* but we have read *corrodens.*

"I am saying all of this," he says, "because I want you to be free of all youthful passions, so that you will revere God and make use of the things that have been given to you by Him." *Before the evil days come,* that is, "before you get old." For old age is in itself a disease, even if no other disease comes in addition. Old people lose the vigor of mind and body. He describes old age with many words and figures of speech: old age has nothing but evil days and is not useful for getting anything done.

2. *Before the sun and the light and the moon and the stars are darkened and the clouds return after the rain.*

Light signifies happiness, darkness signifies affliction and misfortune; thus (Ps. 112:4): "Light rises in the darkness for the upright." Therefore he wants to say: "Before the unhappiness of old age comes, when the sun does not please and light is not a pleasure, when the clouds return after the rain; that is, there is a perpetual sadness and tribulation." In other ages of human life, in adolescence or in youth, there is a certain recurrence of joy; after a storm there comes serenity, after tribulation happiness. But for old people, after clouds there follows rain, one misfortune after another, one storm after another. Thus the poets also have called old age sad.

3. *In the day when the keepers of the house tremble.*

These are descriptions and pictures of old age. He wants to say: "Become accustomed to bearing evils, live in the fear of God, before *the keepers of the house tremble,* that is, "before the hands tremble." For the hands are the protectors of the body, as Aristotle also calls the hand "the tool of tools," because it has many duties and serves the other members of the body, whereas these members have each their own special duties.[5] Our body is a sort of house, in which both the political and the domestic order may be found; the king of this state is the head, its guards are the hands, etc.

And the strong men are bent, that is, "the legs fail and the knees grow weak." For strength is attributed to the bones and the legs, as in the psalm (Ps. 147:10): "The pleasure of the Lord is not in the legs of a man."

---

[5] Aristotle, *On the Soul,* III, ch. 8.

And the grinders cease because they are few.

Extreme old age is toothless. The teeth are the grinders of food, for the mouth is the mill. It is difficult to grind when the teeth have fallen out.

And those that look through the windows are dimmed, that is, "the eyes see very little ahead of themselves." For old age has eyes that are darkening, and all the strength of the senses diminishes in old people.

4. *And the doors on the street are shut and the sound of the grinding is low.*

That is, the mouth hangs and trembles. For the mouth is the door of the heart, as Matt. 15:19 [6] says: "Out of the heart come, etc." Then the throat closes off the voice so that it becomes thin; this is what it means that the doors are shut. For the two lips are the leaves of the door, or the gate, through which our heart goes out as through an entrance into the street. In old people this entrance is closed so that they cannot sing, shout, or speak; indeed, they can hardly draw a breath.

And one rises up at the voice of a bird, and all the daughters of song are brought low.

That is, not only is it difficult for them to speak, but they also sleep badly; for when the humors have dried up, as happens in old people, the source and cause of sleep is lacking.[7] Sleep derives its nourishment from these humors. Therefore they are aroused by every voice of a bird. Meanwhile the young are snoring securely; they sleep through not only the crowing of the roosters or the barking of the dogs but even the thunder.

All the daughters of song, that is, "both ears." This is a Hebraism, like "the son of help or of light or of darkness," about which we have spoken earlier.[8] In the same way the ears are called *daughters of song*, that is, those that deal with songs or that listen to songs. These daughters of song *are brought low*, they become withered;

---

[6] The original has "Matt. 17."

[7] The "humors" were the four bodily fluids whose state and mixture were thought to determine a person's temperament and general well-being: blood, phlegm, choler, and melancholy.

[8] See p. 166 above.

that is, for old people the ears become heavy and deaf, and they take no pleasure in listening to music.

5. *They are afraid also of what is high, and terrors are in the way.*

That is, an old man goes around with his shoulders and head hunched down. For *what is high* in the body are the head and the shoulders. This height, I say, is afraid, that is, it is bent down. He wants to say: "Old people go around after the manner of those who are afraid wherever they go, because they have their head bowed and their shoulders bent." This is what frightened people usually do.

The almond tree blossoms, that is, "the head becomes gray." More than the other trees, the almond stands with gray flowers. Therefore he takes the metaphor of the old man growing gray from this flowering almond tree.

The grasshopper becomes a burden, that is, "such an old man is like a grasshopper, for his whole body is nothing but skin and bone." His bones stick out, and his body is exhausted. He is nothing but a sort of image of death.

And the caper-plant fails, that is, "desire fails." For this is how I prefer to interpret the Hebrew word.[9] He is not referring to sexual desire, which fails especially in old people, but also to every honest desire, as though he were saying: "An old man cannot enjoy anything pleasant, but is useless for everything." Association and conversation with him is nothing enjoyable, but he is a living corpse. You see, then, that he is speaking here about decrepit and useless old age, not about that which is still useful for accomplishing things.

Because man goes to his eternal home, and the mourners go about the streets.

He inserts a passage which compels us to understand this chapter as one dealing with old age itself. He wants to say: "There is nothing left but that man travel to the home of his eternity, that is, to the grave." For the grave is the home of his eternity or of his world, because he travels there and does not return. Meanwhile we

---

[9] The Septuagint had translated ἡ κάππαρις and was followed by the Vulgate, but Luther took the word to refer to the desire supposedly aroused by this plant.

mourn the man who is being carried to the grave; he is carried to the grave with weeping and lamentation. Fear God, therefore, before you come to old age, because then you will have nothing except that they will carry you out with mourning to the grave.

6. *Before the silver cord is removed and the golden fountains are removed.*

That is, "before eating and drinking cease." These are compared to a silver cord and a round piece of gold, a gold circle or ring. For just as a ring or a circle recurs and always comes around, so also eating and drinking continually recur. They are truly a silver cord, for our life depends completely on them and is sustained by them.

Or the pitcher is broken at the fountain or the wheel broken at the cistern.

That is, "before breath and life cease." Our body is a pitcher which always needs to be repaired. The wheel at the cistern refers to the stomach and the other organs which supply nourishment to the body.

7. *And the dust returns to the earth as it was.*

Solomon is looking at the passage in Gen. 3:19,[10] as though to say: "After death the dust returns to the earth as it was." All of us were dust; therefore in death we return to dust as we were before.

And the spirit returns to God who gave it.

Here, too, he is looking at the passage in Gen. 2:7: "And God breathed into man's nostrils the breath of life." He does not define whither the spirit goes but says that it returns to God from whom it came. For just as we do not know whence God made the spirit, so we do not know either whither it returns.

8. *Vanity of vanities, says the Preacher; all is vanity.*

He concludes the book with the same saying with which he began it. He adds a recommendation of his teaching and an exhortation that we not be led astray by erring and varying doctrines but abide in that which has been prescribed. For this is a great source of misery, that when God has awakened His Word and good teach-

[10] The original has "Gen. 2."

ers, immediately heretics and wicked teachers arise, who divert the people to themselves with some sort of rivalry. Thus it was also the concern of the apostles to keep us in their doctrine. Even sound doctrine and the Word of God are forced to endure the perversity. When God has awakened His Word, right away there are heretics and apes who imitate the Word. Moses established the worship of God and certain ceremonies; immediately the apes followed him and erected idols. That is how it is in the arts too. If someone is a good poet, he is obliged to endure his Zoiluses.[11] If he is a good craftsman, he is followed by these pretenders. Thus all the arts have their imitators, that is, their destroyers. But worst of all is the fact that the crowd follows the foolish ones and prefers them to the genuine artists, as Christ said about them (Matt. 24:5): "They will lead many astray." Solomon is complaining about that here.

9. *Besides being wise, the Preacher also taught the people knowledge, weighing and studying and arranging proverbs with great care.*

That is, there was nothing left for the Preacher except that he was wise and taught correctly, but he did not succeed and did not have a following. He was a diligent man, he investigated how to arrange things, he taught diligently. He established many things in an outstanding and brilliant way, but where are the people who listen to it and accept it? Except for words, nothing follows. For either there are no hearers or the wicked teachers and subverters are the ones who succeed.

10. *The Preacher sought to find pleasing words, and uprightly he wrote words of truth.*

That is, he made an effort to be of service with worthy and salutary words, or, as Paul says (1 Tim. 1:15), "words worthy of full acceptance," and he correctly wrote down the words of truth. He did not wrap his teaching in obscurity, as is usually done by those imitators who neither understand correctly nor teach correctly. For as Aristotle says, the mark of one who knows is that he is able to teach correctly.[12] And when Demosthenes was asked how one

[11] See p. 186, n. 17, below.

[12] Apparently a reference to Aristotle, *Metaphysics*, ch. 2, 982, a 14; see also *Nicomachean Ethics*, VI, 1147.

could speak correctly or well, he replied: "If he did not say anything except what he knew well." [13] For he who understands something well is also able to express it well. This is a commendation of the author, as though he were saying: "He taught clearly and well, so that anyone would be able to understand from his book what to think, what to attempt, what he ought and ought not to do."

11. *The sayings of the wise are like spears, and like nails firmly fixed are the collected sayings which are given by one Shepherd.*

12. *My son, beware of anything beyond these. Of making many books there is no end, and much study is a weariness of the flesh.*

Here he exhorts that we not be led astray by erring and varying doctrines, as though he were saying: "You have an outstanding teacher and instructor; therefore beware of new teachers." For the words of this teacher are goads, or spears; that is, they are planted, set in place. Such are the words of David and the prophets. But the words of the bunglers are like foam on the water.[14] On the basis of this passage I conjecture that in this nation there were some ordained men whose task it was to read through the books and true histories, which they were to collect into the annals of the Hebrews while putting the other books into order. Thus they were to establish the authority of the books and approve those that were worthy of being read. Thus there were many authors who wrote bibles, but out of all these books some were received and approved, which we today call the Bible. Therefore he says: "See to it therefore, my son, that you cling to those books which have been received. But despise the others, because they have been despised by these wise men." For it happens that when one good book is published, ten bad ones are also published, as is happening also to us. But the words of the wise are true and firm, words to which one may and should cling, because they are nails firmly fixed and have authority from the men of the congregation. Other books are not like this.

[13] See also Cicero, *De legibus,* II, 19. 47.
[14] An allusion to Hos. 10:7.

Which are given by one Shepherd.

That is, one king, who is the shepherd, has appointed wise men to acknowledge and approve books. These men, I say, recognized the Holy Spirit in this book and approved it for the people. In this way the Gospels were taken up and approved by the fathers; that is, the fathers themselves recognized the Holy Spirit. But one must not infer from this: "Therefore the church or the fathers are above the Gospel," any more than it is valid to say: "I recognize the true and living God and His Word; therefore I am above God and His Word." Just as one is not superior to a prince whom one acknowledges or to a parent whom one acknowledges, so it is here. These men do not teach this shepherd, but they receive from one shepherd. Thus I also distinguish among books and say: "This epistle is apostolic, this one is not apostolic." [15] This is nothing else than that I give testimony to the truth. Now the exhortation follows:

My son, beware of anything beyond these.

That is, "follow the books which have been approved by those who have the Holy Spirit and who acknowledged them to have been given by one teacher and shepherd."

Of making many books there is no end.

Here he touches on the misfortune of human nature, by which everyone imitates these men and good writers, but with great misfortune and discomfiture. Therefore he wants to say: "You are living in a world where you will find innumerable books with which people try to help others. But you stay with the fixed number and cling to Scripture," as has been said above.

Much study is a weariness of the flesh.

He is saying this not about the personal affliction of the writer himself, but about that of his disciples or hearers. It is as though he were saying: "With their many writings and books these men do nothing but bring affliction upon others, even though they wanted to help them, for their readers are always learning and never arrive at the truth (cf. 2 Tim. 3:7). This, I say, is the fruit of their books, to trouble consciences and to vex people. Therefore one must persist and abide in the dogma of the one teacher. One must cling to this

---

[15] See *Luther's Works*, 35, pp. 395—97.

one or to the few who have the true pattern of doctrine. Beware of the others, who are intent only upon seeming to bring in something new and upon being regarded as more learned than everyone else, as is the case with the Sacramentarians and the like. Therefore James says correctly (James 3:1): "Let not many of you become teachers."

13. *Let us hear the conclusion of the whole matter: Fear God and keep His commandments.*

That is, this is the summary of it all: Fear and worship God and keep Him in view; thus you will observe everything that I have set forth in this book. For unless someone fears God, he will not be able to observe any of these things. He has cited examples of men who lived wisely and excellently, without fear, but who, when evil times came, were nevertheless not used to it [16] and brought affliction upon themselves. But those who fear God are able to despise and make fun of every evil and adversity when it comes, and to give thanks if it does not come.

For this is the duty of all men.

That is, this applies to all men and is useful to them all. In other ways of life it is gain that is sought for, but in this one it is godliness. Paul says the same thing this way (Titus 3:8-9): "These are profitable to men. But avoid stupid prattle."

14. *For God will bring every deed into judgment, on account of every secret thing, whether good or evil.*

That is, everything will finally come under judgment, whether good or evil. Prattlers, slanderers, and fools will eventually be confounded, and their dogmas will not endure. So Zoilus was finally thrown down alive from a rock, but Homer still remains the greatest of poets, regardless of all the Zioluses and those who are even worse.[17] In this way all good authors, especially in sacred doctrine, have by the plan of God or the power of God persevered until now.

[16] We have accepted the suggestion of the St. Louis Edition about the meaning of *insolescunt*.

[17] Zoilus was a Cynic of the fourth century B. C., whose writings against Homer became proverbial for their bitterness.

On account of every secret thing, that is, "on account of hypocrisy." For those apes put on a good appearance both in life and in doctrine. Thus Ps. 26:4 says: "I do not sit with dissemblers"; Christ calls them "hypocrites" (Matt. 23:13-29); and Paul says (2 Tim. 3:5): "Holding the form of religion." Therefore God will judge every work, so that what remains is genuine and the pretense under which they had hidden the work is removed. He is not speaking about the Last Judgment, however, but, as is usual in Scripture, about any judgments, whether those by which heretics are judged and punished or those by which other wicked men are judged. They all have their judgment and their time appointed by God which they are compelled to undergo. Thus the pope is being led to judgment today and has almost been judged. Thus also Arius and the other heretics were led to judgment, and the Lord revealed their shame, as Peter says (cf. 1 Peter 2:12), "in the time of investigation." [18]

[18] This account of the death of Arius was derived from Athanasius, Epistle LIV, *Patrologia, Series Graeca,* XXV, 686, although Luther knew it from medieval legends rather than directly from Athanasius.

LECTURES ON THE SONG OF SOLOMON

A Brief but Altogether Lucid
Commentary on the Song of Songs
by Dr. Martin Luther

Translated by
IAN SIGGINS

DR. MARTIN LUTHER'S PREFACE TO THE SONG OF SONGS

MANY commentators have produced all manner of interpretations of this song of King Solomon's—and they have been both immature and strange.[1] But to get at the simplest sense and the real character of this book, I think it is a song in which Solomon honors God with his praises; he gives Him thanks for his divinely established and confirmed kingdom and government; he prays for the preservation and extension of this his kingdom, and at the same time he encourages the inhabitants and citizens of his realm to be of good cheer in their trials and adversities and to trust in God, who is always ready to defend and rescue those who call upon Him.

Moses did the same in Ex. 15. He composed his song about the work being performed at that moment in the Red Sea; and all the songs found in Holy Scripture deal with the stories of their own times. Of this sort are the song of Deborah in Judg. 5, the song of Hannah in 1 Sam. 2, and a good many others, including the majority of the psalms, with the exception of those which contain prophecies about Christ. Doubtless, therefore, Solomon, too, wrote his song about his own kingdom and government, which by the goodness of God he administered in the finest, happiest peace and the highest tranquillity. All this will become clear from the text itself too.

Moreover, since every kingdom, principality, or state which has the Word and true worship of God is forced to sustain many afflictions—to be a laughingstock and abomination to the whole world, to dwell in the midst of enemies, and every single hour to await death like a sheep bound for the slaughter, such a kingdom or state is deservedly called "the people of God" and has every right to place this song, and Solomon's state, before itself as an example, to praise God in the same manner, to glory and rejoice in God, and to proclaim and marvel at His divine mercy and power, by which

---

[1] One medievalist, Jean Leclercq, has called the Song of Solomon "the book which was most read and most frequently commented in the medieval cloister." *The Love of Learning and the Desire for God* (New York, 1962), p. 90.

He protects His own against the snares of the devil and the tyranny of the world.

We use the psalms of David and the writings of the prophets in this way as examples, even though we are not David or the prophets, but because we have the same blessings in common with them — the same Word, Spirit, faith, and blessedness — and because we sustain the same dangers and afflictions on account of God's Word. So we rightly take over their voices and their language for ourselves, praising and singing just as they praised and sang. Thus any state in which there is the church and a godly prince can use this song of Solomon's just as if it had been composed about its own government and state.

And so from this Song of Songs, which Solomon sang about only his own state, there springs as it were a common song for all states which are "the people of God," that is, which possess the Word of God and worship reverently, which acknowledge and truly believe that the power of governments is established and ordained by God and that through this power God preserves peace, justice, and discipline, punishes the guilty, defends the innocent, etc. They praise and proclaim God with thanksgiving for these great benefits.

Again, godly governments and states place no hope or trust at all in riches, power, wisdom, or other human defenses that are neither stable nor lasting, but they console, admonish, and arouse themselves to flee for refuge to God in all their afflictions and dangers and to trust in Him as their true and only Helper and Preserver, who never deserts His people when they suffer persecution for the sake of His name and Word. For it is certainly the case that a people which is zealous in godliness and loves the Word is always exposed to many evils with which it is assaulted by the devil and the world.

This is why this poem is called the Song of Songs, since it deals with matters of the loftiest and greatest kind, namely, with the divinely ordained governments, or with the people of God. It does not treat a story of an individual, as other songs in Holy Scripture do, but an entire permanent kingdom, or people, in which God untiringly performs a host of staggering miracles and displays His power by preserving and defending it against all the assaults of the devil and the world.

What is more, he does not sing of these exalted matters in the common words that people ordinarily use, but he illustrates and adorns his theme with lofty and figurative words to such an extent that when the crowd hears them, it supposes that the subject treated is something very different. For this is the custom with kings and princes: they compose and sing amatory ballads which the crowd takes to be songs about a bride or a sweetheart, when in fact they portray the condition of their state and people with their songs. This is precisely what "Teuerdank" has done in joining "Ehrenreich" to Maximilian as his bride.[2] Or if they speak about hunting, they want to signify by this language that the enemy has been routed and put to flight and that they have gained the victory, as when they say, "The wild boar is speared, the savage beast is taken," and other things of the same sort.[3]

Solomon proceeds in just this fashion in this song of his. He uses magnificent words—words that are worthy of so great a king—in describing his concerns. He makes God the bridegroom and his people the bride, and in this mode he sings of how much God loves that people, how many and how rich are the gifts He lavishes and heaps upon it, and finally how He embraces and cherishes the same people with a goodness and mercy with which no bridegroom has ever embraced or cherished his bride. And thus Solomon begins by speaking in the person of the whole people as the bride of God: "He is kissing me."

[2] *The Dangers and Adventures of the Famous Hero and Knight Sir Teuerdank* was an allegorical poem by Emperor Maximilian I, recounting his own exploits. The emperor is the knight Teuerdank ("Precious Reward" or "Lofty Thinker"), who woos and wins Lady Ehrenreich ("Honored Realm" or "Rich in Honor"), representing Mary of Burgundy. This vain and bombastic allegory was first printed privately at Nuremberg in 1517 and published at Augsburg in 1519.

[3] Cf. *Luther's Works*, 4, pp. 380—83.

DR. MARTIN LUTHER'S BRIEF BUT ALTOGETHER LUCID EXPOSITION OF THE SONG OF SONGS

We take up this book for exposition not from any fondness for display of erudition, like some who lavish every effort upon the obscure books because, of course, on the one hand it provokes praise for their cleverness to have dared address subjects which others flee on account of their obscurity and on the other hand because in the obscure books each of them is free to make divinations and to indulge in speculations or private musings; rather, we take it up in order that after the absurd opinions which have so far obscured this little book have been rejected, we may demonstrate another, more suitable view, useful for life and for a right appreciation of the good gifts of God.

For we know that the purpose of the whole Scripture is this: to teach, reprove, correct, and train in righteousness, so that the man of God may be perfect for every good work, as Paul says in 2 Tim. 3:16-17. Those who fail to observe this purpose, even if they create the impression of erudition among the unlettered by their divinations, nevertheless are ignorant of the true essence of Scripture. Their learning is not unlike bodies infected with dropsy — inflated by inordinate swelling, they give an appearance of vigor, but the swelling is all corrupt and noxious. In the course of this exposition, therefore, we shall direct our reflections to the end that this book, too, may instruct us with doctrine useful for life, and secondly, with consolations.

For we shall never agree with those who think it is a love song about the daughter of Pharaoh beloved by Solomon.[4] Nor does it satisfy us to expound it of the union of God and the synagog,[5] or like the tropologists, of the faithful soul.[6] For what fruit, I ask,

---

[4] This was the interpretation put on the Song of Solomon by Theodore of Mopsuestia.

[5] This was an interpretation favored by most Jewish commentators on the Song of Solomon.

[6] Beginning with Origen, most Christian commentators, both Greek and Latin, had followed this interpretation.

can be gathered from these opinions? So even if this book, amidst all the variety of Scripture, has had its place in the shadows until now, yet by pursuing a new path, we shall not depart from the substance of the thought even if we may perhaps err here and there in details. Accordingly, my view is as follows.

There are three books of Solomon in Holy Scripture. The first, Proverbs, deals mostly with the home and sets forth general precepts for behavior in this life. It does so not as the philosophers of the Gentiles do, but it is diffused throughout with that weightier doctrine of faith and the fear of God, which the Gentiles did not perceive.

The second, Ecclesiastes, is a political book, which gives instruction not only to all in general but especially to the magistrate: namely, that the man who governs other men should himself fear God, perform with vigor the tasks that lie before him and not allow himself to be so discouraged either by the difficulty of the task or by the ingratitude of men that he fails to perform his office.

The third is the book before us, which is entitled "Song of Songs." It rightly belongs with Ecclesiastes, since it is an encomium of the political order, which in Solomon's day flourished in sublime peace. For as those who wrote songs in Holy Scripture wrote them about their own deeds, so in Solomon this poem commends his own government to us and composes a sort of encomium of peace and of the present state of the realm. In it he gives thanks to God for that highest blessing, external peace. He does it as an example for other men, so that they too may learn to give thanks to God in this way, to acknowledge His highest benefits, and to pray for correction should anything reprehensible befall the realm.

CHAPTER ONE

1. *The Song of Songs.*

THE book derives its title either from the subject matter, because it deals with the greatest of all human works, namely, government; or else from the style, because it is written in the fashion of grand oratory. For the poem is entirely figurative, and figures of speech produce grand oratory.

2. *He kisses me.*

He speaks according to the custom of the people of that day. Among us kisses are held in less esteem. However, kisses are signs of love and favor. And so he says *The Lord kisses me*, that is, "He shows favor to this government, He kisses it, He honors it with all manner of blessings and love."

Now, to declare that a realm which to outward appearance was suffering all sorts of afflictions is God's own concern, that it is loved and cherished by God, is certainly the voice of faith. To outward appearance it is not obvious that He kisses the synagog, but rather that He wounds it and hates it. But he adds:

With the kisses of His mouth!

This means that God honors this people with His Word. And certainly this is the treasure which deserves to be extolled first in the political realm, for without it government cannot endure. Paul, too, extols God's gift to this people in Rom. 3:2: "The Jews are entrusted with the oracles of God." Similarly Ps. 147:19 says: "He declares His Word to Jacob, etc." He did not do so to every nation. For it is the Word which distinguishes the godly from the ungodly. It is also through the Word's agency that we come to regard everything we possess either in the domestic or the political realm to be gifts of God and sheer signs of the divine will and favor towards us. Granted that everyone else abounds in all good things, they nevertheless do not understand them to be the gifts of God and therefore cannot avoid abusing them to their own destruction.

For Your breasts are more delightful than wine.

Breasts refer to doctrine, by which souls are fed so that "the man of God may be perfect for every good work" (2 Tim. 3:17). He compares doctrine with wine, of which Holy Scripture declares that it makes the heart glad (Ps. 104:15). Wine is thus metaphorically used for all the world's delights and gratifications.

And this is, so to speak, the voice of an outstanding faith, which declares, "I prefer Your Word to all the pleasures of the world." For we must refer everything to the Word.

3. *For Your name is oil poured out.*

These are very meaningful figures and symbols. *Your name*, that is, "the knowledge of You," is like oil, since it yields a pleasing aroma and is spread abroad through the Word. And this blessing is not hidden away in a corner but is published throughout my whole realm, and it spreads its aroma also to neighboring peoples, like an ointment that is poured out.

So that Your best anointing oils are fragrant.

That is, "where Your Word is, there Your blessings are recognized." For the godly know through the Word that they enjoy the gifts of God and abound in them. But if these are taken away, they know that they are being tried by God, and they bear their cross patiently.

Therefore the maidens love You.

It is a Hebraism that cities are called "mothers" and "daughters." [1] Here he calls Jerusalem a maiden. So the meaning is this: "Through the agency of Your Word it comes about that those who are the godly men on every hand in my kingdom are attracted by these great blessings, set their affections on You, and love You."

So far he has been commending his government for the special reason that it possesses the Word of God. It is therefore an ungodly thing that the external Word is nowadays despised by many who through diabolical revelation boast of the Spirit apart from the oral Word.[2] And yet they know neither what the Spirit nor what the Word really is!

[1] Luther seems to be thinking of such passages as Jer. 50:12.

[2] Cf. *Luther's Works*, 40, pp. 146—49.

4. Draw me after You.

To know and to be able to do are two different things. When we therefore possess the Word, we are not immediately able to follow it, but our flesh, the world, and Satan draw us away from the Word again. Now, therefore, he adds this prayer: "You have given us Your Word, and I thank You for it. Now grant that we may also perform what the Word teaches and follow it in our lives."

No manner of life is without its special burden. Marry a wife: immediately you will discover a flood of ills! You will find things which displease you in your wife and in your children, and the care of the stomach will occupy you. Similarly those who are in government experience a host of evils, for Satan is nowhere inactive. Prayer, then, is all that remains; by prayer let us overcome the various hazards and rocks on which we run aground. For God allows us to be tested by such ills so that the glory of the Word may be demonstrated and the divine power magnified in our weakness. Otherwise there would be no way to demonstrate His glory and mercy.

We shall make haste.

This is emphatic. He does not say "we shall walk" but "we shall run." "If You breathe Your Spirit upon me, then I shall be glad to perform the task of prince, teacher, husband, pupil, etc. Unless You inspire, no one will accomplish anything, no matter how great his zeal and care, especially not in government." Thus we see the most flourishing states ruined rather than sustained by the wisdom of the greatest men.

The King has brought me into His chambers.

He alludes to the way of a groom and his bride and figuratively shows that prayer is heard, for he is picturing God's highest goodwill toward us. "God," he says, "consoles me in the evils I experience in government and reveals Himself to be willing and favorable — just as when a groom brings his bride into his chamber, he certainly does not do so from hatred of the bride!"

In this way he represents that sublime affection which God holds toward those who pray, in that He hears, consoles, cherishes, and enriches them with His own gifts and powers so that each may be able to execute his office more fitly.

We will now exult and rejoice in You;

Thanksgiving follows heeded prayer. "Now I shall exult because You do not forsake me but receive me in Your mercies."

His words *in You* are emphatic. It is as if he were saying: "Outside Your solace and aid one experiences nothing but toils, afflictions, unendurable burdens, griefs, lamentations, etc."

We will recall Your breasts more than wine.

This is part of his thanksgiving, that is: "We shall be grateful, we shall remember Your remembrance, how You love us, seeing that You give us Your breasts." For "to recall" means to preach, to praise, to give thanks. As before, he calls all physical and fleshly joys "wine."

The upright love You.

Twisted men, bent on their own advantage, want to live a life in which they suffer no inconveniences. But if inconveniences do befall them, they are offended and complain with utter impatience.

By contrast, when the upright suffer difficulties and inconveniences, they bear them patiently and pray. Accordingly, when they have been delivered, they acknowledge God's sheer goodwill and love towards them, and so they love God the more fervently.

Next, therefore, Solomon addresses his discourse to the instruction of such crooked men, so that they, too, may learn to triumph over present evils by the same means, namely, by endurance and prayer. For the normal response of those who have been tested and whose prayers have been answered is to teach and instruct others also, as Ps. 116:10 testifies: "I have believed, therefore have I spoken."

ABOUT THE COURSE AND ORDER OF THE BOOK AS A WHOLE

Now, this is the order and course of this song, that it alternates consolations, complaints, prayers, and exhortations. For just as events occur in any legally established state—indeed, just as this life of ours is lived—so Solomon proceeds in this book. He lays out a sort of image of the state and the common life in which by turns consolation follows affliction and new affliction follows consolation as the night the day. Thus in public affairs new storms, new disturbances, and alarms arise constantly, and when they are dispersed, the ensuing period of quiet does not prevail longer, but straightway other tumults and calamities follow. Those who are experienced in government will testify to this state of affairs.

For instance, a rebellion of the people beset David at first. Scarcely had that disaster been put to rights when lo and behold, another ensued, the graver for its being less expected. His most beloved son, Absalom, takes up hostile arms against his father. He is not satisfied with banishing his father from the realm; he violates the royal concubines and also his father's wives. Thus government is like dangerous navigation on a stormy sea.

Consequently Solomon frequently repeats his consolations and exhortations to give encouragement to the hearts of rulers, so that they do not retreat or despair, discouraged by their difficulties, but may learn to lift themselves up by prayer in this manner and to hope for deliverance. And when deliverance has come about, the soul must in this way be prepared again not to succumb to subsequent vicissitudes. For just as valleys follow mountain ridges and the day follows the night, so deliverance follows affliction in constant interchange, and fresh disaster again follows deliverance. Anyone who has observed this rule will understand a good part of this book. And if someone wants to add some allegories later, it takes no effort to invent them!

5. *I am very dark, but comely, O daughters of Jerusalem.*

I have suggested earlier that after his thanksgiving he begins an address.

O daughters of Jerusalem, that is, "You states and adjoining towns, do not be scandalized if everything here is not flourishing."

I am very dark. "Although I am a state founded by God and adorned with the Word of God, yet I seem to be most wretched in appearance, there is no success, and there are very few who desire and maintain public peace. I seem to be not a state but some sort of rabble of seditious men. Do not be offended by this appearance. Turn your attention not to my blackness, but to the kiss which God offers me, and then you will see that I am comely and lovable. For although outwardly I suffer all manner of vexation, yet I am desirable on account of the Word and faith."

The church, too, is similarly undesirable in appearance. It

seems to be lacerated and wretchedly afflicted and exposed to the taunts of all men. But this is our consolation: that our salvation is anchored in the Word and faith, not in outward appearance.

> *Like the tents of Kedar and like the tents of Solomon.*

The tents of Kedar, that is, of the Arabs, are cheap and ugly. By contrast, *the tents of Solomon* are regal and very beautiful.

For this reason I consider that the sentence should be divided as follows: *I am very dark . . . like the tents of Kedar.* "I seem to be like some crowd of Arabs who have no government. For there are many in my people who do not believe the Word. There are many, too, who do not obey the government. It looks more like a jumble of men than a well-ordered state." But nonetheless, *I am comely . . . like the tents of Solomon.* When one takes the inward aspect into account, one will nevertheless discover in that state many godly men who do obey and are good and faithful members of the state, etc.

6. *Do not gaze at me because I am swarthy.*

He continues to exhort in the face of scandals. He warns: "Do not stare at the part of me in which I am ugly, but fix your eyes on my beauty and grace, consider my virtues, not my vices."

Moreover, the man who has learned this lesson should discover in the long run that he has learned and known the greatest art of all. For it is inbred in us that we are more disturbed by some single vice than by all the remaining virtues. Thus today those who are adjudged the wisest men in the world are offended by the many evils, which they undeservedly impute to the Gospel. Yet the magnitude of the blessings we have received from the Gospel, both privately in men's hearts and consciences and publicly in state and household, is appreciated by no one or by very few. For before the revelation of the Gospel, what station of life was there, I ask, that men could assess correctly? Not husband, not wife, not children, not magistrates, not citizens, not menservants, not maidservants were sure that they were established in a way of life that was approved by God. So they all took refuge in the works of the monks.

Similarly, before the light of the Gospel was given, was the use of the arts rightly displayed or recognized? This is clear in the instruction of the young. The proper use of grammar, dialectic, or rhetoric was simply not apparent, so far removed was the possibility of their being taught correctly. If these things happened in the trivial arts, how much more in the weightier arts! The case of theology speaks for itself. Even if the professors of law did have some sort of knowledge of their discipline and its use, yet the deadliest thing of all was that very few of them believed they were in a station of life approved by God. The same could be said of the physicians.

Formerly no one took any notice of these terrible afflictions. Now utterly ungrateful men, forgetting the blessings now present, notice only the bad things. Our inability to enjoy the sight of these great blessings is the just desert of such sheer ingratitude, as it is written (Is. 26:10): "The ungodly will not see the glory of God." But the godly both see the abundant gifts of God and are grateful for them.

Moreover, this rule ought to be observed most diligently in private life as well: if a man banishes the blackness from his eyes, he will see a world full of God's mercy. Thus we read in Ps. 107:43: "Who is wise and will heed these things and understand the mercies of the Lord?" So in everyday human converse you will discover that no man is so bad that he does not possess innumerably many endowments.

The heart, therefore, should be trained to admire the virtues in individual people rather than to be offended by their vices, if any. If someone has vices, the same man has his virtues too—he must, for he cannot abuse all the capacities which he has received from nature! This argument will certainly help to preserve peace of heart. For if you direct your gaze only on the vices and the calamities which occur every day, the heart is necessarily tempted by impatience and hatred. Accordingly, since those evils and those troubles cannot be changed, change yourself and adopt a different outlook; keep your heart free and ignore the distresses at hand. As that excellent saying, which we have often used in Ecclesiastes, advises: "Let it go as it is going, since it wants to go as it is going." [3] But the present benefits and blessings are so numerous and so great that the godly man may easily forget the evils in comparison with them.

[3] See p. 27, n. 15; p. 119, n. 24, above.

Because the sun has scorched me.

The sun signifies tribulation, as Christ indicates in the parable of the seed scorched by the sun (Matt. 13:6). Similarly we read in Ps. 121:6: "The sun shall not smite you by day, nor the moon by night."

Thus he is saying: Lest you be scandalized by any blackness whatsoever, I ask you now not to regard me as responsible for it. It is the sun that has blackened me. In other words, wherever the divine Word and ordinance are found, wherever there is some form of government, there the sun will come and inflict blackness. That is, the devil rises in opposition so that that Word or that state will appear on the verge of total failure. But do not be perturbed, Satan will not prevail.

My mother's sons were angry with me.

It is inevitable in the state not only that there are many tribulations but also that the children rage against their mother, that is, against the state, contrary to the mandate and Word of God. The person who holds governmental authority therefore should be aware that he has been set over seditious citizens, who require only a suitable occasion to stir up sedition, with the result that the very people who ought to have provided help in the administration have a single eye towards overturning and disrupting it. David found this out, and so did the Romans; and I believe that this is the special complaint of all godly princes today.

They made me keeper of the vineyards; but my own vineyard I have not kept!

Here is a grievous lament. He admits that he has the right, power, and title of king; but, he says, the administration is in the hands of others. The vineyard is the people. "I have been set over this people as king and prince. What do I do?" *My own vineyard I have not kept!*

He thus openly confesses that it is impossible to maintain the state by human judgment but that all human wisdom falls far short of what would suffice to sustain so great a task. The reason is obvious: however many good, pious, and wise princes there may be, they could still not alleviate all vices. The malice of the world is so great! And the very men who are in the vineyard oppose and resist and refuse to be ruled.

Then what is to be done? Must one despair of the state on account of such prodigious difficulties and troubles? No, but as far as possible this blackness should be banished from sight, and the mind should busy itself with meditation on the blessings of God, which He both promises in His Word and also displays. Next, one should follow the example of this king in taking refuge in prayer.

7. *Tell me, You whom my soul loves.*

This is a prayer in which he confesses that he lacks the wisdom and strength for administering the state well. In this vein Duke Frederick of Saxony told Staupitz that he knew less and less how to administer his duchy and yet that there was no one to whom he could safely entrust any matter.[4] Similarly Cicero, after the civil war, uttered this cry brimming with indignation and despair: "Oh! that I should have been reputed wise in vain!"[5] Therefore, in accord with Solomon's example, godly princes should pray and say: "O God, Creator and Governor of all, whom my soul loves, show me how the vineyard committed to me is to be tended, etc."

Where You pasture Your flock, where You rest at noon.

Forsaken by his own wisdom and strength, he yearns for God as the Colleague of his reign. "Show me where I may find You, so that You may administer the state together with me. In government I stray as if in night and black fog; You rest at noon. O that I were permitted thus to reign 'at noon,' that is, in complete peace!"

For why should I be like one who is veiled beside the flocks of Your companions?

Veiling was a sign of mourning, as a covered head was among the Romans.[6] So he is praying: "Rescue me from these afflictions. Reduce my cares by Your help, and the things which weary and disgust me by Your presence."

---

[4] See p. 57 above.

[5] See p. 38 above.

[6] Luther is referring to the *lugubria,* or mourning garments, mentioned in such passages as Ovid, *Metamorphoses,* XI, 669.

"Give me heart so that I shall not despair nor succumb to such difficulties. And do this *beside the flocks of Your companions.* I am in a place of eminence amidst the flock of Your companions. They are those who to this day are ruled by Your Word and Spirit. For their sake, I ask, grant success and tranquillity." In this manner he reverts to prayer and to the Word in his great difficulties.

8. *If you do not know, O fairest among women.*

We have heard the lament in which the magistrate complains of the difficulty of administering the state, since even the mother's daughters are hostile. He therefore now portrays the person of the bridegroom consoling those who experience such enormous difficulties and troubles. It is as if he were saying: "You complain about your state, even though there is not a single state in the whole world which can be compared with yours, so does it overflow with all God's highest endowments.

"You have the Word of God, the prophets, saintly judges, saintly kings; do you not recognize this your beauty and fairness?"

But this is the way it goes, in temptation we forget all His gifts because we are intent upon our immediate sorrow or emotion. For temptation swallows everything up, with the result that you see, feel, think, and expect nothing but evil. Even the most learned in Holy Writ, when they are tempted, need someone who will bring them consolation from Holy Writ. So it is necessary that in temptation we should be reminded of the things which have been given us, as Paul says in 1 Cor. 2.[7] Now he adds still further advice.

Follow in the tracks of the flock, and go to pasture with your kids beside the shepherds' tents.

"I can give you no other advice than that you go out and pasture your own sheep, that you exercise your own administrative role, unconcerned about the fact that you also have goats in your flock, that is,[8] evil, shameless, disobedient, seditious citizens. Do not let evil men make you anxious, for pastures exist for the sake of the sheep, and the state is established principally for the sake of good men."

---

[7] The original has "1 Cor. 2," perhaps referring to verse 12 of that chapter or, as the Weimar editors suggest, to 1 Cor. 1:4.

[8] The Weimar text has *i.*, but we have read *i. e.*

But what does He mean when He specifies *in the tracks of the flock?* No doubt He means that he should pay special attention to the example of his forefathers, the saintly judges, kings, and prophets, etc., who were the flock of God, with the result that when he sees that they, too, underwent various trials, he will endure the present disruptions with greater equanimity. David consoles himself this way in Ps. 77:11: "I will call to mind the deeds of the Lord; yea, I will remember Thy wonders of old."

Thus there is no consolation, no solace against evils except the Word of God. "For whatever was written in former days" (Paul says in Rom. 15:4) "was written for our instruction, that by steadfastness and by the encouragement of the Scriptures we might have hope." Christ nailed to the cross, John beheaded, Moses at death's door when his own people wanted to stone him, etc. — they console us so that we bear more calmly the world's outrageous ingratitude, so that we fulfill our office with singleness of purpose and are unconcerned about the goats.

9. *I have compared you, My love, to My cavalry of Pharaoh's chariots.*

This is an amplification of the foregoing consolation. But since there are some periods of war and others of peace, he also divides this amplification into two sections.

This first section should be addressed to a period of affliction and the cross. In tribulation it seems to you that you have been abandoned and defeated. But I have compared you to My cavalry; that is, in My sight you are like a victorious cohort which is equipped to do battle, as are the chariots of Pharaoh, the mightiest of all kings. I think that mention is made of Pharaoh because of all those known to the Jews he was the most powerful king.

This is a consolation of faith, a consolation which is a matter neither of experience nor of sight, for in Solomon's eyes his government is like a worm. Why? Because burdened and disturbed by evils and by its awareness of these evils, it deserts the Word and ignores all of its gifts. But if you look to the Word, all these assertions are perfect truth. It is therefore a most ample promise that God calls the government His friend; but it is not obvious. In appearance it seems rather as if God has deserted it.

10. *Your cheeks are comely like earrings, and your neck like strings of jewels.*

This is the second section of the amplification, dealing with the time of peace. For then the Word of God, which is lost or barely retained in tribulation, is present with us, then we are delighted by the gifts of the Spirit, which in the time of the cross are completely obliterated by our awareness of evils.

We translate *earrings* because these ornaments are divided from each other and arranged in beautiful array. The Hebrew word elsewhere means "lines," or "rows." Moreover, *earrings* and "necklaces" are gifts of the Holy Spirit in the Word. They adorn our neck; that is, the Word is in public use, it is taught, read, heard, and the abundance of the divine promises is possessed everywhere.

11. *We will make you ornaments of gold, studded with silver.*

Ornaments of gold is the same word which we before translated "earrings." But here it denotes the growth of the ornamentation. It is as if He were saying: "We shall augment this adornment and make even golden ornaments for you. The Word will grow more abundant for you if you make use of it."

For the Word is the sort of treasure which grows with handling and distribution but rots with hoarding. It has to be in constant use, for the more it is taught, heard, and learned, the more readily and the more clearly it is understood.

Those ornaments will not be of gold alone, but they will be set off by studs of silver, or vermiculated; that is, the use of the Word is manifold and varied.

In this manner he tells us that as he exercises himself in God's Word and in the examples set forth in the Word, the result is that he finds he has been taught equanimity [9] and is not anxious about the goats that are in his flock. The person who has faith sees and experiences these things. To the person who does not believe, such rich consolations are a game and a joke.

12. *The King is still on His couch.*

The effect of the words of comfort is that that person in government believes the consolation, and this is the unique strength of faith. For the outcome usually is that the heart, conquered by

---

[9] The Weimar text has *aequitatum*, but we have read *aequitatem*.

calamity and present grief, is unable to accept the Word, which promises things so different from experience. Yet faith, however afflicted, remains attentive to the Word and is built up by the Word.

So in this passage he says *The King is still on His couch.* It is as if he were saying: "In my temptation I felt that God had withdrawn very far from me. Therefore I pleaded that He would show me where He pastured His flock. But He has not gone away; He is at hand and reclines at His feast, that is, He cares for me, loves me, protects me, preserves me. He is not planning how to destroy, afflict, or torture me, as I used to feel in my temptation."

My nard gave forth its fragrance.

"My prayer was carried to Him when approach was easy and He still reclined at the feast. Therefore it pleased and delighted Him, and it was heard."

13. *My Beloved is to me a bag of myrrh that lies between my breasts.*

Now he adds his commendation of the comfort and enlarges on the consolation with images of sweetness. "God is not far away, but He dwells in the midst of our life and is like a bag of myrrh in my bosom and in my embraces. That is, He cares for me, protects and comforts me, etc. In short, His feeling for me is like that of a bridegroom for his bride."

It is to be noted, however, that these realities are not palpable. Rather, this consolation remains in the figure of a fragrance. These things are perceived only by smell, in order to express the mystery of faith, namely, that God dwells among His people through a fragrance, that is, through His Word and His name. The faith must needs be great which can believe these things regarding God, that He is between the breasts, that is, that He is very near and close to us, is not angry, etc.

14. *My Beloved is to me a cluster of balsam in the vineyards of Engedi.*

This is a figurative commendation of the consoling discovery that God loves, cherishes, protects, etc., as above.

I think *cluster of Copher* is balsam, and I think so because he adds the words *in the vineyards of Engedi*, which is a city in the tribe of Judah by the Dead Sea, where there are balsam gardens.[10] Accordingly, it is my opinion that the tree was called *Copher* in antiquity, that more recently, however, the name "balsam" has been given it for its value, because balsam is far superior to all other ointments.

15. *Behold, you are beautiful, my love; behold, you are beautiful.*

After trial, when the consolation of the Word has taken hold of the heart, we not only feel that God loves and cherishes us, but we also feel that we please God, that we delight God, and that God takes care of us. In this way conscience and the Spirit give mutual testimony. Conscience feels that it pleases God, and so it praises God. The Holy Spirit approves this faith and in turn commends us. That is what you see expressed by this passage.

Your eyes are the eyes of doves.

The dove has a reputation for simplicity. Accordingly, he is commending the simplicity of faith, because it does not change its mind in tribulation as those do who are without the Word, whose eyes are not dovelike but harlotlike. Their eyes are turned now to this attitude, now to that. We constantly observe this in the enemies of the Gospel. But faith persists in one and the same simple regard for the promises of God and retains a strong hope for its own well-being in the most extreme dangers.

16. *Behold, you, too, are beautiful, my beloved, truly lovely.*

Here is abundance of consolation. The Holy Spirit bears witness in the heart so that we are convinced we are pleasing and beautiful to God. The result therefore is that we in turn also confess that God is beautiful; that is, that He delights us, etc. However, this beauty is not obvious in time of tribulation.

Our couch is green;

17. *the beams of our house are cedar, our rafters are pine.*

All these features are allegorical, and by them he signifies the happiness which he has drawn from consolation. In every state it

[10] See p. 107, n. 6, and p. 181, n. 9, above.

is the case that at every possible danger the government seems to threaten to fall into destruction and ruin.

This is the mood Solomon expresses here. It is as if he were saying: "Formerly I used to think that the whole realm was on the brink of being overthrown. It seemed to be not a kingdom or a state at all but some ancient edifice which would be toppled by the slightest blast of the winds. But now, after the consolation I have received, I see that my government is as firmly established as a house built of cedar, of a material that does not crumble but endures for the longest time. I see also that it is adorned like a bed bedecked with flowers." Just as in temptation no end of trial is in sight, so those who believe the consolation foresee perpetual joy. As he says in Ps. 30:6: "I said in my prosperity, 'I shall never be moved.'"

CHAPTER TWO

THE first chapter contained a thanksgiving for the establishment and the extraordinary endowment of the kingdom. Secondly, it contained a consolation for the magistrate to use during civil dangers and disruptions, even though he sees no success anywhere but sees instead that his best plans sometimes suffer the worst collapse. Solomon urges us to get away from it all and look at the examples of the fathers, not paying attention only to the evils by which we are beset but considering also our blessings, with which we have been honored by God, etc.

In this second chapter there follows a description of another sort of trial sustained by this people over and above their domestic evils—the exceedingly bitter hatred of the world. Just as he taught in chapter one that we should be the sort of men who overcome domestic upheavals, so here he teaches how the godly magistrate ought to protect himself against the hatred of the world.

1. *I am a rose of the field, a lily of the valleys.*

This is a complaint in which he describes the danger. He does so by employing a contrast. Flowers that are nurtured inside walls and enclosures are safe from harm from both man and beast. But we, he says, are like a rose in an open field—anyone has access to it. I do not deny that I am a flower, I acknowledge the gift of the state which God has given me—but oh, that this flower had a hedge around it! For who could count all the dangers to which we are exposed in the midst of the nations, like those who dwell in an open field?

In this light we can call the magistrate "a flower of the field" on account of the innumerable dangers to which he is exposed.

He names the flower which grows on a lower level the *lily of the valleys*, perhaps to distinguish between the higher and lower magistrates. For the fact that there are various species of flowers can also be applied to the diversity of gifts in a sound state. The state itself has the consolation that it is a rose. However, even if it appears from the world's point of view to lack a hedge and stand unprotected, yet so long as it retains the Word and worship of God, it is surrounded and hedged about by the fiery chariots which Elisha showed his servant (2 Kings 6:17). Daniel, too, demonstrates that the angels are the guardians of the state. But only the faithful discern these protections.

2. *As a lily among brambles, so is my love among maidens.*

Here there is a change of person, a usage perfectly familiar to the Hebrews. For the passage above is spoken in the person of the people. Now it is the Lord who speaks. It is as if He were saying: "You are right when you say you are a flower of the field, for you certainly are a flower to Me, even if you seem to be an unprotected flower. But listen to something more: you are a flower among brambles. For I so judge you to be a flower that I judge the rest of the states, all the other realms, to be nothing but brambles, which are raised only to be ready for the flames."

If we understand this section in this fashion, consolation is fittingly joined to the complaint. But it is a consolation only for faith. For if you follow the appearances, the realms of the Gentiles seem to be the most beautiful roses, not brambles, in that they are calm and prosperous, adorned with wealth and splendid victories. By contrast, the state in which the church exists seems to be neglected in God's eyes like brambles, in that it suffers all sorts of pressures. By faith, therefore, we must conclude according to this declaration of God, even though the contrary appears to be the case: other nations are brambles, but this people, however much oppressed before the world, is a rose.

Some have interpreted this verse as not a consolation to the preceding complaint but a confirmation of it: "Not only are you a flower of the field, but you are like a rose among brambles which is pricked [1] on every side to keep it from coming up." But I prefer to take it as consolation.

By a common figure of speech he calls the neighboring cities and peoples of the Gentiles *maidens.*

3. *As an apple tree among the trees of the wood, so is my Beloved.*

These words are spoken in the person of the people, for the

---

[1] The Weimar text has *pingitur*, but it seems preferable to follow the Erlangen text and read *pungitur*.

whole book is as it were a conversation between God and His people, or between conscience and the Word.

The meaning is this: "God, just as Thou dost hold me to be Thine only rose, so I in turn want to embrace, worship, and fear no God but Thee. For even if I see many imposing trees, yet it is only the Apple Tree that delights me." He calls God Apple Tree principally because this tree, among all fruit-bearing trees, has the highest praise.

It is very fitting, then, that God and His people should answer each other in these words. To God a pious people is a rose; to Him we resemble flowers when we preach, pray, and confess. He on His part is a fruitful apple tree to His people; from it His people are fed and enjoy every favor. Whatever other gods may be worshiped or fabricated by men, they are like sterile branches which are fit not for food but for the fire. But it is God's part to provide, feed, defend, govern, pardon, and at length to save.

Among young men.[2]

Interpret this simply as "among the peoples," or else "among those things which are worshiped by men." The Hebrews use the word "son" very broadly.

With great delight I sat in his shadow.

Shadow signifies defense. And this figure is the more apt in that there seems to be no obvious defense for the godly, yet the outcome demonstrates that their defense is very certain and secure, not only against the dangers of the world but even against the gates of hell (cf. Matt. 16:18).

Now, here he adds the reason why he prefers the apple to every other tree: "Because my God is everywhere at hand to help, defend, and provide for me. He is a certain and most sure defense, and so I delight to sit beneath this tree." Moreover by the verb *sat* he signifies perseverance. Those who, like the Gentiles, do not have this Apple Tree wander uncertainly hither and yon and lie open to all Satan's sneak attacks.

And His fruit was sweet to my taste.

This is the second blessing from the Apple Tree which he extols

[2] The Weimar text has *filias*, but *filios* is clearly intended.

here, namely, that not only is the government of a godly people defended by their God but that they receive other blessings of every sort from Him too. These are great when they are applied to the blessings of the Word, in which true nourishment lies, because Scripture furnishes not only the consolation of its promises but in addition various examples and stories by which faith in God is fed and confirmed. The ungodly can expect nothing but dry leaves beneath their trees. But the character of our solace is such that even undergoing death is not a bitter thing.

In this fashion he comforts himself with the favor of God and the preaching of the grace of God in the face of perils and the hatred and anger of men. This is the highest art in all our trials. Accordingly, he will now go on to enlarge upon this awareness of befriending grace by using many words — not that there is any difficulty in the subject matter, but the figures of speech are considerably harder and demand a careful interpreter and one who is at leisure. But I am so occupied with my duties and responsibilities that virtually no leisure time remains for collecting my thoughts.[3] Yet this is a path which deserves to be opened for others so that they may find some apter interpretations.

4. *He brought me to the banqueting house.*

"He not only defends and nourishes me, but He fills me with joy." For "wine makes glad the heart of man" (Ps. 104:15). This gladness is the awareness of God's grace, to which the revelation of the Word recalls us. Some interpreters refer this to temporal blessing.

And His banner over me was love.

Soldiers in camp are assigned according to the order of their banners. So he says: "I recognize my banner, which is love, under this God; I am assigned to this position." If someone wants a different sense here, he can refer the preceding text to conscience and peace of heart, or to spiritual blessings. Again, it could refer to the external and political blessings which God confers on those who have His Word and follow it. As Paul says (1 Tim. 4:8): "Godliness holds promise for the present life and also for the life to come."

---

[3] See Introduction, p. x.

Similarly we read in Ps. 37:19: "In the days of famine they have abundance."

However, it is characteristic of gratitude to refer to God also these physical blessings received, and this is what Solomon does here. For even if other realms also have wealth, power, etc., a better condition nevertheless obtains for Solomon's people in this, that his people conclude that they have the same from God. So we, too, ought to acknowledge our eyes, our ears, and all the other things we have to be the highest gifts and most certain testimonies of God's goodwill towards us. This is Solomon's purpose in using a military metaphor. He represents these benefits as a *banner*, or "sign," to which God summons and musters His people. Moreover, because we feel that these good gifts were given to us by God, and that they were lent to us not for our eternal possession but only for our use, we endure it with a calmer spirit when later they are taken away again. Now Solomon turns to the people.

5. *Sustain me with flowers, refresh me with apples.*

Solomon has consoled himself against the world's hatred by means of the blessings of God, and he has preached these blessings. Now he turns to the whole people and voices his desire that they may do as he does that they may learn to acknowledge these blessings of God and give thanks for them. He expresses this by entreating that flowers or grapes and apples be brought by the others, too, and that he be sustained and refreshed.

However, he has in mind the scandalous fact that the world customarily gives its admiration to magnificence and splendor. It is as if he were saying: "You are offended that my kingdom seems to be far inferior to other realms of Gentile kings. But I beseech you, look under whose shadow I sit, and it will become obvious that our penury outshines the power and wealth of all the nations. So do not spend your wonder on them; rather praise me and recognize this gift of God which we possess. Thus even those of you who are sometimes disturbed by the scandal of weakness will sustain and refresh both me and others."

Some expositors explain the flowers as ministers who understand and adorn these gifts of God,[4] as the patriarchs and prophets

---

[4] Cf., for example, Walafrid Strabo, *Glossa ordinaria, Patrologia, Series Latina,* CXIII, 1137.

adorn the blessing of the kingdom established among the Jews with their highest praises. But the meaning given above seems to me to be simpler.

For I am sick with love.

The comparison is derived from young love, to which supremacy over other emotions is assigned. "Hence," he says, "I ask this because my whole being is on fire with the love of my God out of this consideration of His blessings. Therefore I yearn so greatly that all men should be aware of them and give Him thanks for them."

6. *O that His left hand were under my head, and that His right hand embraced me!*

This, too, is a figure drawn from the love of bride and groom. It is a holy and lawful love, and therefore Satan hates it and tries to impede it even though it is the font of procreation and education.

Furthermore, he includes here two special blessings belonging to this people: the kingdom, or government, which he calls the left hand, and the priesthood, or worship of God. These embraces, he says, make it possible for this rose to endure the thrust of wild beasts and brambles, since it is wholly within the embrace of God, whether you look at the church or the kingdom, for the Word of God is in both. This awareness, or better, this faith, Solomon would like to stir up in other men too.

7. *I adjure you, O daughters of Jerusalem, by the gazelles or the hinds of the fields.*

This is the voice of the bridegroom; He replies to His bride to console her in this faith.

But before we explain the meaning, we must answer the question: Why does He swear by creatures, when that seems to be prohibited in Matt. 5:34-37, where Christ prohibits swearing by heaven or by one's head, etc.? But what that passage means we have demonstrated sufficiently elsewhere.[5]

For the moment it is enough to note that that very passage offers proof of the Jewish people's custom of swearing by creatures.

---

[5] See *Luther's Works*, 21, pp. 99—104; the exposition of the Sermon on the Mount comes from 1530—32.

Well known, for instance, in the books of Kings is the form of oath: "Long live the king!" (1 Sam. 10:24; 2 Kings 11:12), and again, "As your soul lives"[6] (2 Kings 2:4; 4:30). Jacob also swears "by the Fear of his father Isaac" (Gen. 31:53). Similarly we swear by our faith.[7] First, then, these examples reveal that there is no simple prohibition against swearing. Secondly, there is sound enough reason to swear even by creatures when we advance them as signs of God, for that is not to make an idol out of a creature.

Now we shall explain the sense of the present text. *Gazelles* and *hinds* are his names for the holy prophets, the leaders, and the kings among this people, who had been exposed to all the neighboring peoples like hinds in a field. "I adjure you by your forefathers eminent in faith and the spirit." And it is an apt likeness, for he rightly pictures the saintly men of this people by means of beasts that are innocent and constantly exposed to attack.

That you stir not up nor awaken love until it please.

He speaks of sleep because a godly people which lies in God's embrace and experiences God's favor is delighted by these blessings. "Do not shake it from this sleep," He says, "but be still so that it can continue to enjoy this awareness."

8. *The voice of my Beloved!*

This is the bride speaking: she means that she has heard the comforting words of the Groom and His exhortation to His attendants to be quiet and not to create any disturbance. "I perceive the sure effect of this exhortation," she says, "and His Word is not ineffective." For those who otherwise would have caused disturbances are called back to obedience and tranquillity by the Word.

Behold He comes, leaping upon the mountains, bounding over the hills.

9. *My beloved is like a gazelle, or a young stag.*

That is, by means of His Word He leaps from one city to another so that everywhere the effect of His ministration may be felt among

---

[6] The Weimar text has *vivat*, but we have read *vivit*.

[7] In English also, "By my faith" or "On my faith" has been a mild oath at least since the 14th century.

men. By the metaphor of the stag and the gazelle Solomon signifies the progress of the Word, because it spreads its effects to distant places with great swiftness.

Behold, there He stands behind our wall, gazing in at the windows, looking through the lattice.

Here he once more indicates that he has all these possessions in faith. For such a reminder is the Holy Spirit's custom when He preaches the gifts of God so splendidly, in order that we may understand that He is speaking about joy of conscience, not about carnal consolation. "No man has seen God at any time" (John 1:18), but faith is our veil in such a fashion that we with certainty possess the things promised and yet do not see or feel them.

Accordingly, what he has said about the groom, that He leaps from hill to hill like a stag and is present everywhere, keeping all things within His governance and oversight, all this he now refers to faith — that God is truly present, but yet He cannot be seen, He stands behind the wall, He is not perceived by our eyes nor felt by our hand. Thus Christ is present to His church through the Word and sacraments, but He is not perceived by the eyes.

And for those who are occupied in the business of state there is certainly need of this comfort. For although it is impossible to alleviate all ills, however much you want to, we must not on that account think that God does not take care of governments. He is indeed present, yet as one who stands behind the wall and gazes at us through the lattice.

10. *My Beloved speaks and says to me:*

He now says more softly what He has just been saying in an apparently rather sharp fashion. He stands behind the wall, He seems sometimes to have deserted His people, but He does not stand silent. He speaks with me and comforts me so that I may bear patiently whatever vicissitudes befall me from time to time.

Arise, hasten, My love.

These are words of the greatest sweetness. In them the Groom answers His bride as she toils and yet perseveres in faith, in the hope that she will hold fast the sure confidence that she is the beloved of her God even at the very moment when she seems deserted by God. The Jewish realm was certainly shaken violently enough by a host of calamities, and yet the voice of the Bridegroom constantly bore witness to His signal love for His people — even later during the captivity.

My fair one, and come away.

The stress is on the pronoun *My*. It is as if He were saying: "You are fair in My eyes, even though you are utterly contemptible in the world's sight." This beauty is located first and foremost in the Word and gifts of the Holy Spirit and then in the external administration, or government, established by God on the finest laws.

11. *For lo, the winter is past, the rain is over and gone.*

These are words of solace by which Solomon expresses the changing of his fortunes. Springtime is fittingly compared to tranquillity in church and state. By contrast, heresies, seditions, and wars contain and produce no less disfigurement than winter.

Therefore, he encourages the Jewish people to return to gladness, since peace has been procured for church and state by overcoming the trials which have burdened them for some time. It will come to pass that everything in the state and the church which so far has been disrupted and disfigured by tyrants and heretics will grow green and be renewed. God calls His people to this hope and encourages them to embrace it. That is what it means to rise and come to the Bridegroom.

12. *The flowers appear on the earth, etc.*

To the seeds of earth he compares the youthful generation, brought up in peace to worship God and study literature and other skills which are honest and useful in public life.

And the voice of the turtledove is heard in our land.

The *turtledove* is his name for godly people, or the church. For the turtledove more accurately groans than sings. But the result of instruction is this new use for peace, that religion is propagated and men have opportunity to learn the Word of God.

13. *The fig tree puts forth its green figs, and the vines are in blossoms; they give forth fragrance.*

Training and sound doctrine are followed by other good effects, namely, that men become virtuous and live holy lives. And this he symbolizes by the green, or unripe, figs and the sweet fragrance of the flowers of the vine. To this hope Solomon summons his people, who are formed into a kingdom with a divinely delivered worship of God.

14. *O my dove.*

The dove is always the subject of praise in Holy Writ, first of all on account of its simplicity and innocence and then for its fecundity. And Christ's dictum is well known: "Be innocent as doves and wise as serpents" (cf. Matt. 10:16). So the dove is a figure of the church: it is exposed to all injuries, yet it never returns injury, but endures them. Thus Paul urges the Corinthians (1 Cor. 5:8) to walk in sincerity and truth, casting down that profligacy of the human heart which turns everything, whether it be divine or human, to its own advantage. But this is dovelike innocence, to seek the things of God and of one's neighbor.

You who dwell in the clefts of the rock.

We are forced to guess at what Solomon intended here. Some expound this antithetically, as follows: This innocent and godly people does not live proudly like the world and the other kingdoms of the world, but it lives like frightened little birds, driven this way and that, which seek shelter in clefts of stone, etc.[8]

But I prefer to take *the clefts of the rock* as the temple in Jerusalem and the whole worship of God — that according to the Word of God the church performs its sacred rites in Jerusalem, dwells within the walls of the temple as in clefts of the rocks, does not look for groves, vales, etc., like any other profane crowd of idolaters, and that he says *clefts of the rock* emphatically because there is no danger of idolatry there, but rather an assurance of being heard and a sure defense.

[8] An interpretation *per antithesin* was one which sought to identify the unspoken polemic implicit in a verse of Scripture.

Let Me see your face, let your voice sound in My ears.

"Since you are persevering in purity of doctrine and holy worship, practice it in the place I have designated. Sing and teach, praise and give thanks. For your face and your voice delight Me." Indeed, all the works of believers are gratifying and pleasing to God. These are consoling words.

But now immediately a little fox that stirs up fresh troubles will be provided. For even though Satan is totally contaminated, it is not his custom to seek ashes or other ugly places to sit in, but instead he chooses the very cleanest spots. He wants to be among the children of God, as he is in Job 1. Accordingly he stirs up false brethren in the church and seditious citizens in the state. We need therefore to walk cautiously, as Solomon goes on to warn.

15. *Catch us the foxes, the little foxes, that spoil the vineyards.*

We have seen above that the vineyard is the people of God, as Is. 5 also shows. So it is easy to understand who are the foxes whose capture he urges. He speaks of two classes of foxes: foxes and little foxes, in order to indicate the existence of a double danger from astute and malicious men in both government and the church.

The little foxes are false brethren in the church, and also heresies which at first worm their way in so that they can be detected only with difficulty. But those who disrupt public affairs give themselves away immediately by their seditious plans, like bigger foxes, which cannot as readily conceal themselves.

For our vineyards are in blossom.

See how wily Satan is. He seizes the moment when he can do the greatest damage! So under the papacy everything was calm; but after the Word began to be disseminated, seditions and heresies sprang up which spoiled the ripening fruit of the Gospel, while previously both states and churches appeared to be enjoying a profound peace.[9] The more certain, therefore, the effect of the Word is shown to be, the more careful we must be not to yield ground to Satan's wiles.

[9] This was a frequent charge, to which Luther replied in such places as *Luther's Works*, 13, pp. 274—77.

16. *My Beloved is mine, and I am His.*

This is a sort of response in which the bride answers the Groom. She replies that she wants to do this, to persevere in sincerity and to mark out and capture the foxes.

He pastures His flock among the lilies.

17. *Until the day breaks, etc.*

"I shall remain with my Bridegroom as He pastures among the lilies even though night and darkness shall come."

Turn, my Beloved, be like a gazelle or a young stag upon the mountains of Bether.

This is a prayer: "Do Thou also remain with my people and be like a gazelle running on the mountains that Thou mayest visit, tend, and rule individual churches and states."

Although he retains the Hebrew name *on the mountains of Bether,* it should be taken as a descriptive, not as a proper, name, for it means "on the divided or sundered mountains."

CHAPTER THREE

1. *Upon my bed.*

UP to this point we have listened to Solomon singing in general terms about his state, in which he maintained that worship of God which God Himself had established. At this point he begins to digress somewhat in order to carry his account down to his own period and to his own person. For this reason we shall interpret almost all the following verses as pertinent to Solomon himself.

He calls the realm, magistrates and people, his *bed*, on which the Bridegroom, God Himself, lies and rests. This is a familiar figure from the prophet Isaiah: "You have made your beds on every mountain," he says, "and there you have wallowed about with your lovers, etc." (cf. Is. 57:7-10). Isaiah, of course, is speaking about the people's idolatry, and he is referring to their whole religion and their worship centered on mountaintops.

By night I sought him whom my soul loves.

Now when he says that he has been searching, he is referring to the various troubles which so often befall the state. For before Solomon, the kingdom of Israel was tossed about by many, many tempests, as is well known from the history of the kings.

With this he also makes the details of the time agree, that *by night*, that is, in the midst of calamities, he has both sought and longed for what he valued highly, a quiet and stable reign, for it is expressed in the neuter gender.

2. *I will rise now and go about the city, etc.*

These words similarly belong to his description of the passion with which the good king and his whole people longed for tranquillity and an end of evils in state and church.

3. *The watchmen found me, as they went about in the city, etc.*

The guards are the judges and princes. "Among them," he says, "I was looking for what I desired, namely, peace and tranquillity.

"But I found peace neither under Saul and David nor before them under the judges. Whenever a new judge or a new king was given, hope sprang up that the ills of the state would be cured, but I did not find it until I went a little further and came to Solomon. There I finally found what I was looking for, as his name also promises."[1]

4. *I held him.*

As I said before, I take all these statements to be about the person of Solomon. Under his rule the kingdom enjoyed an abundant flowering of peace and every kind of blessing. Yet here these words are not to be taken as if he were writing a hymn of praise to himself. For they are all spoken in the person of the state, as it acknowledges the divine blessings which God has granted through the godly magistrate and gives thanks to God for them. This is the manner in which we are to take the hymn of praise to Solomon written in this chapter.

And would not let him go until I had brought him into my mother's house.

"Home," "chamber," "throne," "palace," and similar terms signify the people, or the realm. It is as if he were saying: "My people is like an empty couch. For how frequent and how grievous are the troubles it has sustained from seditions, wars, feuds, etc.! But after God has given Solomon to his people as king, peace and tranquillity have been born, so that it lies and rests securely on the couch of its mother.

5. *I adjure you, O daughters of Jerusalem, by the gazelles, etc.*

As we have already shown above, this is how he addresses the saintly prophets in this people, yes,[2] he also includes Christ Himself as the Head of all the saints.

6. *What is that coming up from the wilderness like a column of smoke?*

---

[1] The name "Solomon" has frequently been connected with the Hebrew word for "peace," but it probably has another etymology.

[2] The Weimar text has *quia*, but we have followed the Erlangen text and read *quin*.

This text has been made into a hymn concerning the blessed Virgin [3] — obviously so that there may nowhere be any lack of evidence by which to establish the incredible ignorance and blindness of our adversaries!

There is no reference here to the blessed Virgin. It is the Jewish kingdom as it existed under Solomon which is described and commended in such elegant and poetic figures. We may paraphrase: The state and kingdom under Solomon was so very fragrant that all the neighboring realms were filled with the sweetness of its odor, or the celebrity of its fame. It is thus fitly compared to a column of smoke which rises from aromatic incense and fills the whole palace. And by the sweetness of this most pleasing odor the queen of the south was invited to come to Solomon, etc.

Listing various sorts of aromatic substances and saying that the smoke rises from them suggests that various gifts have been resident in this people, wisdom, prudence, patience, faith, etc.

7. Behold, it is the litter of Solomon! About it are sixty mighty men.

Here you see that what was previously God's litter is now called the litter of Solomon. However, we have already said that the litter is the people itself. This, he says, is protected by 60 strong men. They are properly understood to be either the military or those councilors and associates of Solomon who administered the state in peacetime. For it is not possible for one man, even if he is endowed with the greatest wisdom, to be able to carry out all the business of state.

Therefore the one man who is the head of the realm lies on the litter. Around him 60 men holding swords in their hands and expert in warfare stand guard. That is: they are those who are called to administrative responsibility in the state and bring their prudence to bear in the execution of business. Both qualifications are required — that they should be expert and that they should be called. And so he adds:

8. Each with his sword at his thigh.

He indicates the solicitude and care which political administration requires. It is necessary to be attentive to all opportuni-

---

[3] These verses were apparently used in the liturgical observance of some Marian festivals.

ties, at no point to be remiss, and never to be careless. As Paul says (cf. Rom. 12:8): "Let him who rules rule with concern."

9. *King Solomon made himself a palanquin.*

The section of the hymn of praise which we have heard so far is nothing else but a thanksgiving for the litter, that is, for the people. Now here he mentions the palanquin, or seat, which Solomon made for himself. However, he does not intend us to think he is saying this of the materials, but he is comparing to the seat, or palanquin, those laws and judgments by which Solomon governs his people. He praises them for their marks of great distinction: "of gold," that is, wisdom; "of silver," that is, eloquence; "of purple," that is, the ardor of love; "from the cedar of Lebanon," that is, freedom from corruption, so that they might be stable and fixed. But for what purpose?

10. *For the sake of the daughters of Jerusalem.*

Not for the sake of the Gentiles but for the sake of the people of God.

11. *Go forth, O daughters of Zion, and behold King Solomon.*

This little section, too, is extremely fitting for this hymn of praise. It is as if he were saying: "I have shown you what sort of kingdom God has given you under Solomon and the magnitude of the gifts which have been lavished upon you, in that both at home in the state you have laws and judgment and abroad you have peace. Now do this also: notice how these gifts had their beginning. Solomon did not seize his kingdom through tyranny, but his mother crowned him; that is, the kingdom was committed to him by the consent of the whole people. Therefore revere and esteem him, and give God thanks for these His gifts which He has lavished upon you so richly under this king, etc." Moreover, this little section plainly shows that this figurative style which he uses throughout has no other meaning but this, that Solomon wishes to honor his state and to give thanks for it.

CHAPTER FOUR

1. *Behold, you are beautiful, My love, behold, you are beautiful!*

In chapter three we have heard the voice of the bride praising God and giving thanks for the kingdom established through Solomon. In this chapter the Bridegroom makes His response, for these are antiphonal songs.

Moreover, this alternation in which the people and God sing by turns leads to this, that faith is strengthened by a sort of earnest of the Spirit and that it concludes with certainty that these things please God and that it is in grace. Thus earlier the people proclaimed the gifts of God in this kingdom; now faith hears the selfsame thing done by God Himself so that they may be the more roused to give thanks and may learn to understand their gifts more surely and to contemplate them more worthily. So He says: "How beautiful you are, O kingdom of Israel! How holy you are in your certain conclusion that you please your God!" And He begins this description of her beauty from the head.

Your eyes are the eyes of doves.

The eyes signify leaders and teachers. Thus we read in Luke 11:34: "Your eye is the lamp of your body." He calls them doves' eyes; that is, they are remarkable for their simplicity. For above all else, it is demanded of a teacher that he persist in simplicity of teaching and religion.

This, then, is the first feature which God applauds in this people: that they have a priesthood and right worship of God. These are the eyes which deserve the first commendation. Similarly Daniel, in his description of the lion, that is, the kingdom of Babylon, commends the lion because it was standing on two feet like a man, with its head upright, and had the mind [1] of a man (Dan. 7:4). And the meaning of this is that the monarchy was granted to Babylon because of its recognition of God, as the king's own edict testifies (Dan. 6:25-27).

---

[1] The Weimar text has *corpus*, but the Erlangen reading of *cor* would seem in some ways to fit the context better.

But here we should notice that the bride has eyes like doves in the opinion of the Bridegroom. In the world's judgment nothing is considered more disfigured or deformed. For the wisdom of the flesh is simply unable to appreciate this beauty, since even if it sees and hears it, yet it looks at it as if through colored glass.

Behind your veil.

I read it this way: "Your eyes are the eyes of doves behind your locks" — so as to indicate hair hanging down as far as the eyes. That, too, is singularly praiseworthy in a girl. Besides, the hair signifies the adornment of the priesthood, for in the church everything must be done decently and in order. There is a parallel passage in Isaiah: "By means of Assyria the Lord will shave the hairs on the beard" (cf. Is. 7:20). And in another passage he likens a people deprived of the priesthood to a bald head.[2] Some people prefer the hair to mean the rest of the leaders of the people.

Your hair is like a flock of goats which are shorn upon Mount Gilead.

Perhaps he is alluding to the passage in Gen. 31:25, because Jacob camped with his flocks in Gilead on his way back from Mesopotamia. However, it seems more likely to me that he is reflecting on the name of the mountain. Gilead means "mount of testimony." With this name he alludes to the temple, where the sacrifices and the other cultic acts were carried out.

He compares the hair not simply to goats but to a flock of goats in order to signify the concord and agreement of those who teach among the people. Therefore he also calls the goats shorn, not because they have been clipped, but because the hairs are as even as if they had been combed.

2. *Your teeth are like a flock of shorn ewes that have come up from the washing.*

As you know, one commends whiteness in teeth, darkness in eyes. Just as the image of the hair displays the agreement of the teachers among themselves, so also we see that the teeth are ar-

---

[2] It is not clear what passage of Isaiah Luther has in mind: 3:24; 7:20; or 15:2.

ranged in order and give each other help, as it were. But the function of the teeth is to bite.

It is also required of a teacher that he should be powerful in arguing and convincing. However, this should be carried out in such a way that the teeth nevertheless remain white, that is, it should be done without acrimony, without bitterness and hatred, as seeking correction, not revenge. This kingdom, he says, has teachers like this.

All of which bear twins, and not one among them is barren.

He adds this in order to show forth the fruit of their ministry. For twins are brought forth whenever souls are first terrified by the Law and then are raised up again by the promises, or the Gospel.

In the same fashion, those who rightly divide the Word (cf. 2 Tim. 2:15) see the fruit of their teaching in the church. For it simply cannot happen that teaching should go on in the church without bearing fruit, just as the text says: *not one among them is barren.*

3. *Your lips are like scarlet thread.*

Rosy lips are wonderfully fitting in a girl. The lips further signify the office of teaching. They are paired, just as the character of doctrine is also twofold: Law and Gospel. The fact that they are rosy is a symbol of love. For the foremost service of love is to teach rightly about religion.

Again, they are compared to a scarlet thread, or ribbon, by which the hair is gathered, in order to signify concord, just as Paul enjoins (Phil. 2:2): "Be of one mind, etc."

And your mouth is lovely.

The teaching of the ungodly is toil and grief, yes, an "open sepulcher," as the prophet calls it (Jer. 5:16). But this is high praise for the Word of God: it is lovely, because it revives afflicted and contrite hearts. Peter, too, says (John 6:68): "Lord to whom shall we go? You have the words of eternal life."

Your cheeks are like halves of a pomegranate.

Rosy cheeks are also a splendid ornament. They do nothing special, they just glow and are gazed upon, they do not teach like the eyes and the teeth. And so I apply this to the manner of life or the customs of the teachers in the church. The fire of love ought also to glow in them. As Christ says: "Let your light shine before men" (Matt. 5:16).

4. *Your neck is like the tower of David, built with fortifications.*

This also applies to the teachers. For they should not only build but also defend. The time of peace is for teaching. But the time of war is for fighting and resisting Satan and the heretics.

So in this beautiful form he requires a firm and upright neck, which he compares to the tower of David. Nothing that I know of is recorded about this tower in Holy Scripture. But doubtless it was very strongly fortified and built for driving off the enemy. Likewise, it is fitting that a teacher should be equipped to be strong in doctrine, as Titus 1:9 says.

Whereon hang a thousand bucklers.

He adds this to signify the resources with which teachers ought to be equipped against every sort of heretic and against the wiles and deceits of Satan. This was even more necessary in this people because they had a natural propensity to idolatry, to which they were also attracted by the daily examples and customs of the neighboring tribes, even when they themselves were free of false teachers and pseudoprophets.

5. *Your two breasts are like two fawns.*

In addition to the description of the ministry of the Word he has given through the eyes, the teeth, the hair, and the tower, he now applies to it the image of the breasts, an image which aptly pictures those consolations which are made available to terrified minds. As Paul says in 2 Tim. 3:16: "All Scripture is inspired by God and profitable for teaching, for reproof, for correction, and for training in righteousness, etc." There he states unmetaphorically what Solomon here has sketched, as it were, with poetic images.

But what is the connection between breasts and twin fawns? Perhaps he is suggesting that they are not breasts like those of whores but chaste and delicate breasts. In the same way, in Prov. 5:18-19 he calls a wife by this name: "Rejoice with your wife as with a lovely hind."

That feed among the roses.

Yet they feed in the woods. But this is part of the same description, that he means delightful and more delicate breasts, namely, such as derive their fullness not from the crude pasture of grass but from roses.

Here I will issue no warning concerning those impure thoughts which befall youth when they hear such descriptions. For the Holy Spirit is pure and so mentions women's bodily members that He wants them to be regarded as good creatures of God. And indeed, there is nothing in this book that pleases me more than the fact that I see Solomon speaking in such sweet figures about the highest gifts which God has conferred upon His people. He does so in order that an outstanding example of gratitude should be placed before us here. And would that we, too, would learn to praise our God and give such thanks to Him that we called Him our Sun and our Friend, and the church His gazelle, pastured in flowers, etc.

6. *I will hie me to the mountain of myrrh and the hill of frankincense.*

This is a sort of finishing touch with which he concludes the hymn of praise about the ministry of the Word established [3] among this people. For up to this point he has rehearsed almost all the Word's offices, which are likened to the eyes, the teeth, the hair, etc.

Now he adds to this a sort of acclamation: this gift You have given me is like a mountain on which grow myrrh and frankincense, the sweetest fruits. There I shall remain, there I shall take my delight, until the day comes and the shadows are scattered. I shall not grow tired of these gifts, I shall not seek new ones, as impatient spirits are wont. For the more this doctrine is eaten, drunk, seen, and heard, the more its hearers should hunger and thirst for more and hope that they may never hear or see anything else. Those who do not feel this emotion have had no true taste of the Word of God, however much they know to chatter about it.

Myrrh is a symbol of the Word, but frankincense is a symbol of prayer.[4]

---

[3] The Weimar text has *iustitutum,* but we have read *institutum.*

[4] The symbolism of myrrh as the Word of God is not common in the exegetical tradition and may be Luther's own; on the other hand, frankincense is commonly

7. *You are all fair, My love; there is no flaw in you.*

In my opinion, this is a new paragraph, even though it also belongs to the song of praise begun. For he goes on to speak about the fruit and efficacy of the Word, that is, what this ministry of the Word so often preached among the people effects. It is as if he were saying: "So far I have regarded you in only one aspect, namely, in the priesthood. Now I see that you are wholly beautiful and without fault." For the Word which is preached publicly the citizens take back to their homes, and from this Word they learn to govern themselves and their families. And the result is that we discover the sure fruits of the Word everywhere, in the church, in the state, and in the household, because like a leaven the Word pervades all the parts, offices, and ranks of the state.

For when we refer this beauty to the Word, it makes good sense. Thus Christ also says (John 15:3): "You are clean through the Word which I speak to you." And the church today, even though it prays constantly for the remission of sins, is nevertheless utterly pure and without fault, if you keep your eyes fixed on Word, sacraments, faith, and Christ Himself, its Head.

8. *Come from Lebanon, My bride; come from Lebanon. Come from the peak of Amana, from the peak of Senir and Hermon, from the dens of lions, from the mountains of leopards.*

Lebanon is well known. Mount Amana is also well known from Latin writings;[5] Senir is a part of it. These mountains are virtually contiguous, and they are all to the north of Jerusalem.

This is a kind of exhortation that people should keep hold of the Word and not allow themselves to be drawn aside into idolatry by the neighboring tribes. It is as if he were saying: "My kingdom reaches as far as Lebanon, but you, My citizens, beware of the surrounding tribes. Our neighbors are dens of lions and mountains of leopards, that is, for neighbors we have great Gentile empires, but hurry here from Lebanon to Jerusalem and to the temple, where the Word is. In the opposite direction there is nothing but horrible beasts. You may expect extreme dangers from them unless you flee."

taken as a symbol for prayer, as, for example, in Gregory the Great, *Super Cantica Canticorum expositio, Patrologia, Series Latina,* LXXIX, 510.

[5] Cf. Pliny, *Natural History,* V, ch. 22, sec. 18, 80.

9. *You have ravished My heart, My sister; My bride, you have ravished My heart.*

We see in this extraordinary emotion what a joy it is to God and His angels when the people give their assent to the Word and are of one mind. He calls such people "beloved." He calls them *bride.* He calls them *sister.* He says that His heart is as if wounded by love.

With one glance of your eyes.

The emphasis is on the word *one,* to show how very pleasing simplicity, unity, and purity of doctrine are to God. We see how everywhere Christ and the apostles urge and invite to this sort of concord.

10. *How beautiful are your breasts, My sister, My bride!*

The *breasts* can be found not only in the teachers but also in the people. For the saying of Christ is true (Matt. 18:20): "Where two or three are gathered in My name, I shall be in the midst of them." So when in private brother consoles brother, when he announces the remission of sins, that Word is valid and does not deceive. For the Holy Spirit is active through the Word whenever it is rightly and sincerely applied, whether in public or in private.

Your breasts are sweeter than wine.

Every other sort of consolation is nothing if you compare it with those consolations which the Word of God places before us.

And fragrance of your oils than any spice!

Your reputation has a sweeter smell than the reputation of all the nations, for it comes from the Word. For what is the reputation of the whole world compared with the one you have? For you have a remedy not only for business like a lawyer, not only for the body like a doctor, but for the soul, and you raise up and console consciences by means of your bridegroom's ointment. This ointment of the Word cures body and soul and recreates and preserves both.

11. *Your lips are a dripping honeycomb.*

Thus far he has been giving thanks and proclaiming an outstanding gift—that God has instituted government and priesthood among this people.

Now he adds that God has not only instituted these things but has made them prosper, so that the effectiveness and fruit of this arrangement permeate through the whole people, etc.

Honeycomb. The honeycomb is a people that has the ministry of the Word, that is, dialog and mutual consolation. And *dripping honeycomb,* that is, one that spreads in all directions. This sweetness and purity of doctrine pervade the entire people.

Milk. Those who are sick are fed with milk. This is also the function of the Word, for God does not cast away the infirm.

The scent of your garments is like the scent of frankincense.

This people is adorned with the most beautiful virtues, which issue from the Word, and from them there is an odor of frankincense, that is, from them springs the people's renown, and their fame is declared far and wide.

He calls it *the scent of frankincense* because such a reputation conveys something divine. For the highest praise of this people is its very precious adherence to the worship of God.

12. *A garden locked is My sister, My bride.*

Another praiseworthy characteristic of this people! He commends the people because they are bound by most excellent laws, regulated by circumcision and other rites, and what is most important of all, sealed by the promises, by which they are distinguished from all other people. In the same way we Christians are now sealed by the Word, Baptism, and the Sacrament of the Altar, by which we are distinguished from all other races, not just before the world, but rather in God's own judgment.

13. *Your shoots are an orchard of pomegranates with the fruits of the orchard, etc.*

This people is a garden whose outgrowth—that is, shoots which grow out of the earth—are a sort of paradise, full of trees, that is, of saintly men.

Where the Latin text has simply *with the fruits of the orchard,* I take it to mean the sweetest and choicest fruits. The various fruits and trees signify [6] the various gifts and offices among the people — good teachers, magistrates, heads of families, servants and servant girls, young men, old men, etc.

A tree of incense are they who pray faithfully and unceasingly, just as "myrrh and aloes" signify those who mortify their flesh. Thus all kinds of gifts from the Word of God drop down on the hearers.

15. *A garden fountain, a well of living water.*

This is the peroration: you are the true fountain of waters flowing from Lebanon. The city of Jerusalem is called Lebanon by an allegory. It is as if he were saying: "Jerusalem is adorned by God with many gifts both in priesthood and in government, like a fountain which waters other gardens." For by its example other states are also aroused to embrace religious and civil discipline.

16. *Awake, O north wind, and come, O south wind! Blow upon My garden, let its fragrance be wafted abroad.*

He wants this garden to be exercised through trials, so affliction and prosperity alternate. The south wind puffs up with presumption, the north wind dries out by desperation. This is not so that the garden will perish but so that its fragrance will be wafted even further abroad, that the power of the Word may be apparent in the cross.

[6] The Weimar text has *significat,* but we have read *significant.*

CHAPTER FIVE

THIS IS the people's prayer as they acknowledge the blessings and gifts of God. For they ask that the Beloved will now enter the garden which He has so adorned with His praises, that is, that He will continue to bless it and to preserve the gifts He has given already. Similarly the prayer in the Psalms asks: "Strengthen, O God, what Thou hast wrought in us" (Ps. 68:28). Otherwise men's souls will slide into false security and fall.

1. *Let my Beloved come to His garden.*

You, my God, have planted this garden, this government; therefore come, tend and conserve it with Your Word and Spirit, lest it perish from neglect. Eat of its noblest fruits, that is, make it clear to us by Your presence that all these things please You, etc."

I come to My garden, etc.

The prayer has been heard. For He indicates that He is present and tests everything and that everything pleases Him. This is the testimony of conscience which godly men experience in their office and calling; when they serve their calling, they can affirm with certainty that God approves their works and is pleased by them, even if they are somewhat negligent in certain respects, for remission of sins is not excluded here either.

I gather My myrrh.

The *myrrh* is the mortification of the flesh. The spices with their sweet smell are the other good works and the fruits of faith which He says He collects and enjoys.

I eat My honeycomb, etc.

Notice the emphatic manner in which He says that all these things are His. It is as if He were saying: "Your assemblies, your consolations, your works please Me. You please Me by your living, working, speaking, teaching, etc. For even though it is inevitable, in your present state of weakness, that many sins are committed, whether by carelessness or for other reasons, nevertheless, your obedience, however imperfect, is pleasing for the sake of your belief in Christ." As John says (1 John 3:20), "God is greater than our heart." For we have the good quality which is unlimited, opposed to our limited evil quality.

Eat, O friends.

This is an exhortation to the whole church to enjoy these benefits and gifts with gratitude. But they are necessary consolations, scarcely believed even by those whose occupation is in government or the ministry of the church. However, they fortify godly men's hearts so that they will not desert their office through discouragement at the difficulties and ingratitude of men.

2. *I sleep, but my heart is awake.*

A new section begins here. Up to this point he has been describing the very lovely period of peace which flourished under Solomon and has been expressing his thanks for it. Now he looks forward to times to come and sees that because of the sins of the people both the government and the priesthood are to be afflicted in turn by various ills.

For just as there are changes of weather, so war follows peace, happiness follows sorrow, consolation follows affliction — and then some new affliction follows consolation. Solomon deals with these alternations almost to the end of this book and gives a general description of the trials which are to come. "This is the way it must always be in this kingdom; from time to time we shall be tested, exercised by various calamities, etc."

I sleep, and my heart is awake. "I sleep — I am now enjoying a deep peace, I am secure, and everything is calm. Nonetheless, my heart is awake, for I see the sins of the people, I see God threatening evils through His Word. And so I am anxious about the evil to come, etc."

The voice of my Beloved as He knocks!

This is where the cross begins. "The voice of one knocking" is a voice of terror bent on purging clean lest in her smugness she lose her present possessions. For the cross is necessary and useful for us. "He who loves his son increases his whippings," he says in Proverbs (Prov. 13:24).

Open to Me, My love, etc., for My head, etc.

This is an accusation against the bride. "The peace which you have enjoyed up to this point has made you slothful. You lie in bed and let Me stand drenched by the night rains outside the doors; that is, you neglect Me, you administer the government and the priesthood with equal negligence. My head and all My locks are wet; that is, your leaders in both realms go unheeded, etc."

3. *I have put off my garment.*

"I am lying down naked, I cannot get up." This signifies not only the guilt of neglecting the Word, but also rebellion. On account of her sins, she does not wish to obey God submissively in His visitation. She does not want to lose her peace, but she persists in her sins nevertheless. In Ps. 85:10 we read: "Righteousness and peace have kissed [1] each other," for where righteousness is lacking, one should certainly not expect peace.

4. *My Beloved put His hand to the latch.*

Here He wants to constrain her to get up, much as in life. God thrust His hand through the latch opening like this when He sent the Assyrian and when He pressed the people with other calamities. In this way He aroused this government, which was taking its ease and growing negligent because of the long peace. God does not lie: His threats are always followed by their fulfillment.

5. *I arose to open to my Beloved.*

"To open the door" [2] means to display a submissive spirit. She is saying, therefore, that she has submissively borne God's hand.

However, so you will not think that that is easy, she says: "My hands dripped with myrrh, and my fingers dripped with myrrh that found its way to the handle of the bolt." She wants to indicate how difficult it was to conquer the flesh so that she could give her assent to God and not complain but admit the penalty and bear it.

---

[1] The Weimar text has *consolata*, but we have followed the text of the Vulgate and read *osculatae*.

[2] The Weimar text has *hostium*, but we have read *ostium*.

6. *But my Beloved[3] had turned and gone.*

Temptation is portrayed here; and it is added that God seems to abandon us in such evils, nor is any consolation offered to the weary mind.

My soul failed me.

The verb means "it left." It is as if she were saying: "I am gripped by such yearning that I am almost bereft of consciousness. I do not feel that there is any help. Only His Word He left to me; I cling to that, so I am all but abandoned, etc."

7. *The watchmen found me as they went about in the city.*

By *watchmen* here I understand the doctors of the Law, who do not console but terrify even more and bring sins to light. Like those men in Job, they condemn when they should be consoling.

The watchmen can also be taken as those teachers who in time of calamity advise worthless defenses for us to rely on. This is like the worship of saints, indulgences, and other godless nonsense of the same sort which flourished among us.

But afflicted souls cannot be raised up except through the Word of grace. All other forms of solace not only do not help but wound even more and heap up rage (just as here the afflicted people is overpowered).

8. *I adjure you, O daughters of Jerusalem.*

The bride—that is, the people in time of trial, whether it is the Babylonian captivity or something else—has lost its God and is so abandoned at the hands of its adversaries that neither God nor any help is anywhere to be found. Nevertheless, it does not despair for this reason but endures the hand of God in His visitation and calls on other men and exhorts them to prayer. "Daughters of Jerusalem" means "all you who are committed to this worship."

9. *What is your beloved more than another beloved?*

Translate "more than other beloveds." They want to know whom she has as her beloved, that she prefers him to all other beloveds and even though she is deserted does not want to turn to

---

[3] The Weimar text has *illo*, but we have read *ille*.

other defenses and aids. This is the sort of question men will ask who are directed and instructed not by the Spirit of God but by their own reason.

Here, then, she begins a long figurative description of the sort of beloved she has. Now that she has lost him, she describes him for the first time. We are all like this—we are blasé about the blessings we have in our possession, and we neglect them. But when they are snatched from our sight, we seek them enviously, as the poet says.[4]

10. My Beloved is all radiant and ruddy.

This is a figurative description of God, not as He is in His majesty, but as He is in His Word and worship; that is, a God clothed and adorned by the kingdom and the priesthood in this people, etc.

The "radiance" indicates happiness, since on festival days they used to wear dazzling garments. The "ruddiness" means love. It is as if she were saying: "When the priesthood and kingdom were still standing unimpaired, we abounded in very excellent gifts by which God testified to us of His love toward us. Thus everything used to be full of joy and gladness; but now, with the government disrupted and all those excellent gifts taken away, we mourn in wretchedness."

Such is life. Those who have the Word of God have a loving, consoling, gladdening, and beneficent God. But the people complain that they have lost all these things.

Distinguished among ten thousand.

He is the chosen hero and giant who is capable of defending them.

11. His head is the finest gold.

The religion and doctrine which Moses calls the wisdom of this people (Deut. 4:6) is like the purest gold. The cults of other gods are like dross, etc.

His locks are wavy.

At the time when I still had hold of God, I abounded in wor-

[4] Horace, *Odes*, III, 24, 32.

shipers of God and ministers who were very close to the Head, that is, to God. There was a plentiful supply of priests and Levites.

And black as a raven.

The priests were grave men, in whose countenance and gestures there was an agreeable seriousness. Someone may prefer to take the black hair to imply a vile outward appearance, but that is not what I think. For black hair was highly praised among them. So we read in Horace, too: "Worth looking at with dark eyes and black hair." [5]

12. *His eyes are like doves beside springs of water.*

The eyes are guides and leaders of the people who not only worship God and serve Him but also educate and teach simply and faithfully.

The dove is celebrated for its purity, for it will not drink anything but the very purest water. It does this so that it can be on its guard against hawks, whose reflection the water mirrors. Faithful teachers were similarly devoted to being on guard against false spirits. They turned their watchful attention to the pure water, that is, to the Scripture.

But he adds: *eyes bathed in milk*, that is, full of consolations; likewise "eyes dwelling in fullness," that is, displaying a certain joyfulness. Hollow eyes indicate severity, etc. But the eyes of this Bridegroom are full and dwell in fullness, that is, they have a richly provided people, their word is faithfully heeded, their churches and schools are full of pupils.

13. *His cheeks are like beds of spices.*

The cheeks are the whole people's external manner of life, which flows from the Word; it is more vigorous, it yields a sweet fragrance of peace, humility, faith, etc.

His lips are lilies distilling liquid myrrh.

The lips are sweet and full of love; yet they distill myrrh, that is, mortifying doctrine. They teach, accuse, persist, reprove.

[5] Horace, *De arte poetica*, 37.

14. *His hands are rounded gold.*

Among the whole people, he says, there are some who abound in good works. The works of the Law are hands withered, wrinkled, and dry. Here with the sheerest goodwill they do good without any impediment.

His trunk is ivory work.

This means the mass of people, which is like a torso in the body of the church; even though it is weak in itself, so that it needs the help of other members, it is nevertheless white like ivory and incorruptible.

15. *His legs are alabaster columns.*

He contrasts the *legs,* that is, the strong in the church, to the *trunk.*

His appearance is like Lebanon.

The whole people is like Mount Lebanon, planted with the loveliest trees. In it there are various offices, various gifts, etc.

16. *His speech is most sweet.*

His breath is not foul, but He breathes sweet things. That is, these fruits of the church which I have been reciting here please God and are acceptable to Him.

He is altogether desirable.

Not that there are no ungodly men among that people; but because it has the Word, he says that everything is desirable, on the ground that there is no treasure which can be compared with the Word of God. In it the true worship of God is prescribed for us, and remission of sins is promised, so that no sin is left among us.

So she sings the praises of her Bridegroom and bewails the fact that she has been deprived of all these gifts which she had when He was present.

CHAPTER SIX

1. *Whither has your Beloved gone?*

THE bride, sad because she has lost her Bridegroom, has searched for Him in other cities, but has not found Him. The daughters nevertheless promise their own efforts to help her by their prayers, and by joining in the search for the Bridegroom.

2. *My Beloved has gone down to His garden.*

At this point, consolation returns. For she sees that she has not been altogether deserted by the Bridegroom, but that He has gone down into His garden, to tend the garden and gather roses, that is, to increase His gifts to the people even further. For when God deserts us, He does not do it out of anger or hatred towards us, but He is pruning His vine so that it will bring forth fruit more richly (cf. John 15:2). The bride is speaking here about the fruit of trial, the fruit we bring forth in faith and good works through many tribulations.

3. *I am my Beloved's, and my Beloved is mine.*

That is: "He is my Beloved, and I am His beloved." This certainty and trust follow upon temptation. The *roses* are the saints among Solomon's people.

4. *You are beautiful, My love.*

Here the Bridegroom offers Himself to the bride and reveals that He is delighted by her faith because it has not been shattered by its trial so that it blasphemed or abandoned God. And certainly this is a great comfort for our conscience, because it establishes with certainty that patience pleases God and that He takes delight in the sacrifice of a contrite, but not of a despairing, heart, so that even though the flesh takes offense and murmurs somewhat, yet the spirit cries out to God and would rather remain in perpetual trial and even perish than withdraw from God into ungodliness. Thus testing produces hope.

As Tirzah, and comely as Jerusalem.

Tirzah was the seat of the kings of Israel. It is as if He were saying: "My bride, you are as beautiful as Tirzah, a well-fortified city. And you are formed and established like Jerusalem with its excellent laws." It is nothing less than a description of the complete confidence that the church, or the people, feels that all its works are exceedingly pleasing to God.

Terrible as an army with banners.

The church, or people of God, is not only well founded on the worship of God and the laws of the government but is also terrifying to the devil and its other adversaries. For Satan is afraid of us when he sees our heart fortified by the confidence that we believe we are pleasing to God. Our adversaries are also afraid, and it is because they fear the godly that they kill them. As Pharaoh said in Ex. 1:10: "Come, let us deal shrewdly with them, lest they multiply, etc."

5. *Turn away your eyes from Me.*

This could be interpreted two ways. The first is as discouragement: "Turn your eyes away from Me," that is, "so that you do not speculate about My majesty, or else you will be overwhelmed by it." I do not agree with this rendering, for we observe the Bridegroom engaged in a discourse of comfort.

The alternative sense is commendatory and loving: "Turn your eyes away from Me" — "they are so sweet and enchanting, they arouse Me so that I cannot gaze on them further." It is not that He spurns her eyes, but in the fashion of a lover, even while He commands her to turn them away, He desires above all that she will not.

This, then, is a commendation of the orders in the spiritual realm. For the eyes are the teachers, the sort of teachers Elijah, Elisha, etc., were. "They please Me so much," He says, "that they arouse pride within Me." These are extraordinary consolations with which God testifies that He approves the government and the worship of this people, and so their hearts may grasp the complete confidence that they enjoy God's good pleasure, etc.

Your hair is like a flock of goats.

This all goes together with the description above. The *hair,* as I have said, are the priests and Levites, who stand at the head of the people and rule the people with the Word of God.

Gilead means "a heap of testimonies." This is Holy Scripture, which in truth contains a heap of testimonies.

6. *Your teeth are like a flock of ewes that have come up from the washing, all of them bear twins.*

It also devolves upon the office of the teacher to bite and to reprove, not out of private hatred but from love and godly zeal. Thus these are sheeps' teeth. What he adds about bearing twins indicates the fruit of preaching. About the cheeks, see above.[1]

8. *There are sixty queens and eighty concubines and maidens without number.*

So far he has been praising the various offices and ranks of this people. Yet the praise belongs to the Word by which the people is ruled rather than to the people who do the ruling.

Now he gives thanks for the God-given government, which has burgeoned into so many cities and villages. For this is the subject matter to be grasped throughout this whole book — he is talking about the government.

Accordingly, I take the 60 queens to be the wealthier and the 80 concubines the more modest cities which were situated throughout Solomon's entire kingdom, in Syria, Idumea, Palestine, etc., and all used the same body of laws. The maidens are the myriad other cities which were all administered by God-given laws.

The passage in the books of Kings about the huge number of Solomon's wives (1 Kings 11:3) has largely obscured this verse. But they are mistaken who think that Solomon took all these wives because he was so lustful. The Law imposed this necessity upon him, for it enjoined that when a husband died, the next of kin was to take his place. Accordingly, forsaken widows realized that it would be the best arrangement for them if they were among the royal wives or concubines. It was for this reason that Solomon became the husband of so many wives.

9. *My dove, my perfect one, is only one.*

I have said that he is being thankful for the fruit that follows

[1] See p. 207 above.

from the Word. Solomon's administration has not been in vain: there are 60 queens, etc., who all enjoy its benefits. And even though none of these cities is so pure that there are not many dissolute and evil men in it, nevertheless, in every one of them there are some godly men of dovelike simplicity, who respect and obey this government from the heart, who revere and honor it as the highest gift of God since it possesses the Word and the church of God is in it. This is my only one, my one dove, gathered out of the whole realm, etc.

The maidens saw her and called her happy.

Everyone, even the ungodly, is constrained to praise godly and good citizens, who are to be found everywhere in the cities.

10. *Who is this that looks forth like the dawn, fair as the moon, bright as the sun?*

The kingdom of Solomon, constituted in this fashion and adorned by its laws, is celebrated everywhere. It comes forward and brightens the whole world with its fame and glory. Other kingdoms are dark shadows compared with this, because they are besieged by Satan, God has not sent His Word to them nor brightened them with the beams of the knowledge of Himself. And so this government of Solomon's is like the dawn, the sun and the moon in the world on account of the Word.

These are very special consolations, when a people formed into a state can persuade itself that in God's eyes it is the sort of people he describes here. For in the world's eyes we more often than not appear the very opposite, as indeed the history of the people of Israel teaches us.

11. *I went down to my garden to look at the crops of the valley, etc. I did not know, etc.*

New trial follows on the heels of consolation. Up to this point he has been praising his kingdom and giving thanks for it, for he sees his dove; that is, in every city he sees some good men whose godliness and way of life he approves.

Now he turns his attention to another group, and he sees that there is such a huge crowd of ungodly men that by comparison there seem to be no godly or good men. It is ever thus: vices move hearts more vehemently. So special strength is required here, strength which the Spirit of God supplies so that one is not crushed by the appearance of all those evils.

I went down, he says, *into my garden*. "I acted as bishop and visitor to see the effects of my government, and lo! so great was the number of the ungodly that I was constrained to say: 'I did not know,' or 'I did not recognize,' that is, 'I did not recognize my dove.' " For when we add up the numbers, the preponderance of the ungodly is so great that there seem to be no godly men at all.

The same thing happens to us when we visit the churches: [2] we find so many vices everywhere that a man might well despair of the fruit of the Word. And yet that dove remains, even though it is hard to see, because it is hidden by a multitude of evils.

12. *My soul troubled me.*

This passage is quite obscure. Jerome rendered it as belonging properly with the sentence I have just paraphrased, namely, that he went to inspect and search out the fruits but that he does not know, that is, that he finds nothing, because the wicked always form the greater number. If you look, it seems as if the good men are lost and nowhere to be found. But it seems to me that it would be more suitable if we should join the sentences as follows: "I did not know, since my soul ordained me to be the chariot of a noble people." For I take the word "Aminadab" to be a common noun. Moreover, it is a common figure of speech that *soul* is used for "willingness." "My soul placed me on the people's chariot," that is, "I myself wanted to be the chariot of the people. But I do not discover this to be the case either. Certainly I am in a position where I have precedence over other men and rule them. But they are unwilling to be ruled, they prefer not to be subject but to rule and to be princes, etc." This is the usual way of the unbridled crowd.

13. *Return, return, O Shulammite.*

At this point the Bridegroom calls the bride back from surveying these evils, that she may dismiss them and console herself instead

---

[2] Beginning in 1527, a series of visitations had been undertaken to assess the spiritual life of the Evangelical parishes; out of this experience came various manuals, including the *Postils* and Luther's Catechisms.

by examining the good things she has. However, it is no easy accomplishment to be able to overcome our current trial, to recall our mind from sadness by thinking about the gifts we have. But if one's judgment is sound, these gifts always greatly outnumber and outstrip the misfortunes by which we are beset. So he says: "Return, and let us look at you." Turn your eyes away from the misfortunes at hand. Look at yourself, and you will see how great are the blessings and gifts God has bestowed on you.

He calls her *Shulammite*, which means either "perfect" or "at peace," so that by conferring this outstanding accolade on her He may call her back from the sad thoughts she conceived as she stared at her misfortunes. You are "at peace," that is, everything goes well, you abound in all manner of good things. Again, you are "perfect," you lack nothing, since you have a divinely instituted government, you have magistrates who rule and subjects who obey. If there are some evil men among them, do not let them disturb you; rather, consider how great are the gifts you possess, etc.

We, too, should maintain this balance in private life, and patiently endure those trivial faults in our friends or in our wife, since they are balanced by so many other favorable qualities if you think about it in the right way.

What do you see in the Shulammite?

Rather, "Why do you not look at her correctly and as she deserves?" Acknowledge God and the Word of God in her, recognize in her a government established not by human but by divine counsel. What, then, can be criticized in her? God not only has given but also approves the structures of household, government, and church of this people. And even that is not all; He has also promised that He will stand by.

But throngs of the camp.

She is extremely well equipped, so that there is no danger that the huge numbers of the ungodly will overthrow her. God is there, and He governs His people, etc.

CHAPTER SEVEN

1. *How graceful are your steps in sandals, O queenly maiden!*

HERE he describes in song the state thus appointed and adorned. He portrays it as walking, to signify that it not only has excellent gifts but is also putting its gifts to daily use, that the priests are teaching the Word of God, that the government is justly declaring the law, etc. He indicates this by picturing it in sandals. For I do not think he intends an allegory of her being bound and fettered by laws, etc.[1]

The joints of your thighs are like jewels, etc.

It is said that among the Jews it was forbidden for adolescents to read this book. There are some who suppose that this prohibition was designed to prevent adolescents becoming inflamed to lust by reading it.[2]

For myself, however, I think it was forbidden rather for its difficulty, for since it speaks politically throughout, it seems to be of no value to the young, who as yet have no use for worldly affairs. For even adolescents are capable of hearing and speaking about young women without concupiscence if they regard them as God's creation. And the Holy Spirit has a chaste mouth and a pure heart.

Accordingly, He is here speaking about the genital members as about His own creation, which our flesh and concupiscence misuse by their own fault, not by that of the Holy Spirit. I say this so that no one will be offended by this text, which seems to be rather amatory.

It is to be noted that when the Holy Spirit uses allegories, His attention is more on the use of a thing than on its form. So here He makes mention of the reproductive organs like the belly, navel, thighs, etc. in order to describe the fruitfulness of this people.

---

[1] See pp. 191—95 above for Luther's critique of previous interpreters.

[2] See Luther's similar observations on the Book of Genesis, *Luther's Works,* 1, p. 3.

Broader thighs are commended in young women because they are better fitted for childbearing.

Solomon is therefore speaking about spiritual birth in this people, that the youth is being prepared for ministry in church and state. Among us schools are *thighs* of this sort. And for this reason we say that Germany is unfortunate because it lacks such a fitting and elegant junction of the thighs — its schools are lying deserted, etc.

2. *Your navel is a rounded bowl that never lacks mixed wine.*

The power of conception and generation is in the navel. They maintain this view from Job 40:16: "His power is in the navel of his belly." But He means parents and teachers of the young. They are like a bowl which is never empty of wine, that is, their instruction is not worthless.

The Bridegroom thus commends to the bride the gifts she has, so that she may console herself with her endowments and make light of the evils by which she is oppressed.

Your belly is a heap of wheat.

Your instruction and learning are fruitful like a heap of wheat. Roundness is praised in a belly, as is a deeper navel set a little into the belly. *Roses* is his name for Scripture and the laws.

3. *Your two breasts, etc.*

She has breasts with which to feed her offspring.

4. *Your neck is like an ivory tower.*

He calls her neck a tower because it is upright, ivory because it is white and firm.

Now, the *neck* is the people's leaders and magistrates who are uncorrupted and firm, who are not broken in spirit, who are not overcome by hatred, passion, money, etc., but duly perform their office.

Your eyes are like the pools of Heshbon, by the gates of the great.

We read nothing about these pools in Scripture. But the *eyes* are teachers whose waters overflow like pools to comfort the weak both in faith and morals. They are clear eyes, as transparent as pools.

Your nose is like a tower of Lebanon, overlooking Damascus.

A straight nose is also commended; but the Holy Spirit is paying more attention to the use, and so it signifies diligent teachers and magistrates who do not snore but are always vigilant. I think he means some small watchtower facing towards the north.

5. *Your head crowns you like Carmel.*

The highest ranks of the people are the *head,* namely, Solomon with his princes and the high priest. Here they are compared to a very fertile mountain — not for themselves, but for the magnificent promises which both possess.

And the hairs of your head are like the king's purple, etc.

It is a strange figure that he calls the hair "channels," yet if you pay attention to the form, it is not inappropriate to the reality. For women's hair hanging about their shoulders is separated and slightly waved or curled, so that there is some likeness to water flowing out of a channel.

These channels, or hair, are the orders of Levites and the government magistrates, who flow from the high priest and king like hair from the top of the head, flowing down the back to the lower parts of the body.

By the additional phrase *like the purple* he is referring not to the color but to the material. For people have high praise for soft hair, which we compare to silk.

6. *How fair and pleasant you are!*

Here he praises a government adorned by so many gifts.

He calls it *fair* because all its offices are so fitly distributed, *pleasant* because this arrangement adorns it and delights all those who see and hear it.

7. *Your stature is like that of a palm tree.*

The palm does not bend under heavy weight. And you are the same: the nations will not be able to crush you. For your priests teach the Word, and care nothing about the hatred of the world. Your judges follow the law and judge justly, they are not worried by the world's ill will. As 2 Sam. 14:20 says, "My lord the king has wisdom like the wisdom of the angel of God."

8. *I said I will climb the palm tree.*

Prepared and adorned as you are, you please Me so much that I am driven to embrace you.

These are words of special consolation, by which God indicates that everything that He has talked about so far gratifies and pleases Him. For by His Spirit He replies to Solomon's spirit that he is doing the right thing in thus exalting his government by his praises and in giving thanks for it. And He says in loving fashion: "I will climb this palm," that is, "I will lovingly embrace you and your kingdom." The result will be:

Oh, may your breasts be like the clusters of the vine.

"There will be no further need of milk, but I will strengthen your citizens so that they can drink wine, I will make them hardy so that they can not only endure but also overcome vicissitudes, etc."

He makes a connection between the nose and the breasts. The breasts teach, but the nose guards and keeps watch and protects the teaching.

9. *Your throat like the best wine.*

"The praise and thanksgiving which you offer for the government are very pleasing to Me."

Allegorically the throat signifies singing, praising, and giving thanks. "To Me, these actions are like 'wine which goes down smoothly to My beloved'" (for this is how it ought to be translated); that is, "they please Me like this because they are directed to Me. You do not claim your own strength or your own righteousness, but you proclaim Me."

For his teeth to ruminate.

We translate as follows:

Which makes the lips of the aged move.

For the word he uses here means to spread reports and to pour forth speech. So the meaning is this: "Those praises and acclamations in which you celebrate My blessings are remembered and repeated by the old people, who transmit to others their great knowledge of the histories."

11. *Come, my Beloved, let us go forth into the fields, etc.*

Here the bride entreats a new gift, for which she will later give thanks. Under Solomon the kingdom of Israel reached its greatest extent, since he ruled over the peoples of Edom, Palestine, Syria, and Moab.

Since she still has many other peoples abroad (this is what she means by *the fields*), the bride prays that the Bridegroom will give His grace that they, too, may be governed rightly and that the Word may be extended to the neighboring peoples.

12. *Let us go out early to the vineyards, etc.*

We want to see whether among those peoples, too, there are some good men, men who will be useful to the state.

There I will give You my breasts.

We shall teach in those regions also; we shall put our worship and law into practice even among them.

13. *The mandrakes have given forth fragrance.*

He does not mean what we today call a mandrake, but he means a certain sweet and noble fruit, as both Genesis (30:14) and this passage make clear.

The meaning is this: "I have also found the fruit of the Word among the neighboring peoples, who benefit from our religion and government." The Word is never taught without fruit, but it brings forth the best men among the nations also.

All choice fruits, new as well as old.

Poma generally means all the noble fruits of trees. She means that she has an abundance of good citizens, whom she has laid aside for the Bridegroom, that is, the glory of the kingdom of the people of God is not recognized except in the Word. Wherever else you look for it, it is despised. Thus the world not only despises good men but persecutes and hates them. For it is not worthy of recognizing either a godly man or a good work. This is why the bride says *which I have laid up for You*.

CHAPTER EIGHT

WE said at the beginning that this book of Solomon was a sort of hymn in which he sings the divine blessings shown to his people through the Word and expresses his thanks for them. Here he appears to begin his conclusion to this canticle and to pray for the future spread of the kingdom. For he gazes forward to the time of Christ, when the Word and the worship of God would be spread throughout the whole world. This is similar to the prayer in the psalm: "Strengthen, O God, what You have wrought in us" (Ps. 68:28).

1. *O that someone would give You to me as my little Brother, one who nurses at my mother's breast, that I might meet You outside and kiss You!*

The sense is: "O our God, expand this kingdom into infinity." It is already "outside in the field," that is, in the neighboring tribes, and it longs to expand even beyond that.

He pictures the Bridegroom as an infant sucking at its mother's breast. For if you look at other realms into which He was to be introduced, God seemed to be like a little baby in this people. So she says: "You are like a child sucking his mother's milk. Who will give me the privilege that I may see You introduced abroad to all peoples through the Word of the Gospel?"

She adds: *That I might kiss You.* To *kiss* is to give the Word, to possess the Gospel. "When these things take place," she says, "men will no longer despise me. Now we are a contemptible people. But then there will be some in every kingdom of the whole world who will revere and praise me, who will embrace the worship of God and believe the Word of God, etc."

2. *I would lead You and bring You into the house of my mother.*

"Then I shall lead You into the synagog." As it is written about John (Luke 1:17): "He shall turn the hearts of the fathers to the children." For those Jews who believe in Christ have not been turned *away* to us Gentiles, but have been turned *back* to their own fathers, that is, to the faith of their fathers. Afterwards we Gentiles have been received into that family, so that now we are one people.

There You will teach me.

When it is thus openly supported by the Holy Spirit, a perfect ministry of teaching will be instituted.

I will give You spiced wine to drink and the juice of my pomegranates.

Then there will be a richer and more effective doctrine than there ever was under the Law. "I will give You wine which You will drink," that is, "which You will approve." *And the juice of my pomegranates.* Perhaps he adds this to indicate the new character of the doctrine from the various testimonies of the prophets.

3. *O that His left hand were under my head, and that His right hand embraced me!*

So far we have listened to this song of Solomon's in which he has been singing about blessings past and present and praying that in the future the kingdom and its doctrine may be spread through the whole earth. The subject matter of the chapter before us I have called a sort of epilog in which he reviews the things he has been dealing with throughout the book.

Here he uses yet another amorous image borrowed from the marriage embrace. By this image he indicates that this kingdom is in God's protection, and is ruled and directed by God. Since it is true that we are plainly not to be in doubt concerning God's favor towards us, he says:

4. *I adjure you, O daughters of Jerusalem, that you stir not up nor awaken love.*

That is: "You cities, whoever you are under this worship and government of God, take care to be quiet and peaceful, lest you incite disturbance and tumult. Instead, rejoice in this grace and peace, obey the laws, and submit to the magistrates. In religion, too, take care that nothing is thrown into disorder through idolatry or other blasphemous fancies. For these two things are connected.

Peace cannot endure without religion or righteousness, according to the verse of the psalm (Ps. 85:10): 'Righteousness and peace have kissed each other.'"

Earlier,[1] he added a call to witness to his oath, *I adjure you by the gazelles*, so that at least they would be quiet and tranquil out of reverence for the saintly fathers and prophets they had for ancestors. He adds:

Until it please.

I believe he is speaking about the sort of occasion which imposes necessity. "Do not arouse such an occasion yourselves, citizens, but if it is aroused by hostile neighbors, then you should also perform your duty by being vigilant and applying your efforts and strength."

5. *Who is that coming up from the wilderness, leaning upon her Beloved?*

Not only the surrounding tribes but even those who are themselves members of this people marvel at her as she comes up from the desert.

This is the constant preachment of the works of God, that they spring forth as if from the desert and from dry ground. The godless flourish and spring forth as if from a most pleasant paradise where there seems to be nothing that could possess any hint of deformity. By contrast the church and people of God seem to come forth from the desert. For its glory can be seen only in the Word. If it were to come up from a paradise, the world would marvel at it, but the world does not marvel at a desert.

And yet, he says, she is leaning on her raptures, namely, those which the Word provides. For wherever the Word of God is, there of necessity are the Holy Spirit, faith, and other gifts of the Spirit. So he rightly says that she leans and depends on God, whose Word she clings to so pertinaciously. Even if there are some divisions, they are rendered invisible in God's eyes, and only godly men are seen; the others amount to nothing. We should feel the same way about sins and other weaknesses.

At one time I used to make this verse fit the soul and the specu-

---

[1] See p. 216 above.

lative life.[2] But if someone wants to define the speculative life correctly, let him define it as follows: it is to believe and depend on the Word. For those who speculate without the Word are ruined by Satan, as I found out more than once. Therefore let us reject those dreams.

Under the apple tree I awakened you.

This the translator has rendered: "There your mother was corrupted." This is a manifest error. For it has changed a term meaning "pain" into a term meaning "guilt." The word here really means the labor of delivery, or the misery of childbearing, even though in other places it may be used to mean "to corrupt" or "to wound."

The "mother" is the state, and the citizens are her children. "These," he says, "I have awakened under the apple tree; there your mother has borne you or delivered you." The Jewish kingdom was not really very extensive in spatial terms. It is therefore not compared to a small tree, but the seed of the future kingdom of the church, which would spread throughout all lands.

6. *Set Me as a seal upon your heart, as a seal upon your arm.*

The Bridegroom urges the bride to persist in the Word and not to allow herself to be led astray outside the Word either to her own thoughts or to some alien cult. "Come," He says, "let Me be to you like a seal, like a ring by which you will recognize Me and embrace Me from your heart. Look at Me! Fix your eyes and your heart on Me!" "But where are You?" "In the Word," He says, "in Jerusalem and in My temple."

"Affix this seal on your heart, etc."

The fact that He wants to be set not only over the heart but also over the arm signifies faith and love together—that we should both believe and live according to the Word of God. When this is the case, then in truth we walk in divine finery, and wear this seal fitly.

For love is strong as death, jealousy is cruel as the grave.

This reason seems to be anything but appropriate. But since this passage comprises a description of the spiritual life, this

---

[2] See *Luther's Works*, 42, pp. 141—42.

explanation fits very aptly indeed. For since it exhorts that we must hold on to faith and love, it indicates the need for a strong and unbroken spirit because of the various trials which befall the godly. How could such a spirit be better described than by calling it "strong love"? For among all the emotions this one reigns supreme, as not only the honorable and marital love called shows, but also juvenile and mindless passion. What the poet says is true: "Love conquers all." [3] So the Bridegroom is saying: "If you love Me truly, keep hold of My seal, and whatever the grief and vicissitudes you are subjected to by the world and Satan, with this you will conquer. For love is as strong as death, which conquers all things; and envy, or jealousy, is as hard as the grave, which cannot by prayers be moved to give back the dead." We may call jealousy a "fury of love," a fury in which we are enraged by an intemperate love, not by hatred of a person.

But he uses the likenesses of death and the grave to show that godly people will experience death and the grave. As Paul says (Rom. 8:36): "We are being killed all the day long."

Its flashes are the flashes of fire and of flames.

The words translated *and of flames* in the Hebrew are literally "the flame of God." He is indicating the inexhaustible and infinite ardor of a love that cannot be extinguished. For he differentiates the fire of God from other, material, fire, because the fire of God is eternal and inextinguishable. It can be neither lit nor put out by human will. He says: "This fire, which God has lit in you, neither death, nor the grave, nor all the onslaughts of the world and Satan will be able to put out. For love yields to no one, and everything yields to love."

7. *Many waters cannot quench love.*

He speaks of many waters, just as Christ does in Matt. 7:25, when He speaks about the house built on the rock. Not even the force of tempests, he says, will extinguish this love; instead, it will kindle it even more. Those who have earnestly embraced the Word are stimulated as it were by trials and the cross to embrace it even more closely. This, then, is the outcome of all our

---

[3] Vergil, *Eclogues*, X, line 69.

trials: even if they try to tear us away from Christ, the actual effect is to join us still closer to Christ.

If a man offered for love all the wealth of his house, etc.

He urges his people in this noble exhortation to keep hold of the Word with great zeal and care. Just as he has urged them up to this point to endure in their calamities and not to yield, so here his command deals with the opposite extreme—not to let wealth and power transfer their allegiance to another.

It will certainly be the case, he warns, that other lovers will lie in wait for you to seduce, not only by means of the cross and threats but also by promises and wealth. But remember what love does; it despises all wealth, it utterly scorns all allurements. As Augustine says, "The specific gravity of everything is its love," [4] and love cannot be bought at any price.

8. *Our sister is small, and she has no breasts.*

I pointed out above that at the end of this canticle Solomon looks forward to the spiritual kingdom of Christ, because a future kingdom was expected far wider and greater than the physical kingdom of the Jewish people. And it is beyond doubt that these expectations were frequently and thoroughly discussed in everyday conversations. But in this process a misconception arose. The crowd thought that the kingdom of the Christ would be a physical kingdom. They did not understand that Christ would reign through the Word in such a way that the kingdoms of the world would still run their course.

Solomon, then, is saying: "If we look at the extent of the kingdom which Christ will institute through the new covenant, we will be right to compare our present people to a little girl who does not yet have breasts—that is, it is not yet mature enough to preach a Gospel which is to be spread throughout the whole world."

The further significance of the complaint put forward here is this: It is a sort of common voice of all the prophets and saints of the people of the Law, yearning for a release from the prison of the Law into the broad freedom of the Gospel, that God would bring to fruition the promises made about Christ, etc.

[4] Augustine, *Confessions*, XIII, ch. 9.

What shall we do for our sister, etc.?

How intense is the emotion of a heart aflame with the expectation of the coming Christ! As Christ Himself says in the Gospel (cf. Luke 10:24): "Verily, I tell you that many kings and prophets desired to see and hear what you see and hear, but they neither saw nor heard it." So here Solomon, in the person of all the saints, asks: "What shall we do?" It is as if he were saying: "How great and how joyous will the shape of those times be?" He adds:

On the day when she is to be spoken for.

The very lovely meaning and one that is not at all obscure is this: The kingdom of Christ is located only in the Word. For he does not say "on the day when she is to be adorned, when she is to be led into the wedding chamber," but "when she is to be spoken for," namely, in the sweet preaching of the Gospel by the apostles and Christ Himself. By this preaching she will be taught about the grace of God and the remission of sins.

It is as if he were saying: "Today is not a day for speaking but for keeping silent. We are still caught in the prison of the Law and see only a sort of distant glimmer of the Word to be revealed, the Word through which the kingdom of Christ will be spread abroad into the whole world." Now he replies, but very obscurely:

9. *If she is a wall, we will build upon her a battlement of silver.*

These likenesses seem monstrous enough, that he compares his sister to a wall which he wants to adorn with silver battlements, and a door which he wants to decorate with cedar planks. But here, too, I will state my opinion. It seems to me that he compares the people of God, which he calls his sister, to a fortified wall in the time of the Gospel. For through the ministry of the Word the church is fortified like a wall against all false doctrines, even against the gates of hell (cf. Matt. 16:18).

The fact that he mentions not one but many towers, or battlements, which he wants to locate on this wall refers properly to the variety of ministries which are needed in the church. Paul spells this out in Eph. 4. Accordingly, God commends the ministry of the Word among this new people and promises that He will not desert them but build them up, so that ministers will be established as if in watch towers to guard the city.

But if she is a door, we will enclose her with boards of cedar.

Cedar is prized not only for its odor but for its long-lasting qualities, since it does not rot. Hence the expression of Persius "a cedar-quality speech." [5]

The *door* is his name for the teachers, or catechists, in the church, through whom there are some who come in and some who go out every day.

Thus the wall has to do with defense, but the door with doctrine. Paul also uses this figure: "a wide door has opened to me" (1 Cor. 16:9), and by it he means the growth of the church. For when the Word is preached daily, there are always some new people entering whose hearts are inflamed by the Spirit and love of God.

10. *I am a wall, and my breasts are like towers.*

This is the voice of the bride, already in her maturity. For after the giving of the Holy Spirit and the revelation of the Word, the church truly is a wall against the cunning of Satan and the heretics. And it has breasts, firm like towers, by which it teaches, consoles, corrects, etc.

This doctrine and these consolations are very sure and very firm. Souls find their rest in them. In other doctrines they find no rest, as experience shows.

From this I have become in his eyes as one who finds peace.

Where these two things are present—right teaching and defense against wolves—there of necessity follow peace and tranquillity. By contrast, where either or both of these things are lacking, there one waits for peace in vain.

He looks askance at the Law, for there the people were forced to serve under harsh commands. But the doctrine of the Gospel brings true peace, so that men's hearts have no doubt about the mercy of God. And to be sure, the greatest calamity of all is for God to be silent and not to speak. At such a wonderful time as this, after the revelation of such a great light, we ought to have been more grateful.

A peacemaker had a vineyard.

[5] Persius, *Satires*, I, 42.

The translator is mistaken, for I think that both nouns are proper nouns, so that the text should be read as follows:

11. *Solomon has a vineyard at Baal-hamon.*

One is a personal name, the other is a place name, even though "Baal-hamon" is not found anywhere else.

I connect this with what has gone before as follows. At the end of his canticle, Solomon is looking forward to the summit of his people — that is, to the kingdom of Christ, in which the Word of grace would be spread abroad throughout the whole wide world. Because a remnant of the Jews was to be the beginning of that kingdom, Solomon calls the whole church his vineyard and says that it is in Baal-hamon, that is, in an exceedingly great multitude and in a most plenteous place, since Baal means "master" and Hamon means "multitude."

He does this to console his people and to give them hope in the certain fulfillment of the promises that however tiny their kingdom is in comparison with other Gentile realms, it is the seedbed of the future kingdom of Christ, which is a kingdom of the multitude because it is not limited either to one place or to certain persons but is in every place and among all men even to the end of the earth. This sense seems better to me.

Yet there is nothing to stop you from taking this as an epilog to the whole book, one in which he commends his own kingdom and says that however puny it is before the world, it is nevertheless very great in respect to the Word of God. In this way the verses which follow can be applied to external administration, and the histories do indicate that Solomon administered his realm with the highest care and effort.[6] But for the sake of the honor of the Gospel, we ourselves prefer to describe the spiritual kingdom, whose seedbeds Solomon's people were.

He let out the vineyard to keepers.

This vineyard will not lie neglected without cultivation, but it will have its own husbandmen — apostles and other ministers of the Word. Through them the Holy Spirit will adorn the churches with various gifts.

---

[6] Luther is referring to such passages as 1 Kings 3:16-28.

Each one brings for its fruit a thousand pieces of silver.

The definite number stands for an indefinite one. Since a thousand is the highest unit, he means that his keepers come with the richest reward and the amplest fruits. So Peter, Paul, John, etc., appointed as keepers, cultivated this vineyard with most abundant fruit. For the Word of God cannot be taught without yielding every fruit.

12. *My own vineyard is before Me.*

This vineyard is committed to the keepers' charge, but in such a way that God Himself keeps His eye on it. As the saying went, God did not establish the earth and go away.[7] He keeps His eye on it, or rather, He is present in it, when its ministries are discharged, and He is at work. It is the same in government: those who fail to keep their own eyes on the business do not carry out their office very well.

The thousand is for you, O peacemaker, and two hundred for those who keep its fruit.

Here, too, I keep the proper name: "You, O Solomon, may have the thousand." The application to the government is easy. The prince is lord over everything, but those who execute works on the prince's behalf individually receive a reward in proportion to their merit.

But if we look forward to the realm of Christ and the true Solomon, what John has said (John 1:16) becomes quite clear: "From His fullness we have all received." For even if the "keepers" have "two hundred," that is, even if the saints have gifts of their own, Christ is nevertheless the fountain of all gifts.

13. *O you who dwell in the gardens.*

He speaks of *gardens* in the plural, either in a political reference to Solomon's diverse principates or in a spiritual reference to the churches. This is an exhortation that the churches be administered with the greatest faithfulness, for the intimation is that there are those who examine and take note of everything.

---

[7] Cf. Augustine, *De Genesi ad litteram,* Book IV, chapter 12, paragraphs 22-23, *Patrologia, Series Latina,* XXXIV, 304.

Let Me hear your voice.

After pointing out that there are those who pay attention to the bride, He also brings up this point, that she should not be silent but should speak. For this still remains: that the Word of God be assiduously put into practice, so that we are not weighed down by distaste or contempt or hatred of the Word as the Jews grew sick of the manna and looked back to the fleshpots of Egypt (Ex. 16:3).

14. *Make haste, my Beloved.*

Here the bride in turn says farewell to the Bridegroom and asks that He put an end to this captivity to the Law and scatter the unrestricted doctrine of the Gospel on the world as on the changing mountains and be like a gazelle, never standing still in one place.

In this way I understand this book to be about Solomon's state. If I am wrong about this, a first effort deserves lenience. The musings of others have a much larger share of absurdity!

TREATISE ON THE LAST WORDS OF DAVID

2 Samuel 23:1-7

Translated by
MARTIN H. BERTRAM

ON THE LAST WORDS OF DAVID

SAINT Jerome reports that he was moved to translate the Bible anew from Hebrew into Latin by the sneering reproach of the enemies of Christ, the Jews, to the effect that Christians did not have the correct Bible in the version then in use throughout Christendom. The reason given was that a number of words and letters were faulty and altogether different from the Hebrew.[1] Prior to this, others had been induced to translate the Bible for the same reason, for instance, Aquila, Theodotion, Origen, and others, until at that time there were up to six translations, which they called *Hexapla*.[2] And in our day, too, so many are busying themselves with translating that history may repeat itself and there may be so many Bibles in the course of time and so many wiseacres who claim a mastery of the Hebrew tongue that there will be no end to it.[3]

That will inevitably happen if we pay attention to what the Jews say and think of our Bible. After all, they are not in agreement among themselves, and they expound Scripture arbitrarily and quote out of context with their grammar. If we were to heed them, we could never acquire a uniform Bible, since every rabbi claims to be superior to the other. Furthermore, they all have to admit that the words in many a passage are incomprehensible to them. They are far from having one harmonious, perfect, and flawless Hebrew Bible, even from the point of view of grammar, to say nothing of theology, where they are so very incompetent.

Therefore such mockery of the Jews does not disturb me, and their opinion would not impel me to learn a single letter of the

---

[1] Perhaps Luther has in mind Jerome's statements in the prefaces often printed with the Vulgate.

[2] The *Hexapla* was Origen's comparative edition of the Old Testament in six parallel columns, including the original Hebrew, a Greek transliteration of the Hebrew, and four Greek versions.

[3] Luther is referring not only to his own translation of the Bible into German but to the many vernacular and Latin versions that had been produced by this time.

Hebrew language. The reason for that is this: We Christians have the meaning and import of the Bible because we have the New Testament, that is, Jesus Christ, who was promised in the Old Testament and who later appeared and brought with Him the light and the true meaning of Scripture. Thus He says in John 5:46: "If you believed Moses, you would believe Me, for he wrote of Me." Also Luke 24:44-45: "'Everything written about Me in the Law, the Prophets, and the Psalms must be fulfilled.' Then He opened their minds to understand the Scriptures." [4]

For that is the all-important point on which everything depends. Whoever does not have or want to have this Man properly and truly who is called Jesus Christ, God's Son, whom we Christians proclaim, must keep his hands off the Bible—that I advise. He will surely come to naught. The more he studies, the blinder and more stupid will he grow, be he Jew, Tartar, Turk, Christian, or whatever he wants to call himself. Behold, what did the heretical Arians, Pelagians, Manichaeans, and innumerable others among us Christians lack? What has the pope lacked? Did they not have the sure, clear, and powerful Word of the New Testament? What do the factions of our day lack? Do they not have the New Testament, clear and reliable enough? If the New Testament had to be translated in accord with each such stupid devil's mind, how many New Testaments, do you suppose, would we have to have?

If I were offered free choice either to have St. Augustine's and the dear fathers', that is, the apostles', understanding of Scripture, together with the handicap that St. Augustine occasionally lacks the correct Hebrew letters and words—as the Jews sneeringly accuse him, or to have the Jews' correct letters and words—which they, in fact, do not have everywhere—but minus St. Augustine's and the fathers' understanding, that is, with the Jews' interpretation, it can be easily imagined which of the two I would choose. I would let the Jews with their interpretation and their letters go to the devil, and I would ascend into heaven with St. Augustine's interpretation without their letters. For even if St. Augustine cannot say *Kikaion*, as the Jews do, but says *cucurbita* instead in Jonah 4:6, cannot say *venient Hemdath* but says *veniet Desideratus* instead in Hag. 2:7, and many similar things, yet his faith on that account breaks neither neck nor limb, for he knows "the Valiant One,"

[4] The original has "Luke 21."

who is called "Way, Truth, and Life" (John 14:6), of whom, as I said, the prophets foretell and testify.

Furthermore, since the Jews repudiate this Christ, they cannot know or understand what Moses, the prophets, and the psalms are saying, what true faith is, what the Ten Commandments purport, what tradition and story teach and prove. But according to the prophecy in Is. 29:12, Scripture must be to them what a letter is to an illiterate. Indeed, he may see the letters, but he is ignorant of their significance. As the German riddle says: A field of white is sable sown, And men pass by to see what's grown; But many view a growth unknown. However, anyone conversant with and exercised in the art of reading lets his eyes run over a page and catches the meaning even if he does not closely observe every letter and word. Before the other has spelled out one word, he has perused the entire letter. Likewise, a musician may sing the whole song before another discerns and discovers whether so or fa is to be sounded in a key.

Just consider that excellent man Lyra.[5] He is a good Hebraist and a fine Christian. What good work he produces when he, in accord with the New Testament, opposes the Jewish concept. But whenever he follows his Rabbi Solomon,[6] how meaningless and unimpressive it sounds; it has neither hands nor feet, despite his good command of words and letters. Still he surpasses all the the others, both the old and the new Hebraists, who follow the rabbis altogether too strictly. Indeed, in translating and expounding, one need not intentionally strain oneself to transmit the concept of the rabbis and grammarians to us Christians. It is all too prone to stick to us of itself, automatically, just like pitch and glue, even if we deliberately guard against it. For the letters and the stories of the others blind the eyes and induce us occasionally to lose sight of the meaning of Christ where we should not, and thus the Jewish concept insinuates itself unawares, as every translator without exception has experienced. I, too, was not exempt from it.[7]

[5] Many of Luther's expositions of the Old Testament, especially his *Lectures on Genesis* (cf. *Luther's Works*, Vols. 1—8) depended on Nicholas of Lyra (c. 1270—c. 1349).

[6] "Rabbi Solomon" is more usually known as Rashi, who died in 1105; much of Lyra's rabbinical learning came from him.

[7] As such passages as *Luther's Works*, 1, p. 296, suggest, Luther had ac-

In brief, if we do not apply all diligence to interpret the Hebrew Bible, wherever that is feasible, in the direction of the New Testament, in opposition to the interpretation of the rabbis, it would be better to keep the old translation (which, after all, retains, thanks to the New Testament, most of the good elements) than to have so many translations just because a few passages presumably have a different reading or are still not understood. This only confuses the memory of the reader, hinders his study, and leaves him in greater uncertainty than he was before.

To illustrate this, I have decided to discourse on the last words of David, not according to the German translation, in which I followed all the others to avoid the impression that I considered myself the only smart person. No, now I am going to be stubborn and follow none but my own spirit. He who dislikes this may ignore it. It is not the first time that I wrote something displeasing to others. I thank God that I am inured to that. I, on the other hand, do not approve of everything written by others either. Let everyone see how he may build on the foundation with gold or wood, silver or hay, gems or straw. The Lord's Day will bring this to light (cf. 1 Cor. 3:12-13).

1. *These are the last words of David.*

The author means the words of David with which he is determined to die and depart this life. As one is wont to say: "This is my point of view; with it I will abide forever." For these are not the last words that David spoke during his lifetime, nor are they his last administrative speech, but they are his last will and testament. We Germans call this *Seelrecht*,[8] on which a person is willing to die and which is to be executed unaltered after his death. The jurists call it a "last will." [9] A person may live a long time after this has been issued, and he may speak, do, and suffer much subsequently; it still remains intact as his testament, as his last will. In that sense these are also David's last words, that is, his soul's

quired some Hebrew learning through the rabbis but came to distrust their exegesis as his own approach to the Old Testament developed.

[8] *Seelrecht* was the German word describing the provision one made for the salvation of his soul.

[9] Although the term *voluntas* had been used this way in classical Latin, Luther is probably reflecting the usage of Justinian, *Institutes*, I, 5, 1.

testament, even though he spoke many a word, performed many deeds, and suffered much after this. In the following chapters we read, for example, that he took the census of the people, for which he was punished (2 Sam. 24); he installed his son as king (1 Kings 1); he ordered that the temple be built on Mount Moriah (1 Chron. 22); he took a young wench to wife, Abishag, the Shunammite, to warm him (1 Kings 1), because none of his other wives dared to approach him after they had been violated by Absalom (2 Sam. 16:2).

The oracle of David, the son of Jesse.

How modestly David introduces his speech. He does not boast of his circumcision nor of his holiness nor of his kingdom, but he identifies himself simply as *the son of Jesse.* He is not ashamed of his lowly descent, that he was a shepherd. Yes, what is much more, he confesses his birth, in which he, like all men, came forth full of sin and guilty of death, for he wishes to speak of other matters, matters so sublime that no nobility of birth and holiness can be of advantage and no misery, whether sin nor death, can work harm.

The oracle of the man who is assured of the Messiah of the God of Jacob, the sweet psalmist of Israel.

Now David expresses himself clearly. He exalts himself extraordinarily and yet truthfully and without conceit. Here he no longer describes himself as the son of Jesse. This he did not inherit from his father nor learn from him nor acquire through his royal power or wisdom. This was conferred on him from above and without any merit on his part. In that he delights, that he exalts, and for that he is so very grateful. And what is it that he lauds so highly? He says: "In the first place it is that I am the man to whom God promised the Messiah of the God of Jacob, that the Messiah will descend from me, from my blood, from my tribe and family. I am sure and convinced of this not only because this has been promised me by God, whose words are certain and reliable and who will not lie to me, but also because I firmly believe this, because I hold to this unswervingly and immovably, knowing that I cannot be disappointed in this belief, and because I implicitly trust in God's Word with all confidence. Therefore I am cheerful and stand ready to live or to die when and how God wills. I know where I, or my soul, will abide, where I will leave it. I will not have it go astray or linger in doubt or depart wretchedly. I have God's definite assurance regarding His Messiah, and on that account I also have a firm and inflexible faith."

The Hebrew term הָקֻם cannot well be reproduced with one word. St. Jerome says that *constitutum est* approaches its meaning.[10] I should be inclined to translate it with *stabilitus, certificatus, firmatus,* "firmed." However, I am reluctant to use new words; nor does it sound right to say here "firmed of the Messiah, etc." I believe that Heb. 11:1 alludes to the word הָקֻם in this passage, saying: "Faith is the assurance"; in Greek, ὑπόστασις, which we have rendered in German: *Der Glaube ist eine gewisse Zuversicht* ("Faith is a definite assurance"). You cannot express this differently to a German if he is to comprehend it. For faith is and must be a confidence of the heart which does not waver, reel, tremble, fidget, or doubt but remains constant and is sure of itself. A similar idea is expressed in Is. 40:8: "The Word of our God will stand forever." It "stands," that is, it is steadfast, it is certain, it does not give way, it does not quiver, it does not sink, it does not fall, it does not leave you in the lurch. And where this Word enters the heart in true faith, it fashions the heart like unto itself, it makes it firm, certain, and assured. It becomes buoyed up, rigid, and adamant over against all temptation, devil, death, and whatever its name may be, that it defiantly and haughtily despises and mocks everything that inclines toward doubt, despair, anger, and wrath; for it knows that God's Word cannot lie to it. Such is a הָקֻם, "one who is established, substantiated, supremely steadfast, made to stand, able to stand, sure passively as the Word of God is sure actively," as St. Paul declares in 2 Tim. 1:12: "I know whom I have believed, and I am sure, etc.," and as we read in 2 Peter 1:10: "Confirm your call."

Thus David is a הָקֻם who has the assurance of the promise, and who also confidently believes, that the Messiah whom God has promised to the patriarch Jacob (Gen. 49:10: "The scepter shall not depart from Judah until Shiloh comes") would surely issue from his blood. And here the promise of the Messiah given to Jacob is seen anew and more clearly in David (as we shall see further) so that we can henceforth disregard the tribe of Judah and concen-

[10] Jerome had translated *Constitutum est.*

trate our attention on the house of David, from which, and from no other house in the tribe of Judah, the Messiah must most assuredly come. Yet, even though these two, promise and faith, must go hand in hand—for where there is no promise, there can be no faith, and where there is no faith, there the promise comes to naught; but faith is not always uniformly firm but is assailed at times and becomes weak; the promise, on the other hand, as the eternal Word of God, remains equally firm and sure forever and ever—David is called הֻקַם, affirmed," principally for this reason, that he has the firm promise, although he cannot apprehend and retain this without faith. Faith must also be present. So much about the first part.

Secondly, David boasts of being *the sweet psalmist of Israel*, that is, he did not keep this certain promise of the Messiah to himself nor for himself. For faith does not rest and declare a holiday; it bursts into action, speaks and preaches of this promise and grace of God, so that other people may also come up and partake of it. Yes, his great delight impels him to compose beautiful and sweet psalms and to sing lovely and joyous songs, both to praise and to thank God in his happiness and to serve his fellowmen by stimulating and teaching them. Thus David glories in the fact here that he has indited many exquisite, sweet, and melodious psalms about the promised Messiah, which should be sung in Israel to the praise of God and, in fact, have been sung there, in which, simultaneously, both excellent prophecy and a lofty meaning has been preached and imparted to the people of Israel. And as David initiated the writing of psalms and made this a vogue, many others were inspired by his example and became prophets. These followed in David's footsteps and also contributed beautiful psalms; for example, the Sons of Korah, Heman, Asaph, etc.

When David uses the word *sweet* he is not thinking only of the sweetness and the charm of the Psalms from a grammatical and musical point of view, of artistic and euphonious words, of melodious song and notes, of beautiful text and beautiful tune; but he is referring much more to the theology they contain, to the spiritual meaning. That renders the Psalms lovely and sweet, for they are a solace to all saddened and wretched consciences, ensnared in the fear of sin, in the torture and terror of death, and in all sorts of adversity and misery. To such hearts the Book of Psalms is a sweet and delightful song because it sings of and proclaims the Messiah even when a person does not sing the notes but merely recites and pronounces the words. And yet the music, or the notes, which are a wonderful creation and gift of God, help materially in this, especially when the people sing along and reverently participate. In 2 Kings 3:15 we read that the spirit of prophecy was aroused in the prophet Elisha by a psaltery, on which psalms were obviously played after the manner of David. David, too, often banished the evil spirit of Saul or restrained and subdued it with his lyre, as we read in 1 Sam. 16:23. For the evil spirit is ill at ease wherever God's Word is sung or preached in true faith. He is a spirit of gloom and cannot abide where he finds a spiritually happy heart, that is, where the heart rejoices in God and in His Word. St. Anthony also makes the comment that spiritual joy is painful to the devil.[11]

David calls his psalms the psalms of Israel. He does not want to ascribe them to himself alone and claim the sole glory for them. Israel is to confirm them and judge and acclaim them as its own. For it is essential that the congregation of God, or God's people, accept and ratify a word or a song; for the Spirit of God is to dwell in this people, and He wants to be honored and must be honored in His people. In that light we Christians speak of *our* psalmists. St. Ambrose composed many hymns of the church.[12] They are called church hymns because the church accepted them and sings them just as though the church had written them and as though they were the church's songs. Therefore it is not customary to say, "Thus sings Ambrose, Gregory, Prudentius, Sedulius," but "Thus sings the Christian church." [13] For these are now the songs of the church, which Ambrose, Sedulius, etc., sing with the church and the church with them. When they die, the church survives them and keeps on singing their songs. In that sense David wishes to call his psalms the psalms of Israel, that is, the psalms of the church, which has the same Spirit who inspired them in David and which

---

[11] Cf. Athanasius, *Vita Antonii*, ch. 36, *Patrologia, Series Graeca*, XXVI, 896.

[12] Many hymns were ascribed to Ambrose, including the *Te Deum*, but he did write several, of which perhaps the best known is *Deus Creator omnium*.

[13] Pope Gregory I, who died in 604, was responsible for the development of the Gregorian chant; Prudentius, who died c. 410, wrote various hymns that found their way into monastic breviaries; Sedulius (Scotus), a native of Ireland, was a Latin poet of the Carolingian era.

will continue to sing them also after David's death. He sensed in his spirit that his psalms would endure on and on, as long as Israel or God's people would endure, that is, until the end of time. And that is what has happened hitherto and will happen. Therefore they are to be called the psalms of Israel.

2. *The Spirit of the Lord has spoken by me, His Word is upon my tongue.*

Here David begins to speak too strangely and too loftily for me. God grant that I may understand at least a bit of it in spite of that. For here he begins to talk about the exalted Holy Trinity, of the divine essence. In the first place, he mentions the Holy Spirit. To Him he ascribes all that is foretold by the prophets. And to this and to similar verses St. Peter refers in 2 Peter 1:21, where he says: "No prophecy ever came by the impulse of man; but moved by the Holy Spirit, holy men of God spoke." Therefore we sing in the article of the Creed concerning the Holy Spirit: "Who spake by the prophets." Thus we attribute to the Holy Spirit all of Holy Scripture and the external Word and the sacraments, which touch and move our external ears and other senses. Our Lord Jesus Christ also ascribes His Word to the Holy Spirit, as He quotes Is. 61:1 in Luke 4:18: "The Spirit of the Lord is upon Me, etc.," and as he quotes Is. 42:1 in Matt. 12:18: "Behold, My Servant whom I have chosen. . . . I will put My Spirit upon Him." And in Luke 1:35 we read that the Holy Spirit will overshadow Mary, that He will touch her, take her blood and impregnate her, so that the Lord is described as "conceived by the Holy Ghost."

What a glorious and arrogant arrogance it is for anyone to dare to boast that the Spirit of the Lord speaks through him and that his tongue is voicing the Word of the Holy Spirit! He must obviously be sure of his ground. David, the son of Jesse, born in sin, is not such a man, but it is he who has been called to be a prophet by the promise of God. Should he who has such a Teacher to instruct him and to speak through him not be able to compose "sweet" psalms? "Let him who has ears to hear, hear! My speech is really not mine, but he who hears me hears God, and he who despises me despises God (cf. Luke 10:16). For I foresee that many of my descendants will not give ear to my word, and that will redound to their great detriment." Neither we nor anyone else who is not a prophet may lay claim to such honor. But we may do this as far as we are holy and possess the Holy Spirit, namely, in that we can boast of being catechumens and pupils of the apostles, in that we repeat and preach what we have heard and learned from the prophets and apostles and are convinced that the prophets taught this. In the Old Testament such people are called "sons of the prophets." They do not promulgate anything of their own or proclaim anything new, as the prophets do, but they teach what they have received from the prophets. They are, as David says, Israel, for whom he writes his psalms.

3. *The God of Israel has talked to me, the Rock of Israel has spoken; He who rules justly over men, He who rules in the fear of God.*

Now we have three speakers. Above, David remarks that the Spirit of the Lord has spoken through his tongue. There the Person of the Holy Spirit is clearly indicated to us Christians. Whatever Turks, Jews, and other ungodly persons believe we disregard. Thus we have heard that Scripture and our Creed ascribe to the Holy Spirit the external working, as He physically speaks to us, baptizes us, and reigns over us through the prophets, apostles, and ministers of the church. Therefore these words of David are also those of the Holy Spirit, which He speaks with David's tongue regarding two other Speakers. What does He say of these? First of all He speaks of the God of Israel and says that He has spoken to David, that is, has given him a promise. Which Person of the Godhead this Speaker is we Christians know from the Gospel of John. It is the Father who said in the beginning (Gen. 1:3): "Let there be light." And His Word is the Person of the Son, through which Word "all things were made" (John 1:3). The same Son the Spirit by the mouth of David here calls צור, *"Rock" of Israel* and *just Ruler among mankind.* He, too, speaks, that is, the Holy Spirit introduces the Rock of Israel to let Him speak too. Thus all three Persons speak, and yet there is but one Speaker, one Promiser, one Promise, just as there is but one God.

But as the outward working on man is ascribed to the Holy Spirit, so it is the attribute of the Son that He became incarnate and that He was appointed a Lord and Judge over all men and all creation. Ps. 8:4-6 sings: "What is Man that Thou art mindful of Him, and the Son of Man that Thou dost care for Him? Yet Thou hast made Him little less than God and dost crown Him with glory and honor. Thou hast given Him dominion over the works of Thy hands; Thou hast put all things under His feet." Yet there is not a threefold dominion or three rulers, but there is one Lord and one dominion, which the Father has conferred on the Son, yes, on the Man and the Son of Man, but undoubtedly not in this way, that He has eliminated Himself and the Holy Spirit from this dominion. Yet it is called the dominion of the Man which God gives Him. Therefore the same Man who is here called Ruler must be true God, for He has possession of God's kingdom and is therefore equal to God in the one dominion.

For God gives His honor or His own kingdom to no one else. Thus He says in Ex. 20:3: "You shall have no other gods before Me," and in Is. 42:8: "My glory I give to no other, nor My praise to graven images." But now since God bestows on this Man and this Son of Man His honor and dominion, that is, subjects to Him all that has been created as it is subject to Him too; this Man can be no other god or idol but must be the true and natural God together with the Father and the Holy Spirit. If we have the time and are endued with the grace, we shall later discourse on this subject on the basis of more similar passages, especially verses from the Psalms. But first let us dispose of these words of David in which he confesses the two sublimest doctrines of our faith so aptly, that there are three distinct Persons in God, and that one of these, the Son, should become man and receive honor and dominion over all from the Father, that the Holy Spirit, who has previously proclaimed this through the mouth and lips of the prophets, should inscribe this into the heart of man by faith. And this is nothing but the work exclusively peculiar to the Divine Majesty; for it is not the work of man or of angel first to promise this and then to create faith in the human heart. St. Paul declares (Eph. 2:8) that such faith "is the gift of God," effected and bestowed by the Holy Spirit.

Not everybody has the competency to note and to distinguish the three Persons of the Godhead as distinct from one another as he reads Scripture and the Psalms. For if a carnal mind approaches these words here, he will read perfunctorily and cursorily: *The Spirit of the Lord has spoken by me, the God of Israel has talked to me, the Rock of Israel has spoken, the just Ruler among men, etc.* He will not think otherwise than that all these terms refer to God in one Person with a superfluity of words. Or he falls into the Jewish blindness according to which they suppose that David is this just ruler, a ruler in the fear of God. They transform the promise into commands and laws, implying that he who aspires to rule over men must be just and God-fearing, although David enthusiastically and sincerely proclaims that these are words of promise of the Messiah of the God of Jacob and not precepts pertaining to worldly rulers.

Such a person would fare the same way with Ps. 2, in which the three Persons also speak separately, as three individual Speakers. God the Father says (v. 6): "I have set My King on Zion, My holy hill." This King is certainly a Person apart from Him who installs Him as King. And then the words follow immediately (v. 7) "I will tell of the decree." These words sound as if the Father were still speaking, and that is what reason would suggest, though, in fact, it is the King, the Son, as is apparent from what follows (v. 7): "The Lord said to Me, You are My Son, today I have begotten You." That this Person is man is certain, for He is to preach and be the Messiah, as we hear in v. 2: "They rage against the Lord and His Messiah." But that He is God is proved by the words of the Father: "You are My Son, today I have begotten You," as we Christians well know. We find further proof of His Godhead in the fact that God makes "the ends of the earth His possession," together with the Gentiles and whatever the earth contains, which is the equivalent of God's own kingdom.

Furthermore, God orders man to kiss the Son (v. 11), or worship Him and serve Him with awe, concluding with the words: "Blessed are all who take refuge in Him." That can pertain only to God. The fact that not all obey Him in accord with the Gospel does not diminish His dominion over all creatures in the least. He who refuses to be under His grace must be subject to His wrath. He who will not rule with Him must, together with His enemies, be His footstool. He is Judge over the quick and the dead. Do you imagine that because Turk, pope, Jew, and the whole evil host of the world and the devil do not want His grace but rave against it they will on that account escape His might? They will surely be taught their lesson; for "He who sits in the heavens laughs. . . . Then He will speak to them in His wrath" (vv. 4, 5). In brief, He is Lord and remains Lord, as God Himself is Lord; for God has given Him dominion over all. His power is certain and endures. Woe to him who does not accept this by grace. He will encounter this power coupled with wrath in all eternity.

Thus we again find two distinct Persons here, the Father and the Son; and the Holy Spirit is present although not especially mentioned. It is He who composed and put into words this psalm, introducing the Father and the Son in Their own words. Thus the distinctive trinity of Persons in one indivisible divine essence is professed here together with the fact that the Son is Man and Messiah, just as this is professed in the last words of David. A carnal heart will pass over these words casually or suppose that David composed them in his capacity as a pious man about himself or about others. That is what the blind Jews do. But David does not let us attribute these words to him. "These are delightful and charming psalms of Israel," he says, "and I did not make them, but 'the Spirit of the Lord has spoken by me.'" After all, how could flesh and blood, reason and human wisdom, discourse on such sublime and incomprehensible matters? These are sheer foolishness and offense to them.

Now to verify that this is really the opinion of David, that he, as just stated, believed this and died in that belief, we will discuss the words on which he based and by reason of which he indited such lovely psalms. We find them recorded in 2 Sam. 7:11-16 and in 1 Chron. 17:10-14. They read as follows:

> *Moreover the Lord declares to you that the Lord will build you a house. When your days are fulfilled to go to be with your fathers, I will raise up your Offspring after you, one of your own sons, and I will establish His kingdom. He shall build a house for Me, and I will establish His throne forever. I will be His Father, and He shall be My Son; I will not take My steadfast love from Him, as I took it from him who was before you, but I will confirm Him in My house and in My kingdom forever, and His throne shall be established forever.*

The first point made here is expressed in the words *The Lord declares to you that the Lord will build you a house.* This obviously refers to the house of David and signifies that his children are to possess the scepter of Judah until the advent of the Messiah. Enough has been said about this in that little booklet dealing with the Jews.[14] Here we again find the three Persons of the Godhead: first the Holy Spirit, who speaks by the prophet Nathan. We heard before that Holy Scripture is spoken by the Holy Spirit in keeping with the words of David *The Spirit of the Lord has spoken by me.* In like manner He speaks by all prophets. The Holy Spirit, furthermore, introduces the Person of the Father when He says: "The Lord declares to you." And immediately after that He presents the Person of the Son, saying *that the Lord will build you a house.* And yet it is but one God and Lord who speaks through Nathan, makes an announcement to David, and builds his house. All three are but one Speaker, one Announcer, one Builder. It is immaterial whether or not everybody's reason discerns these three Persons in Scripture. I am well aware how the saucy prigs who make bold to instruct the Holy Spirit make annotations here and in similar passages.[15]

Wherever in Scripture you find God speaking about God, as if there were two persons, you may boldly assume that three Persons of the Godhead are there indicated. Thus in the passage under discussion we hear the Lord say that the Lord will build a house for David. Likewise we read in Gen. 19:24: "Then the Lord rained on Sodom and Gomorrah brimstone and fire from the Lord out of heaven." For the Holy Spirit is no fool or drunkard, who would speak one iota, much less a word, in vain. If the Lord, that is, the Son rains fire and brimstone from the Lord, that is, the Father, the Holy Spirit is simultaneously present. It is He who speaks these words by Abraham, or whoever it might be, about the two Lords. And still these three are one Lord, one God, who rains fire and brimstone. Later we shall hear more examples illustrating that.

The second point is contained in the words *When your days are fulfilled to go to be with your fathers, I will raise up your Offspring after you, etc.* Here the text touching on the Messiah really begins. For these words cannot be spoken of Solomon, much less of any

---

[14] A reference to Luther's treatise *On the Jews and Their Lies* (W, LIII, 465—67; *Luther's Works,* 47, pp. 196—99).

[15] This seems to be an attack on several of Luther's opponents who objected to the traditional Trinitarian exegesis of these passages.

other son of David. They must refer to the true, unique Son of David, the Messiah, who was to come after the reign of Judah was ended. *He shall build a house for Me,* He says, *and I will establish His kingdom forever.* This house cannot be identical with the temple of Solomon, for immediately prior to this He says (1 Chron. 17:4-5): "You shall not build Me a house to dwell in. For I have not dwelt in a house since I led up Israel to this day." And in 1 Kings 8:27 Solomon himself declares: "But will God indeed dwell on the earth? Behold, heaven and the highest heaven cannot contain Thee; how much less this house which I have built!" And Is. 66:1 expresses this thought still more forcefully: "Thus says the Lord: 'Heaven is My throne, and the earth is My footstool; what is the house which you would build for Me, and what is the place of My rest?'"

Here God expressly repudiates the Jews' stupid zeal. They boasted that they were erecting a house for God by building the temple, that they were thereby rendering Him a great service. Over this they became proud and stubborn murderers of the prophets. And yet God announces here that He scorns the temple, and that He, instead, demands a humble and contrite spirit which stands in awe before His Word (cf. Is. 66:2); yes, this spirit is to become the temple where He rests. God also rejects all sacrifices and temple worship, saying (Is. 66:3): "He who slaughters an ox is like him who kills a man; he who sacrifices a lamb, like him who breaks a dog's neck; he who presents a cereal offering, like him who offers swine's blood; he who makes a memorial offering of frankincense, like him who blesses an idol." God did not have the temple built that they might haughtily despise His Word and, instead, give themselves to much sacrificing, thus to sanctify themselves; but He had the temple erected that His name, not He Himself, might dwell there, as Scripture declares everywhere. That is, they were to hear His Word there and call upon Him. Thereby He would be honored. But they wanted the reputation and honor of having such a temple be their own, and they murdered the prophets because of their advocacy of God's Word.

Therefore this house, to be built by Messiah, the Son of David and of God, must necessarily be a different, a larger and more glorious, house. For figure it out for yourself; if God is to dwell in this house, it must be much larger and more splendid than heaven and earth, for God is so vast that heaven is the chair on which He thrones and the earth is His footstool. How much additional space would be required to rest His head, breast, and arms? In view of this it is very relevant to ask: "What kind of house of wood and stone would you build Me for My dwelling, when heaven and earth are far, far too small to contain Me?" Holy Scripture, in particular the New Testament, informs us about this house. It is the holy Christian church, which extends to the ends of the earth. Furthermore, it is an everlasting house, a house that will endure and live forever, a house in which God remains and lives and keeps house forever. What a house and temple that will become!

Now let us consider the carpenter, or master builder, of this house. He is to be a man and a son of David, for the text speaks of *one of your own sons* (1 Chron. 17:11). Yet he is to build a house of God which is to be better and more glorious than heaven and earth and, in addition, is to stand forever. Whence will he derive the skill and the power for this? Neither man's nor angel's skill or might can come into question here, for angels cannot create heaven and earth, no, not even the least of the creatures. Much less is man able to do this. Therefore the builder of this house must be true God, who has the actual power of the divine nature to create heaven and earth and even much better things than that; that is, He must be omnipotent God, and yet He is not the Person who says of Him *I will be His Father, and He shall be My Son and He shall build a house for Me.* Here the Persons are clearly and definitely distinguished as Father and Son, as Builder and Master of the house. Still they cannot be two Gods, nor can the Son be a separate or a different God. The First Commandment precludes that possibility, saying (Ex. 20:3): "You shall have no other gods before Me." And (Deut. 6:4): "Hear, O Israel: The Lord our God is one Lord, or God."

We heard before that whenever Scripture speaks of the two Persons of the Father and the Son, the Holy Spirit, the third Person, is also present; for it is He who speaks those words through the prophets. Thus a believing heart finds powerful and well-grounded proof and testimony in this passage that God, the omnipotent Creator of heaven and earth, is the one true God, that there can be no other god beside Him, that there are, at the same time, three distinct Persons, the Father, the Son, and the Holy Spirit yet in this way, that only the Son became Man and David's Son. Undoubtedly the prohibition not to worship more than one God was impressed upon the people of Israel so strictly that they should not be offended when the Messiah should come and be proclaimed and believed to be God, as if He were minded, contrary to Moses, to teach more than one God, or a strange god, but that they should bridle their ears and hearts and be willing to learn how the First Commandment concerning one God is to be understood correctly and thoroughly. The text continues (1 Chron. 17:14):

I will confirm Him in My house and in My kingdom forever.

What does this mean? Let us give ear. As I have said above, the house is to be and to remain forever. Therefore the Master of the house must also be eternal and must be endowed with eternal and divine power. Here He continues His speech to David: "In the house which My Son and yours is to build for Me, He, as well as I, will be Master. He is to be My equal in this one house. I will install Him and decree that He is to own it just as I do." Now, we have heard that this house of God is larger and better and more glorious than heaven and earth. And if David's Son, the Messiah, is Master and Lord of this house, He is certainly also Master and Lord of heaven and earth and far superior to and better than these. For He who is Lord over this house, as God Himself is, must self-evidently be superior and be Lord over heaven and earth, as God Himself is. And that can be none other than the one God, Creator of heaven and earth. From this we deduce that Messiah, David's natural Son, must be true God and no strange god. For, as I have already said, God does not let a strange god be master of His own house. He must and will keep His honor and power for Himself and yield it to no one else. That should demonstrate clearly enough that Messiah, David's Son, is Lord and King in God's own kingdom, or that He is equal with God; for it is certain that God is here speaking of the Messiah.

But if any one insists on imitating the Jews to apply these words *My house* and *My kingdom* to the temple in Jerusalem and to the people of Israel, he may do that without me and on his own. I am well aware that God calls the temple His house. In Is. 56:7 He says: "My house shall be called a house of prayer," which Christ quotes in Matt. 21:13 and in Luke 19:46, etc. And I know that Israel is called God's kingdom. In Ex. 19:6 God states: "You shall be to Me a kingdom of priests" (but with the addition: "if you will obey My voice and keep My covenant"). I am also mindful of the fact that God says in Ezek. 18:4: "The soul of the father as well as the soul of the son is Mine." Yes, I know that the bread that I eat and the wine that I drink are also called God's bread and wine. What is there in heaven and earth that is not His? Thus God declares in Is. 66:1: "Heaven is My throne, and the earth is My footstool; what is the house which you would build for Me? . . . All these things My hand has made, and so all these things come to be." That means: "If I had not previously created heaven and earth, whence would you take lime, stone, wood, iron, and whatever is required for construction? Was that not all Mine first? Where did you get it? What did you do to create it? Yes, who and whose are you yourself? Am I not your Creator?" Thus also David confesses in his beautiful encomium of 1 Chron. 29:14, where he refers to the material for the building of the temple: "All things come from Thee, and of Thy own have we given Thee."

In the very same way God also speaks concerning the sacrifices in the temple, saying in effect in Ps. 50: "What do you propose to offer Me? 'Do I eat the flesh of bulls or drink the blood of goats?' Where did you get your sacrifices, your bulls, your sheep, your goats? Were these not all Mine before? Whose are all the cattle, the sheep, and all other beasts that graze in the pastures throughout the whole world? Did I not create them without your cooperation? From what source would you have taken them for sacrifice to Me if I had not first given them to you?" That is tantamount to saying: "I do not stand in need of your sacrifices, and you must not imagine that you are thereby rendering Me a service, as if I had to have them and could not get along without them. No, this is their purpose: By such sacrifices you are to acknowledge and confess that all that you are and all that you have you have from Me, and that you are thus to honor, exalt, and praise Me as your God and Creator. Yes, for this purpose I have let them be called My sacrifices for a time. But where that purpose is lost, the sacrifices are no longer worth anything."

"In that sense I also called the temple *My house*, not because I had to dwell in it or because you could render Me a service by means of it, but for your sakes I call it *My house*, to afford you a place where you can pray to Me, praise Me, and call upon Me; for this shall not be My dwelling-place but your house of prayer. Yes, it is to be called a house of prayer. But it cannot and must not be called a house of prayer for Me, for I have no one to supplicate and petition, since I am God, who has need of no one. And if My house is used for a different purpose than that of prayer, it is a den of murderers and not My house. That is done by those who imagine that they are bestowing a great favor on Me by the work of building Me a house. They themselves want to be lauded and honored for such a work and such a structure, as if they thereby merited great mercy from Me. Such a house must then be destroyed, devastated, razed as the most disgraceful den of murderers, which is no longer My house but the devil's own hell."

Now, he who would interpret the words *My house* and *My kingdom* in this passage as pertaining to the temple and to the people of Israel must also assume the further burden to adduce good and convincing proof that the temple in Jerusalem and the people of Israel in the land of Canaan have from the time of David until now remained intact continuously, for the text here clearly states that David's house shall remain forever and that the Messiah, David's Son, shall be eternally enthroned in God's house and kingdom. We Christians must concede that we are unable to prove this. We know that God's house, the temple in Jerusalem, has lain in ashes approximately 1500 years, that David's house and kingdom and the people of Israel have also amounted to nothing for about 1500 years, and that they have not had dominion or a kingdom in Canaan. We needs must adhere to our former interpretation and maintain that the words *My house* and *My kingdom* pertain to the eternal kingdom of God, in which He chooses to dwell and reign forever, which His Son and David's, the Messiah, was to build by His divine omnipotence and wisdom.

But let us lend ear to David himself and hear how he understood these words. In 1 Chron. 17:15-16 we read:

Nathan spoke all these words (as given above) *to David. Then king David went in and sat before the Lord and said: "Who am I, O Lord God, and what is my house, that Thou hast brought me thus far?"*

Here David shows that he did indeed understand the words of

God's promise spoken to him by Nathan (1 Chron. 17:13-14): *I will be His Father, and He shall be My Son . . . I will confirm Him in My house and in my kingdom forever.* Therefore he says *Who am I, and what is my house, that Thou hast brought me this far?* "Your promise that my house, that I, my son, should reach such heights as to have him occupy Your own eternal kingdom, be lord and king, is too much glory and honor for me. O Lord God, where are you taking me?" He cannot find words to express himself in his great amazement. He speaks of *thus far*. "Whereto? Whereto? My dear God, am I, that is, my flesh and blood, to sit enthroned in Your eternal kingdom as Your equal? Then my flesh and blood, my son and Your son, must necessarily be true and very God, who sits enthroned as Your equal. O God, where are You taking me?" We read on (1 Chron. 17:17):

Thou hast regarded me as in the form of a Man who is God the Lord on high.

The translation of these words by almost all other Hebraists is far different. Several, however, and among these Bernhard Ziegler, bear witness to me that this passage may and must be translated grammatically as I did.[16] With these words David clearly states that his Son, the Messiah, will surely be true Man, in form, manner, and size like any other man (Phil. 2:7), and yet up above and on high, where there is no manner of men, where only God is and governs, He is to be God the Lord. That is, I say, clearly the opinion of David tersely expressed. In view of this, he says above (v. 16): "Whither, whither are you, dear God, taking me?" And here: "Why do you regard me, unworthy human being that I am, that my son should be King in Your eternal kingdom? David knows full well that no other than the true God is entitled to be King in God's eternal kingdom. And since the son of David is man and a person apart from the Father, who installs him in His kingdom, and since there cannot be two gods or more than one God, David here concludes that his Son, the Messiah, must be true and natural God, and yet none other God than the Father, but a separate Person in the same one inseparable Godhead, and that the Holy Spirit, who

---

[16] Bernhard Ziegler was professor of Hebrew at Leipzig and a frequent consultant to Luther and his colleagues in the translation and exposition of the Old Testament.

as true God speaks these words through Nathan and David concerning the Father and the Son, is the third Person in the same one Godhead.

That is the doctrine and the belief of the New Testament, namely, that Jesus of Nazareth, David's and the Virgin Mary's Son, is true Man and God's natural, eternal Son, one God and three distinct Persons together with the Father and the Holy Spirit. And since David's words in this passage amply reflect that meaning in accord with the general usage of the Hebrew tongue, we Christians must not seek or heed any other significance in them but regard this as the only correct one and look upon all other interpretations as worthless human imagination. The New Testament cannot err, nor can the Old Testament where it harmonizes and agrees with the New Testament.

You may feel tempted to ask here: "If the words of David and Nathan reveal the doctrine of Christ's deity so clearly, how do you explain that neither the holy fathers nor any other teacher discovered or ever mentioned this, and that you recent and young Hebraists just became aware of this now? [17] Why do the Jewish rabbis not discern this?" We reply: After the days of the apostles the knowledge of the Hebrew language was scant and deficient.[18] The dear fathers and teachers contented themselves with the New Testament, in which they found this doctrine and all others in great abundance. The prophets and apostles, however, did perceive the truth of this very well, as we shall hear later. It is perfectly natural that the rabbis did not see this; for he who is blind sees nothing. In Is. 6:9 the prophet says of them: "See and see, but do not perceive." And whoever must learn from them will surely also become blind. To be sure, we, too, would not be able to see it if we could not look the Old Testament straight into the eye because we are illumined by the New Testament. For the Old Testament is veiled without the New Testament (2 Cor. 4:3-4).

Consider our own times, in which we are preaching of the grace

---

[17] Luther is, of course, referring to the Christian exegetical tradition, not only to the Jewish; as his comments indicate, the development of the Biblical support for these doctrines was a contribution of Reformation exegesis to the Trinitarian dogma.

[18] Except for Origen and Jerome, there were few if any of the church fathers who could read Hebrew; except for converts from Judaism, there were few among the medieval doctors who could read it either.

of Christ against our own presumptuous works and holiness. How few there are to see this or to accept it earnestly! Where does the fault lie? It is being preached and taught so lucidly; it is being read, written, sung, painted, and disseminated in every way, so that wood and stone could understand it if these were endowed with but a modicum of reason. And yet, pope, kings, princes, bishops, scholars, lords, noblemen, burghers, and peasants do not see it but pass it by, blind with seeing eyes, deaf with hearing ears; for their heart does not concentrate on what lies close at hand but roves about elsewhere. Thus the prophets also foretold clearly enough in their day that Christ was to be God and Lord over all, as David does here. However, only a few paid this any heed and believed it; the others were blind and deaf to it and followed the voice of their heart and their own fancy. This is termed a mystery, and a mystery it remains. Let him who understands this and is sincere in his belief, thank God and pay no attention to the great multitude of scorners.

Do you not suppose that Isaiah read this text intently? For he says in chapter 9:6-7: "For to us a Child is born, to us a Son is given; and the government will be upon His shoulder, and His name will be called 'Wonderful, Counselor, Mighty God, Everlasting Father, Prince of Peace.' Of the increase of His government and of peace there will be no end, upon the throne of David, and over His kingdom, to establish it and to uphold it with justice and with righteousness from this time forth and forevermore." Here Isaiah takes the words out of Nathan's mouth, as he prophesies that the Messiah will be an eternal King and Father in God's kingdom. And he also calls Him God, for the word אֵל literally, to be sure, means "power"; but when it is a proper name, as here, its meaning throughout Scripture is God, who alone has power. Both Jews and Hebraists have to admit that. Thus Isaiah concurs with David and the New Testament, affirming that Christ is an eternal King and the true God. And it follows that His kingdom must be divine and everlasting, established on the throne of David, etc.

In particular has he studied the concept "everlasting kingdom" in the passage where God says to David by Nathan (1 Chron. 17:14): *I will confirm thy Son in My kingdom forever*, and he feels instinctively that this is spoken, as David says, of a man who must be אֵל, that is, God, up above. For to possess the eternal kingdom of

God and to be King there cannot belong to a mere man, nor can this refer to a transitory, temporal, and earthly kingdom which will terminate and the king of which must die and his children after him. No, here the Son of David is to be an eternal King in the everlasting kingdom of God. And as Isaiah agrees, "of the peace there will be no end," and He, the Son of David, the Child, born and given to us, shall be an "Everlasting Father and a Prince of Peace . . . from this time forth and forevermore." Consequently, He must be God, or אֵל, who is able to bestow and preserve such eternal peace by His divine power.

Isaiah witnesses to the eternity of the Messiah's kingdom in a number of passages; for instance, in chapter 51:4-5: "Listen to Me, My people, and give ear to Me, My nation; for a law will go forth from Me, and My justice for a light to the peoples. My righteousness draws near speedily, My salvation has gone forth." And a little while later he says (v. 6): "My Salvation will be forever, and My Righteousness will never be ended." This is the eternal Righteousness of which Daniel 9:24 says: "Seventy weeks of years are decreed . . . to bring in everlasting Righteousness." This refers to the Messiah; thus all old Hebraists have interpreted it.[19] Mere man or angel cannot be called "eternal Righteousness and Salvation"; no, these terms signify God Himself. And yet He is also David's Son, natural Man, and a Person distinct from the One that speaks about Him and calls Him "My Salvation, My Righteousness." The Holy Spirit is the third Person present; it is He who says this about the other two. In 1 Cor. 1:30 the New Testament speaks of "Christ Jesus, whom God made our Wisdom, our Righteousness and Sanctification and Redemption." That is in accord with Isaiah, and Isaiah is in accord with Paul.

In Is. 60:19-20 we read in like manner: "The sun shall be no more your light by day, nor for brightness shall the moon give light to you by night; but the Lord will be your everlasting Light, and your God will be your Glory. Your sun shall no more go down, nor your moon withdraw itself; for the Lord will be your everlasting Light, and your days of mourning shall be ended." Here it is clearly stated that the Lord and our God Himself will be our everlasting Light. Here the one Lord speaks about the other. Indeed, in the

[19] Luther's phrase *alle alten Ebrei* could refer either to "Hebrews" or to "Hebraists."

entire chapter it is not Isaiah who is speaking but the Lord. It is He who says: "The Lord will be your everlasting Light." Who is the Lord who speaks these words? Without a doubt, God the Father. Who is the Lord of whom He says: "The Lord will be your everlasting Light"? Without a doubt, God the Son, Jesus Christ. For here we find the great name of God, Jehovah, which our Bibles print with capital letters, LORD, in contradistinction to the other names. Who is it who speaks these words by the tongue of Isaiah? Without a doubt, God the Holy Spirit, who speaks by the prophets, introducing the Person of the Father, who, in turn, speaks of the eternal Light, that is, of His Son, Jesus of Nazareth, the Son of David and of Mary.

Such an eternal Light, yes, such a Lord, cannot be a mere angel, nor a man, either. Isaiah's prophecy agrees with the New Testament, in which Jesus often calls Himself a light. In John 1:4-5 we read: "The life was the light of men. The light shines in the darkness, but the darkness has not grasped it." Since this is in agreement with the New Testament, Isaiah's prophecy should cheerfully be interpreted as referring to none other than Jesus Christ, who has not prepared a transitory kingdom under this sun and this moon for us; no, He Himself wants to be our eternal Light, Sun and Moon, Life and Salvation. Thus He says in Is. 51:6 above: "Lift up your eyes to the heavens and look at the earth beneath; for the heavens will vanish like smoke, the earth will wear out like a garment; and they who dwell in it will die like gnats; but My Salvation will be forever, and My Righteousness will never be ended."

My dear friend, tell me, can this and similar verses tolerate the Jews' stupid conception of their Messiah, who is to be a mortal, earthly king on earth, resident in Jerusalem? This is ruled out when God here places in juxtaposition His Messiah and heaven and earth, saying: "The heavens will vanish like smoke" — this will not happen without fire (2 Peter 3:12); "the earth will wear out like a garment, and they who dwell in it will die like gnats." But His Salvation, He says, which is near at hand, His Righteousness, which has gone forth shall remain forever and be an eternal light; for He is the Lord Himself and your God (cf. Is. 51:15). Here you can see whether Isaiah understood the words of Nathan in 1 Chron. 17:13-14, in which he introduces God as saying: *I will be His Father, and He shall be My Son . . . I will confirm Him in My kingdom forever* and David's words (1 Chron. 17:17): *Thou hast regarded me as in the form of a Man who is God the Lord on high,* and (2 Sam. 7:19): *This is the manner of a Man who is the Lord God.* Here the Latin text reads: "This is the law of Adam, O Lord God." This makes no sense.

Let us also consult Daniel, who declares in chapter 7:13-14: "I saw in the night visions, and behold, with the clouds of heaven there came one like a Son of Man, and He came to the Ancient of Days and was presented before Him. And to Him was given dominion and glory and kingdom, that all peoples, nations, and languages should serve Him; His dominion is an everlasting dominion, which shall not pass away; and His kingdom one that shall not be destroyed." Christians understand this verse well. However, now we want to observe how this agrees with the New Testament. He beholds a Son of Man in the clouds, which undoubtedly signifies that His kingdom is not to be of this world, that it is not to be transitory and temporal, but that it is to be heavenly and eternal. He says that "the Ancient of Days," that is, God the Father, gave Him dominion over all, that His power is to endure forever and is not to pass away. This eternity, or this everlasting kingdom, cannot be conferred on any mere creature, neither angel nor man, for it is a divine dominion, God's own dominion. If God were to divest Himself of His eternal dominion and His eternal kingdom, what would He have or have left? He would keep nothing at all, He would destroy Himself since there would then be another in possession of the eternal dominion. Obviously there can be nothing beyond and outside of this eternal dominion. Eternal dominion embraces everything and will not tolerate anything superior to it or anything outside of it. This must be God Himself and nothing else.

This passage from Daniel also [20] powerfully presents the doctrine of the Godhead in three Persons and of the humanity of the Son; for the Person who gives must be distinct from the Person who receives. Thus the Father bestows the eternal dominion on the Son, and the Son receives it from the Father, and this is from eternity; otherwise this could not be an eternal dominion. And the Holy Spirit is present, inasmuch as He speaks these words through Daniel. For such sublime and mysterious things no one could know if the Holy Spirit would not reveal them through the proph-

[20] The Weimar text has *auf,* but the Erlangen text has *auch.*

ets. It has been stated often enough above that Holy Scripture is given through the Holy Spirit. In addition, the Son is nevertheless also a Son of Man, that is, a true human being and David's Son, to whom such eternal dominion is given. Thus we note that the prophets did indeed respect and understand the word "eternal," which God used when He addressed David through Nathan and said (1 Chron. 17:14): "I will install My Son and yours in My eternal kingdom."

Here is where Mr. Smart Aleck, reason, takes offense, presuming to be ten times wiser than God Himself, asking: "How can God take His eternal dominion and bestow it on someone else? What would He be retaining for Himself? Did we not say above [21] that God says in Is. 42:8: "My glory I give to no other, nor My praise to graven images"? And it is particularly impossible for God to bestow this on a human being, who has not existed from eternity, as God has, but who had a beginning in time, who was born and who is mortal, as we Christians confess and preach of Jesus Christ, David's and Mary's Son. The Jews, Mohammed, the Turks, and the Tartars also belong to this category of superintelligent people. With their spoonful or nutshellful of brain they can comprehend the incomprehensible essence of God and say that since God has no wife, He can also have no son. Fie, fie, fie upon you, devil, together with Jews and Mohammed and all who are the disciples of blind, deaf, and wretched reason in these exalted matters, which none but God alone can fathom, which we grasp only in the measure in which the Holy Spirit has revealed them to us through the prophets.

We Christians, illumined by the New Testament, can answer these objections clearly and definitely and say: Christ, our Lord, has two births, or two natures, in one indivisible Person; for He is one Christ and not, as the stupid mind of Nestorius madly maintains, two Christs. According to the first birth, He received, not in time but from all eternity, the everlasting dominion, or the Godhead, from the Father. The Father gave this to Him in its entirety and in its perfection, as He Himself possesses it from eternity. He did not transfer this to Him in the sense that He Himself divested and deprived Himself of it; but He gave the Son the selfsame dominion and none other which He Himself had fully and completely

[21] See p. 277 above.

from eternity and which He retains in all eternity. For there are not two Godheads, but both Persons are one Godhead. The words of Is. 42:8 ever remain true: "My glory I give to no other, nor My praise to graven images." For the Son is no separate god or idol, but together with the Father He is the one true and eternal God.

Christ Himself speaks about this when He says in John 16:15: "All that the Father has is Mine." He does not say: "The Father no longer has anything; I alone have everything now, or: "The Father has everything alone; I have nothing." But He says: "The Father has it all, but, this 'all' that He has is Mine." That is patently saying that the Father and the Son compose one single Godhead. And of this "all" of the Father which belongs to the Son the Holy Spirit also partakes, as Christ says in the same passage: "He will take what is Mine." Which "Mine"? Without a doubt, from the "Mine" which the Father has. Thus the Holy Spirit takes from both, from the Father and the Son, the same complete Godhead from eternity. Christ also says in John 5:26: "As the Father has life in Himself, so He has granted the Son also to have life in Himself," and in verses 21 and 23: "As the Father raises the dead and gives them life, so also the Son gives life to whom He will. . . . that all may honor the Son, even as they honor the Father." All of this is said of the first, eternal, divine birth.

According to the second, the temporal, human birth Christ was also given the eternal dominion of God, yet temporally and not from eternity. For the human nature of Christ was not from eternity as His divine nature was. It is computed that Jesus, Mary's Son, is 1543 years old this year. But from the moment when deity and humanity were united in one Person, the Man, Mary's Son, is and is called almighty, eternal God, who has eternal dominion, who has created all things and preserves them "through the communication of attributes" *(per communicationem idiomatum),* because He is one Person with the Godhead and is also very God. Christ refers to this in Matt. 11:27: "All things have been delivered to Me by My Father," and in Matt. 28:18: "All authority in heaven and on earth has been given to Me." To which "Me"? "To Me, Jesus of Nazareth, Mary's incarnate Son. I had this from My Father from eternity, before I became man, but when I became man, it was imparted to Me in time according to My human nature, and I kept it concealed until My resurrection and ascent into heaven, when it was to be manifested and glorified. Thus St. Paul declares in Rom. 1:4, He was glorified, or "designated Son of God in power." John speaks of this as being "glorified" in chapter 7:39: [22] "As yet the Spirit had not been given, because Jesus was not yet glorified."

Now note that Daniel speaks about the Son of Man, who receives eternal dominion from God, in almost the same way as Isaiah does and as also Nathan and David do, saying that God would install David's Son as King in His eternal kingdom; and, as David states, this is spoken of a man "who is God the Lord on high." O that we Christians would recognize this ineffable grace which both the Old and the New Testament contain in such rich measure! Alas, that we do not rejoice and show forth our gratitude as we should! It would not be surprising if a Christian heart that thoroughly pondered and grasped the import of this would die for joy and again be quickened by joy. How amazing it is that God is man and converses with us humans, that He lives and especially that He dies for us! David grows mute and numb with ecstatic joy; he can utter no more than (1 Chron. 17:16): *What am I, O Lord God, and what is my house, that Thou hast brought me thus far?*

All of this revolves about the words recorded in 1 Chron. 17, on which, as already stated, the last words of David are based, which assert that Christ must be very God and very Man. And whatever further thoughts might well forth from that text we shall consider later with God's help. The prophets that followed David, as well as David himself, derived much proof of Christ's deity and of His humanity from this. Take, for example, Ps. 110:1: "The Lord says to my Lord, Sit at My right hand, until I make Your enemies Your footstool." What else can be the significance of the phrase "to sit at My right hand" than to sit enthroned equal with God, that is, to be seated in the eternal kingdom of God? For Christ does not sit at God's head or at His feet, neither above Him nor below Him, but at His right, as His peer, so that the heaven is also His throne and the earth His footstool. Thus Christ says in Matt. 28:18: "All authority in heaven and on earth has been given to Me," and in Mark 16:19 we read: "He was taken up into heaven and sat down at the right hand of God." And when Christ asks the Pharisees in Matt. 22:43-44: "If Christ is David's son, how is it then that David, inspired by the Spirit" — that is, the Spirit speaks by him — "calls

---

[22] The original has "John 5."

Him Lord, saying, 'The Lord said to My Lord, Sit at My right hand'?" they were unable to make reply.

Today, too, the Jews have no answer and will have none in eternity. To be sure, they blaspheme loudly, but against us Christians, and in their clumsy, malicious mania, also against their own old rabbis and teachers. You can read about this in Lyra on the same passage.[23] But we have the New Testament; it not only agrees with this psalm, and the psalm is similar to it, and, as has been amply stated before, we Christians have enough reason here to interpret the Old Testament as we do; but all other interpretations will inevitably go awry. Christ Himself appears on the scene with His apostles, who testify and prove with an abundance of words and works that this is the meaning. This psalm is, furthermore, one of the passages in which the three distinct Persons dwelling in one Godhead are proclaimed, which is the only interpretation of the prophets and of Christians, given by the Holy Spirit. Jews, Mohammed, and reason can know nothing of this. But here is the Father, who says (Ps. 110:1): "Sit at My right hand." And it is David's Son, Christ, to whom He addresses these words.

Now the Father is not Christ or David's Son, and Christ is not the Father; and yet He is to sit at the right hand of the Father as His equal and partake of one kingdom, dominion, honor, and everything with Him. But God tolerates no peer to share equal honor and dominion with Him. Therefore Christ, David's Son, must be true God and one God with the Father and of equal throne with Him. For there can be no more than one God in accord with the First Commandment, which reads: "Thou shalt have no other gods besides Me." And the Holy Spirit is also present as the one true God. It is He who speaks to us men through David and through all the prophets and reveals and teaches us every truth of the Godhead. Thus David declares (2 Sam. 23:2): *The Spirit of the Lord has spoken by me.* And Christ Himself states in Matt. 22:45: "If David thus calls Him Lord, how is He his Son?" To be sure, without the Spirit he would neither call Him that nor know in what way Christ is his Son and his Lord. The Holy Spirit, however, is not Christ the Son nor the Father. He cannot be another God. It follows cogently that there is but one God and yet three separate Persons, Father, Son, and Holy Spirit, from eternity to eternity.

[23] Apparently a reference to Lyra *ad* Matt. 22:46.

It may perplex some to hear David say: *Who am I? What is my house?* Also: *Thou hast regarded me as a Man who is God the Lord on high* (1 Chron. 17:16, 17). After all, God did not say to David: "You shall be My son; I will establish you in My eternal kingdom." No, God says to David: "Your son shall be My Son; Him will I place in My eternal kingdom" (cf. 1 Chron. 17:13-14). Why does David alter the words of God and refer them to himself, as though he were the man *who is God the Lord on high?* Well, as you hear, David is the father of this Son; the latter is to issue from his family and his blood. Now it is natural that a father glories in the honor that comes to his son as much and more than the son does himself. He wishes every honor and every good thing for his son more than he does for himself. And again, any contumely and dishonor the son experiences saddens the father more than if this were heaped on him himself. Therefore, when he says: *What is my house?* not only David but his whole house exults here over the glory that a Son should issue from their flesh and blood who would sit at the right hand of God.

In history we read of a father named Chilo, who died for joy when apprised that his son had won the victory in the Olympic Games.[24] And we hear of a Roman mother whose son had been reported slain together with many others at Cannae in the war against Hannibal, but who returned home unexpectedly, hale and hearty. In the very moment when she laid eyes on him, she dropped over, dead for joy.[25] David is similarly so overjoyed here that he hardly knows what to say and how to say it. The honor that is to come to his son, his own flesh and blood, affects him as though it had come to him himself.

Moreover, this son of David was at the time still contained only in David's own flesh and blood. Nothing of this son was apparent at this time except David's own person with the flesh and blood from which the son should eventually be born. For all this happened and was spoken in time, before the birth of David's son Nathan, from whose lineage Christ was born (Luke 3:31). In fact, Nathan's mother, Bathsheba, had not yet become David's wife but was still the wife of Uriah. This took place quite a while before

---

[24] Diogenes Laertius, *De vitis, dogmatibus et apophthegmatibus clarorum virorum*, I, 72.

[25] The source of this anecdote is Aulus Gellius, *Attic Nights*, III, ch. 15.

David's fall into adultery. Therefore it is not unfitting for a father to praise and thank God for his son's honor in words like these: "O dear God, who am I and what do You make of me that You honor me so highly and elevate the issue of my flesh and blood to such a lordship? It is I on whom this honor and this joy are bestowed; for, after all, it is my flesh and blood which at present is still in me and with me, but which is to be born some time in the future."

In the prophets our Lord Jesus is therefore often called by the name of His father David. In Hos. 3:5 we read: "Afterward the children of Israel shall return and seek the Lord their God, and David their King; and they shall come in fear to the Lord and to His goodness in the latter days." Here David means our Lord Christ, and He is given equal honor with God and is called the Lord, whom they will seek and honor. They will seek and honor God and their King in the same way, just as we honor the Father and the Son with the same faith. We do not honor the Father with one faith and the Son with a different one. The third Person, the Holy Spirit, is also present here. It is He who utters these words through Hosea and who teaches us to believe.

Likewise, we read in Ezek. 34:23-24: "And I will set up over them one Shepherd, My Servant David, and He shall feed them: He shall feed them and be their Shepherd. And I, the Lord, will be their God, and My Servant David shall be Prince among them." Here Christ is called "David" and "God's Servant." He is called "God's Servant" also in Is. 52:13 and in many other places. And St. Paul, who again and again proclaims Christ [26] as very God, makes Him a servant in Phil. 2:5-7: "Have this mind among yourselves, which you have in Christ Jesus, who, though He was in the form of God, did not count equality with God a thing to be grasped, but emptied Himself, taking the form of a servant, etc." Let us ask the apostle how he can talk so absurdly. If Christ is equal with God, how can He be a servant and assume the form of a servant? If He is a servant, how can He be God and in the form of God? We Christians, of course, know and understand this very well, but the Jews confidently harden themselves with this passage from Ezekiel. They stubbornly insist on their opinion—I am tempted to say, on their madness.[27] Let them go their way.

[26] The Weimar text has *jnen*, but we have read *jn*.

[27] The play on words between *sinnes* and *wahnsinnes* is difficult to reproduce in English.

Similarly, in Jer. 30:8-9 we read: "And it shall come to pass in that day, says the Lord of hosts, that I will break the yoke from off their neck, and I will burst their bonds, and strangers shall no more make servants of them. But they shall serve the Lord their God and David their King, whom I will raise up for them." Here Christ is again called "David." The Jews, both the young and the old, have to interpret this verse as referring to the Messiah. However, they misunderstand the words "the yoke" and "the bonds." They assume that these allude to the Babylonian captivity. But all three chapters in a row speak distinctly of the redemption which the Messiah is to work, that is, the redemption from sin and death, which the Law sets at us, and of which the Jews and reason are ignorant. This is how Christians and whatever has been Christian since the beginning of the world conceive of these words, etc.

Jeremiah in this verse at the same time makes his King David true God. He identifies God with this David and unites Him in one and the same honor which the children of Israel are to render Him. For if this David were not true God, God would not place Him beside Himself and say: "They shall serve the Lord their God and David their King," for it is written: "Thou shalt serve no other God but the Lord your God. Him alone you must fear and serve" (cf. Deut. 6:13-14; 10:20). Thus the words of Jeremiah harmonize with 1 Chron. 17:14-17: "I will confirm your Son in My eternal kingdom, who is Man and who, simultaneously, is God the Lord on high, who is honored and served equally with the Father." And the Holy Spirit, who speaks these words through Jeremiah and teaches us to believe and understand them, must be the third Person present here. And this is one God, beside whom we honor and serve no other.

This should be sufficient about the text of 1 Chron. 17, on which David's last words are based to show that Christ is God and that He is Man, descended from David. Now we may again revert to David's last words and bring them to a close, in which he professes that Christ is his Son and in which he praises Him as his God, in accord with the verse (1 Chron. 17:17): "Thou hast regarded me as a Man, who high above, or up above, or on high is God the Lord" *(qui superne vel in supernis vel in excelsis est Dominus Deus).* When our Latin text uses the vocative case and says *Domine Deus,* this makes no sense, just as little as its rendition of 2 Sam. 7:19

does: *Ista est lex Adam, Domine Deus.* It would be better to say: *Ista est lex vel forma hominis, Domini Dei; seu, qui sit Dominus Deus, etc.* Enough has been said about that now. However, since this is such fine subject matter and we, unfortunately, are such a small number together with the apostles and prophets, who concern themselves with Christ, the crucified David and eternal God, we want to discourse further on David's last words before we conclude them and take leave of them. This we do for the strengthening of our faith and in defiance of all devils, Jews, Mohammedans, papists, and all other enemies of this Son of David.

In the first place we want to give Moses, the fountainhead, the source, the father, and teacher of all prophets, a hearing. We want to test him to see whether we find him to be a Christian, whether he supports our position, since Christ Himself mentions him by name and says in John 5:46: "Moses wrote of Me." And if he wrote of Christ, he must, of course, have prophesied and proclaimed Him and enjoined all prophets who followed him to write and to preach of Christ. This they have done diligently, so that all Jews, young and old, know that a Messiah was to come. But Moses lies buried and is hidden from them, and no one knows where he is interred. Therefore we shall authorize and commission two faithful and reliable legates, or ambassadors to look for him, find him, rouse him, and fetch him hither. These two are the evangelist John and the apostle Paul. I wager that these two will hit the mark and not miss. However, I do not want you to forget what I said earlier, namely, that I would like to discuss here the proposition: Wherever the Hebrew text readily yields to and harmonizes with the New Testament, this is and must be the only right interpretation of Scripture.[28] All else, whatever Jews, Hebraists, and anybody else may babble against this to make it agree with their stippled, tormented, and coerced grammar, we must certainly consider sheer lies.

All right! John begins his Gospel with the words: "In the beginning was the Word, and the Word was with God, and the Word was God. He was in the beginning with God; all things were made through Him, and without Him was not anything made that was made." This is the speech of St. John, or rather, of the Holy Spirit, who quickens all things. Now let us see whether John is able to

[28] See p. 270 above.

find Moses with these words and to raise him from the dead. Moses has a very acute sense of hearing. He steps forth immediately and says: "Here I am; for just as you, John, speak about the Word, I, too, have spoken and still speak about the Word. You are taking the words out of my mouth. In the beginning of my book I, too, said of creation: 'And God said, "Let there be light"; and there was light. . . . And God said, "Let there be a firmament in the midst of the waters." . . . And God said, "Let the waters under the heavens be gathered together into one place, and let the dry land appear." . . . And God said, "Let the earth put forth vegetation, plants yielding seed." . . . And God said, "Let there be lights in the firmament of the heavens to separate the day from the night,"' etc." (cf. Gen. 1:3, 6, 9, 11, 14).

Here Moses is in accord with John, saying that there was a Word in the beginning of creation, through whom God said, that is, created and made, everything. Moses is not muttering or stammering here. These are not ambiguous and obscure words. The grammar is definite, too, on this point, that where there is a speaker, there is also a λογ, a word, or speech. We care not if the Jews, heretics, and Mohammed dream up their own interpretation here in opposition to the Christian belief. We have Moses' text and grammar on our side. This states plainly and clearly that God spoke in the beginning before the advent of any creature and that there is a Word through whom God says everything. This is affirmed in John 1. The dear fathers, Hilary, Augustine, Cyril, and others dealt with this Gospel amply and forcefully, rendering any further discourse on our part superflous. Their books are still extant.[29] For the present it suffices that we see and hear for ourselves how spontaneously and naturally and manifestly and exactly Moses agrees with John. Even blind reason cannot deny this but, in accord with definitive grammar, must concede that they speak one and the same language about the Word, through whom God created and made everything in the beginning.

Both of them, Moses and John, wish to indicate by which means, with which tool, or from what God made such a great

[29] Luther may not be referring to specific passages in these church fathers; but such passages are: Hilary, *De Trinitate*, I, 10, *Patrologia, Series Latina*, X, 31—32; Augustine, *De Trinitate*, II, 5, 9, ibid., XLII, 850; Cyril, *Expositio sive commentarius in Joannis Evangelium*, I, 2, *Patrologia, Series Graeca*, LXXIII, 29—37, and *passim*.

work, the whole universe. There was no material at hand, no wood or stone; there was absolutely nothing available with which the world was created. It was solely the Word, through whom it was made. The Word, however, was not made, but was with God from the beginning when He made all things, as Moses here says: "God said, 'Let there be'" this and that, etc. By the Word, he says, all things came into being. But there can be nothing with God outside of creation which is not God Itself. It follows that the Word must be God Himself, as great and as mighty as God Himself, since all things were made by Him. And yet, this cannot be the Person who speaks the Word. The speaker and the Word must be two separate beings. And again, these cannot be two gods because there is only one true God. There is of necessity only one Creator of heaven and earth, not two or three creators, or gods. Thus Moses and John concur in their testimony that God and the Word are surely two distinct Persons and that these two are, nonetheless, but one Creator and God, indivisible in the one divine essence.

This is how David read and understood Moses when he wrote in Ps. 33:6: "By the Word of the Lord the heavens were made, and all their host by the Breath of His mouth." He says that the heavens and all that is in and on it are "made." My dear man, made out of what? Out of nothing. By what? By God's Word and the Breath of His mouth. Does not David's speech here coincide with that of Moses? Does he not wish to say with practically the same words that God said, "Let there be the heaven," and the heaven came into being? But if the heaven with all that is therein came into being and was made by God's Speech, or Word, then the earth with all that is therein indubitably also came into being and was made by the same Word. Now, the Word is not the heaven nor the earth, nor anything that is in them, nor anything that is made together with these by the Word. Therefore it must be God Himself, and, at the same time, a Person apart from the Speaker, who makes all things through the Word, united in one indivisible essense of divine power, might, and effect. But if we have the Word, it is easy to discover the third Person in David's speech: "All their host by the Breath of His mouth."

The author uses the word "made" only once, saying: "By the Word of the Lord the heavens were made, and all their host by the Breath of His mouth." He mentions three distinct Persons, namely, the Lord, His Word, and His Breath; and yet he does not set up more than one Creator, without any differentiation. All things are made. By whom? By one Creator, who is Lord, Word, and Breath. The Lord does not do His own work separately, the Word does not do His own work separately, and the Breath does not do His own work separately. All three distinct Persons are but one Creator of the work of each. And each one's work is that of all three Persons as that of one Creator and Master. For as the Lord creates the heavens, the Word creates the same and no different heavens, and the Breath creates the same and no different heavens. It is one essence that creates, and it is one creation that all three Persons create. And again, just as the Lord creates the host of the heavens by His Spirit (as the text says: "And all their host by the Breath of His mouth") thus the Breath creates the same and no other host of the heavens, and the Word creates the same and no other host of the heavens.

Therefore a Christian must here take careful note not to mingle the Persons into one Person nor to divide and separate the one divine essence into three Persons, as Athanasius sings in his Creed.[30] For if I ascribe to each Person a distinct external work in creation and exclude the other two Persons from this, then I have divided the one Godhead and have fashioned three gods or creators. And that is wrong. Again, if I do not ascribe to each Person within the Godhead, or outside and beyond creation, a special distinction not appropriate to the other two, then I have mingled the Persons into one Person. And that is also wrong. Here the rule of St. Augustine is pertinent: "The works of the Trinity toward the outside are not divisible." [31] The works performed by God outside the Godhead must not be divided, that is, one must not separate the Persons with regard to the works and ascribe to each its distinct external work; but one must distinguish the Person within the Godhead and yet ascribe, externally, each work to all three without distinction.

Let me illustrate this with an example. The Father is my God and Creator and yours, who created you and me. This same work,

---

[30] A reference to the so-called Athanasian Creed's "without confusing the Persons or dividing the divine Substance."

[31] Cf. Augustine, *De Trinitate*, II, ch. 5, sec. 9, *Patrologia, Series Latina*, XLII, 850.

[W, LIV, 58]

your creation and mine, was also performed by the Son, who is also my God and Creator and yours, just as the Father is. Likewise, the Holy Spirit created the selfsame work, that is, you and me, and He is my God and Creator and yours as well as the Father and the Son. This notwithstanding, there are not three gods and creators, but one God and Creator of us both. With this creed I guard against the heresy of Arius and his ilk, to keep me from dividing the one divine essence into three gods or creators and to help me retain in the true Christian faith no more than the one God and Creator of all creatures.

On the other hand, when I go beyond and outside of creation or the creature and move into the internal, incomprehensible essence of divine nature, I find that Holy Scripture teaches me — for reason counts for nought in this sphere — that the Father is a different and distinct nature from the Son in the one indivisible and eternal Godhead. The difference is that He is the Father and does not derive His Godhead from the Son or anyone else. The Son is a Person distinct from the Father in the same, one paternal Godhead. The difference is that He is the Son and that He does not have the Godhead from Himself, nor from anyone else but the Father, since He was born of the Father from eternity. The Holy Spirit is a Person distinct from the Father and the Son in the same, one Godhead. The difference is that He is the Holy Spirit, who eternally proceeds both from the Father and from the Son, and who does not have the Godhead from Himself nor from anyone else but from both the Father and the Son, and all of this from eternity to eternity. With this belief I guard against the heresy of Sabellius and his ilk, of Jews, Mohammed, and all others who presume to be smarter than God Himself. Thus I refrain from jumbling the Persons together into one Person, but I retain, according to the true Christian belief, three distinct Persons in the one divine and eternal essence, all three of which are, over against us and all creatures, one God, Creator and Worker of all things.

Perhaps all of this is too abstruse or subtle for us Germans and should, more reasonably, be confined to the universities. But since the devil whips his tail about in these last days and would fain stir up all sorts of heresy again; and since the world, even aside from this, hankers and longs to hear something novel and is weary of the salutary doctrine, as St. Paul prophesied (2 Tim. 4:3); and since the door has thereby been left open for the devil to bring in what he will: it is useful and necessary that at least a few, both laymen and scholars, especially pastors, preachers, and schoolteachers, also learn to reflect on such vital doctrines of our faith and to express them in German.[32] But may he for whom this is too complicated stay with the children and confine himself to the Catechism and pray against the devil and his heresy, against the Jews and against Mohammed, lest he succumb to temptation. But since we have entered upon this subject, we will cite more illustrations of this doctrine for those who are interested, and demonstrate that the one Godhead is not to be divided nor the Persons intermingled. This we do to strengthen and to profess our faith.

When St. John baptized our Lord in the Jordan, heaven opened and the Holy Spirit descended physically in the form of a dove, and the Father's voice was heard to say: "This is My beloved Son; with whom I am well pleased" (cf. Luke 3:22; 2 Peter 1:17). Here we find a dove, a creature which not only the Holy Spirit but also the Father and the Son had created. As I was saying: "The works of the Trinity to the outside are not divisible," whatever is creature has been created by God the Father, the Son, and the Holy Spirit as one God. Still, the dove is called only Holy Spirit, or, as Luke says, it was only the Holy Spirit, who descended in the form of a dove. And the Christian Creed would by no means tolerate that you say of the dove: That is God the Father, or: That is God the Son. No, you must say: That is God the Holy Spirit, although God the Father, the Son, and the Holy Spirit are but one God. You may say very correctly of the dove: That is God, and there is no God beyond that one. And yet it would be incorrect for you to say: That is God the Father; that is God the Son. You must say: That is God the Holy Spirit.

In like manner, the voice that says "This is My beloved Son, etc." is a creature created not only by the Father but also by the Son and the Holy Spirit. As I was saying: "The works of the Trinity, etc." Outside the Godhead all creatures are created equally by all three Persons as by one God, and over against the creature all three Persons are one God. And again, with regard to the three Persons the creature is but one work and not three works. And yet

---

[32] On the difficulty of Trinitarian terminology in German, see, for example, *Luther's Works*, 34, p. 202.

this voice is called, and is, none but the Father's. As a Christian you cannot say of the voice: That is God the Holy Spirit or that is God the Son. No, you must say: That is God the Father, although God the Holy Spirit and God the Son and God the Father are but one God. You may say very correctly of this voice: That is God, and there is no God beyond that. But it would be incorrect to say: That is God the Son or God the Holy Spirit. No, you must say: That is God the Father.

Of Christ's humanity we say similarly: It is a real creature created by the Father, the Son, and the Holy Spirit. We would not permit the Creed to state that the Father alone or the Son alone or the Holy Spirit alone created this creature, or humanity; this is "an indivisible work of the Trinity," a work which all three Persons created as one God and Creator of one and the same work. Thus the angel Gabriel says to the Virgin Mary in Luke 1:35: "The Holy Spirit will come upon you, and the power of the Most High will overshadow you." "Not only the Holy Spirit," says he, "will come upon you but also the Most High, that is, the Father will overshadow you with His power, that is, with His Son, or Word. And 'the Child to be born of you' will be called the Son of the Most High." Thus the entire Trinity is present here as one Creator and has created and made the one work, the humanity. And yet it was only the Person of the Son that united with the human nature and became incarnate, not the Father nor the Holy Spirit.

Of this Man you cannot say: That is God the Father or that is God the Holy Spirit; but you must say: That is God the Son, although God the Father, the Son, and the Holy Spirit are one God, and although you can say very correctly of the Man: That is God, and there is no other god beside Him. And yet it would be incorrect to say: That is God the Father or God the Holy Spirit. No, you must say: That is God the Son, as St. Paul declares in Col. 2:9: "For in Him the whole fullness of deity dwells bodily." And yet the Father and the Holy Spirit are not thereby deprived of their Godhead but are one God together with the Son and Man Christ. Here you observe how the three Persons are to be believed as distinct within the Godhead and are not to be jumbled together into one Person and that, for all of that, the divine essence is not to be divided to make three gods. Viewed from without, from the point of view of the creature, there is but one Creator, so completely one that even the creature forms which the three Persons individually take are the single work of all three Persons of the one God.

To make such a profound matter somewhat intelligible, the doctors, particularly Bonaventure, adduce a crude illustration.[33] If, for example, three young women would take a dress and put it on one of their number and this one would also take part in clothing herself with this dress, then one could say that all three were dressing her; and yet only one is being attired in the dress and not the other two. Similarly we must understand here that all three Persons, as one God, created the one humanity, clothed the Son in this, and united it with His person, so that only the Son became man, and not the Father or the Holy Spirit. In the same way we should think also of the dove which the Person of the Holy Spirit adopted and of the voice which the Person of the Father adopted; also the fiery tongues on the Day of Pentecost, in which the Person of the Holy Spirit was revealed; also the wind and whatever else is preached in Christendom or in Holy Scripture about the operation of the Holy Spirit.

Here one might reasonably ask: Why, then, do we say, or rather, why does Holy Scripture teach us to say: "I believe in God the Father, Creator of heaven and earth," and not to mention also the Son as Creator? Also, why do we say: "I believe in Jesus Christ, who was conceived by the Holy Ghost?" Also, why do we say that the Holy Spirit quickens us and that He spoke by the prophets? Here the peculiar and distinctive works are being assigned externally to each Person by way of differentiation. This is perhaps too subtle too for simple Christians who want to adhere to their plain faith that God the Father, the Son, and the Holy Spirit are one God, etc. However, it is necessary to discourse on this subject in Christendom and to learn to understand it in order to withstand the devil and his heretics. In the first place, it is certain that God wants to be known by us, here on earth by faith, yonder by sight, that He is one God and yet three Persons. And according to John 17:3, this is our everlasting life. To this end He gave us His Word and Holy Scripture, attested with great miracles and signs. We must learn from it. To attain that knowledge of God, it is surely necessary that He Himself instruct us, that He reveal Himself and appear to

---

[33] Neither the Weimar editors nor we have succeeded in identifying this reference to Bonaventure.

us. By ourselves we could not ascend into heaven and discover what God is or how His divine essence is constituted. Well, for this purpose He employs visible elements in His creation, as Scripture teaches us, so that we may comprehend this; for invisible creatures do not make an impression on our senses.

Accordingly, you must view the creature in two different ways; in the first place, as a creature, or work, per se, absolutely, created or made in this or that way by God. In that sense all creatures are God's work, that is, the single work of all three Persons without distinction. This we have already heard. For in that respect they manifest no distinctive revelation of the three Persons, since they are all the same single work of the three Persons as of the one God. Secondly, you must view the creature not per se, absolutely, but relatively, according to each one's function, as God uses them toward us. Here God takes His creature, which all three Persons as one God have created, and uses it as an image, or form, or figure, in which He reveals Himself and in which He appears. Here distinctive images, forms, and revelations of the three separate Persons come into being. Thus God employs the dove to become an image, or revelation, of the Holy Spirit. This is a distinctive image, which does not portray the Father or the Son but only the Holy Spirit. The Father, the Son, and the Holy Spirit want the dove to depict and reveal distinctively only the person of the Holy Spirit, to assure us that God's one essence is definitely three separate Persons from eternity. That is why Luke 3:22 states: "The Holy Spirit descended upon Him in bodily form, as a dove."

In the same way, we say of the Son that He is revealed to us in His humanity, or, as St. Paul says in Phil. 2:7, "taking the form of a servant, being born in the likeness of men." And this form, or humanity, is not the image, or revelation, of the Father or of the Holy Ghost, although it is the same single creation of all three, Father, Son, and Holy Spirit, but it is the peculiar and special form and revelation of the Son alone. For thus it has pleased God, that is, Father, Son, and Holy Spirit, that the Son should be revealed to and recognized by humankind in this form, or figure, of humanity as a Person apart from the Father and the Holy Spirit in one eternal essence of divine nature. In like manner we should profess that the Father was revealed to us in the voice. This form, or figure, is not a revelation of the Son or of the Holy Spirit but only of the Father, who in that distinctive form wants to manifest Himself to us as a Person distinct from the Son and the Holy Spirit in one, indivisible divine essence.

You may also choose a crude example illustrating this from grammar. When the priest baptizes or absolves, he uses the words: "In the name of the Father and of the Son and of the Holy Spirit." All of these words in our mouth are the creation and work of God (as we and all that we have are), and not one word is distinctively only that of the Father, or of the Son, or of the Holy Spirit, but it is the work of all three Persons, the single creation of the one God. However, in accordance with this interpretation, or revelation, you must not say that the words "of the Father" signify all three Persons, but specifically only the Father, and the words "of the Son" specifically only the Son, and the words "of the Holy Spirit" specifically only the Holy Spirit—all in one Godhead. Thus these words, or their interpretation, reveal to us that there are three distinct Persons in the one Godhead. For the priest does not say: "In the names," as of many, or as though each Person had a special name and essence. No, he says: "In the name," as in the name of one being and yet three distinct Persons.

Accordingly, you observe that the creature must be considered in a twofold manner, as a reality and as a symbol, that it is something per se, created by God, and that it is also used to signify or teach something else, something which it is not of itself. Smoke is a reality, a thing per se and at the same time a sign of something else, something which it is not but which it indicates and reveals, namely, fire. St. Augustine comments at length on this in *On Christian Doctrine*.[34] But here in this sublime subject it means more. For the humanity of Christ is not a mere sign or a mere figure, as the dove and the voice also are not empty figures or images. No, the humanity in which God's Son is distinctively revealed is complete, it is united with God in one Person, which will sit eternally at the right hand of God, as was promised to David in 1 Chron. 17:12 above. The dove is a figure assumed for a time by the Holy Spirit to reveal Himself, but it was not united with Him forever. No, He again shed this form, as angels, too, adopt human form, appear in it, and later again abandon it. The same is true of the voice of God the Father. There is no promise

[34] Augustine, *Christian Doctrine*, I, 2.

involved that it should be so forever, but it is a temporary revelation.

When we confess in the children's Creed: [35] "I believe in God the Father Almighty, Creator of heaven and earth," we do not mean to imply that only the Person of the Father is the almighty Creator and Father. No, the Son is likewise almighty, Creator, and Father. And the Holy Spirit is likewise almighty, Creator, and Father. And yet there are not three almighty creators and fathers but only one almighty Creator and Father of heaven and earth and of us all. Similarly, the Father is our Savior and Redeemer, the Son is our Savior and Redeemer, and the Holy Spirit is our Savior and Redeemer, and yet there are not three saviors and redeemers, but only one Savior and Redeemer. Likewise, the Father is our God, the Son is our God, and the Holy Spirit is our God, and yet there are not three gods, but only one God. Likewise, the Holy Ghost sanctifies Christendom, so does the Father, so does the Son, and still there are not three sanctifiers, but only one Sanctifier, etc. "The works of the Trinity to the outside are not divisible."

All of this has been said so that we may recognize and believe in three distinct Persons in the one Godhead and not jumble the Persons together nor divide the essence. The distinction of the Father, as we have heard,[36] is this, that He derived His deity from no one, but gave it from eternity, through the eternal birth, to the Son. Therefore the Son is God and Creator, just like the Father. But the Son derived all of this from the Father, and not, in turn, the Father from the Son. The Father does not owe the fact that He is God and Creator to the Son, but the Son owes the fact that He is God and Creator to the Father. And the fact that Father and Son are God and Creator they do not owe to the Holy Spirit; but the Holy Spirit owes the fact that He is God and Creator to the Father and to the Son. Thus the words "God Almighty, Creator" are found as attributes of the Father and not of the Son and of the Holy Spirit to mark the distinction of the Father from the Son and the Holy Spirit in the Godhead, again, the distinction of the Son from the Father and the Holy Spirit, and the distinction of the Holy Spirit from the Father and the Son; namely, that the Father is the source, or the fountainhead (if we may use that term as the fathers do) of the

[35] "Children's Creed" was Luther's term for the Apostles' Creed.
[36] See p. 303 above.

Godhead, that the Son derives it from Him and that the Holy Spirit derives it from Him and the Son, and not vice versa.

Beyond this internal distinction of the Persons, there is also the external difference, in which the Son and the Holy Spirit are revealed. The Son is revealed in humanity, for the Son alone became man, He alone was conceived by the Holy Spirit, was born of the Virgin Mary, suffered and died for us, as our Creed informs us. However, it is also correct to say that God died for us, for the Son is God, and there is no other God but only more Persons in the same Godhead. Only the Holy Spirit was diversely revealed in the fiery tongues, in the gifts, in the variety of languages and miraculous signs, etc., although the humanity was created by all three Persons, and the fiery tongues and the gifts of the Holy Spirit are the creation and work of all three Persons, as we have heard sufficiently for the present. We have precious books on this subject by St. Augustine, Hilary, and Cyril at our disposal. And this article of faith remained pure in the papacy and among the scholastic theologians, and we have no quarrel with them on that score.

Some people worry and wonder whether they are addressing the Person of the Father or the Divine Essence when they pray the Lord's Prayer. It is not at all surprising that strange thoughts come to a person in this extremely mysterious and incomprehensible article of faith and that occasionally one of these goes away and a word miscarries. But wherever the basis of faith remains intact, such splinters, chips, or straws will not harm us. But the foundation of faith, as we have heard,[37] is this, that you believe that there are three Persons in the one Godhead and that each person is the same, one, perfect God, in other words, that the Persons are not intermingled and the essence is not divided but the distinction of Persons and the unity of the essence is preserved. For it is this mystery, of which, as we read in 1 Peter 1:12, the angels cannot behold and wonder their fill in all eternity and about which they are in bliss through all eternity. And if they were able to satisfy their longing, their happiness would end too. We, too, shall behold this, and it will make us eternally blissful, as the Lord says in John 17:3: "And this is eternal life, that they know Thee the only true God, and Jesus Christ, whom Thou hast sent." In the meantime, faith must cling to the Word, for reason cannot do otherwise than assert that

---

[37] See p. 302 above.

it is impossible and contradictory that there should be three Persons, each one perfect God, and yet not more than one God; that only the Son is Man; that he who has the Father and the Son will surely learn to know the Holy Spirit from the Father and the Son.

You have heard earlier that the Father is the God and Father of us all, that the Son is the God and Father of us all, that the Holy Spirit is the God and Father of us all, and that, for all of that, not more than one God is our Father. For the essence is undivided, therefore no matter which Person you may mention, you have named the one true God in three Persons, since each Person is the same, one, perfect God. In this you cannot err or go wrong. For Jesus Christ is no other God or Father or Creator than the Father or the Holy Spirit, even though He is a different Person. The same is true of the Father and of the Holy Spirit. Hence it would not only be incorrect but also impossible and futile for you to restrict the name "Father" to the Person of God the Father and to the exclusion of the Son and the Holy Spirit; for that would be dividing the Divine Essence and eliminating the Son and the Holy Spirit. That is out of the question. For according to such a manner of personal paternity, the Father has no more than one Son, and the Son has no more than one Father. He is not such a Father to you, and you are not such a Son to Him. No, this is the only-begotten Son of the Father from eternity, as Ps. 2:7 says: "The Lord said to Me, 'You are My Son, today I have begotten You.'" But you are a temporal son of all three Persons, of one God, and may be 30, 40, or 50 years of age, depending upon the time of your birth and baptism.

As the works of the Trinity to the outside are indivisible, so the worship of the Trinity from the outside is indivisible. Whatever God does to the creature is done by all three Persons without distinction. For there is one Divine Essence of all three Persons, and what we or the creature do to each Person of the Godhead we do to the one God and to all three Persons without distinction. In relation to us He is one God; within Himself He is distinctive in three Persons. Thus Christ Himself says in John 14:9-10: "Philip, he who has seen Me has seen the Father; how can you say, 'Show us the Father'? Do you not believe that I am in the Father and the Father in Me?" And in John 5:23 we read: "All may honor the Son, even as they honor the Father." And in John 10:30: "I and the Father are one." We mean to say: "One entity, one essence, one

God, one Lord." At this point "the Jews took up stones again to stone Him" (John 10:31). In John 5:17-18 we read: " 'My Father is working still, and I am working.' This was why the Jews sought all the more to kill Him, because He not only broke the Sabbath but also called God His Father, making Himself equal with God, etc."

I am going to discontinue this subject now. It had been my intention to write an essay, but I have fallen into preaching. Read the Gospel of St. John; it teaches this all in rich measure. We have established that Moses agrees with St. John in the assertion that the Word was in the beginning, that by Him all things were made; that this Word cannot be a creature or anything created and yet is something distinct from God, or a Person different from God, whose this Word is. For since He was not made but all things were made by Him, He must be God, Creator of all things, for it is certain that outside of creation, which is made, there can be naught but God, who makes it. And yet the Word, the God and Creator by whom all things are made, is distinct from the Speaker, or from Him who speaks the Word. Thus Moses is now our witness; he has become a Christian and is teaching the same doctrine that we Christians teach, namely, that God had a Word in the beginning, by whom all things were made, just as John writes.

Now let us briefly lend an ear also to the other legate, St. Paul, how he salutes Moses and appeals to him. In Col. 1:15-17 he has this to say of our Lord Jesus Christ: "He is the image of the invisible God, the firstborn of all creation; for in Him all things were created, in heaven and on earth, visible and invisible, whether thrones or dominions or principalities or authorities—all things were created through Him and for Him. He is before all things, and in Him all things hold together." To be sure, these words cannot be spoken of Christ according to the human nature; for He was not man "before all things." At present it is only 1543 years ago that He became man. This is indeed a mighty and powerful verse in proof that Christ is eternal God, Creator of heaven and earth, and that to the present day and forevermore everything exists and is preserved and is made by Him, also all that is exalted in heaven and on earth, angels and spirits, the visible and the invisible. On this point Paul is in perfect agreement with John, who says (1:3): "All things were made through Him, and without Him was not anything made that was made." If Moses hears and approves the words of John, he surely also gives ear to and agrees with these words of Paul and says: "Yes, my dear Paul, in Gen. 1 I recorded the same truth which you and John voiced, namely, that all things are created by the Word."

In 1 Cor. 10:4 Paul says furthermore: "They drank from the spiritual Rock which followed them, and the Rock was Christ." If Christ was contemporaneous with the children of Israel and accompanied them, if it was He from whom they drank spiritually and on whom they were baptized spiritually, that is, if the children of Israel believed in the future Christ as we do in the Christ who appeared; then Christ must be true and eternal God. For you cannot believe in angels—that is an honor to which God alone is entitled. Nor can the angels be our spiritual food; God Himself must be that. Likewise, in 1 Cor. 10:9 Paul writes: "We must not put Christ to the test, as some of them did and were destroyed by serpents." What do we make of that? Does not Moses write again and again that it was the Lord Jehovah, the one true God, whom the children of Israel put to the test? In Ex. 17:2 he says: "Why do you put the Lord to the proof?" And in Num. 14:22 the Lord declares: "They have put Me to the proof these ten times." If this is the Lord of whom Moses writes, how can it be Christ, of whom St. Paul writes? But they must both be correct; for the Holy Spirit does not contradict Himself.

It follows cogently and incontrovertibly that the God who led the children of Israel from Egypt and through the Red Sea, who guided them in the wilderness by means of the pillar of cloud and the pillar of fire, who nourished them with bread from heaven, who performed all the miracles recorded by Moses in his books, again, who brought them into the land of Canaan and there gave them kings and priests and everything, is the very same God, and none other than Jesus of Nazareth, the Son of the Virgin Mary, whom we Christians call our Lord and God, whom the Jews crucified, and whom they still blaspheme and curse today, as Is. 8:21 declares: "They will be enraged and will curse their King and their God." Likewise, it is He who gave Moses the Ten Commandments on Mount Sinai, saying (Ex. 20:2, 3): "I am the Lord your God, who brought you out of the land of Egypt . . . You shall have no other gods before Me." Yes, Jesus of Nazareth, who died for us on the cross, is the God who says in the First Commandment: "I am the Lord your God." How the Jews and Mohammed would rant if they heard that! Nevertheless, it is true and will eternally remain true. And he who disbelieves this will tremble before this truth and burn forever.

Here is Moses, who states so lucidly that all things were created by the Speech, or the Word, of God. And in Ps. 33:6 [38] David declares: "By the Word of the Lord the heavens were made." If the heavens are made by the Word, then every other creature is also made by Him; for he who makes one creature makes them all, and he who does not make them all is unable to make any. Thus Moses and David agree with John and Paul, and both join them in saying: "All things were made and created by the Word, or by Christ." Now, if all things were made by Him and if nothing was made without Him, as the text of all four declares, Moses, David, John, and Paul; then what they call "all things" must include and not exclude the exodus from Egypt and whatever else happened in the midst of the people of Israel, yes, all that everywhere has taken place since creation, and still takes place, and will take place. These are powerful and important words which declare that all is made by Him and, as Moses puts it, "God said, and there was." Even if Moses does not use the name "the Son" or "Christ" grammatically, he nonetheless names and professes the Speech, the Word, by whom all things are made. Thereby he indicates that in God there is one who speaks and another who is the Word, and yet there is but one Creator of all creatures. Something had to be reserved for the New Testament too, so that in it the Father, the Son, and the Holy Spirit might clearly be named, whom the Old Testament calls the Speaker, the Word, and the Spirit of the Lord.

Therefore it is of no avail to Jews, Turks, and heretics to feign great religious zeal and to boast against us Christians of their belief in the one God, the Creator of heaven and earth, and that they devoutly call Him Father. These are nothing but inane and empty words with which they take the name of God in vain and misuse it contrary to the Second Commandment. Thus Christ says to the Jews in John 8:54-55: "It is My Father who glorifies Me, of whom you say that He is your God. But you have not known Him." It is indeed extremely inconsistent to call God "Father" and not to

---

[38] The original has "Ps. 54."

know who He is. For if you were to ask such a very saintly Jew, Turk, or heretic whether he belives that this one God, Creator of heaven and earth (whose name they exalt so piously and whom they call Father—although all this falsely), really is a Father and has a Son in the Godhead outside of creation, he would be horrified in his great holiness and would regard this as frightful blasphemy. And if you would ask further whether the same, one God, Creator, Father (as they call Him with their lying mouths) is also a Son, who has a Father in the Godhead, he would stuff up his ears in his great zeal, gnash his teeth, and worry that the earth might swallow you and him. And if you continue to ask whether the same, one God, Creator, and Father (as they boastfully call Him) is also a Holy Spirit, who has the Father and the Son, from whom He derives His divine essence, this superholy man would run away from you as though you were the vilest devil just come from hell.

Here you can note that they do not know what God is. When they speak of God, Creator, and Father, they do not know what they are saying. For if God is not to be the God (as Holy Scripture teaches us) who is a natural Father, who has a natural Son, and both have a natural Holy Spirit, all in one divine essence, God is nothing; He is no God at all. Consequently they have no God, except that they sinfully and shamefully misuse the name of God and fabricate their own god and creator, who is to be their father and they his children. They rob God of His natural Fatherhood, of His one natural Son, and of the natural Holy Spirit, that is, of the entire true Godhead. Instead, they impute to God their vain dream and their lies of God, Creator, and Father. Yes, they confer on their fabrication, that is, on the devil, this holy name of God. The devil is their god and father, the father of all lies. At the same time, they presume to be the dearest little children and the holiest saints.

It is a settled matter, and thus God Himself revealed Himself to us, that He is one God, Creator, and Father of heaven and earth; that this same, one God, Creator and Father of all the world, is a natural Father of one Son in the Godhead; that this same, one God, Creator and Father of all the world, is one natural Son of the Father in the Godhead; that the same, one God, Creator and Father of all the world, is a Holy Spirit, proceeding from the Father and the Son in the Godhead. For the three distinct Persons are one God, Creator and Father of all the world. And each Person is the same complete, one God, Creator and Father of all the world. And when you call upon Jesus Christ, saying: "My dear Lord God, my Creator and Father, Jesus Christ, one, eternal God!" you need have no concern that the Father and the Holy Spirit are resentful on that account, but you may know that you immediately call upon all three Persons and the one God, no matter which Person you may address. You cannot call upon one Person without including the others, since there is one indivisible divine essence in all and in each Person. On the other hand, you cannot deny any one Person without denying all three and without denying God entirely, as we read in 1 John 2:23: "No one who denies the Son has the Father."

I say it is not wrong but laudable if you invoke Jesus Christ thus. The church sings similarly of the Holy Spirit: "Come, O Father of the wretched."[39] However, it is better to observe and not disregard the order of the Persons, as the apostles do and as the church, emulating them, does when they mention the name of the Father in supplication or prayer, for example, in the Lord's Prayer, etc. For He is fountainhead or the wellspring (so to say) of the Godhead in the Son and the Holy Spirit, and when the Father is mentioned, the Son cannot be divorced from Him but must simultaneously be named and meant. Likewise the Holy Spirit is named and meant together with the Father and the Son, because none of the Persons can be a separate God apart from the others. Thus say St. Paul (2 Cor. 1:3) and St. Peter (1 Peter 1:3): "Blessed be the God and Father of our Lord Jesus Christ, the Father of mercies." Christ Himself always gives precedence to the Father in the Gospel and ascribes everything to Him, and yet He says (John 5:23): "That all may honor the Son as they honor the Father," and (John 16:15): "All that the Father has is Mine." The only difference is this, that the Father is the first Person, from whom the Son derives everything, and not vice versa. However, the fact that a sin may be committed distinctively against the Father or against the Son or against the Holy Spirit is related to the revelation of the Persons and not to the division of the essence. We have dealt a little with this subject above, and elsewhere it has been treated more in detail.

[39] These are the opening words of the second stanza of the hymn "Veni, Sancte Spiritus" of Stephen Langton, who died in 1228.

But what is to be our attitude over against St. John's further statement about the Word: "The Word became flesh"? That, I suppose, cannot be harmonized with the Word about which Moses writes: "God said, Let there be light!" or David says: "By the Word of the Lord the heavens were made." Moses, or (as we believe) the Word Himself, commands on Mount Sinai (Ex. 20:4; Deut. 5:8): "You shall not make yourself a graven image or likeness of anything that is in heaven above, or that is in the earth beneath." John does not make an image but a creature and a man, saying (John 1:18): "The Word became flesh." Paul does the same when he declares (Rom. 1:3; Gal. 4:4) that He was David's Son, or Seed, born of a woman. Therefore Moses must be speaking of another Word, a Word by whom all things were made. Nothing can be created by man, who himself is a creature. Paul and John are contradicting themselves when they make Him a man and yet say that all was created by Him.

Let us see whether we can find a similar statement in Moses. In Gen. 3:15 he writes that God said to the serpent: "I will put enmity between you and the woman, and between your seed and her Seed; He shall bruise your head, and you shall bruise His heel." It is obvious that God is not speaking of an ordinary serpent here, which slithers through the grass or the water and devours young frogs, but of a serpent which at that time was a beautiful and very intelligent animal. It was not merely able to speak but also to discuss profound divine questions and commands, just as though it had learned it in heaven. This gift was imparted to no other creature except to angels and men. And by means of this gift, the serpent wrought such harm as to lure man into sin and eternal death with the glittering pretense of God's name. This was not a common and silly little snake, such as eat little frogs, but a snake that devours the entire world. It was the cursed devil who dwelt in the snake, who brought death into the world through sin. Of this murderer, teacher of sin, and world-devourer God is here speaking and saying that his head will be crushed, that is, that his power, death and sin, will be destroyed and life and righteousness be restored.

And that is to be effected by the Seed of the woman. As the devil worked man's fall through a woman who issued from man without the participation of a woman, thus the Seed which will issue from a woman without the participation of a man will bring about the devil's downfall. This Seed of the woman will have to be a man, or a son, for in scripture the seed of man obviously means the offspring, the son of a man. The unusual feature in this passage is that this Child, or Man, is called "Seed of a woman." Otherwise the word "seed" regularly refers to the seed of a man, or a father. We read, for example, of Abraham's seed, of David's seed, etc. Throughout Moses and the prophets the word "seed" means the man's seed. Thus Moses here agrees with Luke and Matthew, stating that this woman is to be a virgin who will become a mother solely through her own seed and without the cooperation of a man. And since this is in accord with the New Testament, we Christians, following the previously acknowledged rule,[40] concede no other interpretation either to the Jew or to the devil.

In brief, it is certain that this Seed of a woman is to be a man. But, in addition, He must also be God, lest Moses be accounted an idolatrous prophet of the devil; for he imputes to this Seed the power which is proper to no creature but to God alone, namely, to abolish death and the murderer, sin and God's wrath, and to restore righteousness and life. My dear friend, no angel individually or all angels collectively will be able to do that. This calls for a mightier and more exalted man than all angels and creatures. I repeat, Moses must be a damned and idolatrous prophet if he attributes to the seed of a woman works such as strangling and overcoming death and sin, raising from the dead, and justifying, when this seed of a woman is a mere creature and not the one God Himself, who alone can quicken, as John 1:4 says of the Word: "In Him was life."

Reason itself must, of course, admit that he who is competent to crush death underfoot is also able to restore life, that he who can destroy sin can restore righteousness; for the removal of death is nothing else than restitution of life, and the remission of sin is nothing else than restitution of righteousness, of which the serpent, that is, the devil in the serpent, basely defrauded Adam and Eve together with all their descendants and all the children of men. It was he who through his lies brought sin and death down upon them. The text in Gen. 2:17 reads clearly enough: "Of the tree . . . you shall not eat, for . . . you shall die." Against this the Liar and Murderer replied: "You may indeed eat of it without suffering death. In fact, you will become like God and know everything."

[40] See p. 268 above.

As I said before, all of this speaks about the sin and death which the serpent caused and ushered into the world. Therefore the crushing of the serpent can mean nothing else than the demolition of his work and power, as St. Paul says in 2 Tim. 1:10: "Christ abolished death and brought life and immortality to light." We pay the commentaries no heed which Jews, Mohammed, and others scribble and scrawl. It suffices us that Moses is in agreement here with the New Testament.

This interpretation, that the Seed of a woman must be God, who should crush the devil's head, was held also by Adam and Eve. For according to Gen. 4:1, when Eve had given birth to Cain, she perhaps supposed that because he was the first man born on earth he would be the foremost, and she assumed that he was to be the Seed of the woman and that she was to be that woman, or mother.[41] This prompted her to exclaim: "I have the Man, the Lord!" as though she were to say: "This is undoubtedly the Man, the Lord, the Seed of woman, of whom God spoke, etc." She calls the child Man and Lord, or God; for here we find the great and proper name of God, Jehovah, which indicates nothing else than God alone in His nature or essence. And איש, when used alone and without the accompanying word for woman, does not simply designate a male such as all men are, but an ideal and outstanding man, as we Germans, too, say: *Das ist ein Mann! Das will ein Mann werden!* ("He is every inch a man!") Similarly, Eve means to say here: "I have borne a son, who will develop into a real man, yes, he is *the* Man, God Himself, who will do it, crush the serpent, as God assured us." How is this possible? How could the idea come to her which induced her to say of this child: "I have the Man, the Lord," if she had not understood God's statement to mean that the woman's Seed would have to be God, who would carry out what God had told them?

Without a doubt Eve was not the only one to interpret these words thus. Very likely Adam discussed this with her long before this, and they cherished this verse and drew comfort from it against sin and death, which were to be abolished by this Seed and replaced by the forfeited innocence and life. In the absence of that

---

[41] See also Luther's discussion of Gen. 4:1 in the *Lectures on Genesis* (*Luther's Works*, 1, pp. 241—43), where this interpretation of the words of Eve does not appear in so explicit a form.

comfort they would have despaired. And it is not God's will or way that His eternal Word, such as this is, should be spoken in vain and understood by no one. In Is. 55:11 He says: "My Word shall not return to Me empty, but it shall accomplish . . . that for which I sent it." Now, there were only two people here who could understand it. Therefore they must have understood it profitably, blissfully, and correctly, entirely as we Christians do and before us all prophets did.

But our poor, unhappy Mother Eve was mistaken in her assumption that she was that woman simply because there was no other woman on earth beside her. In her great desire and longing, she hoped that her son was to be the Seed, the Man Jehovah. She was too impatient and hasty; but no one can reprove her for her desire to be rid of sin and death, that is, of the devil, so soon. However, God had not said to her: "Your seed is to do it." Nor had He said to Adam: "Your wife's seed is to be the One." No, He reads their proper text to both of them, one that all children of men will still feel to the end of time. But to the serpent God turned and said: "As for you, on the other hand, I will provide Him who shall crush your head. He will be the Seed of a woman. I will fell you haughty, powerful, evil spirit by the Son of Man, so that all men in turn will run you down and tread you underfoot as you have now done to Adam and Eve." This our dear Lord Jesus Christ did, does, and ever will do, who together with God the Father is one Jehovah. Amen.

Someone may interpose here: How do you account for it that no Christian or Jew has seen such a meaning in this passage? All other translators do it differently. The Latin reads: "I have gotten a man through God." [42] Other Hebraists say: "I have gotten the Man from the Lord." That does not interest me now. Above, I repeatedly reserved the right to decline having a teacher here and to present my own views in the translation. If it pleases no one else, it is sufficient that it pleases me. The little Hebrew word אֵת means "the." As all grammarians will agree, it is the accusative case article. In Gen. 1:1 Moses, for instance, says: "In the beginning God created אֵת heavens and אֵת earth." Translated, this reads: "the heavens and the earth." And so it goes on in this and the following chapters. For instance: "Adam knew אֵת Eve, his wife." Likewise: "She bore

[42] The Vulgate had translated *Possedi hominem per Deum*.

אֶת Cain." Likewise: "And again, she bore אֶת Abel, his brother." Likewise: "Adam begat אֶת Seth, Seth begat אֶת Enosh, etc." In the same manner Eve said here after she had given birth to Cain: קָנִיתִי אִישׁ אֶת־יְהֹוָה, "I have gotten the Man, the Lord." For as I already said, she hoped that Cain would be the Seed promised by God to crush the serpent's head.

I am convinced, if the most rabid Jews, who crucified Christ, or the still viler ones of today, who would fain crucify Him still more ruthlessly — a story is current about Jews and Turks who recently crucified a cat in Budapest, Hungary, and then carried it about with many blasphemous words in derision and disdain of our Lord Jesus Christ [43] — I say, if such wicked and venomous crucifiers of God and of cats could believe, or if they, even without belief, would acknowledge grammatical truth in languages generally, they would declare: "Yes, you accursed Goyim, if it were true that the Seed of the woman is God and Man, then we would be well aware that this text, where Eve says: "I have gotten the Man, Jehovah," agrees uncommonly well with that idea, and we freely admit that the language would easily and precisely yield the meaning that this Son is that Man and God the Lord. Any other interpretation, such as "I have gotten the Man by the Lord or from the Lord or with the help of the Lord," is forced and constrained and unsuitable and does not comply with the true nature and character of the language, and no one can prove the contrary. Yes, that is what those evil people would have to confess. But since they cannot tolerate the truth that God became incarnate through a woman, this text and all of Scripture must be mistaken, or they must give it an entirely new face.

All other Hebraists would also be obliged to admit this if they scrutinized the text closely and if they believed that this Seed of the woman is Jehovah, that is, God and man. For the fact that this little word אֶת means "the" and denotes the accusative case has been demonstrated, authenticated, and admitted by all Hebraists, Jews and Christians, in all grammars. However, that it could also mean *ad, de,* or *cum,* from, with, or by, has not yet been proved and indeed never will be proved. For in reply to the examples they adduce from Rabbi Kimchi [44] or from Scripture, one can with good

[43] We have been unable to obtain further information about this report.

[44] Apparently a reference to Rabbi David Kimchi (c. 1160—1235), whose

reason say that the study of the Hebrew tongue has really never again come into its own and that the Jews cannot know the meaning of all the words as the subject reveals them; much less do they know the force of phrase, figure, and idiom, but they doubt, equivocate, fidget, and search as an inept organist gropes for the keys, or organ pipes, and queries: "Are you the right one, or are you the right one?"

As the teachers of the Latin language say, there is a vast difference between speaking an idiomatic Latin and speaking a grammatical Latin, so there is also a great dissimilarity between speaking idiomatic Hebrew and speaking grammatical Hebrew. They may speak grammatically, though haltingly, but to speak a pure, good, and fluent Hebrew is no longer possible. Anyone learns German or any other language much better from oral conversation at home, in the marketplace, or from a sermon than he does from books. Written characters form dead words; oral speech forms living words. These do not go into writing as accurately and well as the spirit, or soul, of man can express them orally. In his *Prolog* Saint Jerome writes of Demosthenes and Aeschines and Livy: "The live word has a certain secret power." [45] Particularly unwarranted is their claim that אֶת may mean as much as *de, a, ab*, that is, "from"; for example: "I have gotten the man from the Lord." The examples in Gen. 44:4 and Ex. 9:29: "Having gone out אֶת city," and the like, do not solve the problem. It is perfectly correct to say: "Having left the city, he set up stones for an altar"; that is, appositively.

But when Moses writes in Gen. 5:22 and 6:9: "Enoch walked אֶת God," "Noah walked אֶת God," they translate: "Enoch and Noah walked with God." That is a poor translation, and it also does not sound right. Whither did they walk with God? Toward the east or toward the west? It must read: "He walked God" in the accusative. As the Latins also say: "He lived a Sardanapalus"; "they imitate the Curii and live the orgies of Bacchus"; "he strips off his father." In this way "Noah walked God," that is, he walked the godly way, he led a godly life, he did and performed the work of God. In Gal. 1:10 St. Paul speaks similarly: "Am I urging God or men?" that is,

---

grammatical and exegetical work served as a source for the early Christian Hebraists such as Reuchlin.

[45] These words appear in the so-called "helmeted preface," which was printed in many editions of the Vulgate.

"Am I teaching divine or human truths?" In the same place (Gal. 2:20) he says: "The life I live," and in Rom. 6:10: "The life He lives He lives to God." The same is found in 1 Peter 4:2. I commend all of these passages and more to the attention of the Hebraists; for instance, Gen. 39:2: "The Lord was אֶת Joseph, with Joseph." Here we Germans, I suppose, have to say "with Joseph," although this does not really reproduce the sense of the accusative case, and yet this is the sign of the accusative in Hebrew, and that it shall remain. May that suffice on this verse, in which Eve, or rather Moses, agrees with the New Testament that this Seed of the woman is Jehovah. That is the way it was understood by her and by Moses; otherwise they could indeed have employed a different expression.

The words of Moses in Gen. 22:18, containing God's promise to Abraham and confirmed with an oath, are also pertinent here: "By your Seed shall all גּוֹיִם (Gentiles) of the earth be blessed." Here we find the word גּוֹיִם, with which the present-day Jews — if indeed they are Jews [46] — calumniate and curse us just because we glory in this blessing, which God promised to Abraham, saying: "All גּוֹיִם shall be blessed in your Seed." However, they, these circumcised saints, want to see us Gentiles damned and claim that they are the only seed of Abraham. But because they curse the Gentiles and want to be a seed through which all the Gentiles are cursed, it is manifest that they are not Abraham's but the devil's seed. For God, whose judgment is just and certain, says that Abraham's seed will not curse the Gentiles, as they do, but that all the Gentiles will be blessed through him. And this has now been true for approximately 1543 years, and it will be true forever.

This is not a human blessing, one of mere words, as when we wish one another a good morning or a good evening. That is the only way man is able to bless. Nor is it a devil's blessing, with which sorcerers bless children, cattle, and the like to make them prosper and to shield them from harm. Nor is it a Jewish blessing which purports to be effective and perform miracles through Schamhaperes and their sorcery with letters and figures or with the

---

[46] Elsewhere, too, for example, in the *Lectures on Genesis* (*Luther's Works*, 2, pp. 359—62), Luther seems to have expressed doubts even about the physical descent of the Jews of his time from Abraham.

tetragrammaton of God's name. [47] That is like the blessing of the Turks and also the devil's blessing and idolatry. They bless themselves in battle with letters and words to make themselves proof against sword and all other weapons. Nor is it a papistic blessing, which bewitches water and wax to produce holy water and Agnus Dei, and which is to endow them with supernatural powers and thus aid them. No, this is a divine blessing which God alone can and will impart. Such a blessing is not a mere empty word which expresses and wishes us a good morning without actually giving us that, but this blessing gives and supplies what it stipulates. For instance, when God blessed all men and animals in Gen. 1:28, saying: פְּרוּ וּרְבוּ, "Be fruitful and multiply," this was not just an idle speech, but the fulfillment followed immediately, and man and beast became fruitful and multiplied until they filled the earth. And this blessing is still effective and will be so until the end of the world. For by virtue of it we are what we are and have what we have in body and soul, in goods and in all that exists or ever will exist.

Thus the divine blessing, promised to Abraham's seed, is also an active, real, and live blessing, which provides what the blessing promises. It is promised and issued against the curse under which the serpent brought us through Adam's disobedience and sin. Here the promise of the Seed of the woman is renewed, and henceforth it is to be known as Abraham's Seed. Later it was called David's Seed, and finally the Virgin's Seed. Therefore the blessing in the Seed of Abraham here means the same as earlier (Gen. 3:15): The Seed of the woman shall crush the serpent's head, that is, He shall remove sin and death and restore innocence and life. For sin and death are the curse under which we would have to languish eternally if we were not again blessed by this Seed, that is, if we were not again made alive and righteous, holy and blessed. Yes, thus we are blessed in this Seed of Abraham. Indeed, on account of this blessing we glory in being גּוֹיִם, we accept it by faith, we are very haughty, proud, and arrogant over against the devil and his power, over against death and sin and whatever else there may be. We sing and say: In the Seed of Abraham, of David, of the woman Mary we have remission of sin, ablution of sin, redemption from sin, liberation from death and every other evil; for it is He "whom God made our Wisdom, our Righteousness,

[47] Cf. *Luther's Works*, 4, pp. 151—78; 47, p. 256.

and Sanctification and Redemption" (1 Cor. 1:30), our Blessing, our Consolation, our Life, and our Joy in eternity. May God be praised for this forever. Amen.

And if this Seed of Abraham produces and works such a powerful and effective blessing among the Gentiles, He cannot be a mere man, able to wish a person a good morning and no more—something all men are able to do, but He must be the one true and natural God, who is able to administer this blessing mightily. For to abolish sin and death, to bestow righteousness and life, is not the work of a human being or of an angel, but to do this is the exclusive domain of the one eternal and divine Majesty, the Creator of heaven and earth. And again, if He is to be Abraham's Seed, that is, his child and son, He cannot only be God, but He must also be a true and natural man, proceeding from the flesh and blood of Abraham; that is, He must be both God and man in one Person. Furthermore, since He is not the Person who says to Abraham of this Seed and Person: "In your Seed shall all the Gentiles be blessed," He must be a different and distinguishable Person, for He who says to Abraham: "In your Seed, etc." is not Abraham's Seed, but He is referring to another who is to be Abraham's Seed. We naturally conclude that these are two different Persons. And yet there remains but the one undivided God in His one divine essence. The third Person is also at hand. It is He who expresses these words about the two Persons orally through Moses or the angel. As we said before, the utterance of the oral word is the special function and the distinctive revelation of the Holy Spirit; just as Christ's humanity is His particular and special revelation.

We Christians further infer from this that the mother of this Seed of Abraham must be a virgin who would conceive Him without sin from the Holy Spirit and give birth to Him. For if He were to be conceived from a man, as other children of Adam are, He would have to be conceived in sin, as Ps. 51:5 laments about all of mankind: "Behold, in sin did my mother conceive me, etc." If that were true, then He Himself would stand in need of another seed to bless Him, that is, to redeem Him from sin and death; then He could not be a blessing to us nor bestow a blessing on us. But on this subject St. Paul is our eloquent preacher, especially in Romans and Galatians (Rom. 3 and 4; Gal. 3), where he proclaims and teaches the Seed of Abraham and David in such a masterly fashion that it is superfluous for us Christians to treat of this further at this time; for this is our daily bread, the constant subject of our sermons, of our reading, and of our singing.

Behold, what a good Christian Moses is, to agree so fully with St. Paul and the entire New Testament. Should the cursing Jews and the seeds of the devil not be prone to stone such a heretic, as they were often tempted to do in the wilderness? Should he be their prophet and teacher? Oh, with such heresy he is not worthy of having a circumcised saint lend his superholy ears to hear the mention of his name. It must be execrated together with the accursed Goyim, to whom he promises such a great and joyous blessing. To be sure, Moses does not exclude the Jews with the words "all Goyim," for the children of Israel, too, are often called Goyim in Scripture. No, they exclude themselves, as David prophesied of them in Ps. 109:17-18: "He did not like blessing; may it be far from him! He loved to curse; let curses come on him! He clothed himself with cursing as his shirt (the garment closest to his body), may it soak into his body like water (through flesh and blood), like oil into his bones (through marrow and bones)!" Now, I trust, we Christians understand Christ's words in John 5:46: "If you believed Moses, you would believe Me, for he wrote of Me." He indeed wrote of Christ throughout his entire book, in which he speaks of God and Messiah. We will now also comprehend the passage in John 8:56: "Your father Abraham rejoiced that he was to see My day; he saw it and was glad." Where did he see it? In this verse, where he heard that his Seed was to be God and man, who would bless all Gentiles, redeem them from sin and death, and give eternal life and holiness and blessedness. He felt the same joy which David experienced above, in 1 Chron. 17:16, when the same Son was promised him.

We will cite Moses just once more, from Ex. 33. When God was wroth with the people because of the golden calf; when He refused to accompany and befriend them further but wanted to put Moses in charge and assign an angel to him; when He did not want to speak to the people any longer but communicated only with Moses, who said (Ex. 33:18): "I pray Thee, show me Thy glory!" then the Lord replied (vv. 19-20): "'I will make all My goodness pass before you and will proclaim before you in the name of the Lord; and I will be gracious to whom I will be gracious and will show mercy on whom I will show mercy. But,' He said, 'you cannot see My face; for man shall not see Me and live.'" Just study this text and, disregarding the devilish treatment rabbis and Jews accord it, see whether, in accordance with unadulterated language usage, it is in agreement with the New Testament. Here the Lord informed Moses, who desired to view His glory, that this was impossible; but, at the same time, He promised Moses that He would let all His goodness pass before him. One Person, the Father, who speaks of the Son (who is all the Father's "Goodness," by whom He made all things), Him Moses, that is, His regime and His people of Israel, is to see, not in His glory but just in passing, here in this life. For the Moses of these stories and visions is not the Moses who was born to his father Amram, not the private citizen Moses, but the called prophet and head of the people of Israel, to whom God gives the Law.

Immediately a different Person says: "I will proclaim before you in the name of the Lord." Here you perceive that the Lord will preach before Moses, that is, before the people of Israel, in the name of the Lord. What does that mean: "I, the Lord, will preach in the name of the Lord"? Does this not involve two distinct Persons? One Lord who preaches and one in whose name the first Lord preaches? But this Preacher, who is a Lord, must necessarily become a man if He is to preach before Moses and Israel. For God commanded the office of the ministry to man, for example, to the prophets and the apostles, through whom God proclaims His Word to us. And from the following words we can gather what the content of the sermon is to be: "I will be gracious to whom I will be gracious, and will show mercy on whom I will show mercy"; that is, "I will not preach as you, Moses, are obliged to preach. For you must proclaim the Law as follows: 'I command you today to do and to observe this and that. If you fail to comply, you will fare badly.' I, however, will proclaim that no man can become pious or be saved before the Lord by the Law; for no one keeps the Law as is his duty. Therefore your sermon produces only wretched people; it shows them their sins, on account of which they cannot keep the Law." That is why St. Paul calls this an office of transgression and of death in 2 Cor. 3:6, 9; Gal. 3:19.

"But My message in the name of the Lord reads: 'The Lord wants to do it Himself, and man's own merit and righteousness will count for naught. He who will attain righteousness will do so solely by grace and mercy. He who seeks grace and mercy without advancing his own merit will receive it.' That is the meaning of the words: 'I will be gracious to whom I will be gracious' (Ex. 33:19). This text does not mean that I am gracious to him who has the Law or who boasts of merits, but I am a gracious God to him who glories in My mercy." Thus this verse is not addressed principally and most directly against wretched sinners who are caught by the Law, but it is directed severely and bluntly against the stiffnecked, rigid, and brazen pride of man's own righteousness. Behold, that is preaching in the name of the Lord; that means, God will do what Christ preaches; and He preaches sheer grace, saying in John 7:19: "None of you keeps the Law" and in John 8:24: "I told you that you would die in your sins, for you will die in your sins unless you believe that I am He," that is, the Jehovah, the First, who is God Himself, and in John 1:17 we read: "The Law was given through Moses; grace and truth came through Jesus Christ."

Now compare this meaning of Moses' text in this passage with the New Testament, and tell me whether it does not agree with it closely, without pressure, and easily. It is not necessary to force and torture any word with odd explanations that militate against the normal meaning. The words in their common meaning in Hebrew agree with our Christian faith, which teaches us in the New Testament that Jesus Christ is Jehovah, God and Man, and that He was the Preacher of the people of Israel. In Rom. 15:8 St. Paul calls Him "a Servant to the circumcised," a Preacher of the circumcised people of Israel. And Christ Himself declares in Matt. 15:24: "I was sent only to the lost sheep of the house of Israel." He also forbade the apostles to go among the heathen. And here He says to Moses: "I will proclaim before you." He says as it were: "For My person, I will be a preacher only among your people, the circumcised Israel, especially of the wretched people whom you have humbled with the Law." Thus we read in Is. 61:1: "The Lord has anointed Me to bring good tidings to the afflicted." The Gospel is nothing else but the Word of Christ, of God's Son, in which He proclaims sheer grace and mercy to us in the Father's name, who sent Him for that purpose and who Himself works all things in us through Him.

This is the "passing" before Moses and his people. In it He has taken note of us, and all the goodness of God has been shown to us, without exposing and displaying the glory of His divine being to view. That does not belong to this life; only after we have died will this take place, for He says (Ex. 33:20): "Man shall not see Me and live." This does not forbid that man will ever behold God; on the contrary, this holds out the promise of the resurrection of the dead, when we will see Him. These words pertain only to this life. "Man," He says, "shall not see Me and live." "To be sure, man may see Me, but it will not happen while he is still alive. He must first die and enter into a different life. There this privilege will no longer be denied him. There he will comprehend that I was gracious to him to whom I was gracious, and that I was not at all gracious to him because of his own righteousness nor of the works of the Law."

I am well aware that the Hebrew word קָרָא, "to preach," may also mean to call, to name, to read, as Lyra and Burgensis bear witness,[48] according as it is construed with a particle in one direction or another. But the way it stands here with the little word "in," it usually means to preach. See Gen. 4:26; 12:8; 13:4. It is indifferent to me if rabbis or contentious Hebraists do not accept this. I am satisfied, as I have often said, if Moses' words, in accord with the best usage of the Hebrew language, coincide and agree so nicely with the New Testament, instead of with the forced interpretation of the rabbis, that everybody (even if he is not a Christian but is conversant with the language) must say: "Indeed, if the Christian belief is correct, Moses' words surely reflect their interpretation; for these words agree with nothing else so well and so surely as with the New Testament." And in this manner I should like to free the whole Hebrew Bible for the Jews from their shameful and blasphemous commentaries. However, this is not one man's work. It is enough that I set an example for others who are more learned than I am, or that I have demonstrated my good will, inducing them to improve and enlarge on this.

Moses continues his report with these words (Ex. 33:21-23): "And the Lord said, 'Behold, there is a place by Me where you shall stand upon the rock; and while My glory passes by, I will put you in a cleft of the rock, and I will cover you with My hand until I have passed by; then I will take away My hand, and you

[48] Lyra *ad* Ex. 33:19.

shall see My back; but My face shall not be seen.'" Here, too, there are two Persons named Jehovah speaking. One says: "While My glory passes by." This is the Father, who speaks of the passing by of His glory, that is, of His Son. And the Son Himself says that it is He who is passing by. As we heard before, this is all said of Christ, God and man, who walked here on earth.

The other matter about the "place by Me" and all that is said about the cleft of a rock and of covering Moses with His hand until He should pass by I understand to mean that God for the sake of the future Rock, Christ, protected and preserved the people of the Law, or Israel, in His patience because they could not keep the Law. That is the tenor of St. Paul's words in Rom. 3:25, which say that the sin which remained under the Law is in divine forbearance forgiven in this time, when Christ has appeared and "passed by," etc. But since this "passing by," God has withdrawn the hand of such forbearance and the protection of the rock. For the Law is done for and fulfilled, and we no longer require the forbearance and the protection of a future Christ. Yes, he who believes that Christ is still to come and who wishes to stand with Moses in the cleft of the rock under God's protecting hand is damned. The rock and the hand are removed, we now have the Lord and His "passing by," up to whose time the protection and the forbearance of God were to endure. Now we look after His passing and see what He has done for us, that is, we see His back, we see what He left behind for us, namely, that He, God and man, died and rose for us. Thus Christ's humanity might be termed His back. In this we recognize Him in this life until we arrive at the place where we shall also behold His face and His glory.

In Ex. 34:5-7 Moses depicts the Lord as that type of a preacher: "And the Lord (Jesus Christ) descended in a cloud and stood with him (Moses) there, and proclaimed in the name of the Lord. The Lord passed before him, and proclaimed (preached), 'The Lord, the Lord, a God merciful and gracious, slow to anger, and abounding in steadfast love and faithfulness, keeping steadfast love for thousands, forgiving iniquity and transgression and sin, but who will by no means clear the guilty, visiting the iniquity of the fathers upon the children and the children's children, to the third and the fourth generation.'" In this passage the Latin Bible is completely wrong, whoever it was that did it. It substitutes

"Moses" where it should have "the Lord." [49] Perhaps this expert translator thought it unbecoming that the Lord should preach and proclaim the Lord, that this was more fitting for Moses. The translation of Burgensis appeals to me. He holds that the Hebrew text reads thus: "And the Lord passed before him and proclaimed (or preached) the Lord, the Lord God, the Merciful One, the Gracious One." He used the accusative case. In German we would say: He preached concerning the Lord, the Lord God. However, the meaning is and remains the same. For in German the expressions "to preach the Lord" and "to preach concerning the Lord" are synonymous.

Now, this is another clear text that states that the Lord is a Preacher and that He preaches in the name of the Lord. Two Lords are mentioned here, and yet they are not two Gods or Lords. Yes, he says that the Lord indeed does preach concerning the Lord, concerning the Lord, concerning God. Twice we find the word "Lord" and the word "God" is added to these. That makes three, and yet they are not to be three Gods. Above, we explained the meaning of the statement that the Lord preaches in the name of the Lord; namely, that Jesus Christ is the Preacher, God and man, sent by God, who has preached to Moses, that is, to Moses' people, in the name of His Father and concerning His Father about sheer grace and mercy and told them that no man can be justified by the Law because no one keeps it. He delivers the selfsame sermon here in different words, saying: "The Lord stood with Moses and proclaimed." Why does He stand with Moses and not above him or far from him? The two preaching offices, the Law and the Gospel, must stand side by side even though their objectives are different. Moses preaches of sin and kills thereby. Christ preaches of grace and quickens thereby. However, grace is ineffective if the sin is not first revealed and recognized through the Law. In Matt. 11:5 the Lord Jesus says Himself that He preaches the Gospel to the poor and to the lost sheep of the house of Israel, that is, to those who because of the Law feel that they are lost.

And now, what does the Lord preach in the presence of Moses and before Moses? He says that He preaches of the Lord, Lord

---

[49] The Vulgate of Ex. 34:5 reads: *Cum descendisset Dominus per nubem, stetit Moyses cum eo, invocans nomen Domini.*

God, the Gracious and Merciful One, etc., that is, that three Persons are one God, before whom one's own merits, based on the Law, lack all validity. These count for nothing before Him and, in fact, are nothing. Only pure grace and mercy, goodness and faithfulness count before Him; He forgives sin, transgression, and iniquity. Before Him no one is innocent. And now, if you would hold to God and call Him by His right name, for it is recorded here that He is a Forgiver of sin, that He is gracious and merciful, and that no one is innocent in His sight, you must not parade your merits before Him, no matter if you are Moses, John, or whoever you will, but you must join St. Paul in Rom. 3:23 and say: "All have sinned and fall short of the glory of God," or "they may not say that they are innocent and righteous before God." If they do that, the last words of our quotation will be applicable to them: "He visits the iniquity of the fathers to the fourth generation." And as Christ also says (Mark 16:16): "He who does not believe will be condemned."

Take note that we do not find the words of the First Commandment here, Ex. 20:6: "Showing steadfast love to the thousandth generation of those who love Me and keep My commandments." In place of this, we read here: "No one is innocent before Him," that is, no one loves Him and keeps His commandments save those alone who boast of no merits, but who call and believe God gracious and merciful and a Forgiver of sin, and who plead guilty and petition God in the Lord's Prayer: "And forgive us our debts, as we forgive our debtors." That is nothing else than preaching pure grace, that is not preaching what we ought to do, as the Ten Commandments demand of us, and what never gets done, but what God in His mercy wants to do for us and has done for us, as the New Testament teaches and testifies. There we have the Preacher, who manifests Himself to Moses and foretells what He will preach in the New Testament. And what He prophesied to Moses in that day we see fulfilled in the New Testament, namely, that no one can be righteous and blessed by means of his own righteousness, but solely by God's grace, which is proclaimed to us by this Preacher, God's dear Son.

The words that follow this passage relate how Moses implores God to go with them and not forsake them, and how the Lord replies that He will escort them, do great miracles, etc. God is again reconciled with the people, He renews His covenant and writes new tables for them; in brief He summarizes the Old Testament commandments and the worship ordinances, to show how they should live and act. But we find no mention here of grace and forgiveness, as we did above. This is the situation: Moses now has the comforting assurance of the New Testament, when the Lord Himself will preach and govern. And now that this people has been entrusted to him that he may teach and rule it until the days of the New Testament, he prays that the Lord may remain with him and accompany him. "For," says he, "what am I to do? It is a stiffnecked and evil people (Ex. 34:9). And if You are not with us and forgive sin and bear with us patiently until You Yourself appear as the Preacher of grace, we are lost forthwith. We must have Your divine forbearance and Your protection in this regime, in which we are to preach Your law and yet will not keep it." It is the very same message that chapter 33 contains about the sheltering hand of God in the cleft of the rock.

For God replies (cf. v. 10): "All right, I will do it. I will make a covenant with your entire nation. I will perform miracles, the like of which have never before been witnessed in the whole country and among all the Gentiles. And all of the people among whom you are shall see how wonderful the work of the Lord is that I will do with you. See to it that you keep what I command you today, etc." All of this is spoken of the Old Testament and of Moses' people. The same is true of the following words which speak of the expulsion of the Amorites, Canaanites, Hittites, etc., all of which took place in Old Testament days. The Lord deliberately avoids the term "My people"; He calls them Moses' people, "your people," and "the people among whom you are." "Yet, true to My promise," He says, "I will hold My hand over them, protect them in the cleft of the rock, and perform miracles such as were never wrought among all the Gentiles." And this came true. Read the Old Testament from beginning to end, and you will discover how many great miracles the Lord performed in the midst of these people from the days of Moses to those of Christ. He did this even though they, with the exception of those who understood Moses and placed their hopes in Christ, were not His people, that is, not the people of grace but of the Law. The great multitude were nothing but work-righteous, stiffnecked, and zealous promoters of the Law.

But mark how the text clearly indicates that the Lord who is conversing with Moses is Jesus Christ, the future Preacher of the New Testament. For He here differentiates between Himself and the Father, saying (Ex. 34:10): "All the people among whom you are shall see the work of the Lord which I will do." Behold, it is the Lord's miraculous work of which He speaks and which He will do just as the Lord does it. Thus He says in John 5:19: "Whatever the Father does, that the Son does likewise," likewise (v. 17): "My Father is working still, and I am working," likewise (v. 21): "For as the Father raises the dead and gives them life, so also the Son gives life to whom He will." That indeed puts John in accord with Moses, and Moses with John. In fact, the two almost agree word for word. There are obviously two distinct Persons here, Father and Son, as John calls them, and the Lord who speaks of the Lord and performs the Lord's wondrous works, as Moses expresses it. And yet this is but one work, and not two different kinds of work. Therefore it cannot be more than one Lord and God.

The Lord continues to address Moses in the same passage (v. 23), saying: "Three times in the year shall all your males appear before the Lord God, the God of Israel." Here the Lord again speaks of the Lord God, the God of Israel. For these are not Moses' words, but the Lord's, who is conversing with Moses, and who commits the Old Testament to his care, which He will protect and patiently bear until the day of His own future "passing by." Of this we have said enough above.[50] Now, if rabbis and Jews interpret all this differently and sneer at my conception of it, it is as it should be; God's enemies shall not understand God's Word. But their expectorations on this text do not deserve that sow or ass read them even if they could. Moses' countenance has horns [51] and shines too brilliantly for them to look at it (2 Cor. 3:7). We, however, have a Moses whose words, unforced and according to the natural use of language, agree so genuinely and so charmingly with the New Testament. And even though it is Moses' lot to rule over these perverse and base people in his days of the Old Testa-

[50] See p. 328 above.

[51] The Vulgate translation of Ex. 34:29 *(cornuta esset facies sua)* had been responsible for this idea, most familiar perhaps in Michelangelo's statue of Moses.

ment, he, at the same time, prophesies mightily concerning Jesus Christ, our Lord, that He is true man and that He, together with the Father and the Holy Spirit in distinctive Person, is one true God, who does all that the Lord does. Enough of that. We will be glad to be called fools and unlearned in Scripture. We will let Jews and Turks abide in their dreamland with their great wisdom.

All right, let every one believe what he will. I, for my part, know and am convinced that I and all Christians have Moses on our side, that he is a sincere Christian, yes, a teacher of Christians. It matters not that he was at that time still cowled and attired in the Old Testament, as though he were no Christian but a devout monk. Thus St. Bernard is a monk in his vocation but a true and sincere Christian in his belief, who does not depend, insist, and rely on his cowl and his order, as the majority do, but builds solely on the mercy of Jesus Christ, as he himself often testifies.[52] Similarly, Moses lets the rest boast of the Law and circumcision; he goes along with them dressed in this cowl, but his heart, his faith, and his profession are always Jesus Christ, God's Son, etc. And if we have Moses, the teacher and the chief, on our side, then his disciples, the prophets, will follow him in crowds and join us; for they do not believe, profess, and teach differently than Moses, their teacher, does. But where will we seat all these dear guests? This little book is too small to contain them all; even Moses cannot find enough room in it.

This is what we will do: We will go to them and dine with them. Their kitchen and cellar are better stocked than ours. They can offer us meat and drink in abundance and dine us sumptuously. In other words: Let each one take the prophets in hand, read them diligently, and note where the Lord, Jehovah, Jesus Christ, speaks distinctively and where He is spoken of. You have now heard that it is He who speaks with Moses on Mount Sinai, who guides Moses and the people, and who performs miracles. And although He does not act alone here, but the Father and the Holy Spirit work with Him and do the same work, He nevertheless reveals Himself in those words and deeds to show that He is a Person distinct from the Father in the one, divine essence. And whoever observes so much in Scripture (which not everybody does) that he notices where one Person speaks of the other, indicating that

[52] See, for example, *Luther's Works*, 22, p. 52, n. 42.

there are more than one present, will soon discern which is the Person of the Father and which is that of the Son. And if you have mastered the distinction of the Father and the Son, then the distinctive presence of the Holy Spirit is also established immediately. By way of illustration we cite Ps. 2:7: "You are My Son, today I have begotten You," and Moses here in Ex. 33:19: "The Lord preaches in the name of the Lord," and Gen. 19:24: "Then the Lord rained . . . brimstone and fire from the Lord." Here you readily notice that the Lord who let fire rain is the Son, and that the words "from the Lord" denote the Father; for the Son is from the Father and not vice versa. In Hos. 1:7 we read: "I will have pity on the house of Judah, and I will deliver them by the Lord their God; I will not deliver them by bow nor by sword, etc." In Zeph. 3:9 the Lord says: "Yea, at that time I will change the speech of the peoples to a pure speech, that all of them may call on the name of the Lord and serve Him with one accord." In Ps. 45:7, 11 we read: "Therefore God, your God, has anointed you with the oil of gladness above your fellows. . . . And the king will desire your beauty. Since He is your Lord, bow to Him," and in Jer. 23: 5-6: "Behold, the days are coming, says the Lord, when I will raise up for David a righteous Branch, and He shall reign as King and deal wisely, and shall execute justice and righteousness in the land."

But where the Person does not clearly identify itself by speaking and apparently only one Person is involved, you may follow the rule given above and be assured that you are not going wrong when you interpret the name Jehovah to refer to our Lord Jesus Christ, God's Son. A fine illustration for this is Ps. 50:1: "Thus says the Lord: Where is your mother's bill of divorce, with which I put her away?" Here the word "Lord" designates the Person of the Son, although His Person is not distinctively mentioned. Thus it is interpreted by Lyra and also by others. I was very pleased many years ago to see Lyra write so definitely: " 'Thus saith the Lord,' that is, Jesus Christ." [53] And if you read the entire chapter following this verse (for Isaiah is not uttering a single word here, but all is spoken by the Lord), it will be found that the Person of the Son, Jesus Christ, is talking here, and not only according to

---

[53] Lyra writes *ad* Is. 50:1: " 'Thus says the Lord,' that is, our Savior Jesus Christ, addressing the unbelieving Jews."

His deity but also His humanity. For He says (Is. 50:6): "I gave My back to the smiters, and My cheeks to those who pulled out the beard; I hid not My face from shame and spitting. For the Lord God helps Me, etc." Read the whole chapter, and you will discover that it is God the Lord who suffers and receives help from the Lord God. This is proof that Christ is true God and man.

An example which does not clearly differentiate between the Persons is Heb. 1:6, which quotes from Ps. 97:7: "And again, when He brings the Firstborn into the world, He says, 'Let all God's angels worship Him.'" There is no particular sign, aside from the introductory words: "The Lord has become King; let the earth rejoice," that this psalm is speaking of Jesus Christ, God's Son. The Jews, of course, as well as every unspiritual person, will not concede that this refers to Christ. However, the Spirit professes that no one has become King but the Son. Ps. 2:6 bears this out, saying: "I have set My King on Zion, My holy hill." Also 1 Chron. 17:14: "I will confirm Him in My kingdom forever." Ps. 97 proves Him true God, saying (v. 7): "All the angels of God shall worship Him." In Hebrew this passage reads: "All ye gods, worship Him." But the word "gods" found here cannot refer to God, who is not many, but just one God. Therefore this signifies the angels. But He whom they worship is God, Jesus Christ, God's Son. Hence they who hold that this psalm speaks of Christ, as the Epistle to the Hebrews does, do not do wrong, despite the fact that they do not see the distinction of the Person.

When the same epistle (1:10) quotes from Ps. 102:25-26: "Thou, Lord, didst found the earth in the beginning, and the heavens are the work of Thy hands; they will perish, but Thou remainest, etc.," reason again finds no sign here of any distinctive reference to Jesus Christ, as the Epistle to the Hebrews does; I suppose it would have found clearer passages in the Psalter, but I believe that we are given examples of this type to spur us on to seek Christ in Scripture, since He is assuredly God and Creator together with the Father and the Holy Spirit. Thus anyone who affirms that Christ is He who created heaven and earth is certainly not mistaken. And yet we must diligently look for the distinctive revelations pertaining to the Person of the Son and carefully examine the words that indicate and reveal His Person. He who does not have a better example may simply accept the words of God's promise to David in 1 Chron. 17:12, that his Son Messiah shall build God a house and be Lord and King in this forever. Many psalms revolve about that theme. Also our Ps. 102 prophesies of such a house and building. It fervently implores the Lord to come and build Zion. This cannot have the physical Zion in mind. That was already erected at the time, and, moreover, that was not the house of God nor the Zion David's son was to build and in which he was to be King. Earlier we heard that the Builder and Lord of this house must be God and also David's son. Therefore the Epistle to the Hebrews correctly applies this psalm to the Person of Christ, who, of course, is one God and Creator with the Father and the Holy Spirit, but who is revealed distinctively and as a Person separate from the Father in the building of God's house and kingdom. Thus it is also a mark of identification of Christ, God's Son, to be called Abraham's Seed, in whom all Gentiles are to be blessed, and whom they will obey. We read in Gen. 22:18; 49:10: "To Shiloh the Gentiles will be obedient," and in Ps. 2:8: "Ask of Me, I will make the nations your heritage." This psalm, too, speaks about such a kingdom among the Gentiles, and in doing so it describes the Person of the Son, etc.

In brief, all three Persons are one God, one Lord, one divine majesty, nature, and essence. However, at times the Person of the Father is distinctively revealed, occasionally that of the Son, and then again that of the Holy Spirit. No matter which Person is made manifest, it is still the one God in three Persons. We must know the Divine Majesty aright, lest we believe blindly and wildly, as Jews, heretics, and Mohammed do, that God is but one Person. God resents that. He wants to be acknowledged as He reveals Himself. And God is particularly concerned about our knowledge of the revelation of His Son, as seen throughout the Old and the New Testament. All points to the Son. For Scripture is given for the sake of the Messiah, or Woman's Seed, who is to remedy all that the serpent has corrupted, to remove sin, death, and wrath, to restore innocence, life, paradise, and heaven. Just as Adam had primarily sinned against the Son in his fall, although he simultaneously offended all three Persons as one God, so God, in turn, let only His Son become man in contradistinction to the other persons, so that Adam might rise again through this same Son, by the sin against whom he had been brought to fall. And yet this raising up or redemption is the work of all three Persons as of one God.

For when the serpent, the devil, wanted to effect Adam's downfall, he set him in particular against the Son, saying: "You will be like God." That was an offense against the Son of God. Both the devil and Adam wished to dispossess the Son of His honor; for only the Son is like God, or only He is "the image of the invisible God," as we read in Col. 1:15, and the image of His divine essence, who "bears the very stamp of God's nature," as Heb. 1:3 tells us. The devil himself had experienced this fall in heaven and with his angels had learned his lesson from his opposition to the same image, the Son of God. He had not been content to be the most beautiful image of God among all the angels (though not born from eternity, but created and with a beginning), but he had aspired to become also the inner, natural image of God, equal with the Son. This is the way the fathers interpret the passage in Is. 14:12-14 addressed to the king of Babylon: "How you are fallen from heaven, O Day Star, son of Dawn! . . . You said in your heart, 'I will ascend to heaven . . . I will make myself like the Most High.'" For this reason the Person of the Son has been revealed distinctively and made man, that we might again rise in Him and through His humanity, we who had sinned against His deity and had fallen. Thus all of Scripture, as already said, is pure Christ, God's and Mary's Son. Everything is focused on this Son, so that we might know Him distinctively and in that way see the Father and the Holy Spirit eternally as one God. To him who has the Son Scripture is an open book; and the stronger his faith in Christ becomes, the more brightly will the light of Scripture shine for him.

Now, if you believe and understand that Christ is very God and very man, as Scripture teaches us, then see to it that you do not separate the Person of Christ nor intermingle the two natures or the divine and the human essence into one essence, but that you differentiate between the natures and preserve the one Person. For many wiseacres have come to grief on this point, that they have insisted either on uniting deity and humanity into one nature or on dividing them into two Persons, as Nestorius and Eutyches and their like did.[54] The Jews and Turks presume to be

---

[54] Luther had gone into this history at greater length in his treatise of 1539

extraordinarily smart, supersmart, and look down upon us Christians as great dolts. If Christ is God, they say, how can He die like a man, for God is immortal? If He is man, how can He be God's Son, for God has no wife? Here the saying is pertinent: Money implies honor, said the frog, and sat down on a penny. Here these wise, yes, wise, wiser, wisest people, the Turks and the Jews, teach us that God cannot die and that He has no wife. How could we stupid Christians ever acquire such profound wisdom if these great and supergreat teachers would not instruct us, apprising us silly ducks and geese of the fact that God has no wife and that He cannot die? It would not at all be surprising if the earth on which Jew or Turk deigns to tread would leap over the heavens with them, overjoyed to bear such a genius; and if the heavens, in awe of such wisdom, would tumble down with stars, suns, and moons and fall to the feet of Jew and Turk or into the abyss of hell; for it indeed reflects unfathomable wisdom that God has no wife and that He cannot die! O Lord God, Christians understand none of these things! Who would provide a wet nurse for God? Where would He get a nursemaid? Who would bury Him? Who would furnish the music and dance at His wedding? Who would read Requiem Mass for Him? Fie on us Christians to worship a mortal God and make Him a married man! Blessed, blessed are Mohammed and the rabbis who inform us otherwise! No, shame on you, you senseless Mohammed! Should you be called a prophet, who are such an uncouth blockhead and ass?

All right, let these miserable fools go their way and think themselves smart until they are surfeited with it. But you cling firmly to the Christian faith, taught us by Scripture, that Jesus Christ is true God and God's Son, and also true man, David's and Mary's Son, and yet not two Sons, two men, two Persons, but one Son, one Person, of and in two distinct natures, deity and humanity. For just as you, as we heard earlier in the doctrine of the Godhead, must guard against jumbling the three Persons into one Person or separating the essence, or nature, into three Gods, but must retain the three distinct Persons in one divine essence; so you must here beware lest you separate, or divide, the one Person into two Persons or mingle the two natures into one nature, but you must

On the Councils and the Church (W, L, 594—95; *Luther's Works*, 41, pp. 108 to 110).

preserve the two distinct natures in one Person. And just as the two natures unite in one Person, thus also the names of the two natures unite in the name of the one Person. In Latin this is known as "communication of idioms or properties." [55] By way of illustration: He who is called Man and who was born of the Virgin Mary and was crucified by the Jews must also be called the Son of God. And we must say that God was born of Mary and was crucified by the Jews; for God and Man are one Person. There are not two Sons, the one of God, the other of Mary, but He is just one Son, God's and Mary's.

If you were to concur with Nestorius and say that God, or Jesus, God's Son, was not born of Mary nor crucified by the Jews but that this was experienced only by the Man, Mary's Son, then you would create two Persons, you would split the one Person into two, so that there would be one Person who is born and crucified and another Person who is not born and crucified. Each nature would thus become a Person in itself, and there would be two distinct Sons. This is tantamount to saying that God did not become man but that He remains God, a Person in Himself, apart from the man, and the man a person in himself, a person apart from God. That will not do; it will not hold its ground against Scripture, for it says in John 1:14: "And the Word became flesh," and in Luke 1:35: "The child to be born will be called holy, the Son of God." And the Catechism states: "I believe in Jesus Christ, God's Son, conceived by the Holy Ghost, born of the Virgin Mary," etc. It does not say that God's Son is a different Person but the same one who was born of Mary and became her son.

On the other hand, if you were to say with Eutyches that the man Jesus, Mary's son, is not Creator of heaven and earth, or that he is not God's Son, who is to be worshiped, you would again divide the Person and split it into two persons. Just recently a silly bloke opened his big mouth and exclaimed that we Christians lived so precariously, worshiping a creature as God. That stupid fool does not read Scripture nor any books but dreams of such sublime matters in his own ignorant head. He is a conceited smart aleck. Nestorius separates the persons, tearing the humanity away from the deity and making each nature an independent person. In consequence, only the man Christ was crucified. Eutyches,

[55] Cf. *Luther's Works*, 22, pp. 491—98.

however, tears the humanity away from the deity, also making each nature an individual person.[56] The result is that God must be worshiped divorced from and apart from the human nature. But Scripture and the Creed speak thus: When we worship the Man born of Mary, we do not worship a detached person, a person apart from and outside of God, a separate, independent person. No, we worship the one true God, who is one God with the Father and the Holy Spirit, and who is one person with His humanity.

He who does not share that view must be confused and muddled in Scripture, unable to yield to any of its statements. For in Scripture Messiah is called God's Servant, Is. 42:1: "Behold My Servant . . . in whom My soul delights," and Is. 52:13: "Behold, My Servant shall prosper." In Ps. 22:6 He is even called "a worm, and no man." And what is still more loathsome, in Ps. 41:4 He is called a poor sinner: "I said, 'O Lord, be gracious to Me; heal Me, for I have sinned against Thee!'" In Ps. 69:5 we read: "O God, Thou knowest My folly; the wrongs I have done are not hidden from Thee," in v. 9: "The insults of those who insult Thee have fallen on Me," and in Ps. 40:12: "For evils have encompassed Me without number; My iniquities have overtaken Me, till I cannot see; they are more than the hairs on My head; My heart fails Me." Here reason, Jew, and Mohammed shout at us Christians: "How can that be understood as speaking of God? How can God be a servant? How can He be a wretched sinner?" O God, what nonsensical, stupid, and monstrous people we Christians are before such exalted, wise, and holy people who worship no creature but only the one God!

Reason admittedly does not find that in its Bible, that is, in its chimney flue, its dreamland. Nor do the Jews find this in their Bible, that is, in the Talmud, under the sow's tail, where they study their Schamhaperes. Neither does Mohammed find it in his Bible, that is, in his bed of harlotry; for that is where he did most of his studying. Thus this contemptible, filthy fellow boasts that God, that is, the devil, had endowed him with so much physical strength that he could bed with as many as 40 women and yet remain unsatisfied. Indeed, his choice book, the Koran, smells and savors of his

---

[56] We have translated the text as it stands; but Eutyches, who died in 454, had not, as Luther says, "separated" the two natures in Christ but had asserted only one nature after the incarnation.

studies in that Bible, the carnality of harlots. He looked for and found the spirit of his prophecy in the right spot, that is, in the mons Veneris. And it is surely not surprising that he who pores over such books knows nothing of God, or Messiah. Thus they also do not know what they are saying and what they are doing.

Thanks and praise be to God in all eternity that we Christians know that Messiah is God's one eternal Son, whom He sent into the world to take our sins upon Himself, to die for us, and to vanquish death for us. Thus Is. 53:6, 10 says very clearly: "All we like sheep have gone astray . . . and the Lord has laid on Him the iniquity of us all. . . . He made Himself an offering for sin, etc." Therefore we exult and rejoice that God's Son, the one true God together with the Father and the Holy Spirit, became man, a servant, a sinner, a worm for us; that God died, and bore our sins on the cross in His own body; that God redeemed us through His own blood. For God and Man are one Person. Whatever the Man does, suffers, and speaks, that God does, suffers, and speaks; and, conversely, what God does and speaks, that the Man does and speaks. He is both God's and Mary's Son in one undivided Person and in two distinct natures. The devil and his pander and whoremaster Mohammed and his Schamhaperists, the Jews, may be offended at this; they may blaspheme and curse (whoever cannot refrain), but all of them will tremble eternally for this in the depth of hell with howling and gnashing of teeth. God willing, that day is not far removed. Amen.

For the time being I will discontinue here discoursing on these sublime doctrines on the basis of the Old Testament. I hope that this may suffice to exhort our Hebraists to wrest the Old Testament from the rabbis wherever possible, regardless of their interpretations, commentaries, or grammars. These rabbis are very often at variance with one another and do not know where they stand. They are prone to equivocate with words and sentences to suit their stupid interpretation, even though the letter harmonizes readily with the New Testament, and it is certain that Jesus Christ is Lord over all. To Him Scripture must bear witness, for it is given solely for His sake. It was not my intention to quote the New Testament extensively this time since all of this has been proven there so clearly for approximately 1500 years. (That is the reason, too, why the Jews reject the New Testament.) This is particularly clear in the Gospel of St. John, in which practically every other word, as it were, proclaims that Jesus is God and Man in one Person. This same John, together with the other apostles, evangelists, and many thousands of their disciples, were also Jews, or Israel and Abraham's seed by birth, much more purely and more definitely than the present-day Jews, or Israel, are. No one knows who the latter are or whence they came.

Now, if we are willing to believe the Jews, or Israel, it is far more reasonable to give those Jews, or Israel, credence, who have for approximately 1500 years to date governed the church publicly in all the world, who have overcome devil, death, and sin, who have interpreted the writings of the prophets, and who have continuously worked miracles through their disciples. I repeat that it is far more meet that we believe such true and acknowledged Jews and Israelites than these false and unknown Jews or Israelites, who have wrought no miracle these 1500 years, who have interpreted no writings of the prophets, who have perverted everything, who have done nothing in the open but underhandedly and clandestinely, like children of darkness, that is, of the devil, have practiced nothing but blasphemy, cursing, murder, and lies against the true Jews and Israel, that is, against the apostles and prophets. And they continue this daily and thus prove that they are not Israel or Abraham's seed but venomous and devilish foes of the true Israel and Abraham's children and in addition despoilers, robbers, and perverters of Holy Scripture. Therefore it behooves us to recover Scripture from them as from public thieves wherever grammar warrants this and harmonizes with the New Testament. The apostles furnish us with many precedents for this.

I shall now come back to the last words of David, with which I began this booklet. In this way I shall bind the beginning and the end of this wreath together. I have digressed and meandered enough. Others can and will, I hope, improve on this and diligently seek and find the Lord Jesus in the Hebrew Old Testament; for He lets Himself be found there very readily, especially in the Psalter and in Isaiah. Try it according to the rule given above, and I am sure that you will agree with me and thank God. Well, I began this booklet with the thought that David's last words should be interpreted and understood in the light of Christian doctrine thus: [57]

[57] See p. 286 above.

[W, LIV, 94]

1. *The oracle of David, the son of Jesse, the oracle of the man who is assured of the Messiah of the God of Jacob, the sweet psalmist of Israel:*

2. *The Spirit of the Lord speaks by me, His Word is upon my tongue.*

3. *The God of Israel has spoken to me, the Rock of Israel has said, He who rules justly over men, He who rules in the fear of God.*

As stated before,[58] there are three speakers involved here: the Spirit of the Lord, the God of Israel, and the Rock of Israel; and yet there is but one Speaker. With reference to the third Speaker, the Rock of Israel, we read: "The Ruler among men, the Ruler in the fear of God." This Ruler is Messiah, as the Chaldean text, too, shows. In the Hebrew the following words are interrelated: "the Rock of Israel, the just Ruler, the Ruler in the fear of God." But it is certain that צוּר יִשְׂרָאֵל means the Rock of Israel and designates God Himself. And yet He is Messiah, the Man and Ruler in the fear of God. The Hebrew word מוֹשֵׁל used here means ruler. It does not mean lord in the sense in which God is Lord, but as men are rulers and govern. Wherever this term is used for God, you may unhesitatingly assume that Jesus Christ is meant. For example, Gideon says (Judg. 8:23): "I will not rule over you, and my son will not rule over you; the Lord will rule over you." In Ps. 22:28 we read: "Dominion belongs to the Lord, and He rules over the nations," and in Ps. 59:13: "God rules over Jacob to the ends of the earth." Ps. 8:6 also speaks that way of Christ: "Thou hast given Him dominion over the works of Thy hands; Thou hast put all things under His feet." That is stating the same thing which David does here when he calls Him the Rock of Israel (that is, God) and a just Ruler (that is, Man) over all that God made. This means that He is equal with God and simultaneously is Man.

David calls Him a just Ruler. This does not pertain to earthly and temporal justice. On this theme David elsewhere composed a beautiful psalm, namely, Psalm 101, where he says: "I will sing of loyalty and of justice." No, here he speaks of the eternal justice Messiah ushered into the world, whereby He redeemed us from sin and justified us. For in the words that follow David speaks of "the everlasting covenant" which God made with the house of

---

[58] See p. 276 above.

David. This is also the meaning of Is. 55:3: "I will faithfully keep for you the grace promised David," and Ps. 89:2: "For Thy steadfast love was established forever, Thy faithfulness is firm as the heavens." Earthly justice is far too fickle to fit this description. Earthly justice at its best—and it seldom is that—hardly preserves external peace, fends off murder, robbery, adultery, theft, etc. And granting that it does that, man is not justified thereby before God. God may temporarily and bountifully reward these virtues here on earth with riches, honor, power, happiness, etc. Before God all of this is slight, trivial, and perishable rubbish which He gives even to His enemies, and that in richer measure than He does to His dear children, who have a more precious reward to expect of which the world is ignorant.

Therefore there is no basis in fact to the rabbis' and their successors' interpretation that this passage refers to David, that he was to be just and lead a godly life, being established as king and ruler. No, this is a far different man, this Man who rules justly and in the fear of God. David did not make a single person righteous and God-fearing through his reign, not even himself, nor did Moses accomplish this with his law. See Rom. 3:20. But all are made righteous and God-fearing through this Ruler, Messiah, and this Rock of Israel, Jesus Christ. Thus Zech. 9:9 exclaims: "Rejoice greatly, O daughter of Zion. . . . Lo, your king comes to you, humble; just and having salvation, and riding on an ass." And Paul says in 1 Cor. 1:30-31: "Whom God made our Wisdom, our Righteousness and Sanctification and Redemption; therefore, as it is written, 'Let him who boasts, boast of the Lord,'" and not of our own righteousness, wisdom, etc.; for that is His domain, and for that reason He was made Ruler—He was to perform such works among men, make them righteous and return them to the fear of God, to the state of innocence and obedience from which we had fallen in Paradise through the cunning of the serpent. It is unnecessary for us to expatiate on this righteousness and on this fear of God here; for our justification and our salvation by Christ alone and out of sheer grace is the daily theme of our sermons. Now follows

4. *He dawns on them like the morning light, like the sun shining forth upon a cloudless morning, like rain that makes grass to sprout from the earth.*

David compares the dominion, or the kingdom, of Messiah, who is to restore and reinstate righteousness and the fear of God, with the charming and lovely activity of spring. For because the sun moves far from us, winter locks up the earth in frost, ice, snow, etc., so that all the trees are bare, all vegetation withers, nothing is verdant, nothing blooms, nothing bears fruit, and all the world looks like a vast expanse of death. But when the sun again begins to return to us toward summer, creation is again unlocked, everything greens and blossoms again, all is fragrant, all is renewed, the earth is again, as it were, quickened and gladdened. All men, also the heathen, regard spring as the gayest season of the year. Vergil writes: "This is the most beautiful time of the year." [59] He is of the opinion that the world had its beginning in spring. This is in accord with Holy Scripture, for Moses fixes April as the first month of the year. Similarly, the dominion and kingdom of grace is also a joyous and happy time, in which Messiah makes us righteous and God-fearing, so that we green and bloom, emit fragrance, grow, and become fruitful. For He is the Sun of Righteousness, which again rises for us. Thus Mal. 4:2 says: "But for you who fear My name the Sun of Righteousness shall rise, with healing in its wings." Therefore He also chose to rise physically from the dead in spring, or in April, in that merry season, and to establish His reign, although He was born in winter, that is, subjected Himself to the sin, to all forms of misery and the death of Adam for our sakes, and thus endured the harsh winter for 33 years.

For just as the prophet David here by the season of spring typifies the blessed time of grace, which dawns on us through Messiah, his Son, so he also suggests that the season of winter indicates the opposite, namely, the time of wrath under original sin, which we inherited from Adam. In that way God symbolized sin and grace to us in His creation as a lasting reminder until the Last Day, when years, earth, and heaven will change. Sin and grace are to be proclaimed to us daily and annually by summer and winter, if we but have ears to hear and eyes to see. In accord with such spiritual interpretation, Adam first lived in the charming season of spring, for he, too, was physically created in spring, in the beginning of the year; but through sin he soon called spiritual winter down upon his head, which Christ, the dear Sun, again dispelled,

---

[59] Vergil, *Eclogues*, III, 57.

reinstating spring. And now this is the order: He who lives in spring will never die; he who dies in winter will never live. In other words: "He who believes and is baptized will be saved; but he who does not believe will be condemned" (Mark 16:16). For the Sun, which David here foretold, sets on the latter but rises on the former.

David has more news to impart to us than just these facts expressed by summer and winter. He is more particularly interested in conveying to us the mystery that Messiah's reign is to be different from that of Moses. Moses' rule is that of the Law, which not only fails to remove sin, but it even multiplies sin, that is, it reveals sin and shows how monstrous and enormous and culpable it is. That frightens man, and now he, as it were, becomes inimical to God's judgment and His law, by which he is condemned and killed in his sin. St. Paul discusses this so beautifully in Romans and Galatians (Rom. 3; Gal. 3). It is Mount Sinai, on which there is lightning, thunder, rain, and earthquake, as though heaven and earth were to crumble. And though this is really the season of spring, the sun is hidden much farther behind the dark clouds than in winter, when it does occasionally shine brightly but with insufficient strength. For the heathen who live in the unknown sins of winter without a knowledge of the Law are much more secure than God's people, who must endure the thunder and lightning of the Law even in the season of spring. For wherever the Sun, Christ, does not shine brightly, spring, too, transmits no joy, but Moses with his law invests everything with terror and death. Thus the phenomena of the weather in the heavens are also eternal prophets. Occasionally the Law also rushes in upon our conscience and takes us unawares, although we live in the time of grace.

But in the days of Messiah, says David, when the צוּר יִשְׂרָאֵל Himself will reign to justify us and to save us by grace, it will be as enchanting as the most delightful time in spring in the wake of a refreshing, warm rain, that is, following the preaching of the comforting Gospel, immediately after which the Sun, Christ, rises in our hearts through true faith and devoid of Moses' clouds and thunder and lightning. Then all luxuriates, greens, and blossoms, and the day is filled with joy and peace, the like of which is unknown to the rest of the year. For here winter, clouds, sin, death, and all terrors are overcome, and a joyous, beautiful Easter Day is now celebrated into eternity. Behold, that is what David means when he compares his Son's, Messiah's, rule to a day in spring, when it rains early in the morning and then the sun rises in all its splendor and makes everything green and blooming and fragrant and live and merry. Ask yourself if this is not the best and happiest time of the year. There follows

5. *Yea, does not my house stand so with God? For He has made with me an everlasting covenant, well-ordered and secure.*

On the basis of 1 Chron. 17 we said earlier [60] that these words: *Does not my house stand so with God?* mean: O, what am I and what is my house to God? After all, it is not a house which would be deserving of such inexpressible honors before God, a house from which Messiah, צוּר יִשְׂרָאֵל, God's Son, the just Ruler among men, should be born." In these words David bows low in deep humility and marvels that such great things should come from his flesh and blood. The other subject, regarding the everlasting covenant with the house of David, I have treated quite adequately in the booklet on the Jews and thereby have given others an incentive to expand and improve on it.[61] The following two words, עֲרוּכָה and שְׁמֻרָה, *well-ordered and secure,* were chosen deliberately for instruction and for comfort. For if you take a glimpse at history, it will seem to you that God has forgotten His covenant and not kept it. David's house and that of his descendants lies desolate and disorganized. Yet it was not only maintained up to the time of Messiah, but it was also kept in order and secure against all devils and all men. No one was able to overthrow or subdue it, but, as promised, all were obliged to leave the scepter of Judah unimpaired until the advent of Messiah.

However, after Messiah came, His kingdom, the church, when viewed externally, impresses one as more desolate and disordered. It seems that there is no more dismembered, wretched, and ineffectual dominion or reign than the Christian church, Christ's kingdom. On the one hand the tyrants rend and devastate it with fire, water, sword, and every type of violence; on the other hand, factious spirits and heresies uproot and destroy it. Besides, false

[60] See p. 286 above.

[61] Cf. *On the Jews and Their Lies* (W, LIII, 417—552; *Luther's Works,* 47, pp. 137—306).

Christians do the same with their evil life. They make it seem as though there were no more disgraceful and disorderly rule on earth. And all of these work with the one aim in mind—rather, the evil spirit works through them—to annihilate Christ's rule, or at least, to make it a miserable, muddled affair. In brief, Christ acts as though He had forgotten about His dominion, it seems that He' can be found nowhere, and neither עֲרוּכָה nor שְׁמֻרָה is visible to reason. And yet it is עֲרוּכָה בַּכֹּל and שְׁמֻרָה, all is *well-ordered and secure*. And even though this is hidden from our view, He sees it who says in the Song of Sol. 8:12: "My vineyard, My very own, is for Myself," in Matt. 28:20: "Lo, I am with you always, to the close of the age," and in John 16:33: "Be of good cheer, I have overcome the world." At the same time we also observe that there always has been and always is a people that honors the name of Christ, that has His Word, Baptism, the Sacrament, the Office of the Keys, and the Spirit against all the gates of hell. There follows

For all my help and enterprise is that nothing grows.

David wishes to say: "I am also a lord and king, ordained by God before all kings; I have waged many wars; fortune has smiled on me; with God's help and miraculous deeds victory and triumph have been mine; I have done well in my reign and have governed efficiently; I have founded and established the kingdom well; I have administered justice; I have also suffered much over this. But this kingdom of mine, yes, the kingdoms of all earthly kings too, compared with the kingdom of my Son, Messiah, the צוּר יִשְׂרָאֵל, must be considered nothing but a withered twig which never grew and greened. For neither I nor any other king ever achieved victory over death, sin, hell, devil, and world; nor has any king in his rule ever made people righteous, God-fearing, and eternally blessed. We are poor, needy, and simple lords in our kingdoms; but my Son, Messiah, the צוּר יִשְׂרָאֵל is the Man who gained the victory over sin, death, devil, hell, world, and everything else. He has a kingdom that is a kingdom, in which He works this and effects this, that He justifies and saves His own eternally. This is real flourishing and blooming and fruitbearing, and it can never dry up.

I translated the word חֵפֶץ with *enterprise* after the example of Solomon in Eccl. 3:1: "For everything there is a season, and every undertaking (that is, enterprise) has its hour." For that is idiomatic. After all, you must undertake something and not go idle; you must do something to earn a living. Therefore *enterprise* designates all sorts of projects which a person pursues in this life. The philosophers also call them "intentions," "resolutions," and "purposes," because one person may be pleased to undertake, or do, this, another that. For חָפֵץ really means "to be pleased to," to "wish to," "to have an inclination or a desire to" do a certain thing. He who is not disposed to do a thing will either not do it or do it in a way that is worth about as much as not doing it.

6. *But the sons of Belial are all like thorns that are thrown away; for they cannot be taken with the hand;*

7. *but the man who touches them arms himself with iron and the shaft of a spear, and they are utterly consumed with fire in their dwelling.*

Here David is prophesying of the Jews who would not accept this Lord and Messiah. He calls them בְּלִיַּעַל, or, as we are accustomed to say, "Belial." In German that means *unnütz* ("worthless") or *schädlich* ("harmful"). In worldly government we call such people worthless and base knaves who are bent on working harm. But David is here speaking in the spirit and about the kingdom of Christ. For there it is the vogue to esteem the enemies of Christ's kingdom, such as Jews, heretics, heathen, highly. For even today Jews, Mohammed, pope, and factious spirits imagine they render God the greatest service when they inflict harm on the true Christians. They resent being called בְּלִיַּעַל; they want to be regarded as the worthiest. Thus Jer. 23:32 says about the false prophets: "They do not profit this people at all," that is, they are the most pernicious when they would be the most useful. In brief, the Christians are "Belial" and children of the devil; these, however, are the only children of God. Whatever they do is right—until God expels them and consumes them with the fire of His wrath. This we witness in the present-day Jews. What a terrible fire of divine wrath has overtaken them!

David likens them to the thistles among the grain in the field, which, in my opinion, the Lord Jesus calls ζιζάνια in Matt. 13:25. We translated that into German with the word *Unkraut* ("tares"). Ambrose in his *Hexaemeron* says: "Degenerating from wheat seed to its own kind."[62] In German we call these *Trespen* ("bromegrass"). But Christ is here speaking of a more noxious plant, one that is uprooted in the harvest and destroyed by fire, and He uses practically the same word as David does, who also separates his thistles and burns them with fire. Therefore ζιζάνια must be what David here calls קוֹץ, the large, noisome, thorny thistles or the other type of thistles which our peasants call *toll Graet* ("deadly nightshade"), which are sorted out with scythes, sickles, rakes, and pointed sticks in the harvesttime, for this cannot be done with the bare hand. They serve no other purpose than to be burned. Bromegrass, however, is used as fodder for the cattle. Thus the hardened Jews are such evil, prickly thistles and *toll Graete*. Neither God's benefactions nor His miracles could convert them and cannot convert them now; but with the iron and spear of the Romans they were ejected and consumed with physical fire together with their city in their own dwelling. Over and above that, wherever they are in exile, they are still burning within themselves with the spiritual fire of divine wrath. Thus David foretold its destruction and final perdition to this people, which was imposed on them because they would not accept this King. The Lord prophesied the same in Luke 19:43-44; Dan. 9:26; and Zech. 14:2.

Let this be my translation and exposition of David's last words according to my own views. May God grant that our theologians boldly apply themselves to the study of Hebrew and retrieve the Bible for us from those rascally thieves. And may they improve on my work. They must not become captive to the rabbis and their tortured grammar and false interpretation. Then we will again find and recognize our dear Lord and Savior clearly and distinctly in Scripture. To Him, together with the Father and the Holy Spirit, be glory and honor in eternity. Amen.

---

[62] Ambrose, *Hexaemeron*, Book III, ch. 10, sec. 44.

Index

Abimelech 153
Abishag 271
Abraham 88, 93, 280
  blessing of 323 f.
  Seed of 318, 323 ff.
Absalom 25, 56, 62, 118, 143, 200, 271
Abstinence 32 f., 93
"According to the mouth" 97 f.
Accusative, sign of, in Hebrew 320 ff.
Adam and Eve 24, 319 f.
Aesop
  Fables 61 n., 96, 101
Affection(s)
  changelessness of 20 f.
  depraved 8, 10 f., 19
  subject of Ecclesiastes 10 f., 12
Affirmative statement 47
Affliction 25, 63; *see also* Cross
  alternates with consolation 199 f., 204 f., 235, 237, 246
  faith does not change mind during 209, 243
  on account of God's Word 191 f.
Alcibiades 105 n.
Alexander 19 ff., 43, 86, 101
Amazons 130 f.
Ambition 69 f., 96; *see also* Striving, human
Ambrose 274 n.
  Hexaemeron 352 n.
Ammonites 139
Ancestors, imitating of 17, 21, 42, 206
Ancient of Days 291
Angel(s) 81, 212, 308, 310, 313, 318, 326, 337
Anger
  in sense of sorrow 110
  in the heart 117, 178
  wisdom, source of 28
Anselm 176 n.
Antiochus IV, Epiphanes 115 n.
Antony, Mark 41 n., 103 n., 104, 105 n.
Anxiety 7, 10 f., 24, 28, 46 f., 70, 93, 150
Apostles 262 f., 276, 287, 299, 344
Apostles' Creed 275, 306, 309 n., 342
Appearance
  and heretics 187
  judging on basis of 60, 196, 200, 212, 349 f.
Aquila 267
Arabs 201
Arians 163, 268
Aristotle 103
  De anima 59 n., 179
  Metaphysics 183 n.
  Nichomachean Ethics 183 n.
Arius 187 n., 303
Arts 9, 152, 165, 183, 201 f.
Assurance 272 f.
Astronomy, study of 9
Athanasian Creed 302 n.
Athanasius
  Epistle 187 n.
  Vita Antonii 274 n.
Atlas 143 n.
Augustine 63 f., 268, 310
  Christian Doctrine 308 n.
  Confessions 11 n., 30 n., 259 n.

De Genesi ad litteram 20 n., 263 n.
Le Trinitate 300 n., 302 n.

Babbler 62, 162 f.
Babylon 227, 339
Balsam 107 n., 208 f.
Banner 214 f.
Bathsheba 296
Beast 3, 57 ff., 61
Belial 351
Belisarius 115 n.
Belly servers 67, 166
Bernard of Clairvaux 335
Bernard of Cluny
  De contemptu mundi 4 n.
Bible 184; *see also* Scriptures; Word of God
  German translation of 270
  Holy Spirit recognized in Books of 185
  versions of vii, 36 n., 267
Birth 50 f., 108
Blesilla 4, 31
Blessing(s) 11, 214 f., 240
  giving thanks for 215 f., 227
  of Abraham 323 f.
  received from Gospel 201 f.
Blindness, spiritual 288
Body 179 ff.
Bonaventure 68 n., 306
  Commentarius in Ecclesiasten, Opera 18 n., 19 n.
Books 184 f.
Boredom 8, 10, 20, 32, 34, 155

Breath of God 301 f.
Brenz, Johann x, 3 n.
Bride 193, 198, 216 f., 233, 243, 247 f., 257 f., 261
Bridegroom 193, 198, 205, 216 f., 222, 227, 243, 257 f.
Bundle of sticks 69
Bunglers 65 f., 184
Burgensis 329, 331

Caesar Augustus 39, 42, 45, 116 n.
Caesar, Julius 10 f., 17 f., 20 f., 39, 90 n., 103 f., 117 f., 143 n.
Gallic War 102 n.
Cain, birth of 24, 319 ff.
Calling 151, 201 f., 236
Candace 131
Cannae, battle of 296
Carthusians 32
Catullus
Carmina 145 n.
Certainty of grace 3 f., 144 f., 148, 227, 243
Chance 132
Charlemagne 69 n.
Charles V 39 n., 152
Chilo 296
Christ; *see also* Messiah; Son (of God)
and true meaning of Scripture 268, 339
baptism of 304
called David 297 f.
called God's Servant 297
contemporaneous with children of Israel 313
deity of 287 f., 299 ff., 312
guides Moses and the people 332 ff.
humanity of 277, 286 f., 291, 294, 305 ff., 330
kingdom of 259 f., 262, 288 f.
speaks with Moses on Mount Sinai 325 ff.

Sun of Righteousness 347 f.
the Word 276, 299 f., 312 ff., 317, 341
two natures of xii, 292 f., 325, 339 ff.
Church; *see also* People of God
false brethren in 221
fortified like wall against false doctrines 260 f.
fruits of 242
God's dwelling-place 282
pictured as dove 220
purity of, through Word 232
songs of 274
terrifying to Satan 244
undesirable in appearance 200 f., 349 f.
utterly pure and without fault through Word 232
well-ordered and secure 350
Cicero 5, 11, 17 f., 24 f., 38, 39 n., 41, 104, 204
De amicitia 126 n.
De divinatione 26 n.
De legibus 184 n.
De natura deorum 26 n.
De officiis 122 n.
Commodus 72 n.
Communication of attributes 293
Community of goods 68 f.
Complaint 211
Concord 69, 228 f., 233
Confidence that works are pleasing to God 244, 255
Conscience 3, 70, 80, 133, 209
terrors of 273
testimony of 236
Consolation 64, 206 f., 212, 230, 233, 237, 243, 325

after affliction 199 f., 204 f., 235, 246
happiness drawn from 209 f., 214
Contempt
for created things 8
for world 4, 9, 31, 176
Contentment with present 7, 10, 13, 21, 30, 65, 86, 101, 133, 143
gift of the Holy Spirit 43, 47
Contrite spirit 281
Counsels of men 4, 9 f., 14, 24, 34, 44
hindrances to 62
ineffective as republic of Plato 75
Craftsmen, envy among 63 f.
Crates of Thebes 89 n.
Created things 4, 49
attitude toward 8, 93
contempt for 8
goodness of 14 f.
Creator 300 ff., 309
Creature 8, 40, 50, 302 ff.
viewed per se and viewed relatively 307 f.
Cross 25, 108 f., 206, 235, 237 f., 258 f.; *see also* Affliction
Cyril 310
Expositio sive commentarius in Joannis Evangelium 300 n.

Dangers 90, 160 f., 174, 211
David
amazement of 286
and psalms of Israel 274 f.
deep humility of 286, 349
firm faith of 272 f.
glories as father in his son 296 f.
house of 280, 296
joy of 286, 294, 296, 326

INDEX

lowly descent of 271
name of Christ 297 f.
Dead
 outside of space 150 f.
 sleep of 147 f., 150
Death 44, 182, 258
 better than day of birth 107 f.
 better than human misery 63
 time of 50 f., 59
Deference 157 f.
Delight 50
Delilah 131
Demosthenes 5, 24, 38, 39 n., 41, 104, 132, 322
Deuteronomy, Book of x
Dietrich, Veit xi
Dinner parties 29
Dio Cassius
 History 72 n.
Diogenes 89 n.
Diogenes Laertius
 De vitis, dogmatibus et apophthegmatibus clarorum virorum 296 n.
Dion of Syracuse 22 n., 41
Dissembling 83 f., 187
Divine Essence 275, 279, 301
 and Lord's Prayer 310 f.
 not to be separated into three Persons 302, 305, 310, 340
Doctrine; *see also* Purity of doctrine
 called purest gold 240
 compared with wine 197, 255
 good effects of 220
 must be defended 230
 new things in 43, 116, 140, 184 ff., 303
 of Christ's deity in Old Testament 287
 of Proverbs 195
 varying 184 ff.
Dog and his shadow 61, 96, 101

Domestic matters, success in 35, 37
Dominion 49, 277 ff., 291 f., 345
Door 261
Doubt 3, 272
Dove 209, 220, 227, 241, 246, 304, 307
Dreams 77 f., 81
Drones 65

Earrings 207
Ecclesiastes ix f., 4 f., 6 ff.
 principal conclusion of 46 f., 92 f., 186
 purpose of Book 7, 10 f., 195
 subject of 10 f., 12 f., 22, 144
Education 71 ff., 176 f., 202, 250
Ehrenreich 193 n.
El 288 f.
Elbe 17, 65
Elements, four 15, 17
Elisha 274
Endeavors, vain 7 f., 9, 14, 94, 102 f.; *see also* Striving, human
Envy
 destroys a happy life 178
 of craftsmen 63 f.
 of lot of another 98
Epicureans 3
Epicurus 88 n.
 Fragments 89 n.
ἐπιείκεια 129
Erasmus
 Praise of Folly 127 n.
Erfurt, riots in 159 n.
Erlangen text 291 n.
Eth 320 ff.
Euclid 74 n.
Euclio 67
Eutyches 339, 341, 342 n.
Evangelical admonitions 64
Evils
 alternate with times of peace 237
 and God 55, 120
 becoming accustomed

to 92, 109, 176 f., 186
 children not disturbed by 117
 offense of, in face of virtues 201 f.
Example 17 f., 22, 33, 43, 49, 147, 153, 174, 186, 192, 214
Experience 23, 28, 47, 105
Eye(s)
 in old age 180
 insatiability of 19, 67, 86, 99
 oblique 133
 sight of 100 f.
 signifies teacher 227, 241, 244, 250
 treasure of 11

Fabius, Quintus 159 n.
Faith
 and interpretation of Bible 268 f.
 and love together 257 f.
 and promise together 273
 as definite assurance 272
 as veil through which God is seen 218
 does not change mind in tribulation 209, 243
 effected and bestowed by Holy Spirit 277
 in God's nearness 208
 of David 272 f.
 speaks and preaches of the promise 273
False teachers 221, 239, 260 f.
Fate 41, 55, 102, 143
Father (God)
 distinction of 303, 309
 first Person 316
 name not to be restricted to Person of God the Father 311
 voice of 304 f., 306 ff.
Fear of God 55, 81 f.,

124, 145, 178, 186, 195
Figures of speech 9, 12 f., 105, 107, 113, 139, 170, 193, 196, 212, 214, 249
Fire of thorns 114, 352
First Commandment 282 f., 295, 313 f., 332
Folly
  success of 38 f.
  wisdom and 38 f., 99
Fool 38 f.
  definition of 65 f., 76
  hears only what he wants to hear 155, 157
  indications of 78
  laughter of 114
  runs away from adversity 112
  sacrifices of 75 f.
  world ruled by 159
Foxes 221
Francis I 39 n., 151
Franciscans 9
Frankincense 231 n., 234
  symbol of prayer 231
Frederick (III) the Wise 34 n., 56 f., 83 n., 90 n., 139 n., 159, 167 f., 204
Free will 49, 133

Gazelle 217 f., 222, 264
Gellius, Aulus
  Attic Nights 296 n.
Generations, succession of 15, 97
Generosity 115, 171 f.
Gentiles 41, 212, 255, 278, 323, 338
Germany
  and the Gospel 44, 64, 144 f.
  condition of government in 25, 165 f.
Giving 115, 171 f.
Glory 26, 326 f.
  in sense of wealth 157
God
  and marriage 4, 35

and reason for confounding our plans 82
approves what we do 148
as Bridegroom 193
as King 40 f.
author of good and evil things 55, 120
Breath of 301 f.
called Apple Tree 212 f.
church His dwelling-place 282
Colleague of Solomon's reign 204
Creator 300 ff., 309
faith in nearness of 208
fear of 55, 81 f., 124, 145, 178, 186, 195
figurative description of 240 ff.
Forgiver of sin 332
Giver of happiness 54
in three Persons 277 f., 280, 282, 291 f., 301 f.
keeps eye on preaching in vineyard 263
knowledge of, everlasting life 306 f., 310
moments of life and death fixed by 51
must give benediction for success 47, 73
right hand of 294 f.
seen through veil of faith 218
will set things straight 56 f., 84 f., 92, 119
works of 14 f., 21, 55 f., 119, 143, 173 f., 256

Goliath 5
Good intentions 26
Good works 74, 77, 107, 135, 147, 169, 172, 174, 236 f., 242
Gospel
  and Germany 44, 64, 144 f.
  compared to spring-

time 348 f.
effect of on wicked people 74
foretold 260, 262
hindered by foolish preachers 65 f.
magnitude of blessings received from 201 f.
not heeded by all 124
recognized as God's Word by fathers 185
Word of Christ, of God's Son 328
Government 5, 245; see also State
  and history 43
  as divine ordinance 8, 169, 248
  care of details in 167 f.
  concern for 24, 225 f.
  condition of, in Germany 165 f.
  exists for sake of good men 205
  good to overlook some things 123 ff., 158 f.
  greatest of human works 196
  persevering in obedience to 136 f.
  reform of 27, 56 f., 64 f., 119, 143
  respect for 169
  woman in 130 f.
Goyim 321, 324, 326
Gravity of conduct 110 f.
Greedy man 43, 87 ff., 92; see also Miser
Gregory I 274 n.
  Dialogi 58 n.
  Super Cantica Canticorum expositio 231 n.

Hair 228, 241, 244 f., 251
Happiness 53 f., 240
  compared to light 92
  drawn from consolation 209 f., 214
  gift of God 54
  necessary for youth 177
  of fools 114

INDEX

of the spirit 112
over the present only 120
running away from 30
with grave countenance 111
without planning 31 f., 37 f.
Health 11
Hebraism 40, 53, 97, 101, 117, 120, 136, 147, 152, 164, 166, 180
for superlative 13
Hebrew 14, 16, 36, 37, 50, 58, 81, 120, 136, 166, 272, 273, 276, 288, 289, 319, 320, 321, 322, 323, 324, 329, 345, 348, 349, 350, 351, 352
Hebrew language 7, 213, 267, 287, 322
Heir 45, 94 f.
Heliogabalus 72 n.
Hercules 143 n.
labors of 5
Heresy
and easy conscience 80 f.
attitude toward 84, 120, 155, 163 f.
gives disorderly appearance to church 349 f.
"in the time of investigation" 187
resources against 230, 304
source of misery 182 f., 219
worms its way like little foxes 221
Herodotus
History 42 n.
Hesiod
Works and Days 63 n.
Hilary
De Trinitate 300 n., 310
History
and ordinance of God 103
and promise of God 349

course of 102
government and 43, 71
Holy Spirit 275 f., 279, 295
bears witness in heart 209
Breath of God 301 f.
chaste mouth of 231, 249
effects and bestows faith 277
"Father of the wretched" 316
gives ability to be content 43, 47
in the form of dove 304 f., 306 f., 308
not apart from oral Word 197
Person distinct from Father and Son 303
recognized in Books of Bible 185
works ascribed to 276
Holy water 324
Homer
Iliad 130 n., 156 n.
Hope, best thing among mortals 146
Horace
De arte poetica 117 n., 241 n.
Epistles 133 n.
Odes 87 n., 157 n., 240 n.
Satires 68 n.
Sermones 10 n.
Hour 50, 350
of death 50 f., 59
House of God 74, 77, 139, 281 ff., 284 f., 338
Hugh of St. Victor
In Ecclesiasten Homiliae 49 n.
Human affairs, administration of 7, 160
crookedness of 26 f., 143
not carried out by schemes of wise men 102

subject of Ecclesiastes 12
Humors 180 n.
ὑπόστασις 272

Ideas 4 f., 33
Idleness 65, 106 f., 114, 123, 150, 238
Idolatry 232
Ignorance 80 f.
Immortality of soul 59, 61
Impatience
in trouble 106
of heretics 5
under slander 115 f.
Ingratitude 106, 115 f., 119, 141, 145, 170
Insatiability 19 ff., 34 f.
Interpretation 57 f., 191—95
importance of faith in 268 f.
of Old Testament 268, 270, 287, 299, 318
of Song of Solomon 191, 214
per antithesin 220 n.

Jehovah 290, 313, 319 f., 321, 323, 328, 336
Jerome 4, 31, 79 f., 107 n., 108, 115 n., 247, 267, 272 n., 287 n.
Commentarius in Ecclesiasten 4 n., 15 n., 63 n., 147 f.
Epistle (to Paulinus) 53 n.
Prolog 322
Jerusalem 23
as example of religious and civil discipline 235
fall of 141 n., 285, 352
Jesse 271, 275
Jewish commentators xi, 194 n., 267 ff., 278, 292, 319, 329, 343
Jews
and belief in one God,

Creator, Father
314 f.
and correct Bible 267 f.
and crucified cat in Budapest 321
and Moses 326
classed with Turks 339 f.
compared to true Jews 344
destruction of, foretold 352
John, on the Word through whom God created 299 ff.
John the Baptist
and baptism of Jesus 304
silence of Jesus over murder of 27
Joseph in Egypt 70, 97 f.
Judah
scepter of 280 f., 249
tribe of 272 f.
Judgment 137
Justice 56 f., 83 f., 124
Justification, attributed to works 74, 111
Justinian 115 n.
Institutes 270 n.
Juvenal
Satires 88 n., 96 n.

καιρός 52
Kimchi, Rabbi David 322 n.
King
child as 165 f.
cultivator of earth 85
cursing of 169
education of 71 f.
God as 40 f.
keeping commands of 135 ff.
Kingdom of Christ 259 f., 262, 288 f.
Kisses 196, 254
Knowledge
as experience 28, 105
of nature 9
of self 122
sorrow result of 22 f., 28, 105

teaching of 183
wisdom modified by 28
Koheleth 12
Koran 342 f.

Lacedemonians 42
Langton, Stephen 316 n.
Last will and testament 270
Last Words of David x f., 270, 279, 294, 298, 344, 352
λάθε βιώσας 89
Laughter 31 f., 110 f., 149
of fools 114
Law 70, 81, 264, 327 ff.,
Laws
and prudence 125 f.
moderator of 128 f.
praise of 226, 245
use of 122 f.
Leclercq, Jean
The Love of Learning and the Desire of God 191 n.
"Let it happen as it happens" 27, 29, 119, 202
Life
enjoyment of 10, 29 f., 36 f., 53, 98, 148 ff.
everlasting 58, 306 f., 310
to live well 44, 71, 100, 109
under the sun 14 f., 58
Light 289 f.
Christ as 289 f.
symbol of happiness 92
Listening
at windows 127
of fools 155 ff.
to Word of God 76 ff.
λόγος 300
Lord's Prayer 310, 316, 332
Love 29 f.
faith and 257 f.
first service of, to teach rightly about religion 229
should glow in teach-

ers 230
strong as death 257 f.
Love or hate 3, 144 f.
Lucian of Samosata
De morte Peregrini 60 n.
Luther, Martin
Against Latomus 133 n.
Catechisms 247 n.
Lectures on Genesis 269 n., 319 n., 323 n.
On Monastic Vows 79 n.
On the Councils of the Church 339 n.
On the Jews and Their Lies 280 n., 349 n.
Postils 247 n.
Table Talk 12 n.
Luther's Works x, xi, 5 n., 9 n., 15 n., 16 n., 20 n., 27 n., 57 n., 71 n., 77 n., 79 n., 83 n., 87 n., 112 n., 125 n., 128 n., 129 n., 133 n., 139 n., 144 n., 151 n., 152 n., 159 n., 168 n., 185 n., 193 n., 197 n., 216 n., 221 n., 249 n., 257 n., 269 n., 304 n., 319 n., 323 n., 324 n., 335 n., 339 n., 341 n., 349 n.
Lycurgus 42
Lyra; see Nicholas of Lyra

Man 175 f., 319
Manichaeans 268
Manlius, Titus, Torquatus 166 n.
Marian festivals 225 n.
Marius, Gaius 41 n.
Marriage
and misery 106, 198
gift of God 4
success in 35
Mary of Burgundy 193 n.

INDEX

Matthias, king of Hungary 70 f.
Maximilian I
  The Dangers and Adventures of the Famous Hero and Knight Sir Teuerdank 193 n.
Melanchthon, Philip x
Messiah 271 f., 278 f., 280 f., 283, 299
  called worm and poor sinner 341
  Help of Israel 350
  Jews' conception of 290, 298
Miracles 333
Mirror 100 f.
Miser 53, 67 ff., 86 f., 90, 95 ff.; *see also* Greedy man
Misery 8, 13, 22, 32, 34, 44, 63, 95 ff.
  heresy source of 182 f., 219
  in marriage 106, 198
Mohammed 340, 342 f., 351
Monasticism 4, 32, 83
Monks 5, 32, 66, 79, 83, 104, 146, 176 f.
Moses
  and God's "passing by" 327 ff., 330, 334
  guided by Christ in wilderness 332 ff.
  hears Christ on Mount Sinai 325 ff.
  was he a Christian 299 f., 312, 326, 335
Mourning 108 f., 182, 204
  house of 112
Music 36 f., 273 f.
Myrrh 208, 227 n.
  as mortification of flesh 235, 236, 238, 241
  symbol of the Word 231

Nabal 141
Name 102, 106 f., 197, 308

Nathan 280, 286 f., 288, 290, 292, 294
Natural law 5
Nature
  changes in 17
  knowledge of 9, 18
Nero 34, 43, 45, 72 n.
Nestorius 292, 339, 341
New Testament
  cannot err 287
  clear and reliable 268
  Moses and 333
  proclaims that Jesus is God and Man 343
  something reserved for 314
New things 20 f., 164
  in doctrine 43, 116, 140, 184 ff., 303
Nicholas of Lyra 79 f., 269 n., 295 n., 329 n., 336 n.
Nothing 14, 21 f.

Oath 135, 217 n., 256
Obedience 135 ff., 237
Office of the ministry 4, 228 ff., 327
  discouragement in 237
  variety of ministries 260
Ointment 10, 107, 149, 157, 197, 209, 233
Old Adam, sameness of 21
Old age 98, 117, 179 f.
Old Testament
  cannot err where interpretation harmonizes with New 287, 295, 299, 318
  full of miracles 333
  to be interpreted in direction of New 268, 270, 299
  veiled without New 287
Oppression 62, 83
Order
  of God 121
  of Persons in Godhead 316
  way of life 58, 120 f.

Origen 194 n., 287 n.
  Hexapla 267 n.
Ovid
  Amores 10 n., 116 n.
  Ars amandi 109 n.
  Metamorphoses 204 n.
  Tristia 128 n., 133 n.
Ox
  absence of anxiety in 45
  and plowing 83
  wants saddle 133

Parcae 143 n.
Patience 116
Patrologia, Series Graeca 187 n., 274 n., 300 n.
Patrologia, Series Latina 4 n., 20 n., 49 n., 53 n., 58 n., 177 n., 215 n., 231 n., 263 n., 300 n., 302 n.
Paul, on divinity of Christ 312 f.
Peace 26, 46, 195, 207, 224 n., 237
Peace of Cambrai 39 n.
Peasants' War 90 n., 125 n.
Pelagians 268
Pellicanus, Conrad
  De modo legendi et intellegendi Hebraeum 112 n.
Pentecost 306, 310
People of God; *see also* Church
  as bed or litter 223, 225
  asked to give thanks for blessings 215 f., 227
  distinguished from other people 23, 234, 246
  pictured as bride 193
  pictured as vineyard 203, 221, 262 f.
  ratify and accept psalms as their own 274
Perseverance 116, 213

Persius
  Satires 18 n., 261 n.
Person
  and distinct external work 302 f.
  denying one denies all three 316
  of Father 276 f., 280, 282, 286, 293
  of Holy Spirit 276 f., 280, 286 f., 289, 295, 297 f., 301
  of Son 276 f., 278, 280, 286, 292 f., 305
  special distinction within Godhead 302, 305, 309
  undivided 339 f., 343
Persons 276 f., 280, 282, 289, 295, 301 f., 315, 327
  distinctive forms and revelations of 307, 316
  distinctive works assigned externally to each 306
  external difference of 310
  not to be mingled into one Person 302 ff., 304, 340
  order of 316
Philip of Macedon 39
Philosophers 3, 17, 18, 55
  believed in chance 132
  classed with monks 146
  on immortality of soul 59, 61
Philosophy 3, 9
Pit 150, 160
Planning 22 f., 26, 30, 71 f., 82
  and happiness 31 f., 37 f.
Plato 22 n., 75, 103
  Meno 132 n.
  Phaedo 59 n.
Plautus
  Aulularia 67 n.
  Trinummus 109 n.

Pleasure 10, 29 f.
  and appointed time 53
  enjoyed in God 98, 149
  garden of 36 f.
  in toil 8, 46 f., 92 f., 110
Pleonasm, Solomonic 13, 16
Pliny
  Natural History 66 n., 232
Plutarch
  Lives 19 n., 39 n., 90 n., 103 n., 105 n.
Political office 4, 7, 56 f., 65, 83, 110, 223
Poor 83, 90, 95 f., 100, 167, 172
Prayer 198 f., 204, 208, 222, 231, 236, 253 ff., 285, 316
Preacher
  Christ 328 ff.
  title of Ecclesiastes 12, 23
Preachers
  God's eye on 263
  hindering Gospel 65 f.
  indignation over unfaithfulness of 92
  serve all for the sake of the remnant 146
  should stick to preaching 151
Present 11, 44, 54
  contentment with 7, 10, 13, 65, 86, 101, 133, 143
  happiness over 120
Promise 276
  and faith 273
Prophets, sons of 276
Prudence 33, 125
Prudentius 274 n.
Psalms 273 f.
ψυχικῶς 99
Publilius Syrus
  Sententiae 88 n., 168 n.
Punishment 11, 23 f., 48
  delay in 140 f.
  for those who despise the Word 25, 80
  for those who will not

hear 125, 136 f.
  war as 138
Purgatory 147
Purity of doctrine
  neglected by descendants 43
  threatened by false brethren in the church 221
  very pleasing to God 233

Rabbi Solomon 269 n.
Reason 5, 240, 279, 292, 295, 310 f., 342
Rebellion 200, 203, 238
Rebuke 113, 119 f., 169, 241, 245
Reform
  attitude toward 27, 64 f., 119, 143
  of wickedness in government 56 f.
Rehoboam 43, 72
Repair work 167
Reuchlin 112 n., 322 n.
Revised Standard Version 36 n.
Ribbeck, Otto, ed.
  Scenicae Romanorum Poesis Fragmenta 78 n.
Right hand of God 294 f.
Righteous man 121 f., 126, 134
Rock 276, 313, 330, 345
Roman empire 26, 42, 156
Rörer, George x
Royal road 42, 74, 77, 111, 122
Ruler 276 ff., 345 f.

Sabellius 303
  186 n.
Sacrifice(s)
  in temple 281, 284 f.
  of fools 75 f.
Saint Louis editors 73 n.,
Sallust 88
  Catiline 102 n.
Sapor 71 n.
Satan 65, 244, 317 f., 339

INDEX

Schamhaperes 323, 342 f.
Scriptures; *see also* Bible; Word of God
   and many books 185 f.
   and metaphors taken from nature 9
   attributed to Holy Spirit 275, 280, 292
   called heap of testimonies 245
   open book to him who has Son 268, 339
   purpose of 194, 206
   stories in, to strengthen faith 214
Second Commandment 314
Sectarians 43, 84, 140, 144, 155, 186
Sedulius 274 n.
Seed of Abraham 318, 323 f.
Seed of the woman 24, 317 ff.
Seelrecht 270 n.
σεμνότης 110
Septuagint 36 n., 181 n.
Serpent 317 f., 339
Sex 130, 132
Shulammite 248
Silvanus 177
Sin and grace 347
Slander 115, 163
Slaves 36
Small Catechism 304, 341
Social existence 68 f., 106, 146, 177
Socrates 132
Solitary life-style 4, 68 f., 89, 106 f., 177
Solomon
   and peace 224 n.
   catalog of works of 33, 36 f., 94
   discourses of 12
   many wives of 245
   special style of 7, 12 f., 193, 196
   tents of 201
   three Books by 195
   wisdom given to 11, 22 f., 28
   yoke of 144

Son (of God)
   Adam's sin against 338 f.
   Everlasting Light 289 f.
   Gospel of 328
   King 278, 288
   Light and Life 290
   of David 281, 283, 285 f.
   only-begotten Son 311
   Person distinct from Father 303
   Righteousness and Salvation 289 f.
   Son of Man 277, 290 ff., 294
   true Man 286 f., 291, 305 ff., 330
   wrath of 278 f.
Song of Solomon x f., 191 n., 195
   and impure thoughts 231, 249
   ideas about 194 f.
   order of Book 199 f.
Songs
   in Scripture 191 f.
   of the church 274
Sophocles
   Oedipus Coloneus 63 n.
Sorrow 30, 91 f., 178
   better than laughter 110 f.
   result of knowledge 28, 105
   result of wisdom 22 f.
Soul 59 f., 61, 109, 150
   in sense of willingness 247
Springtime 219 f., 347 f.
State 5; *see also* Government
   and afflictions on account of God's Word 191 f.
   compared to apple tree 257
   compared to rusty iron 162
   praise of 226
   solicitude for 24, 225 f.

   wretched in appearance 200
Staupitz 57 n., 83, 204
Stoics 127
στοργή 258
Strabo, Walafrid
   Glossa ordinaria 215 n.
Streams 16 f., 97
Striving, human 8, 10, 14, 17 f., 22
   changelessness of 20, 101 f.
Study 64 f.
Success in domestic matters 35, 37
   benediction for 47, 73
   in marriage 35
   of folly 38 f.
Suetonius
   Lives of the Twelve Caesars 72 n., 116 n.
Sultan 136
Sun 9, 14, 177, 347 f.
   existence under 14 f., 23, 58
   function of 16 f., 96
   in sense of tribulation 203
Sword, power of 85
Synagog 254

Talmud 342
Tantalus 67
Teaching; *see also* Office of the ministry
   false 221, 239
   first service of love 229
   of knowledge 183
Temerity 7, 39, 41
Temple 75, 220, 228, 232, 281, 283 ff.
Temptation 239, 304
   and consolation from Holy Writ 205
Ten Commandments 269, 313, 332
Terence
   Adelphoe 106 n.
   Eunuchus 87 n., 154 n.
   Phormio 99 n., 160 n.
Tetragrammaton 324
Teuerdank 193 n.
Thales of Miletus 122 n.

Thanksgiving 10, 199, 215 f., 227, 231, 252
Themistocles 154 n.
Theodore of Mopsuestia 194 n.
Theodotion 267
Theologians 4
Things 4, 8 f., 11, 13, 31, 49, 88
  new 20 f., 164
Thraso 87 n., 156, 159
Three Speakers 276, 278, 345
Three women and one dress 306
Time 49 f., 152 f.
  and space 150 f.
  appointed by God for correcting faults 57
  appointed for pleasure 53
  appointed for toil 52
  in God's hands 54 f., 73, 152
  of death 50 f., 59
Timon of Athens 105 n.
Toil
  allotted share of 98
  and appointed time 52
  as tribulation 14
  does not make rich 88
  enjoyment in 8, 46 f., 92 f., 110
  for the wind 91
  misery in 164
  without care 70, 150
Toleration 126
Torquati 166
Tower of David 230
Tranquillity 11, 29, 48, 142, 219, 223 f.
Trinity xii, 275, 279, 302, 305
  works of, toward outside not divisible 302, 304, 309, 311
  worship of, from outside indivisible 311
Trouble makers 65 f.
Troubles
  foreseen 161
  impatience during 106

of public official 56 f., 223
of state or household 5, 24, 110, 204
sufficient for the day 10, 25, 46, 71
Turks 340
Two natures in Christ xii, 292 f., 325, 339 ff.
Tyranny 139

Ulysses 5
Ungodly
  preponderance of 246 f.
  vexed by similarity to beasts 61
Uprightness in external matters 133

Valerian 71 n.
Vanity 4, 11, 34, 82
  meaning of word 13 f.
  possession of impious 48
  realm of 15 f.
  vastness of 18 f., 129
Vergil
  Aeneid 38 n., 43 n., 102 n., 108 n., 156 n., 159 n.
  Eclogues 258 n., 347 n.
  Georgics 114 n.
Vespasian 141
Vineyard 203, 221, 262 f.
Virgin birth 325
Virtues 234
  and vices 202, 246 f.
Vitae Patrum 9, 177 n.
Vows 79 f.
Vulgate 181 n., 267 n., 298 f., 320 n., 322 n., 330, 331 n., 334 n.

War 21, 26
  as punishment 138
  temerity and wisdom in 41
  victory in 39, 151, 156
Warning
  against despisers of Word 80
  against idolatry of

neighboring people 232
  against varying doctrines 184 ff.
Water, perpetual flow of 17, 97
Wealth 8 f., 37, 86 f., 89 f., 93 f., 259
  compared to wisdom 119
  enjoyed as though it were a picture 68, 87
  glory of 157
Weimar
  editor(s) 27 n., 205 n.
  text 37 n., 48 n., 59 n., 64 n., 73 n., 97 n., 105 n., 110 n., 112 n., 128 n., 205 n., 212 n., 213 n., 217 n., 224 n., 227 n., 231 n., 235 n., 238 n., 239 n., 297 n.
White garments 10, 149, 166
Will of God 24 f., 28, 40, 65, 148
William IV, duke of Bavaria 90 n.
Wind 91
  and operation of Holy Spirit 306
  cause of 16, 173
Wisdom
  and folly 38 f., 99
  and will of God 25
  better than might 153 f., 156
  brings sorrow 22 f.
  makes happy countenance 134
  modified by knowledge 28
  negative 132
  source of anger 28
  spiritual 148
  superior to wealth 119
  to administer 8, 20, 33, 36 f., 46
Woman 8, 130 f.

INDEX

military service of 100
not created for ruling 130 ff.
Word
all things created by 299 ff., 312 ff.
as Person of Son 276, 299 f., 312, 317, 341
Word of God; *see also* Bible; Scriptures
and counsels of men 10, 24 f.
and giving to poor 172 f.
and Holy Spirit 197
and purity of church 232
and speculative life 257
brings affliction to state 191 f.
firm and sure forever 272 f.
followed by offense 75, 203
followed by presumption and despair 74
grows through use 207
is swift as a gazelle 217 f., 222, 264
listening to 76 ff.
neglect of 25, 76, 238, 264
possession of, and ability to follow 198
prayer for spread of 253 ff.
rightly divided 229
sure fruits and effects of 232 ff., 242
Works of God 14 f., 21, 55 f., 119, 143, 173 f.
spring forth from dry ground 256
Works of human life 23, 36
and confidence of pleasing God 244, 255
approved by God 148
definite time for 51 f.
justification attributed to 74, 111
without anxiety 70
World
belongs to pious 48, 53
compared to rusty iron 161 f.
contempt for 4, 9, 31, 176
hatred of 211, 214
lies in wickedness 140, 145
never changes 117 f.
ruled by fools 159
thicket of thorns 67

Youth 176 f., 231

Zeal in religion 76, 245, 314
Ziegler, Bernhard 286 n.
ζιζάνια 352
Zoilus 186 n.

INDEX TO SCRIPTURE PASSAGES

Genesis

1 — 313
1:1 — 320
1:3 — 276
1:3, 6, 9, 11, 14 — 300
1:26 — 49
1:28 — 5, 324
1:31 — 56, 101
2 — 49 n.
2:7 — 182
2:17 — 318
2:18 — 8
3:15 — 317, 324
3:16 — 131
3:17-19 — 150
3:19 — 14, 182
4:1 — 24, 319
4:26 — 329
5:22 — 322
6:9 — 322
12:8 — 329
13:4 — 329
19:24 — 280, 336
22:18 — 323, 338
29:17 — 100
30:14 — 253
31:25 — 228
31:53 — 217
39:2 — 323
42:38 — 150
44:4 — 322
44:29 — 150
47:12 — 97
49:10 — 272, 338

Exodus

1:10 — 224
9:29 — 322
12:4 — 98
15 — 191
16:3 — 264
17:2 — 313
19:6 — 284
19:8 — 82
20:2 — 47
20:2, 3 — 313
20:3 — 47, 277, 282
20:4 — 317
20:6 — 332
32:34 — 81

33 — 333
33:18 — 326
33:19 — 328, 329 n., 336
33:19-20 — 326
33:20 — 329
33:21-23 — 329
34:5 — 331 n.
34:5-7 — 330
34:9 — 333
34:10 — 333, 334
34:29 — 334 n.
38:8 — 100

Leviticus

27:14-25 — 79
27:28-29 — 79

Numbers

14:22 — 313
16:30 — 21

Deuteronomy

4:6 — 240
5:8 — 317
6:4 — 282
6:13-14 — 298
10:20 — 298
23:3 — 139
32:11 — 9

Judges

5 — 191
8:23 — 345
9:53 — 153
11 — 79

1 Samuel

2 — 191
2:22 — 100
10:6-7 — 151
10:24 — 217
16:23 — 274
25:13 — 141

2 Samuel

7:11-16 — 279
7:19 — 291, 298

13:21 — 110
13:30 — 110
14:20 — 251
16:2 — 271
18:9-15 — 143
23:1-7 — xi
23:2 — 295
24 — 271

1 Kings

1 — 271
3 — 36
3:11-12 — 22
3:16-28 — 262 n.
4:7 — 46
4:22 — 46
4:26 — 46
7 — 36
8:27 — 281
11:3 — 245

2 Kings

2:4 — 217
3:15 — 274
4:30 — 217
6:17 — 212
11:12 — 217
20:13 — 107

1 Chronicles

17 — 294, 298, 349
17:4-5 — 281
17:10-14 — 279
17:11 — 282
17:12 — 308, 338
17:13-14 — 286, 290, 296
17:14 — 283, 288, 292, 337
17:14-17 — 298
17:15-16 — 285
17:16 — 286, 294, 326
17:16, 17 — 296
17:17 — 286, 291, 298
22 — 271
29:14 — 284

2 Chronicles

9:4 — 28

INDEX

10:4 — 144
15:7 — 147 n.

Job

1 — 221
1:12 — 136
1:21 — 91
13:14 — 66
14:5 — 51
15:32 — 141
40:16 — 250

Psalms

1:2 — 50
2:2 — 278
2:4, 5 — 279
2:6 — 278, 337
2:7 — 278, 311, 336
2:8 — 338
2:11 — 278
7 — 81
8:4-6 — 276
8:6 — 345
13:3 — 92
22:6 — 342
22:28 — 345
22:29 — 44
26:4 — 187
27:1 — 92
30:6 — 210
33:6 — 301, 314
33:10 — 25
37:19 — 171, 215
37:26 — 171
38 — 173 n.
40:12 — 342
41:4 — 342
42:1 — 9
45:7, 11 — 336
49:10 — 44
50 — 284
50:1 — 336
50:14 — 82
51:5 — 325
55:23 — 141
58:9 — 114
59:13 — 345
68:28 — 236, 254
69:5 — 342
69:9 — 342
73:2 — 75
77:11 — 206
85:10 — 238, 256
89:2 — 346
97:7 — 337
101 — 345
102 — 338
102:25-26 — 337
103:5 — 9
104:15 — 197, 214
104:22-23 — 14
104:23 — 88
107:4 — 165
107:43 — 202
109:17-18 — 326
110:1 — 294, 295
110:4 — 58, 120
112:4 — 179
116:10 — 199
118:12 — 114
119:66 — 28
121:6 — 203
127:2 — 88
139 — 173
139:15 — 173
147:10 — 179
147:19 — 196

Proverbs

5:18-19 — 230
6:6 — 9
6:10-11 — 66
7:10 — 134
7:13 — 134
10:22 — 88
13:24 — 238
14:30 — 178
16:14-15 — 170
17:12 — 156
18:2 — 155
19:17 — 171
21:29 — 134
31:19 — 66

Ecclesiastes

1:4 — 97
1:5 — 97
1:7 — 97
1:8 — 3, 86, 99, 129
1:9 — 34, 55
1:15 — 143
1:16 — 21
1:18 — 105
3:1 — 350
3:19 — 3
4:17 — 74 n.
5:18 — 8, 110
7:18 — 145
9:1 — 3
9:7-9 — 10
9:11 — 8
11:28 — 116 n.
12:11 — 12

Song of Solomon

8:12 — 350

Isaiah

3:24 — 228 n.
4:1 — 148
5 — 221
6:9 — 287
7:20 — 228
8:21 — 313
9:6-7 — 288
14:12-14 — 339
15:2 — 228 n.
19:11 — 166
26:10 — 202
29:12 — 269
40:8 — 272
42:1 — 275, 342
42:8 — 277, 292, 293
50:1 — 336 n.
50:6 — 337
51:4-5 — 289
51:6 — 289, 290
51:15 — 290
52:13 — 297, 342
53:6 — 343
55:3 — 346
55:11 — 320
56:7 — 283
57:7-10 — 223
60:19-20 — 289
61:1 — 275, 328
65:17 — 20
66:1 — 281, 284
66:2 — 281
66:3 — 281

Jeremiah

5:16 — 229
17:9 — 19
23:5-6 — 336
23:32 — 351

30:8-9 — 298
50:12 — 197 n.

Ezekiel
16:49 — 90
18:4 — 284
34:23-24 — 297

Daniel
6:25-27 — 227
7:4 — 227
7:13-14 — 291
8:23 — 134
9:24 — 289
9:26 — 352

Hosea
1:7 — 336
3:5 — 297
10:7 — 184 n.

Amos
4:11 — 124
6:1 — 139

Jonah
1:3 — 136
4:6 — 268

Habakkuk
3:1 — 81

Zephaniah
3:9 — 336

Haggai
2:7 — 268

Zechariah
9:9 — 346
14:2 — 352

Malachi
4:2 — 347

Matthew
4:4 — 173
5:16 — 230
5:34-37 — 216
5:45 — 115, 146
6:10 — 25
6:16 — 30, 134
6:29 — 157
6:34 — 10, 25, 46, 71
7:3 — 122, 126
7:3-5 — 169
7:6 — 154
7:25 — 258
10:16 — 220
10:22 — 116
11:5 — 331
11:6 — 75
11:27 — 293
12:18 — 275
13:6 — 203
13:25 — 351
15:19 — 180
15:24 — 328
16:18 — 213, 260
17:5 — 77
18:20 — 233
18:28 — 136
21:13 — 283
22:43-44 — 294
22:45 — 295
22:46 — 295 n.
23:10 — 77
23:13-29 — 187
23:23 — 124
23:26 — 76
24:5 — 183
25:24-30 — 123
26:24 — 62—63
28:18 — 293, 294
28:20 — 350

Mark
14:21 — 63
16:16 — 332, 348
16:19 — 294

Luke
1:17 — 254
1:35 — 305, 275, 341
2:34 — 75
2:37 — 100
3:22 — 304, 307
3:31 — 296
4:18 — 275
6:35-38 — 171 n.

6:38 — 171
10:16 — 275
10:24 — 260
10:42 — 76
11:34 — 227
12:20 — 123
19:43-44 — 352
19:46 — 283
24:44-45 — 268

John
1 — 300
1:3 — 276, 312
1:4 — 318
1:4-5 — 290
1:14 — 341
1:16 — 263
1:17 — 328
1:18 — 218, 317
2:24 — 27
4:37 — 34
5:17 — 334
5:17-18 — 312
5:19 — 334
5:21 — 334
5:21, 23 — 293
5:23 — 311, 316, 334
5:26 — 293
5:46 — 268, 299, 326
6:68 — 229
7:19 — 328
7:30 — 49
7:39 — 294
8:24 — 328
8:54-55 — 314
8:56 — 326
10:30 — 311
10:31 — 312
11:9 — 96
12:35 — 96
14:6 — 269
14:9-10 — 311
15:2 — 243
15:3 — 232
16:15 — 293, 316
16:21 — 49
16:33 — 350
17:3 — 306, 310
21:21 — 133

Acts
8:27 — 131

INDEX

14:17 — 53
26:14 — 102, 158
27:21 — 163

Romans

1:3 — 317
1:4 — 294
3 — 325, 348
3:2 — 196
3:20 — 346
3:23 — 332
3:25 — 330
4 — 325
6:10 — 323
8:16 — 148
8:20 — 14
9:16 — 55
10:16 — 124
11:35 — 40
12:8 — 226
12:15 — 30
13:2 — 136, 137
13:14 — 10
15:4 — 206
15:8 — 328
16:18 — 67

1 Corinthians

1:4 — 205 n.
1:30 — 289, 325
1:30-31 — 346
2 — 205
2:12 — 205 n.
3:12-13 — 270
5:8 — 220
9:26 — 91, 152
10:4 — 313
10:9 — 313
13:5 — 67
14:9 — 91
15:58 — 147
16:9 — 261

2 Corinthians

1:3 — 316
2:15 — 107
3:6 — 327
3:7 — 334
3:9 — 327
4:3-4 — 287
6:10 — 44, 112
9:6 — 171
9:7 — 171

Galatians

1:10 — 322
2:20 — 323
3 — 325, 348
3:19 — 81, 327
4:4 — 317
6:4 — 68 n.
6:10 — 174

Ephesians

2:6 — 60
2:8 — 277
4 — 260
5:33 — 82
6:7 — 135

Philippians

2:2 — 229
2:5-7 — 297
2:7 — 286, 307
2:12-13 — 55
4:6 — 7

Colossians

1:15 — 339
1:15-17 — 312
2:9 — 305

2 Thessalonians

3:12 — 148

1 Timothy

1:7 — 78
1:15 — 183
3:4 — 110
4:4-5 — 8
4:8 — 214
6:7 — 91
6:8 — 149
6:17 — 53

2 Timothy

1:10 — 319
1:12 — 272
2:15 — 229
3:5 — 187
3:7 — 185
3:13 — 85
3:16 — 230
3:16-17 — 194
3:17 — 197
4:2 — 113

4:3 — 303
4:7 — 152

Titus

1:9 — 230
2:14 — 135
3:8-9 — 186
3:10 — 84, 120, 155

Hebrews

1:3 — 339
1:6 — 337
1:10 — 337
7:1-17 — 58
11:1 — 272

James

3:1 — 77, 186
3:15 — 99

1 Peter

1:3 — 316
1:12 — 310
2:12 — 187
2:13 — 170
2:23 — 27
4:2 — 323

2 Peter

1:10 — 272
1:17 — 304
1:21 — 275
3:12 — 290

1 John

2:23 — 316
3:8 — 173
3:20 — 237
5:19 — 145

Jude

4 — 100
8 — 78

Revelation

21:5 — 20—21

APOCRYPHA

Ecclesiasticus

15:14 — 50

Luther 66483

THE McQUADE LIBRARY
MERRIMACK COLLEGE
North Andover, Massachusetts

DISCARD

DEMCO